Medicolegal Library 5

Edited by A. Carmi

Psychiatry - Law and Ethics

Edited by
A. Carmi S. Schneider A. Hefez

With Contributions by
G. Ammon L. V. Annis U. Aviram A. Avnat C. A. Baker
Y. Bar-El J. Bazak I. Burbiel A. Carmi S. B. Cohen
H. H. Cohn S. Davidson B. C. Dimond G. Dreifuss
G. Dixon A. Elizur A. Eser G. Ferguson D. A. Frenkel
Y. Ginath L. Gostin D. Griepenstroh A. F. Halmosh
S. S. Herr E. Johanson Y. Kitamura A. A. Kuforiji
N. Laor N. S. Lehrman A. Levy U. Lowental
G. W. Lynch L. Mathers R. R. Mayer T. Mitsuishi
M. Moser R. Moses T. M. Napier L. S. Nelson
J. R. Rappeport P. Rodenhauser R. R. Rogers
S. Schneider C. P. Seager S. P. Segal N. P. Sheehy
D. Shnit P. Silfen M. Torem E. Totsuka I. Treves
M. S. Tropper S. Tyano J. Wagner M. A. Watson F. Weil
Y. Z. Zadik G. Zlotnik

Springer-Verlag
Berlin Heidelberg New York Tokyo

Judge Amnon Carmi
P.O.B. 6451, Haifa 31063, Israel

Prof. Dr. Stanley Schneider
Summit Institute
Wurzweiler School of Social Work, Yeshiva University
Michlala, Jerusalem Womens's College
P.O.B. 7446, Jerusalem, Israel

Prof. Albert Hefez
9 Zinger Str., Kiriat Bialik, Israel

ISBN 3-540-15742-5 Springer-Verlag Berlin Heidelberg New York Tokyo
ISBN 0-387-15742-5 Springer-Verlag New York Heidelberg Berlin Tokyo

Library of Congress Cataloging in Publication Data. Main entry under title:
Psychiatry - law and ethics. (Medicolegal library ; 5) 1. Forensic psychiatry-Addresses, essays, lectures. 2. Insanity-Jurisprudence-Addresses, essays, lectures. 3. Psychiatric ethics-Addresses, essays, lectures. I. Carmi, Amnon. II. Ammon, Günter, 1918. III. Series.
K487.P75Z97 1986 614'.1 86-14715

Typesetting, printing and bookbinding: Appl, Wemding
2119/3140-543210

Table of Contents

List of Contributors

G. Ammon
Prinz-Friedrich-Leopold-Str. 21, D-1000 Berlin 38

L. V. Annis
c/o Leigh Mathers, Units 22, Forensic Service
Florida State Hospital, Chattahoochee, FL 32324, USA

U. Aviram
School of Social Work, University of Tel Aviv, Tel Aviv, Israel

A. Avnat
c/o M. S. Tropper, Geha Psychiatric Hospital, Petah Tikva, Israel

C. A. Baker
c/o Leigh Mathers, Unit 22, Forensic Service
Florida State Hospital, Chattahoochee, Fl 32324, USA

Y. Bar-El
Kfar Shaul Psychiatric Hospital, Givat Shaul, Israel

J. Bazak
7 Narkis Street, Jerusalem, Israel

I. Burbiel
Menterschweige, Geiselgasteig Str. 203, D-8000 München 90

A. Carmi
P.O. Box 6451, Haifa 31063, Israel

S. B. Cohen
401 Peachtree Street, N. E. Atlanta, GA 30308, USA

H. H. Cohn
36 Tchernichowsky Street, Jerusalem 92585, Israel

S. Davidson
Shalvata Hospital, Hod Hasharon, P.O.B. 94, Israel

B. C. Dimond
Polytechnic of Wales, Treforest, Mid Glamorgan
Wales, Great Britain

G. Dixon
402 East Park Avenue, Tallahassee, FL 32302, USA

G. Dreifuss
62 Margalit Str., Haifa 34464, Israel

A. Elizur
Shalvata Hospital, Hod Hasharon, P.O.B. 94, Israel

A. Eser
Gunterstalstr. 73, D-7800 Freiburg

G. Ferguson
Faculty of Law, University of Victoria, Victoria, Canada V8W 3H7

D. A. Frenkel
Horkania, Jerusalem, Israel

Y. Ginath
Beer Sheva Mental Health Center, P.O.B. 4600
Beer Sheva, Israel 84170

L. Gostin
Oxford University, Center for Criminology Research 12
Bevington Rd, Oxford OX2 6OH, Great Britain

D. Griepenstroh
Bleibtreustr. 48, D-1000 Berlin 12

A. F. Halmosh
26, Yphtach Hagilach Str., Beer Sheva 84234, Israel

S. S. Herr
190 Montrose Avenue, South Orange, NJ 07079, USA

E. Johanson
Brinkvagen 7, S-8-90248 Umea

Y. Kitamura
c/o Totsuka E., 404 Naito-cho House, 1-121
Naito-cho Shinjuku-ku, Tokyo 160, Japan

A. A. Kuforiji
Department of Law, University of Ibadan, Ibadan, Nigeria

N. Laor
Yale School of Medicine, Child Study Center, 333 Cedar Str.
New Haven, CT 06510, USA

N. S. Lehrman
Roslyn, NY 11576, USA

A. Levy
Shalvata Hospital, Hod Hasharon, P.O.B. 94, Israel

U. Lowental
Eshkol Boulevard 22, Apt. 3, Jerusalem 92-585, Israel

G. W. Lynch
John Jay College of Criminal Justice, 444 West 56 Street, NY, USA

L. Mathers
Unit 22, Forensic Service, Florida State Hospital, Chattahoochee
FL 32324, USA

R. R. Mayer
8 Rakafot Street, Rehovot 76608, Israel

T. Mitsuishi
c/o Totsuka E., 404 Naito-cho House, 1-121
Naito-cho Shinjuku-ku, Tokyo 160, Japan

M. Moser
Tel Aviv University, Tel Aviv, Israel

R. Moses
Summit Instiute, Shimony 44, P.O.B. 7446, Jerusalem 91073, Israel

T. M. Napier
Nothern Central Hospital, Sheffield 55, 1AU, Great Britain

L. S. Nelson
Department of Psychiatric Medicine, East Carolina University
School of Medicine, Greenville, NC, USA

J. R. Rappeport
University of Maryland, School of Medicine, MD, USA

P. Rodenhauser
Wright State University, School of Medicine, Dayton
OH 45435, USA

R. R. Rogers
Harbor, UCLA Medical Center, Torrance, CA 90509, USA

S. Schneider
Summit Institute, Wurzweiler School of Social Work
Yeshiva University Michlala, Jerusalem Women's College
P.O.B. 7446, Jerusalem, Israel

C. P. Seager
Nothern Central Hospital, Sheffield 55, 1AU, Great Britain

S. P. Segal
University of California, Berkeley, CA 94710, USA

N. P. Sheehy
Department of Applied Psychology, UWIST
Llewyn-Grant Ponylan, Cardiff CF 3 7UX, Great Britain

D. Shnit
School of Social Work, University of Tel Aviv, Tel Aviv, Israel

P. Silfen
Bar-Ilan University, Department of Criminology
Ramat-Gan, Israel

M. Torem
P.O.B. 927, Dayton, OH 45401, USA

E. Totsuka
404 Naito-cho House, 1-121, Naito-cho Shinjuku-ku
Tokyo 160, Japan

I. Treves
Shalvata Hospital, Hod Hasharon, P.O.B. 94, Israel

M. S. Tropper
Geriatric Center, Rishon-le-Zion, Israel

S. Tyano
Geha Psychiatric Hospital, Petah Tikva, Israel

J. Wagner
c/o M. S. Tropper, Geha Psychiatric Hospital, Petah Tikva, Israel

M. A. Watson
c/o S. P. Segal, University of California, Berkeley, CA 94710, USA

F. Weil
1, Biram Street, Haifa 34986, Israel

Y. Z. Zadik
13, Yecheskel Street, Ramot Remez, Haifa 32207, Israel

G. Zlotnik
Ronvej 15, 2600 Glostrup, Denmark

I. Introduction

The Abnormal Approach to Abnormality

A. Carmi

1 Introduction: The Need for Normology

Criminals represent a minor group of individuals in the community. Criminals necessitate the employment of an enormous group of qualified professionals: judges and juries, prosecutors, lawyers, policemen, jailers, social workers, and probation officers, and even members of parliament, who produce criminal laws. A few criminals attract the attention of the whole population by thus activating the "seventh republic," the press, radio, and television. Kojak and Agatha Christie constitute integral parts of human culture; crime and punishment are indispensable components of our life in society. Human society is expected to produce criminals in case all the old ones are executed or made to repent. Criminals join the angels in building the structure of our "normal life."

If we need criminals, why do we condemn them? Go forth and reflect that we need them so much because we are in need of the process of condemnation.

Law is a sanctioning discipline, psychiatry is a therapeutic one. Each of these two disciplines is concerned with those who deviate [1]. The law deals with the difference which exists between society and the nonconforming individual. Psychiatry is interested in the difference between the patient and other men. The phenomenon of difference is the topic of our present work. Human beings are alike in many respects, such as their anatomy and physiology and their psychological structure. Human beings differ in many other respects, and each group of people consists of majorities and minorities. It is our view that to be different, or to be different from the majority, is not to be deviant. "Deviant" behavior is a natural phenomenon. Nonconformity seems to be a consistent characteristic of human society [2]. In order to explain abnormality one should understand and know normality. We should consider the need to study normality and develop the field of "normology".

Normology should deal with the man in the middle, the member of the silent majority. Campbell et al. refer to the forgotten man, who does his job, obeys most of the laws, gets along with his neighbors, and is in fact the source of stability and continuity [3].

Abnormality is a social distinction established to separate undesired behavior from more accepted patterns of conduct [4]. The hidden desires of the normal community should be ascertained in order for abnormal behaviour to be understood. The criminal law and the criminal's behavior cannot be explained unless one understands the inner – often aggressive – impulses of legislatures, judges, prosecutors, and the public at large [5]. The silent majority constitutes and activates a "majorityranny". This sociopsychological phenomenon deserves multidisciplinary studies, training, and approach.

2 Who is Normal?

Studies of IQ in different parts of the world show that the highest mean IQs are generally obtained by Mongoloid populations originating in Japan and China [6]. Are the Japanese, who on the average exhibit IQs significantly above those of the Americans and the British, "normal" or "abnormal"? The answer depends on the different reactions of the various readers. Japanese may feel pride and satisfaction, whereas Americans will consider the need for modification of the IQ tests. What is normal drinking? In France or Italy moderate drinking is normal. In Iran any imbibing of alcohol is abnormal. Abnormality depends on the cultural values of the defining persons. Prostitution is not accepted in some cultures, but is accepted in others [7].

Society's reaction to sexually deviant behavior emphasizes the fact that the rules for normality are formed and fixed by psychological impulses rather than by objective external factors. According to the Kinsey report, 37% of the total male population surveyed reported at least incidental overt homosexual experience to the point of orgasm between adolescence and old age. Despite the fact that it occurs in all age-groups and apparently in all cultures, homosexual behavior represents a form of activity that is socially unacceptable to one degree or another [8]. Here the definition of normality is not based on reality but shapes it. The power of such psychological impulses is so strong as to direct the behavior of the deviant people, too. They tend to adopt the general conception although they know that it lacks both reason and justice.

The so-called social nudists are isolated in society at large, but they are able to participate in their own group and activate it. Consider the following response of a nudist to an interviewer's question: "I told you about this one on the sun deck with her legs spread. It was not a *normal* position. *Normally,* you wouldn't lay like this" [9]. Apparently, this lady had not abandoned the general abnormal approach to normality.

The same applies to racial discrimination. With respect to the misleading assumption of inherent black inferiority in America, sociologists indicate that both blacks and whites have been born into a prison which they did not make and from which they have been unable to escape [10].

3 Mathematical Formulae

Statisticians study in great detail how the individuals in a group differ from each other. Experience has taught them that for many distributions drawn from large populations the histograms approximate to what is known as a "bell-shaped curve" [11], which is also called a "normal" curve. But what about Alexander Bell, who found himself on the peak of the normal curve? Standing there alone, should he be regarded as abnormal? The answer lies in the common approach rather than in the study of the curve.

An average shows the central value of a group of observations, describing both the quantitative data obtained from a sample and the population from which the sample is drawn [12]. The average is expected to typify the whole set of items, being always close to the center of the concentration of the measurements [13]. The average acts as a group of individual values, showing the individuals' general size in the group [14] and describing the distances between them and other individuals of same sample. Averages can be - and often are - misleading. It is incorrect to assume that because a certain human behavior is widespread, it should be regarded as normal [15]. Central tendency is a natural phenomenon; it is not a moral ideal.

The mathematicians apply various kinds of averages. The arithmetic mean is the most familiar index of central tendency of given data [16]. It is the sum of a set of specific measurements divided by the number of measurements in the set [17]. The arithmetic mean is the center of gravity, a point of balance. As such it may psychologically serve as an important mechanism for giving satisfaction to those who wish to apply it. However, the arithmetic mean does not thereby become normal, and the criteria for normality are fixed by external, nonarithmetic considerations.

The median is a point on a scale such that half the observations, which are arranged in order from smallest to largest, fall above it and half below it [18]. The median is influenced only by the number of items and not by their values in the series. The median corresponds to the middle individual [19], but it does not determine his normality. The cases fall into each of two intervals with equal frequency, but each individual, including the median, is separated from the others by the same number of subintervals. Where five patients take five different doses of the same medicament, the "median" patient will not be regarded as normal.

The mode is that measurement which occurs most frequently [20]. The mode is used in preference to other averages if the purpose is to indicate the most typical value of the series. Thus, where the first prisoner had previously been found guilty of one crime, the second prisoner of two crimes, and the third and the fourth of three crimes each, then the relevant mode will be three crimes. Does it mean that prisoner number 3 is normal? What is the message of this mode?

The mathematicians may bring about understanding; they will describe and explain the phenomenon of frequency more correctly and accurately. They are not supposed to change the course of events, just as photography is not expected to affect its objects.

The statistical conception of deviance relates to the infringement of the modal values and the behavior of a given group at a given time [21]. The mode, mean, and median serve as the measuring rods for conformity and deviance [22]. We have tried to indicate that these means are able to show the place of the individual on the human map, but not to determine his value.

4 The Scientific Approach

Geneticists refer to genetic abnormality [23]. The genes are organized on chromosomes, of which there are 23 pairs. The incidence of Down's syndrome or trisomy (a third chromosome) 21, is 1 in 666 births. Edwards' syndrome is due to trisomy of an E group (16-18) chromosome. Ninety percent of children born with this syndrome die within a year, and the survivors are grossly defective. Abnormalities of many other kinds have been recognized as well.

Every human being will die when his time comes. Dead people will never be regarded as abnormal. Only living people may endanger their neighbors; only living people may be classified as abnormal. The geneticist tries to predict who will live and what he will look like. He does not relate to the value of such life. He does not add his own feeling to the scientific data he supplies.

Physicians, unlike the geneticists, take part in the establishment of certain kinds of relations with their patients. They are interested in their patients as patients. Professionally, they do not deal with healthy people [24]. Diagnostic classification and etiological analysis, which are required for the purpose of treatment, cannot be made or justified unless some pathology can be shown. The doctor will look for an organic basis or for any underlying cause indicating an abnormal functioning. Any deviance will thus be regarded as an individual pathology [25]. Doctors tend to classify their patients as being ill or defective. Their future relations will necessarily be affected by this process. The patients will need medical care; they will also need other kinds of help. Their needs will affect the interest of their fellowmen. This is where the public at large will start to be annoyed. This is how the medical profession plays a role in the formation of general societal attitudes.

The psychologist confronts a still harder task. Usually, the psychologist is comparing his patients profile with some "typical" profiles. He possessses typical profiles which have been acquired by way of experience, supplied norms, and theoretical considerations [26]. If psychology has failed successfully to cope with the dilemma, the reason lies perhaps in its tendency to concentrate on research into the abnormal, rather than to develop the psychology of the normal. Abnormal psychology deals with mental states which do not coincide with or reach real integration [27]. "Integration" means individual wholeness, with all the parts functioning together [28]. All relevant parts are expected to be together and to work together, and not to be easily divided or uncoordinated or work one against the other.

No satisfactory tests of integration have been worked out, and abnormality can be gauged only roughly [29]. Too many factors affect human behavior, most of which are beyond our knowledge. Moreover, where human (psychologist's) mind defines human (patient's) mind, each mind affects the other, and it is impossible to localize each separate effect. Thus the psychological approach to abnormality must necessarily consist of scientific as well as nonscientific elements.

The sociologists hold the view that deviance is a social rather than a behavioral or biological matter [30]. Defining an individual as a delinquent or as mentally ill is viewed as an interpersonal process in which the definer makes a value judgment about the behavior of the person being defined [31].

5 The Sociological Approach

Social norms have three properties. They involve patterns of behavior, they have normative quality, and they carry sanctions [32]. The object of the social norm is to regulate the individual's activities [33]. It expresses the idea that an individual ought to behave in a certain way [34]. The rules of law are a particular order of norms [35]. Law is perceived, at least partly, as the institutionalized form of preexisting norms. A norm is valid if it corresponds with the actual feelings and demands of the community [36], if it is accepted by the common consciousness of the people [37]. The norm expresses the behavior, thinking, and attitudes which the community expects of each individual [38]. The law as a normative system lays down what must be done [39]. It expresses the legislature's will that certain acts should be performed by certain persons in certain circumstances [40]. The formation of legal norms constitutes a long continuing process. In the words of Holmes: "In law, as in a magic mirror, we see reflected not only our own lives, but the lives of all men that have been" [41]. Norms are thus regarded as resulting from endless choices made by the various members of the community through time [42]. The acquisition of norms by individuals also involves a continuous process of learning or socialization [43].

One may wonder whether the interests of the majority should overcome and overrule the interests of the minority. However, the common conception which states that the law is really formed by the accumulated interests of the majority should be open to discussion too. The legal system does not operate as a value-neutral arena in which conflicts are solved according to principles of pure justice [44]. There is no will of the state, but the wills of individuals who govern it [45]. The law represents a codified behavioral standard as formed by persons possessing access to the legislative process [46]. Such persons belong to groups which, due to their political or economic power, are capable of having their views incorporated into the official views of the society [47]. The law represents an institutionalized tool of those groups which are more powerful than others [48].

The inevitable conclusion is that conceptions of what ought to be legal and the contents of the legal norms are extremely variable, not only according to time, place, and society but also with respect to the governing groups.

Every society requires each of its members to conform to its standards [49]. Conformity usually refers to the activity which is consistent with the behavior patterns of the group [50]. Conformity means social alikeness, doing what one's society wants one to do [51]. Common practice demonstrates "normality" [52]. Conformity satisfies a common interest of both the community and the individual. Human beings tend to conform to group norms because of their longing for congruity [53] and because of their wish to reduce ego anxiety [54].

Two other psychological processes operate within the individual, comprising the shortcomings of personality and the original impulses on the one hand, and the mechanisms of adjustment and the internalized group of norms on the other hand [55]. Infantile gratifications and frustrations are the earliest pressures toward conformity [56]. The young child is subjected to an inexorable process of indoctrination in the group norms under a pedagogical technique of awarding or withholding rewards or punishments. This process is reinforced by the approval or disapproval of the social group through its social, cultural, religious, and political mechanisms. The interaction of personality and the environment leads to potential conformist or nonconformist conduct [57]. Within this frame work an important role is played by the law. Its function is to enforce community values through governmental action.

The law consists not only of the norms to be adopted or obeyed, but also of the retribution to be meted out in the case of contravention. The connection between the contravention and its punishment is a hidden but powerful factor which motivates and justifies the whole process. The members of the community are thus divided into two groups: the good, who conform, and the bad, who do not conform. Those who do not conform are to be punished. Modern criminology is aware of the fact that there are people who are ready to conform but cannot. Liberal legislations are now prepared to offer every individual any treatment that will enable him to conform to the common standards [58]. Apparently, the public at large has not yet reached the stage of fully and willfully accepting these views. And in any case, every community insists that its norms should be the only guidelines for individual behavior, and that normality is the only model to be adopted.

6 The Determination of Normality

Social norms constitute an accumulation of decisions made by the community over a long period of time [59]. The public at large determines not only the norms but also the deviance. The individual is dependent upon both the norms set by others and the judgments of others [60]. The judgment that an actual behavior is what it ought not to be in relation to the norms, and that it is "bad," is a value judgment [61]. A behavior may look abnormal to a layman, though it does not necessarily look abnormal when viewed through the special lens of the psychiatrist. Deviance works as a process by which the group and its organs of social control interpret and define behavior as deviant [62]. Whether an act is deviant depends on how other members of the group react to it. Deviance is a property inherent not in certain forms of behavior, but in the interaction between the person who commits the act and those who respond to it [63]. The degree to which other members will respond to a given act as deviant varies greatly, and depends also on who commits the act and who is harmed by it [64].

The critical variable in the deviance process is the whole community rather than the individual. The actual behavior is filtered through the community screen [65]. Deviance cannot be understood without reference to societal reactions to it [66]. Deviant behavior is behavior that people so label [67]. Deviance expresses the idea that some people are out of line with most others in the community [68]. It constitutes a disjunction between the roles and expectations of the individual and those of the group [69]. It describes the departure of the individual from the modal behavior of the group or from the accepted rules [70].

The criminal law is conceived as a system of social control over the citizens [71], applying punishment for crimes. Kant urged a mystical connection between the harm done to society by the crime and the degree of punishment. Apparently, punishments express more than the actual harm which was caused by the criminals. Any contravention arouses a reaction of disapproval by the group [72].

However, one should not disregard the satisfaction in punishing felt by the punishing agencies and by the public at large. The punishing process gratifies a number of psychological perversities among the members of the group. Moreover, deviance may itself be, if properly controlled, an important condition for preserving community welfare, and even for keeping the social order intact [73]. It may also work as a social adhesive, uniting the members of a group in concern about the individual's problems [74].

Norms are not formed by "good" citizens, but constitute the compromise produced by conflicting powers. A criminal is a molder of his environment rather than a mere product of that mold [75]. The social group may even indirectly benefit from its deviant members, but it tries to limit the flow of behavior of all the members within its domain [76]. This process implies a constant interaction between the individual and his surroundings, each making demands on the other [77].

7 Stigmatizing the Deviants

There is no universally accepted definition of what constitutes deviant behavior [78]. Deviance is too complex to have one cause or explanation [79]. In any case, by describing someone as a deviant we express a certain kind of attitude which has a stigmatizing property [80]. A derogatory attribute is imputed to the social image of the individual [81].

Deviance constitutes a threat to the sacred traditions and to the common conceptions. Deviance is in itself a frustration to members of the dominant groups [82]. The anxiety created by the behavior or conditions of the deviants is threatening to the "normals" and produces reactions [83]. These reactions are to define deviance and attack deviants. The behavior of the stigmatizer rather than that of the stigmatized should be learned in order to understand the phenomenon of deviance. Shoham indicates the release of frustrations and resentment through the subconscious mechanisms of transference and scapegoating, which serve as the catalyst for the psychic formation of social stigma; he also indicates the inner aggression and the projection of guilt as the stigmatizer's own deviant guilt tendencies, which bring about the same results [84]. The differences arouse fear; the powerlessness of the deviant turns him into a target.

8 The Insane

The individual's actions are sometimes so bizarre and deviate so much from ordinary behavior that they create difficulties for his fellowmen. The latter will then be apt to label them as crazy and treat him as deviant. Gross deviations are recognized in all societies as showing or expressing abnormality. The more severe a behavior disorder, the more likely it is to be considered abnormal [85]. There seems to be wide disagreement among psychiatrists in assigning people to a particular diagnostic group [86]. Different schools employ different concepts of mental abnormality, and apply different definitions to similar conditions [87].

The sociological approach includes under the term "mental abnormality" all types of deviation from the social norms [88]. Mental illness is considered to be a social status rather than a disease [89]; in the words of Szasz: "We call people mentally ill when their personal conduct violates certain ethical, political and social norms. This explains why many historical figures, from Jesus to Castro, and from Job to Hitler, have been diagnosed as suffering from this or that psychiatric malady" [90]. The severely handicapped have always been identified as such because of their difficulty in adapting themselves to social demands [91]. And the judgements of the psychiatrists could not be far removed from those of the common man of the society in which the psychiatrists and the patients lived [92].

The statistical approach focuses on average behavior and determines what deviates from the statistical average [93]. This approach conceives the middle range as normal and its extremes as deviant [94]. One may wonder, however, whether a given individual might be thus diagnosed as being sick or well, as human behavior is not always – if at all – quantifiable [95].

Another approach equates normality with health. Behavior is regarded as normal when no manifest pathology is present [96]. Anything that does not function according to its design is abnormal. Adult and mature behavior is normal, infantile and immature behavior is abnormal [97]. Thought disorder has always been regarded as one of the main criteria of mental illness [98]. The World Health Organization refers to mental subnormality as "incomplete or insufficient general development of the mental capacities" [99].

The legal definitions of abnormality are usually artifical and superficial, and are not based upon the best that is known in the field of abnormality [100]. Lawyers feel that they cannot cope with this issue without the help of a psychiatrist [101]. They ask the psychiatrist to diagnose nonconformist behavior which seems to them to constitute an overt manifestation of a psychiatric illness [102]. They may perceive healthy persons as those who are reasonably free from undue discomfort and disability [103], and they seek the psychiatrist out as emissary to their unreasonable brethren [104]. The troubled patient troubles his neighbors. Finkel writes about the fear of the "other," "this strange stranger in our midst, our kin but not kind, who spurs the community of reasonable men to action" [105]. Mentally disordered people were always treated as outcasts and hardly distinguished from criminals [106]. This widespread fear of mental illness has been known throughout the history of mankind's ignorance [107].

Psychiatry has found it too difficult to cope with this phenomenon of fear and ignorance. Referring to the youngster who is dishevelled in appearance, wears no socks, whose clothes are dirty, talks to himself, and sometimes has a menacing look, Finkel states: "In a literal and aesthetic way, our eyes, ears and nose may be affected. In a moral way, our sense of values may be jostled. Yet he lays no hand on us. The question is: May we lay hands on him?" [108]. The answer seems to be simple, if we label him as abnormal.

9 The Criminal

Two hundred and forty criminals were interviewed for a total of several thousands of hours. While considering the following major findings, try to replace the criminals with respected citizens whom you know personally.

- The criminal is tremendously energetic [109].
- The fear of death is very strong, persistent, and pervasive in the criminal mental life [110].
- The criminal fears being reduced to "nothing" [111].
- The criminal is ordinarily angry [112]. (How would you feel behind thick walls?)
- Nearly all criminals are intensely sentimental toward their mothers [113].
- Most criminals had been exposed to religious ideas and training [114].
- Perhaps the most striking difference between criminals and noncriminals was that the former took the basic religious teachings extremely literally.

- The criminal emphasizes his total difference from other people [115]. (Does not each of us enjoy doing the same?)
- The criminal criticizes others, but angrily rejects any criticism of himself [116]. (Is this not a normal human trait?)
- When the criminal is held accountable for a crime, he portrays himself as a victim [117]. (Do not all respected victimologists share the same view?)

And what about the criminal's failures to put himself in another's position [118], to consider injury to others [119], to assume obligation [120], or to trust other people [121]?

One writer indicates that the criminal has many thoughts about violating the law [122]. How can such phenomena really be measured, and what about the dreadful thoughts of many innocent citizens? In Freedman's words [123]: "A reservoir of homicidal aggression resides in the mass of man which can be tapped whenever it is attached to a suitable public symbol. The existence of a symbol rather than the existence of the thoughts makes the real difference."

Another writer tries to distinguish between mentally ill and normal criminals by arguing that normal criminals are able to mend their ways if taught a lesson by punishment [124]. Penologists may wonder whether recidivism is not a common phenomenon and whether this argument will not necessarily bring about the result that recidivists will be exempted from responsibility as they did not or could not learn their lesson.

All attempts to show that offenders as a class can be sharply distinguished from law-abiding citizens with respect to their social origin, physique, intelligence, or environment have seemingly failed [125]. There are as many classes as there are criminals [126]; there are many kinds of criminals, with all sets of traits [127]. It is now believed that there is no such thing as anthropological criminal type. The physical and mental constitution of both criminal and law abiding persons of the same age and class are very much the same [128]. The range of crimes is very wide, too. It extends from gross physical violence to minor infractions of the law. Moreover, what is and what is not criminal is defined by each legislature and by the laws of the power at present in force [129].

Crime is varied and complex, possessing no single face, and limited to no one particular social group [130]. Criminality is taken by various psychiatrists to be a means of maintaining psychic balance or as an effort to rectify a psychic balance which has been disrupted [131]. What about the psychological need for balance which activates the psychiatrists? Does he not share the common need to label that kind of behavior which constitutes a hidden threat to him? Psychiatrists may be helpful due to their better understanding of human behavior. However, establishing psychiatric criteria for criminal responsibility is a logical impossibility, as moral responsibility is a metaphysical term about which no science, including psychiatry, can say anything scientific [132].

Recently, major attention has been given to physiopsychological explanations of criminal behavior, as well as to socioenvironmental, sociocultural, and social-psychological explanations [133]. We should look for a multifactor approach, taking into consideration the fact that each criminal act entails different behavior and cultural conditions [134].

Plato in his *Republic* [135] refers to the wild beast in us, casting off shame and prudence, which will not shrink from any deed of blood. Such a beast does not exist, of course, but this "Platonic hate" is rooted deep in our hearts.

Jean Paul Sartre said that hell is other people. Hell is not other people, but it may well be found in other people. Many myths, uncertainties, and ambiguities dominate the popular attitude toward the criminal [136]. The "average" citizen expresses a pathological fear of criminal behavior [137]. The definition of behavior as "criminal" is a form of stigmatization [138], which is used by frightened citizens as means of self-defense. The criminal is regarded by society as an undesired man [139], and his behavior is seen as intolerable and therefore to be responded to with sanction. Some criminologists are more interested in the question why some individuals fail to inhibit those kinds of actions that are socially proscribed than in discovering the manner in which criminal habits are acquired [140]. Criminality is defined by deviation from the ordinary social structure. It is the going against the tide which arouses the majorityranny.

The offender is not some species of animal which could be described by markings and habits. Such descriptions will always remain theoretical and superficial [141]. Delinquents can certainly not be regarded as abnormal individuals [142]. One should carefully consider Durkheim's statement that criminality is a normal function of human life [143].

10 Hillel's Rule

We do not claim that there are no insane patients or criminals. Our cities contain many offenders and mentally ill, as well as many lawyers and psychiatrists. Psychiatry and criminology have made substantial contributions to the study of these phenomena.

Our purpose was to show that each of us reacts to his neighbor, educates him, studies his behavior, stigmatizes him. Our purpose was to show that the forgotten citizen is nothing but a wolf in sheep's clothing, and that majorityranny is applied by silent majorities. Time has come to consider our own behavior and to study the phenomenon of abnormalizing other people.

Old Rabbi Hillel used to say:
"Do not do to others what you would not wish to be done to yourself."
We wish to do to ourselves what has been done by us to others.

References

1. Freedman L (1955) Conformity and non-conformity. In: Hoch P, Zubin J (eds) Psychiatry and the law. Grune and Stratton, New York, p 41
2. Ibid, p 52
3. Campbell J, Sahid J, Stang D (1970) Law and order reconsidered. Praeger, New York, p 57
4. Knudten R (1974) Crime in a complex society. Dorsey, Illinois, p 279
5. Shoham G (1976) Social deviance. Gardner, New York, p 138
6. Lynn R (1978) Ethnic and racial differences in intelligence: international comparisons. In: Osborne T, Noble C, Weyl N (1978) Human variation. Academic, New York, p 283
7. Redlich F, Freedman D (1975) The problem of normality. In: Allen R, Ferster E, Rubin J (eds) Readings in law and psychiatry. Hopkins, Baltimore, p 56
8. Feldman P (1979) Abnormal sexual behavior - males. In: Eysneck H (ed) Handbook of abnormal psychology. Pitman Medical, London, p 131
9. Weinberg M (1973) Becoming a nudist. In: Rubington E, Weinberg M (eds) Deviance, the international perspective, 2nd edn. MacMillan, New York, p 299
10. Sawry J, Telford C (1971) Psychology of adjustment. Allyn and Bacon, Boston, p 334
11. Newmark J (1977) Statistics and probability in modern life. Holt, Rinehart and Winston, New York, pp 39, 222
12. Guilford J (1965) Fundamental statistics in psychology and education, 4th edn. McGraw Hill, New York, p 43
13. Ferguson G (1971) Statistical analysis in psychology of education, 3rd edn. McGraw Hill, New York, p 44
14. Moroney M (1965) Facts from figures. Penguin, Baltimore, p 34
15. Kubie L (1948) Psychiatric implications of the Kinsey Report. Psychosom Med 10: 97
16. Hays W (1973) Statistics for the social sciences, 2nd edn. Holt, Rinehart and Winston, New York, p 219
17. Ferguson, op cit, p 45
18. Ibid.
19. Hays, op cit, p 217
20. Guilford, op cit, p 55
21. Shoham, op cit p 93
22. Ibid, p 92
23. Shields J (1979) Heredity and psychological abnormality. In: Eysneck, op cit, p 543
24. Mercer J (1973) Labeling the mentally retarded. In: Rubington, op cit, p 77
25. McGuire R (1979) Classification and the problem of diagnosis. In: Eysneck, op cit, p 8
26. Ibid, p 19
27. Taylor W (1954) Dynamic and abnormal psychology. American Book Co, New York, p 2
28. Ibid, p 66
29. Ibid, p 63
30. Friedson E (1973) The production of deviant populations. In: Rubington, op cit, p 125
31. Mercer, op cit, p 78
32. Rushing W (1975) Deviant behavior and social process. Rand McNally, Chicago, p 2
33. Hall J (1938) Readings in jurisprudence. Bobbs-Merrill, Indianapolis, p 201
34. Kelsen H (1966) On the pure theory of law. Israel Law Review 1: 36
35. Chamblis W, Seidman R (1971) Law, order and power. Addison Wesley, Massachusetts, p 8
36. Holmes OW (1971) Theories of punishment and the external standard. In: Goldstein A, Goldstein J (eds) Crime, law and society. The Free Press, New York, p 27
37. Ross A (1974) On law and justice. University of California Press, Berkeley, p 71
38. Knudten, op cit, p 288
39. Chambliss, op cit, p 59
40. Raz J (1970) The concept of a legal system. Clarendon, Oxford, p 75
41. Holmes OW (1921) Collected legal papers. Harcourt, New York, p 186
42. Chambliss, op cit, p 37
43. Shoham, op cit, p 26
44. Chambliss, op cit, p 503
45. Hall, op cit, p 199

46. Knudten, op cit, p 54
47. Chambliss, op cit, p 65
48. Ibid, p 504
49. Taylor, op cit, p 65
50. Freedman, op cit, p 43
51. Taylor, op cit. p 66
52. Freedman, op cit, p 46
53. Shoham, op cit, p 19
54. Ibid, p 92
55. Feldman, op cit, p 436
56. Freedman, op cit, p 44
57. Carr L (1950) Delinquency control. Harper, New York, p 161
58. Taylor, op cit, p 64
59. Erikson K (1973) Notes on the sociology of deviance. In: Rubington, op cit, p 29
60. Byrne E, Maziarze E (1969) Human being and being human. Prentice Hall, New Jersey, p 239
61. Kelsen, op cit, p 1
62. Kitsuse J (1973) Societal reaction to deviant behavior. In: Rubington, op cit, p 17
63. Becker H (1963) Outsiders: studies in the sociology of deviance. Glencoe, New York, p 14
64. Ibid, p 13
65. Erikson, op cit, p 27
66. Lemert E (1951) Social pathology. McGraw Hill, New York, p 75
67. Becker, op cit, p 9
68. Sagarin E (1975) Deviants and deviance. Praeger, New York, p 10
69. Shoham, op cit, p 21
70. Ibid, pp 4, 88
71. Chambliss, op cit, p 189
72. Ross, op cit, p 91
73. Erikson, op cit, p 28
74. Shoham, op cit, p 141
75. Yochelson S, Samenow S (1976) The criminal personality. Jason Aronson, New York, p 104
76. Erikson, op cit, p 28
77. White R, Watt N (1973) The abnormal personality, 4th edn. Ronald, New York, p 90
78. Rushing, op cit, p 1
79. Shoham, op cit, p 105
80. Ibid, p 3
81. Ibid, p 69
82. Blalock H (1967) Toward a theory of minority-group relations. Wiley, New York, p 205
83. Schur E (1971) Labeling deviant behavior. Harper and Row, New York, p 109
84. Shoham, op cit, pp 72–73
85. Redlich, op cit, p 56
86. McGuire, op cit, p 5; Wilson E, Deming J (1979) Statistical comparisons of psychiatric diagnosis of some Massachusetts State hospitals during 1925. Q Bull Mass Dep Ment Dis 11: 1–15
87. Clarke AM, Clarke AD (1979) Mental subnormality. In Eysenck, op cit, p 212
88. Healy W (1969) The individual delinquent. Patterson Smith, Montelair, p 442
89. Scheff T (1973) Screening mental patients. In: Rubington, op cit, p 193
90. Szasz TS (1974) Law, liberty and psychiatry. Collier, New York, p 17
91. Clarke, op cit, p 212
92. Redlich, op cit, p 56
93. Ibid, p 55
94. Romano J (1950) Basic orientation and education of the medical student. JAMA 409: 143
95. Redlich, op cit, p 55
96. Sabshin M (1975) Psychiatric perspectives on normality. In: Allen et al., op cit, p 58
97. Redlich, op cit, p 55
98. Payne R (1979) Cognitive abnormalities. In: Eysenck, op cit, p 420
99. WHO (1954) The mentally subnormal child. WHO Technical Report Series n 75, Geneva
100. Healey, op cit, p 442
101. Scheff, op cit, p 193

102. Freedman, op cit, p 42
103. Romano, op cit, p 143
104. Finkel N (1980) Therapy and ethics. Grune and Stratton, New York, p 3
105. Ibid
106. White, op cit, p 6
107. Reed C, Alexander I, Tomkins S (1967) Psychopathology. Wiley, New York, p 684
108. Finkel, op cit, pp 18–19
109. Yochelson, op cit, p 255
110. Ibid, p 259
111. Ibid, p 265
112. Ibid, p 268
113. Ibid, p 291
114. Ibid, p 297
115. Ibid, p 315
116. Ibid, p 363
117. Ibid, p 366
118. Ibid, p 372
119. Ibid, p 374
120. Ibid, p 376
121. Ibid, p 387
122. Yochelson, op cit, p 248
123. Freedman, op cit, p 45
124. Board R (1967) An operational conception of criminal responsibility. In: Reed et al., op cit, p 786
125. Trasler G (1979) Criminal behavior. In: Eysenck, op cit, p 67
126. Quinton R (1910) Crime and criminals. Longmans, New York, p 259
127. Healey, op cit, p 161
128. Goring C (1913) The English convict, a statistical study. Wyman, London, p 440
129. Trasler, op cit, p 67
130. Knudten, op cit, p 9
131. Feldman, op cit, p 436
132. Board, op cit, p 789
133. Knudten, op cit, p 279
134. Ibid, p 89
135. Plato, Republic Book 9, 571, C, tr. Francis Cornford
136. Knudten, op cit, p 37
137. Ibid, p 38
138. Cressey D, Ward D (1969) Delinquency, crime and social process. Harper, New York, p 115
139. Healey, op cit, p 160
140. Trasler, op cit, p 68
141. Healey, op cit, p 160
142. Ibid, p 4
143. Knudten, op cit, p 279

II. Psychiatry and Society

The Responsibilities of Psychiatrists to Society: The Dual Loyalties

R. R. Rogers

Introduction

The psychiatric profession prepares its practitioners to view two opposites as equally true and to accept the world not as good or bad, black or white, but rather as shaded. Intimate knowledge of the intricacies of the human dimension does not permit dichotomies into good or bad. Our patients teach us, for instance, that their grandiose defensiveness hides their fear of facing or acknowledging their feelings of inferiority. Our patients also teach us that their rigid adherence to schedules and patterns represents their fear of chaos and fragmentation. Their preoccupation with cleanliness represents a frantic effort to camouflage their fascination with dirt, etc.

As we learn to accept this seeming paradox in our patients, we gradually mature into accepting this within ourselves. We learn to recognize that our need to be successful represents our fear of being insignificant. Our adherence to professional societies is an attempt to protect ourselves from the awesome loneliness of the burden of being solely responsible for the lives of one and many patients. We even learn to accept that our high ideals for helping mankind are nothing but a mask behind which we hide our destructive and aggressive impulses, and to respect this within ourselves and others.

In our profession we have developed a fancy language to sanction the cover-up which we engage in. We call them defenses and we are grateful for having them. But having to recognize these defenses within our patients and acknowledging them within ourselves makes life somewhat more difficult for us. We have to (at times) look starkly at many of our conflicts, including the conflict between our dual loyalties to society: the professional and the personal.

Legal Issues

Example 1. A prominent child psychiatrist was called to refer a 2½-year-old girl who had told her mother that she had been sexually molested by her father. The psychiatrist had not yet seen the little girl but had talked to the mother, who revealed the communication, which reflected the child's familiarity with sexual experiences. Such knowledge was indicative that this 2½-year-old child had had a sexual experience. The child psychiatrist attempted to refer this child to another psychiatrist, because of the long distance they would need to travel and "in order not to impose any additional hardship on this child" (the referring psychiatrist's overt statement). The psychiatrist to whom she attempted to refer the child asked if she had reported the suspected sexual child abuse to the proper authorities. She replied she had not, and expressed shock at having to do so. She stressed that she had not seen the little girl, but had only talked to the mother, and that the father of the little girl was a physician. She added that a child of this age would most likely be expressing fantasies and not events. When the physician to whom she attempted to refer the child persisted in informing her that it was her legal responsibility to report the case and then to treat or to refer, she said "but this would be unethical in terms of confidentiality." She was then confronted by two arguments from the physician to whom she attempted to refer the patient: (a) that being a physician did not entitle her to break the law, and (b) that protecting this little girl from further sexual abuse was more important than "protecting" the mother's confidentiality (the mother was not even the patient). Of course, the referring physician (after this conversation) had the additional burden of facing her real motivation for attempting to refer the child to someone else. Was she truly wanting to protect this child from the burden of long travel time to and from appointments, or was she attempting to protect herself from the burden of contacting the proper authorities and the conflict between her professional responsibility of confidentiality and her legal responsibility?

Ethical Issues

Example 1. A 17-year-old girl was referred to a psychiatrist because of feelings of insecurity, fear of mental illness, and bouts of depression. The psychiatrist happened to be someone keenly interested in a research project on children of Holocaust survivors. It so happened that the girl was the daughter of a survivor and the therapist concentrated her examination and treatment of this girl into the sector of her being the daughter of a survivor. The patient (who did not know about the research project of her therapist) experienced as "bewildering and artificial" her psychiatrist's overwhelming interest in this particular aspect of her life, namely what she knew or did not know about her mother's concentration camp experience and how this affected her, etc. Indeed, she felt that her therapist was "more interested" in her mother's background, well-being, and feelings than she was in her, the patient. Such feelings aggravated existing rivalry between mother and daugher. They also hindered therapy for this girl, since she felt the therapist's interest in her as a person was not genuine.

Example 2. Another psychiatrist had a more subtle dilemma: he was keenly interested in a research project on children whose mothers had died in childbirth. He found himself accepting much more readily the referrals of these patients than of others. He then pursued with these patients the theme of how their knowledge of having lost a mother in childbirth had affected their perceptions of themselves.

Both of these psychiatrists would have been behaving perfectly ethically had they officially notified their patients that they had accepted them as patients because of their specific interests in the particular research projects. There still would have been the dilemma of whether or not to accept fees and whether the specific interest of the therapist might not contaminate the therapist's ability to see the "entire" patient from the patient's perspective.

While legal and research issues represent clear-cut ethical dilemmas, choosing, accepting or refusing, and treating patients can be ambiguous and complicated for psychiatrists. Our personalities are our essential tools. These "tools" are never objective. Other medical specialists accept or reject patients on the basis of external factors (hospital bed availability, diagnosis, fees, time availability, etc.).

Psychiatrists are not only influenced by their intimate feelings about these aforementioned criteria, but they also have to acknowledge to themselves why they accept or reject a particular patient. This is not an easy task. We all have predilections, positive and negative experiences which cast a shadow over our professional objectivity. We reach out toward or reject patients who are like ourselves. We are prejudiced against or in favor of patients who remind us of an important figure in our background. We have emotional calendars for certain psychological events and circumstances which become reignited through our patients' experiences. The professional, personal, and societal roles cannot easily be disentangled from each other. They are interwoven and intermeshed.

Nuclear Issues

Nuclear weapons have been with us for several decades and the public's awareness of these issues has been dormant until recently. Indeed, Lifton [1] has coined the term "psychic numbing" to define the human reaction to the acknowledgment of the existence of nuclear weapons. In a paper "On Emotional Responses to Nuclear Issues and Terrorism" [2], this author has talked about the fact that we lack an emotional platform for nuclear issues because they lie outside our sensory experiences and are beyond our human capacity to encompass. This was so until 2 years ago, when an active, vociferous antinuclear campaign from the pulpits and campuses changed the reactions of the public. People have now moved from failure to acknowledge to fear. Physicians and psychiatrists in particular, because of their humanistic concerns, have been among the first to alert the public to the danger of a nuclear holocaust. We feel responsible as citizens of this planet for alerting people to the dangers of nuclear war. What about our responsibilities as psychiatrists to people (some of them our own or our colleagues' patients) who live in constant anxiety about the world coming to an end and doomsday being near, when we promote films which show Hiroshima and a potential holocaust? When we tell people, especially children and adolescents, that the world is likely to be destroyed by nuclear weapons, what do we do to their impetus for building relationships, building careers, building and believing in the future?

Psychiatrists, like other adults, are easily inclined to embrace a cause for the sake of our children. But psychiatrists like all adults frequently use children as tools for promoting personal causes.

Nuclear issues have raised a second dilemma concerning professional and societal responsibilities. An organization in the United States, Physicians for Social Responsibility, has been actively compaigning for people to sign up for a nuclear freeze referendum in their respective states. For this purpose physicians were encouraging their colleagues (psychiatrists among them) to distribute literature and give encouragement to their patients. This raised specific problems for psychiatrists: We are not supposed to impose our world view, our opinion, our agenda, our politics, and our motivation on our patients. Can we dismiss psychiatric ethics for the sake of a cause as lofty as a nuclear freeze campaign?

Political and Money Issues

Our political convictions and our attitudes about money are dependent to a great extent on who we are, from where we come, when and how we were raised, and who our parents are, what they are like, and where they come from. Our feelings about money and politics are intimate and fierce. We do not submit these inclinations to objective scrutiny. We usually do not even acknowledge them to ourselves. We rarely examine them. This set of circumstances – unresolved childhood experiences covered by background justification, wrapped with the rationalization and fierceness which political and money issues evoke in us – easily leads to the establishment of priorities among our loyalties without objective reasoning. Many of our stances toward money are disguised and displaced childhood agendas.

Our political agendas are an adult camouflage of our external and internal experiences. They (money and politics) are the instruments via which we relate our intimate self to the small and wider groups of our world. The way we utilize these instruments often represents a compromise between our manifest and latent loyalties.

Child Psychiatric Issues

Child psychiatry offers a multitude of dilemmas to the practitioner. One of these is the continuous need to perceive the child as one's patient and to view the parent only from the point of view of the parenting role for this particular child. The child psychiatrist, though, remains a general psychiatrist and perceives the emotional distortions in the parent.

The child psychiatrist, however, also remains a physician who experiences his role of having to alleviate the hurt in the child as well as in the parent. This is not an easy task because often both (the parents and the child) replay for the psychiatrist their rivalry for individual attention by the therapist. People engaged in rivalries frequently perceive the opponents' loss as their gain and vice versa. Unfortunately, adults who have grown up with a hunger for nurturance cannot sufficiently nurture their children, in spite of their determination to do so.

There is another ambiguity which frequently arises in child psychiatry. Child psychiatrists, being adults and having had several years of training in adult psychiatry, and having spent all their medical school years and internship (with only a brief interlude in pediatrics) with adult patients, are easily inclined to accept the parent or parents as primary patients and dismiss their attention and care from the child. It is often easier to understand the parent, diagnose his problems, and treat him than to focus directly on the child. The intricate and intimate relationship between parents and children and the reciprocal reverberations of symptoms tend to lead the child psychiatrist to treat the parent rather than the child. The knowledge that most general psychiatrists cannot treat emotionally ill children and that child psychiatry is the medical specialty of greatest shortage, as enumerated by the U.S. Surgeon General, creates some guilt in child psychiatrists when they accept the parents rather than the child as patients. But these issues are not simple. For example, a 7-year-old second-grader was referred by his pediatrician. The reason for referral was given as his intolerably loud and disturbing behavior. The boy's mother, a very obese and loud woman, "shouted" to the examining psychiatrist, "Billy is so loud the teacher complains that he shouts louder than all the children in the class, if not in the school." This mother was frustrated not only with Billy (as we will call him), but also with his little brother, who had had multiple physical ailments, particularly ear troubles, throughout his early childhood. Billy had spent much of his early years sitting with mother in doctor and hospital waiting rooms. Attention had been focused on his little brother, except when he obtained negative attention through his disturbing behavior. He had become very good at it. But the mother's frustration was much more than her anger at her two little boys (one sickly and one noisy). Her worst feelings of frustration stemmed from a sense of being "chained" to her husband. He was a strikingly handsome, athletic man, who worked in a factory on the night shift and slept during the day. Since he needed quiet in order to sleep, she had the unenviable choice between keeping the two boys quiet (an impossible task) or taking them to her mother, who then bossed her and her sons.

These were the overt dilemmas: psychiatric evaluation of this family revealed that both mother and father bitterly resented their low economic status and the missed opportunities which had led to them. Father had been chosen to play professional baseball, but when he had to go out of town for a training period, he refused to go because he was scared of losing Mrs. C., who at the time was his girlfriend. On superficial evaluation it seemed incomprehensible that so strikingly handsome a man would be paralyzed by fear of losing a woman who was so obese, loud, and physically unattractive. Psychiatric evaluation of Mr. C. revealed him to have the remnants of a fully fledged, untreated separation anxiety centered on his mother; this anxiety of phobic proportions he had displaced onto his wife. Whom should the child psychiatrist treat in this case: Billy, his mother or his father, or the entire family? Just as the child psychiatrist was deliberating on these issues, the father was diagnosed as suffering from essential hypertension, a condition which truly endangered his life and his ability to continue to provide for his family and to be a father to these two little boys. Because of the economic strain on this family, the psychiatrist attempted to refer them to a clinic where lower costs would have enabled several family members to be treated. The father could not accept this because of the attachment which he had by now formed to this psychiatrist and because of the reawakened hurt: "Had I only become a professional baseball player we could live like they do, rolling in money, and I could afford anything and everything for my family and myself," he said.

Dilemmas of confidentiality arise with particular poignance in child psychiatry. Child patients are told by their therapists that they should trust the therapist with their intimate communications in order to learn to understand themselves. The therapist on occasion may learn that a teenage girl is pregnant, a preadolescent boy considers suicide, a 7-year-old girl is actively involved in stealing, etc. In such cases as rape and sexual molestation or physical abuse it is now somewhat easier for the child psychiatrist to make decisions even when they are unpalatable. The law demands an immediate verbal report when the psychiatrist suspects child abuse, followed by a written report with in 36 hours. The psychiatrist cannot break the law any more than any other citizen. Nevertheless, "the adversary" role in which the psychiatrist has to place himself vis-à-vis his patient presents a dilemma. At a recent conference a law enforcement officer vehmently declared that the matter is simple:

"when you hear about suspected child abuse, you excuse yourself and call the police." For a psychiatrist this is not as simple as for a law enforcement officer. The patient has come to us for help. It is true we help our patients when we protect them from harming children or others, but we have a hard time exposing them to the punitive arms of the law because we feel their hurt. Each parent who abuses his child was abused by his parents when he was a child. The parent becomes the abuser because of the unresolved hurts from his having been abused. As citizens we are compelled not only to obey the law, but also to protect society from the hurts potentially inflicted by our patients. As physicians, particularly as psychiatrists, we find it difficult to help punish people because of their illness and their hurts.

Conclusion

When one practices psychiatry, one lives and feels many lives. The intimacy with which our patients entrust themselves to our care enriches our human experience. It is impossible to expect such enrichment without being prepared also to assume the burden it places upon us. It is a heavy burden. The most difficult one, however, is the obligation to look at ourselves and our faults and shortcomings, including accepting our excuses, defenses, rationalizations, intellectualizations, and motivations. We have to have empathy not only for our patients and society but also for ourselves. The multiplicity of our loyalties, especially the duality of our loyalties towards society and our profession and the duality of our loyalty towards our patients and ourselves, raises questions within ourselves. This is what enhances our ability to raise questions within our patients to help them to perceive themselves and their society in a corrected way.

References

1. Lifton RJ (1967) Death in life: Survivors of Hiroshima. Random House, New York
2. Rogers RR (1980) On emotional responses to nuclear issues and terrorism. Psychiatr J of the University of Ottawa 5 (3): 147–152

Political Psychiatry

G. W. Lynch

In February 1983, the Soviet Union resigned from the World Psychiatric Association. The letter of withdrawal, sent to the Association's headquarters in Vienna, took the Soviet Society of Psychiatrists and Neuropathologists out of the world body.

The action of the Soviet Union came 5 months before the July Convention of the World Psychiatric Association, which was expected to act on two proposals: one by the National Psychiatric Association of the United States to suspend the Soviet affiliate, and the other by the British Psychiatric Association to expel it. The President of Britain's Royal College of Psychiatry, Dr. Kenneth Rawnsley, stated in an interview that be believed Moscow had withdrawn because "it would have found it difficult to cope with the possibility of a humiliating debate in the full glare of public debate" [1].

The action of the Soviet Union also came 1 week after the publication of a revealing and critical cover story in the *New York Times Magazine* of January 30, 1983, entitled "The World of Soviet Psychiatry" [2]. Some speculation concerning the Soviet move suggested that Moscow believed that there had been too much conciliation on the part of Soviet psychiatrists and that they had been improperly complying with Western requests for data on specific cases. Only recently (December 1982), after a prolonged refusal to give information about purported cases of abuse, Soviet psychiatrists submitted information on seven cases. They also concurred with the proposal to hold an international inquiry into the allegations.

By withdrawing from the World Psychiatric Association, the Soviet Union avoids the probability of censure or suspension in July and sharply curtails professional contacts, date exchanges, and the likelihood of other specific charges of alleged abuses in Soviet psychiatry.

The Soviet move has been long in building. Over the last few years, a number of American and Soviet writers have made the allegation that the Soviet government is engaged in a deliberate plot to remove all political dissidents and intellectuals from the mainstream of Soviet society. In an effort to accomplish this end the Soviets, they allege, use psychiatry as a legitimate front to disguise the punitive and repressive actions of the Soviet government against its citizens. These allegations have been documented in the writings of such prominent Russian authors as Alexander Solzhenitsyn, Andrei Sokhorov and, most recently, Alexander Podrabinek. In addition, several Western psychiatrists, Boris Segal, Paul Chodoff, and Rita Rodgers, have written articles which call attention to the misuse of psychiatry in the Soviet Union [3].

In its annual meeting in Mexico City in December 1971, the World Congress of Psychiatry held unofficial discussions with Soviet psychiatrists concerning specific reports which had been forwarded to Western psychiatrists from Soviet civil rights activist Vladimir Bukovsky. The reports were exact copies of psychiatric diagnoses of six dissenters who were examined by Soviet doctors and subsequently committed to special hospitals. Bukovsky solicited the opinions of Western psychiatrists in order to subject the judgment of Soviet doctors to closer professional scrutiny. His motive for circulating these reports to the West was to gain "outside" professional support to substantiate his charges against Soviet psychiatry. Soviet psychiatrists interviewed on this matter at the Mexico City meeting neither denied nor affirmed the authenticity of these reports. Rather, they denied the allegations that psychiatric hospitalization is being used in the USSR to suppress political dissent and dismissed these charges as part of the ongoing cold war plot [4].

On 9 December 1971, the American Psychiatric Association, through a resolution of its trustees, put the Association on record as "opposing the misuse of psychiatric facilities for the detention of persons solely on the basis of their political dissent, no matter where it occurs" [5]. Although their statement was the result of international concern over mounting evidence that the Soviet Union is using psychiatry as a political tool of the state, it acknowledged that such misuse was not unique to the Soviet state. There can be no balanced discussion of the misuse of psychiatry for political purposes in another country without first examining the subject with regard to American psychiatric practices. Specifically, the question has arisen as to whether a democracy, which is based on a constitution and provides protection for its citizens through a Bill of Rights, is capable of allowing the kind of gross perversion of psychiatric ethics alleged to be associated with totalitarian regimes.

In order to answer this question, we must review briefly the common law traditions and practices which have shaped the role of psychiatry in contemporary Anglo-American law. Essential to any discussion of psychiatric jurisprudence are the legal provisions concerning a defendant's mental competency to stand trial and the defense of insanity. While both of these provisions have been held up as representing an enlightened view of criminal responsibility, in practice they have also provided governments with a means of abusing due process.

One of the most vocal critics of the interplay which has developed between American psychiatry and the law is Thomas Szasz, an American psychiatrist. In his book *Psychiatric Justice,* [7] Szasz has propounded the thesis that psychiatry, when used by the state in the legal process, provides the government with an effective weapon against the individual citizen. Specifically, he focuses on the common law rule that a mentally incompetent defendant may not be subjected to a criminal trial. The rule states that a person accused of a crime is mentally fit to stand trial only if he understands the charges against him and the nature and object of the proceedings, and can assist counsel in his defense [6]. In the American legal system the determination of a defendant's mental competence (or incompetence) to stand trial is strongly influenced by the opinions of psychiatrists who conduct the examination for the court. Szasz argues that the use of psychiatrists by the court seriously distorts the notion of the psychiatrist as an advocate for his client and provides the state with another method of controlling social deviants. This is the basis for his contention that psychiatry is used to further the ends of the state rather than serve the needs of the individual. Szasz maintains that the majority of psychiatrists who are solicited to assist the state will render judgments favorable to the state.

While the procedures to determine mental competency by a court appear to comply with due process. Szasz notes two major violations. First, the declaration by the court that the defendant is in fact mentally incompetent to stand trial results in a postponement of the trial and commitment to a psychiatric institution. When this occurs the defendant is denied his constitutional right to a trial. Even though the incompetency rule allows the accused to be tried at a later date when deemed competent, the defendant is effectively denied his right to stand trial and resolve his guilt or innocence when he chooses. Insofar as the Sixth Amendment of the United States Constitution provides that "In all criminal prosecutions, the accused shall enjoy the right to a speedy and public trial . . .," the mentally incompetent defendant is denied this constitutional right. Secondly, the practice of automatic commitment to a psychiatric facility for indefinite duration can be construed as punishment without official adjudication [7]. Furthermore, Szasz contends that the use of psychiatrists in the courtroom gives the state added power over the accused, since it can repeatedly move to have the defendant incriminated as mentally incompetent to stand trial.

As an example of this power he cites the experience of Mr. Louis Perroni in a New York court [8]:

> In June 1955 Mr. Louis Perroni was arraigned but was not indicted. Instead, at the request of the District Attorney, the Onondaga County Court Judge before whom he appeared ordered him to undergo pretrial psychiatric axamination to determine his fitness to stand trial. He was examined by two court-appointed psychiatrists, found incapable of standing trial, and committed to the Matteawan State Hospital. In June 1961, after spending approximately six years at the Matteawan State Hospital, Mr. Perroni and his attorney obtained a favorable ruling in one of their numerous *habeas corpus* hearings. Mr. Perroni was returned to court in Onondaga County. But again, despite the decision of a State Supreme Court Judge in Duchess County that Perroni was fit to stand trial, the District Attorney moved that he was not fit and should be examined by psychiatrists. Again the court concurred, ordered the examination, declared Perroni unfit to stand trial, and recommitted him to Matteawan.

Szasz also cites the cases of the American poet Ezra Pound and General Edwin Walker as examples where the government used the mental incompetency proceedings to discredit the political ideology and values of the accused. In each case the defendant held a political view which was embarrassing to the American government. More recently, Richard Moran in his book *Knowing Right from Wrong, the Insanity Defense of Daniel McNaughtan* [9] offers a revised view of the origin of the insanity defense in Britain. Moran claims that the attempted assassination of Prime Minister Sir Robert Peel (which instead resulted in the death of Edmund Drummond) by Daniel McNaughtan was a political act. The efforts of the Tory government in England in 1843 to persuade the court to interpret McNaughtan's crime as the product of a diseased mind were essentially self-serving. By regarding him as a criminal lunatic the government was able to divert attention from the political cause he represented.

Moran writes [9]:

> Finally, the McNaughtan case demonstrates how psychological descriptions can function to distract attention away from moral, political, or social conflicts which might otherwise be considered important. The court's interpretation of McNaughtan's crime as the product of a diseased mind served to discredit him and the political ideas he represented. By regarding McNaughtan

> as a criminal lunatic incapable of knowing right from wrong, the court indicated that an explanation for his behavior would have to be sought in medical or psychological terms rather than in political theory.

Thus it was in the government's best interests to support a rule which would relieve a defendant of criminal responsibility if it could be shown that he was incapable of knowing right from wrong when the crime was committed. The McNaughtan Rules dominated the American law on criminal responsibility until 1954. At that time the Durham decision proposed a broader measure of criminal responsibility than the "right from wrong" test. Both the McNaughtan and Durham tests are responsible for introducing psychiatry into the courtroom.

The legal-psychiatric practices of Western common law countries are clearly susceptible to political influence. Szasz and others who have studied commitment proceedings claim that psychiatrists working for the government usually recommend commitment. However, there is no proof that mental hospitalization has been initiated and carried out with psychiatric compliance as a matter of state or governmental policy [10]. Rather, the use of psychiatrists by the state in court proceedings leads to a situation where the psychiatrist's professional judgment is suspect. Szasz states:

> "... whenever the physician is employed by someone other than the patient his loyalty and responsibility to his employer must be frankly recognized" [11].

Thus the role of the psychiatrist brought into the court to substantiate the claims of either judge or prosecutor in a competency hearing is one of an adversary rather than that of advocate for the client. It is possible that the psychiatrist views the accused as a threat to the state and can justify his actions as protecting the community. The civil commitment proceeding is a good example of a due process court hearing which relies upon the professional judgment of a psychiatrist to assess the dangerousness of the patient. Those who are considered dangerous to themselves or others are ordered by the court to psychiatric hospitals for compulsory medical treatment. In effect, psychiatrists are requested by the courts to predict the future behavior of individuals on the basis of information derived from an examination.

The question arises as to just how accurate these predictions are. In 1969 Dershowitz reviewed the few studies on psychiatric prediction of antisocial behavior and concluded that psychiatrists were prone to overprediction [12]. He found that for every correct prediction of violence, there were numerous erroneous predictions. Similarly, Litwack and Ennis found that there is no empirical evidence that psychiatrists can predict dangerous behavior [13]. The failure accurately to predict who is dangerous results in a high number of false positives, that is, persons who are not really dangerous nonetheless ending up in psychiatric hospitals. The problem of prediction is exacerbated by the lack of reliability of psychiatric diagnoses. Studies indicate that psychiatrists often disagree in their judgments and diagnoses. A review of several studies on the reliability of psychiatric diagnosis showed that the changes of a second psychiatrist agreeing with the first were little better than 50-50 [14]. These studies suggest that the courts have entrusted psychiatry with a task it is not capable of handling.

Chesler has written extensively on the treatment of women in psychiatric theory and practice. She maintains that psychiatry, as a male-dominated profession, has neglected to examine the psychological problems of women in a sociopolitical context. Psychologists continue to view such problems as depression, anxiety, and aggressiveness as caused by individual pathological factors. Chesler contends that these problems are not at all pathological but rather symptomatic of a dissatisfaction with the social role ascribed to women. However, women who have experienced these problems see themselves as »neurotic« or »psychotic« and in need of professional help [15]. Often these women have ended up being committed to psychiatric hospitals for mental illness. In her book *Women and Madness,* [15] Chesler explains how psychiatry manipulates the female psyche to force it to adhere to the social norms.

More recently, penologists, sociologists, and psychologists have raised the question of the role of the psychiatrist in penal institutions. They question whether a psychiatrist who is working for the state can really function as an advocate for his patient. A particular situation where this question has received attention is at the Patuxent Institute for Defective Delinquents in Maryland. At Patuxent offenders are committed for an indeterminate period and released only after they have been judged fit by staff psychiatrists. Similarly, psychiatrists are used by the armed forces to determine the psychological competency of those who hold rank, to assess an individual's potential for promotion, and to predict the loyalty of those entrusted with top military secrets. To what extent does their allegiance to the military influence their professional opinions and judgments [16]?

All of the above-mentioned issues and others are the subject of a spirited debate going on in the United States at all levels of society. President Reagan has called for the defendant to prove insanity, rather than the state. Many prominent psychiatrists are calling for the total abolition of the insanity defense because of its susceptibility to abuse, its variability in practice, and the unreliability of diagnoses of future dangerousness. The public at large responding to polls appears disenchanted with the insanity defense, particularly in the cases of the murder of John Lennon and the attempted assassination of President Reagan. Out of this intense debate a new approach to the bringing to justice of the mentally and emotionally disturbed seems to be evolving. Whether the debate will stop at putting the burden of proof of insanity on the defendant or at striking down the defense completely and considering insanity along with other issues after the trial has been concluded is as yet unclear.

Although there is evidence, therefore, to support the misuse of psychiatry in America and other Western democratic countries, it is neither as prevalent nor as strong as the evidence from the Soviet Union. According to the American psychiatrist Chodoff, the reason for this is not that American psychiatrists are necessarily any more virtuous than their Soviet colleagues, but rather because of certain safeguards inherent in the structure and the organization of our society.

These safeguards are [17]:

1. In America the state is not the only source of employment for psychiatrists and a psychiatrist does not have to do what he understands the state expects of him, either explicitly of implicitly, at the cost of giving up his profession.

2. The United States is a more open society than the Soviet Union and the values of American Society favor the ethic of individualism rather than of communalism. There is more tolerance for dissent in the United States and, in addition, there are many kinds of checks, including potentially adverse publicity, on the actions of American psychiatrists.
3. The institution of judicial review, which does not exist in the Soviet constitution, opens an avenue for the review by an impartial third party of all cases of involuntary hospitalization in the United States, forcing psychiatrists to justify their committing a patient to involuntary hospitalization, and serving as a check on the psychiatrist's authority to make such a commitment a lasting one.

The conclusion of Chodoff and other American psychiatrists is that the role of American psychiatry with respect to being the guardian of state and societal values differs from that of psychiatry in the Soviet Union.

Over the last few years both American and Soviet writers have discussed the use of Soviet psychiatry as a means to further the political aims of the state. Probably the most extensive work on this subject has been done by the Russian Alexander Podrabinek. His book entitled *Punitive Medicine* [18] describes the process by which political dissidents are judged mentally ill and involuntarily committed to psychiatric hospitals. Clearly, in Podrabinek's view the state has come to rely on psychiatry to stabilize political life. It has discovered that political dissidents can be dealt with through involuntary hospitalization and that this procedure is far more effective than a criminal trial. Ever since the Soviets became involved with the West in "the politics of détente," they have been more concerned with their image abroad. Consequently, they have deliberately disassociated themselves from the brutal and repressive measures characteristic of the Stalinist era. Podrabinek contends that the current practice of labeling dissidents as mentally ill allows the Soviet government to avoid the publicity which surrounds a public trial. Thus Soviet psychiatry operates as an arm of the state and is subject to government control. He points out that cases where seemingly sane people have been declared insane on the basis of political pretext and committed to institutions are common throughout Russian history. As an example he cites the case of Peter Chaadayev (1794–1865), who was an outstanding Russian philosopher. Chaadayev published the "Philosophical Letter" in 1836 and shortly afterward he was officially pronounced insane by the authorities. His writing was viewed as an unpatriotic attack on Soviet nationalism and a threat to the future existence of the state. Count Benhendorf, chief of the gendarmerie, in a letter to Prince Golitsyn, the military governor of Moscow at the time, dismissed the contents of the publication as the product of a lunatic. He wrote [18]:

> But the inhabitants of our capital, always known for their sweet reason and pride in the dignity of the Russian Nation, understood immediately that this kind of article could not possibly have been written by a sane compatriot, and therefore so the rumors say – did not direct their indignation toward him, but on the contrary, expressed their genuine sympathy for the mental disorder that has befallen him, which can be the only reason for his writing such absurdities ...

Although Podrabinek documents several other incidents similar to the Chaadayev case in prerevolutionary Russia, these events occurred in the nineteenth century and were not yet part of a systematic political strategy to declare sane people mentally ill. The systematic use of psychiatry for political purposes began after the Russian Revolution of 1917. Chodoff and Segal, both American psychiatrists, discuss the case of Major General Pyotr Grigorenko [19]. Grigorenko was arrested in 1964 for delivering an anti-Stalinist speech and turning out leaflets critical of the regime. He was declared mentally disturbed and sent to a psychiatric hospital for 15 months. After his release he continued his protest activities and was arrested again in May 1969. Grigorenko was examined by a psychiatric commission in Tashkent, who found no positive evidence of mental illness. The conclusions of the Tashkent commission were rejected by psychiatrists at the state-run Serbsky Institute, who upon conducting their own examination stated that Grigorenko was of unsound mind and required compulsory treatment in a psychiatric hospital. Their diagnosis stated that Major General Grigorenko was suffering from "a pathological paranoid development of personality" with the presence of reformist ideas [20]. Chodoff, who has read the reports of the Grigorenko examination, points out that most of the information in the report focuses on his political activity and very little is said about interpersonal and work relationships. Furthermore, all psychological abnormalities reported are tied to the political views of Grigorenko. According to Chodoff, the decision of the authorities to subject the General to a second examination was based on the knowledge that psychiatrists at the Serbsky could be relied on to produce a finding of mental illness.

Podrabinek offers an interesting theory to explain the increased use of psychiatric hospitals during Stalin's reign. At that time party bosses were being regularly replaced by the authorities (Committee for State Security; KGB) and, rather than face the firing squad, they persuaded the government to create a network of special psychiatric hospitals in order to save their own lives [21].

Probably the most scathing evidence of abuse and violation by physicians who operated and staffed Soviet psychiatric hospitals during the Stalinist period comes from information produced by a special investigation committee. The documents of the investigative committee (1955–1956), which have never been published or released in the West, contain documented evidence that Soviet psychiatric hospitals were admitting mentally healthy people. Above all, the committee established the existence of a criminal alliance between psychiatrists at the Serbsky and the state security agencies [22]. This alliance is purported still to exist and is currently the subject of criticism by Western psychiatrists. They view this kind of collaborative relationship between psychiatrist and government as a violation of the code of ethics for psychiatry. In their view this arrangement interferes with the professional code which holds that the individual needs of the patient are more important than the welfare of the state.

To explain the co-optation of psychiatry by the government it is necessary to examine Soviet bureaucracy. Segal points out that psychiatry, like all other Soviet institutions, is completely subordinate to the state. Soviet psychiatric hospitals are under the jurisdiction of the Ministry of the Interior and often the chief doctors and directors of these institutions are members of groups which have political authority. They serve in these groups along with members of the KGB and, in fact, the chief physicians hold military rank. Consequently, all of their actions are coordinated with military chiefs and accountable to the KGB. Also, the promotion of chief physicians in the Soviet political hierarchy is indirectly based on the degree of cooperation between the physician and the KGB. According to Podrabinek, this practice influences psychiatric diagnosis and treatment. Psychiatrists are always conscious of how their decision will be viewed by the authorities. This political awareness has led to several situations where the needs of the patient are subordinated to the personal career ambitions of the chief physicians [23].

In addition to the apparent collaboration between the state and the physicians of the various psychiatric hospitals, the laws and procedures governing involuntary commitment have been criticized. Podrabinek and others who have studied the laws agree that the Soviet Penal Code and the Penal Law Procedure Code are written broadly to protect the interests of the state against anti-Communist sentiment.

For example, article 70 of the Penal Code, which is most frequently used to convict political dissidents, reads [24]

> Agitation and propaganda conducted for the purpose of damaging or weakening Soviet power, or committing certain especially dangerous crimes against the State, or dissemination, for the same purpose, of slanderous insinuations denigrating the Soviet state and social system as well as dissemination of, or the manufacturing and storing of, literature of the same content for the same purpose are punishable by deprivation of freedom of from six months to seven years with exile of from two to five years, or without exile, or by exile of from two to five years.
> The same acts committed by a person previously convicted of especially dangerous crimes against the State, as well as those committed during time of war are punishable by deprivation of freedom for a term of from three to ten years and possible exile of from two to five years.

Compulsory medical measures are officially regulated by specific articles in the Penal Code and through administrative practice.

Article 58 is central to the issue of psychiatry and the law and reads [25]:

> Persons who committed socially dangerous acts in a state of insanity, or those who committed such acts in a state of sanity, but became insane prior to sentencing or while serving their sentences, whereby they were unaware of their actions or unable to control their actions, are subject, on the decisions of the court, to the following compulsory medical measures:
> 1. Commitment to a general psychiatric hospital.
> 2. Commitment to a special psychiatric hospital.

The leading Soviet psychiatrist is Dr. Andrei V. Snezhvesky, who is head of Moscow's Institute of Psychiatry. It was he who lead the delegation to the 1977 congress of the World Psychiatric Association in Hawaii. It was there that he had to listen to the strong criticism of Soviet psychiatry, as the conference voted to condemn "the systematic abuse of psychiatry for political purposes in the U.S.S.R." [26].

The prominence Snezhvesky holds today is based partly on his definitions of the various forms of schizophrenia, which have been broadly adopted throughout Soviet psychiatry. His most controversial diagnosis is "sluggish schizophrenia," which represents a slow, continuous mental deterioration. It is this diagnosis that has been used most prominently in the cases of the dissidents. The problem it presents to Western psychiatrists is that the diagnosis is made on the basis of nonpsychotic characteristics which show mild emotional or behavioral deviations and might even be judged normal, but are certainly not psychotic by Western standards. The pervasiveness of Snezhvesky's topology in the Soviet Union and its easy use in the cases of dissidents has led to the charge that it was created for that purpose. But that charge is regarded as too facile an answer by most observers.

A more plausible explanation must take into account the entire Soviet society and its attitude toward dissenters. Reich holds [27] that to dissent in a society which officially prohibits it is seen and experienced by the nondissenters as peculiar, upsetting, and strange. It is not too far a step from "strangeness" to sluggish schizophrenia, with the KGB, the psychiatrists, and the court finally believing that the diagnosis is appropriate for the phenomenon they have observed and experienced as out of the normal range. He does not necessarily see an all-embracing plot based on making diagnoses which are known to be false. It is rather a pervasive mind set which demands such conformity of itself that the dissenter's nonconformity evokes strong reactions. These reactions tend to exaggerate the seriousness or potential seriousness of the problem and thus the misdiagnosis.

Thus under Soviet law people are arrested for certain political crimes such as "anti-Soviet agitation" or "the spreading of deliberate fabrications discrediting the Soviet political and social system." Soviet law requires a psychiatric examination if an investigator or prosecutor has reason to question the accused person's mental stability. The psychiatric examination is conducted by a commission of not fewer than three psychiatrists at the Serbsky Institute of Forensic Psychiatry. Upon completion the results are reviewed by a court and, if the court accepts the commission's judgment, the accused can be sentenced to an indefinite period of detention for further psychiatric examination in a psychiatric hospital. The accused is never informed of the findings of the commission, nor is he permitted to participate in the court hearing. In fact, article 184 of the Penal Law Procedure Code states that the ruling of forensic psychiatric examination and the examination's conclusion need not be announced to the accused if his mental condition renders it impossible. As a result of article 184, the rights of the accused with respect to the examination (which are provided for separately in article 185) are withheld on the grounds that the announcement of an examination may be traumatic to the subject who is suffering from mental illness [28]. In comparing the Soviet commitment process with American civil commitment procedures, one cannot help but notice the absence of due process in the Soviet judicial system.

While Podrabinek is convinced that Soviet psychiatry is nothing more than an instrument for political repression, Western psychiatrists have avoided such sweeping criticism. Instead, they emphasize that the practice of psychiatry must be understood and judged within the political context of a totalitarian state. In a totalitarian state there is little tolerance for political dissent. The bureaucratic structure which exerts great control over its members also demands ideological conformity. Therefore, it is plausible that Soviet psychiatrists, who have been accused of using their authority to legitimize the current actions of the government toward political dissidents, believe they are acting in accordance with their Marxist-Leninist beliefs [29]. In their view, those who denounce the political system of their country might very well be suffering from delusional psychopathology. Hence commitment to a psychiatric institution is justifiable on the basis of this type of "sickness." On the other hand, as has been pointed out in this paper, there is evidence that Western psychiatrists have also not acted with the best interests of the defendant in mind. The role of the psychiatrist representing the state in civil commitment proceedings, competency hearings, and predictions of future dangerousness must raise continuing ethical issues. In the final analysis the misuses of Western psychiatry occur to a much lesser extent and in a more subtle form than the overt and repressive practices in the Soviet Union.

Western psychiatrists often believe that Soviet psychiatrists are deluding themselves in diagnosing dissent as schizophrenia. Unfortunately, there will be even less chance for dialogue and debate now that the Soviet Society of Psychiatrists has withdrawn from the World Psychiatric Association. We are yet to know if the gestures of conciliation and discussion proffered by the Soviet psychiatrists were unacceptable to the Soviet political authorities, thus leading to the rupture from the world body. Whatever the reason for the withdrawal, one can now hope that the Soviet Union will find a wiser and more constructive way to express itself over the criticism of its psychiatric practices. The responsibility of the rest of us, I believe, is to find ways to reestablish discussions with Soviet psychiatrists on the issues without compromising a fair evaluation of those issues.

Acknowledgment. I gratefully acknowledge the valued assistance of Mr. Paul Dynia, a doctoral candidate in the Ph. D. Program at John Jay College of Criminal Justice, for his thoroughly reviewed and detailed research, upon which this paper is based.

References

1. The New York Times, February 11, 1983, p 8
2. The New York Times (1983) The world of Soviet psychiatry. 30 January
3. Chodoff P (1974) Involuntary hospitalization of political dissenters in the Soviet Union. Psychiatric Opinion 11: 5–19; Rodgers R (1974) Psychiatric hospitalization of political dissenters. Psychiatric Opinion 11: 20–24; Segal B (1977) Soviet approaches to involuntary hospitalization. International Journal of Social Psychiatry 23: 94–102
4. Chodoff, Involuntary hospitalization, p 6
5. Ibid, p 16
6. Encyclopedia of crime and justice (1983) Competency to stand trial. The Free Press New York
7. Szasz T (1965) Psychiatric justice MacMillan New York, pp 19–36
8. Ibid, p 143
9. Moran R (1981) Knowing right from wrong, the insanity defense of Daniel McNaughtan, The Free Press, New York p 5
10. Chodoff, Involuntary hospitalization, p 17
11. Szasz, Psychiatric justice, p 56
12. Dershowitz A (1969) The psychiatrist's power in civil commitment: a knife that cuts both ways. Psychology Today February: 47
13. Ennis BT, Litwack T (1974) Psychiatry and the presumption of expertise: flipping coins in the courtroom. California Law Review 62: 693–752
14. Ibid, pp 699–708
15. Chesler P (1972) Women and madness Avon, New York p XX
16. Chodoff, Involuntary hospitalization, p 19
17. Ibid, p 18
18. Podrabinek A (1980) Punitive medicine. Karoma, Ann Arbor, p 55
19. Chodoff, Involuntary hospitalization, pp 11–13
20. Ibid, p 12
21. Podrabinek, Punitive medicine, p 69
22. Ibid, pp 70–71
23. Ibid, pp 9–22
24. Ibid, p 22

25. Ibid, p 117
26. Reich W (1983) The world of Soviet psychiatry. The New York Times Magazine, 30 January, pp 20–50
27. Ibid, p 25
28. Podrabinek, Punitive medicine, p 69
29. Chodoff, Involuntary hospitalization, pp 15–16

The Prostitution of Psychiatry: The 1930s in Germany and the 1980s in America

N. S. Lehrman

The behavior of psychiatrists in Nazi Germany was symptomatic of crimes that were perpetrated. Violating their sacred Hippocratic oath, these "doctors of infamy" killed hospitalized patients they had sworn to care for. Their crimes represented the culmination of a long political process through which German psychiatry and medicine were deliberately demoralized. Aspects of similar processes exist in contemporary America. They can be found in other countries also, such as the Soviet Union, but problems there will not be discussed here, since they have been considered elsewhere [1].

Nazi psychiatry, under the leadership of the Swiss psychiatrist Carl Jung [2] – still honored in America – provided much of the ideological basis for Germany's acceptance of Hitler's horrors. Labeling dissent as Jewish or communist and as the product of a biologically different psychology helped to permit Nazi criminality to go unchallenged – especially when it went unpunished. Indeed, that criminality was sometimes consciously glorified, as in the "Horst Wessel Song," the Nazi hymn extolling a pimp and thug who was murdered in a brawl.

Injuring the innocent and exculpating terrorists and other criminals represent two key aspects of psychiatry in pre-Hitler and Nazi Germany; examples of such acts can also be found in contemporary America. Awareness of history, and of today's similarities to yesterday, can help prevent yesterday's horrors from being repeated.

Psychiatry Injures the Hospitalized Innocent

Psychiatry's most important social task has always been the care and treatment of the hospitalized mentally ill, especially the insane. Although data are scarce, statistics suggest what many older individuals, psychiatrists especially, have long suspected: that treatment results today are significantly worse than 30 years ago. It was recently pointed out, for example, that around 1950 corrected rates of readmission of schizophrenics within 5 years of original admission were 56% and 48% in a public system and a private hospital respectively, whereas studies since the advent of drugs report readmission rates of 70% or even more [3]. That results are poorer today is suggested also by the large number of mental hospital dischargees, "zombies," on the streets of our large cities: demoralized human beings who represent public nuisances, objects of pity, and easy prey for petty criminals.

The process through which psychiatric patients are often demoralized and made worse by the fragmented and incompetent care they are given in both our private and public mental hospitals is demonstrated all too vividly in Sheehan's touching account of "Sylvia Frumkin" in her book *Is There No Place on Earth for Me?* [4].

Wrongful deaths in public mental hospitals have also become a national scandal. New York State established a special Commission on the Quality of Care for the Mentally Disabled because so many were occurring. The treatment received by Judith Singer at Staten Island's South Beach Psychiatric Center is illustrative. This 19-year-old girl, dead 6 days after admission, was treated during that brief period in four different places by 13 different physicians. She was given 34 injections, because the staff did not know how to win her confidence so that she would take oral medication. Seven different major psychopharmaceuticals were used, including the most toxic, lithium, on this struggling youngster, who was tied down in restraints through almost her entire brief hospitalization, during which she lost 23 Ibs. [5].

At Manhattan Psychiatric Center, another New York State facility, 27-year-old Pablo Martinez died from "asphyxia by compression of the neck while being restrained" by hospital staff. He was still hostile and adversary to them a full month after his admission, and they responded murderously when he assaulted one of them again. The *New York Times* account [6] mentions no disciplinary or legal action either against the staff who choked this patient to death or against the professionals and administrators whose incompetence permitted a hostile relationship to continue so long between the patient and those treating him.

One of the most important causes of these increasingly poor results, which produce the staff demoralization called "burnout," is the fragmentation of care, both horizontally and vertically. A "team" assumes responsibility for the patient's treatment, although a physician is always held responsible when things go wrong. And both team and doctor are changed frequently, particularly when the patient is most vulnerable: when entering or leaving the hospital.

The assignment to nonpsychiatrists of the responsibility for organizing care is another reason for the increasingly poor results. The clinical needs of patients are subordinated more and more to the organizational desires of those providing care; bureaucracy thus takes precedence over service, causing harm rather than help to those supposedly served - as in Nazi Germany, and its mental hospitals particularly.

Psychiatry Injures the Innocent in the Community

American psychiatry has injured innocents in the community in two different but related ways, both of which assist political power's not infrequent lawless attempts to silence dissent or creativity. Sometimes psychiatry actively assists those silencing attempts, as in Soviet Russia, by stigmatizing the individuals being targeted. More frequently, it refuses to consider the possibility that the psychological distress some patients experience might be caused at least partly by the psychological harassment to which they are being subjected. Real external causes are ignored in favor of "internal psychological reality" stemming largely from childhood. Unrecognized but effective silencing of dissent and creativity through such well-meaning but irrelevant psychiatric treatment often results.

Crippling the Creative

Psychiatry almost destroyed the professional career of Hyman H. Gordon, a 69-year-old dermatologist of previously impeccable reputation. In 1975, when he considered himself "more creative" than ever in his life, as manifested by his many contributions to medical literature, a psychiatric diagnosis was imposed upon him which stopped those contributions short by undermining his ability to earn a living.

He continued, unceasingly and sometimes frantically, to fight the psychiatric "witch-taint" applied to him, but how does one prove he is not suffering from an implicitly permanent "personality disorder"? His marriage broke up, and the civil liberties organizations, which should have helped fight this outrageous attack on his most fundamental rights, have ignored him. When Dr. Gordon's name was mentioned, a key executive of one such organization warned this author to be "careful" because the doctor is allegedly "disturbed."

Minor difficulties with superiors had been occurring at the Kaiser-Permanente Foundation in California, where Dr. Gordon had been working, and they demanded that he return to duty following surgery on his foot sooner than was either proper or customary. He protested and they demanded that he see a psychiatrist. He called the psychiatrist himself, who then came to Dr. Gordon's hospital room. The dermatologist was quite outspoken during the interview about his superiors' harassing demand that he return to work before he was physically able to do so.

After a half-hour visit, the psychiatrist diagnosed him as suffering from a "paranoid personality disorder," following which Dr. Gordon was involuntarily placed on "chronic sick leave . . . due to chronic illness." When he asked the Foundation's Medical Director what chronic illness he was allegedly suffering from, he received a note, which the Medical Director refused to sign, claiming he had an "emotional disability." This followed shortly after that same Medical Director's memo of congratulations to Dr. Gordon for a clinical study the latter had published, and for his receiving second prize from the journal *Cutis* in its annual manuscript contest.

Since being smeared in 1975 with his psychiatric witch-taint, Dr. Gordon, then 61, has had to sell his home and to move five times, and his wife had to give up three positions to follow him. She finally left him because he refused to stop seeking vindication. He sued for negligent infliction of mental distress, among other injuries, and won $ 50000 in money damages at the end of 1980. But he is still left with the "paranoid personality disorder" stigma and, blackballed, has been unable to find suitable work since August 1980.

Pummeling the Protestant

Portia Parker is a 47-year-old divorced black woman, with no previous psychiatric history, who had often successfully insisted on being treated lawfully and respectfully by the New York City Welfare Department, on whose rolls she had long been a client. Her 11-year-old son was veritably kidnapped from her recently by these authorities, largely on the basis of a psychiatric diagnosis made by a psychologist. Her attorney was not even permitted to make a copy of the report.

The youngster was then placed in a Catholic Charities foster home in a remote part of the city, whose location the authorities refused to tell Mrs. Parker. After he had been there 3 weeks, he was badly injured in an automobile accident. Mrs. Parker visited him each day during his month in the distant hospital, but after his discharge his whereabouts were kept secret not only from her but also from her attorney. On examination in October 1982, she was remarkably self-controlled, considering the harassment she had endured at official hands - which her attorney confirmed. She insisted that her religious faith - she is a devout, Bible-reading Protestant - had been a great source of strength to her, but her statement that she heard God's voice was a major element in the psychologist's determination that she was mentally incompetent to care for the youngster. When asked about that voice, however, she described it as something within herself which strengthens her and helps her differentiate right from wrong.

Liquidating the Leftist

Arnold Parker was a Harvard-trained Jewish attorney - a much-decorated European theater infantryman during World War II and an active left-winger both before and after it. His psychiatric treatment during the McCarthy period of the early 1950s was largely responsible for his suicide.

By 1952 he had married, fathered three children, and started his own practice. The times were turbulent: stories of "communist conspiracy" filled the media, and left-wingers Julius and Ethel Rosenberg had been sentenced to death for allegedley passing atomic secrets, about the very existence of which there was considerable question even then. And each week in Boston's newspapers, ex-Communist Herbert Philbrick was unveiling new horror stories, complete with new names, out of his *Three Lives* in the left there before, during, and after World War II.

Parker had not been named, but the possibility that he might be shook him greatly, particularly since he was beginning to rethink his own political concepts as well as being concerned about making a living for his family. Odd interferences seemed to be occurring also with his mail and telephone - or were they only in his head? Because of his distress, he began treatment with a prominent Boston psychoanalyst, who characteristically focused on the past rather than on the here and-now. The possibility that the doctor's office might be wiretapped in order to destroy Mr. Parker, and perhaps others, was not even dreamed of. But this was before the break-in at the office of Daniel Ellsberg's psychiatrist.

Parker's valid fears of governmental authority in the present - such as the congressional committees roaming the land and carrying out inquisitional hearings - were seen as really stemming from his fear of his father, a strict, fair man, whom I knew well. A breach between them was thus established. His wife was, of course, excluded from the treatment, thus impairing another important supportive relationship.

His agitation and mood swings became increasingly severe, largely because his real pain from present harassment and his valid fears for the future were systematically shunted aside by his psychoanalyst's focus on the past. The week before Senator Joseph McCarthy's scheduled hearings in Boston, he hanged himself.

Hitler's *Mein Kampf,* published in 1925/1926, described his tactic of "unleash[ing] a veritable barrage of lies and slanders," among other attacks, "against whatever adversary seems most dangerous, until the nerves of the attacked person break down" [1]. Jews have long been vigilant against attacks on them both individually and collectively; Golda Meir is reported to have insisted that "anyone who is *not* paranoid does not know Jewish history."

But American psychiatry systematically denies the existence of such attacks upon specific patients, with former leftists in the profession being among those doing so most vociferously. The denial by the supposed psychological experts of victims' own valid perceptions of their persecution greatly increases their agitation – as with both Dr. Gordon and Mr. Parker. Some psychiatrists then use this increased agitation to show how sick the victim really was, thus evading responsibility for their own passive behavior, and avoiding facing their own cowardice.

The Nazis also blamed their victims [8] to justify the mistreatment inflicted upon them – including murder. Although the Nazis' acts were positive acts committed against the victims, and American psychiatrists' acts are only acts of omission, the denial in both situations of the doctor's obligation to help his patient – beyond merely listening passively – has harmed innumerable victims of persecution mistakenly seeking psychiatric assistance.

Psychiatry's Exculpation of Terrorists and Other Criminals

The verdict of "not guilty by reason of insanity" given on the case of John W. Hinckley Jr. after his carefully premeditated assassination attempt on President Ronald Reagan and others is merely the most visible of the many cases in which psychiatry has exculpated or condoned criminality or mitigated its punishment – with or without the insanity defense. A young killer by arson was recently spared prison and sent to a New Jersey Roman Catholic home for women instead, partly on psychiatric recommendation [9], while a man from East Northport, Long Island, who admitted making obscene, anti-Semitic telephone calls – over 1000 during a 6-month period – was given a conditional discharge provided that he would "continue the psychiatric treatment he said he has been receiving since shortly after his arrest" [10].

The disparity between the actual verdict on Hinckley and his punishment and what they should have been is only the most striking example of the disparity between the treatment received by the perpetrators of many premeditated crimes in whose cases psychiatry has played a significant role, and those handled by our judicial and penal processes in their usual, nonpsychiatric way. Indeed, the Hinckley verdict itself may almost represent a psychiatric green light for terrorism, discouraged in no way by the Reagan administration, since it implies that any perpetrator of terroristic acts can claim insanity with a significant likelihood of subsequent exculpation, especially in jurisdictions requiring the prosecution to prove sanity "beyond a reasonable doubt" when insanity is claimed.

Sentence Disparities: Pre-Hitler Germany and Arsonist Peter Burkin

Wide disparities in juridical handling, of terrorism particularly, were occurring in Germany long before Hitler came to power. These disparities played an important role in undermining the criminal justice system there and people's trust in it: this was a major factor facilitating the ultimate Nazi takeover. The late Fredric Wertham pointed out in 1949 [11] that in 1919–1920 327 political murders were committed in Germany: 314 by fascists and 13 by antifascists. After the 13 antifascist murders, eight death sentences were pronounced; there were 22 convictions (1.69 per murder) and the sentences imposed added up to 177 years in jail: 13.6 years per murder.

Very different – and markedly condoning – consequences followed fascist murders. Not a single death sentence was pronounced for any of these 314 killings, and all of them together produced only five convictions: 0.015 convictions per murder. All the sentences imposed added up to 31 years: 0.099 years, or 36 days, per murder.

A similar bias in the United States is suggested by a comparison of the disparate legal and penal treatment given Kathie Boudin, the daughter of the distinguished civil liberties attorney Leonard Boudin, who was involved in an October 1981 hold-up murder, and Peter Burkin, a "Right to Lifer" who torched an abortion clinic. Miss Boudin has been subjected to cruel and "unique" [12] handling, including solitary confinement, all allegedly for her own security, before even being brought to trial, while Burkin was in and out of incarceration relatively quickly.

Burkin was tried in November 1979, 9 months after he had stormed into an abortion center in Hempstead, New York with a lighted torch in one hand and an open can of gasoline in the other. His was the first arrest after 26 firebombings of abortion clinics throughout the nation [13]. At the trial, he claimed he was not guilty of attempting to burn the clinic down, since that was not his motivation. He insisted he was really seeking only to kidnap a physician to demonstrate his antiabortion views, the arson having occurred accidentally.

His obvious self-contradictions at the trial were accepted by the jury as evidence of mental illness rather than of lying. Little effective refutation had apparently been offered by the office of the District Attorney who was reelected with Right to Life Party support. Burkin was found not guilty of attempted murder and of arson with intent to kill – the major charges – and not guilty by reason of insanity on one count of setting a fire and one count of reckless endangerment. He was hospitalized for less than 2 years and has long been at large in the community. Press coverage of this trial – in contrast to that of Hinckley's – was relatively scant, with no mention at all of his release from hospital. The lack of public response to this outrage thus becomes understandable.

The Psychiatric Hunting License

The "psychiatric hunting license" concept, that mentally ill individuals are automatically exempt from responsibility for criminal acts they commit, was formulated in 1949 by Wertham [11]. He described hired killer Martin Lavin, who repeatedly played crazy after being arrested, and then rapidly became "sane" after having been found not guilty by reason of insanity. Returning to the streets, he then resumed his murderous career, which was only terminated in a shoot-out, where he murdered one policeman and was killed by another.

The falseness of the notion that mental illness – or, more specifically, insanity – automatically removes criminal responsibility has been known for centuries. In 1760 John Monro, Superintendent of London's Bethlehem Hospital, was asked at a murder trial whether "lunatics" know what they are doing. "Sometimes, as well as I do now" [14], was his accurate reply.

Despite the facts, American psychiatry has campaigned long and loudly over the past four decades for the increased introduction of psychiatric considerations into the criminal law. These considerations, based on psychiatry's supposedly greater knowledge of the criminal mind, seem almost always to produce assertions that the perpetrator is less responsible for his actions than the law would otherwise regard him.

Murder, Psychiatric Style

Deliberate murder has been committed with the apparent hope that "mental illness" would exculpate the killer and get him released as quickly as Burkin was – and as Hinckley might have been, had it not been for media attention.

Dennis Sweeney, who was described as "crazy" and having been "hearing voices" for some time, deliberately journeyed from Connecticut to New York City to shoot and kill former Representative Allard Lowenstein [15]. Lowenstein was one of the most effective Jewish political leaders then active in America; his constructive vigor can be compared to that of Germany's Walther Rathenau, another outstanding and assassinated Jewish leader.

Sweeney's babblings apparently convinced the prosecution not only that he was insane, but also that he was therefore not responsible for his actions – despite Monro's statement over 220 years earlier. Sweeney was found not guilty by reason of insanity, in proceedings conducted behind closed doors, and has apparently been hospitalized since. Should his delusions – whether real or faked – clear, he will then presumably be released, as Burkin was.

The handling of Sweeney overlooks another fundamental lesson the German experience could teach us: that the mentally ill, and the insane in particular, are both less competent and more manipulable than the rest of us. In 1933, the Nazis planted a crazy Dutch communist, Marinus van der Lubbe, in the *Reichstag* (German parliament building) with a small torch just before the building suddenly went up in flames. At the trial, the accused Bulgarian communist, Georgi Dimitrov, "the only man in recorded history to have made [Hitler's *Reichsminister*] Goering turn publicly red in the neck," pointed at van der Lubbe and "exclaim[ed] . . . 'This miserable Faust! Who is his Mephistopheles?'" [16]. This question was apparently never asked after the Lowenstein murder.

Mark Chapman's carefully premeditated murder of ex-Beatle John Lennon represents another crime for which exculpation via an insanity plea had apparently been planned, with a skillful publicity campaign having apparently been set up before the murder to facilitate that exculpation. The American media's uncritical credulity in this case gravely undermined its credibility in general, and the peculiar blocking of attempts to bring key facts about this murder to public attention warrants scrutiny also. Seeing Chapman as sick, rather than as vicious, which the media still do despite his conviction for murder, continues to hide the possibility that a criminal conspiracy was operating here behind a carefully constructed facade of mental illness.

The Berwid Murder: A Frame-up Which Failed

Focused terrorism, anti-Semitism, and possibly conspiracy all came together with Adam Berwid's murder of his ex-wife Ewa in December 1979, while on authorized pass from Pilgrim Psychiatric Center. Here a deliberate attempt was made to exculpate a man of premeditated murder by blaming psychiatrists, and then using that blame both to terrorize and prostitute the specialty. This particular attempt ultimately failed.

Key movers in that unsuccessful effort were the prosecutor in the Burkin case, Nassau County District Attorney Dennis E. Dillon, supported by the Right to Life Party; New York State's Mental Health Commissioner, James A. Prevost; John A. Talbott, candidate for the presidency of the American Psychiatric Association and editor of its major journal, *Hospital and Community Psychiatry;* and others. The coverage of *Newsday,* Long Island's daily newspaper, apparently actively fostered these efforts, and the other media, including the *New York Times,* cooperated passively or were seduced, or both. Teresa Carpenter's Pulitzer-prize-winning *Village Voice* story contained lurid but unprovable details and pivotal inaccuracies, and placed primary blame on "two careless doctors" – "elderly" Dr. Blumenthal especially. She also predicted that Berwid, if ever "found capable of standing trial, [would] almost certainly be acquitted by reason of insanity." CBS's *Sixty Minutes* account, while deeper than any other media report, hardly scratched the surface.

Adam Berwid's attempts physically to harass his wife Ewa in 1977, after she had decided to divorce him for his assaultiveness, were met by her obtaining court orders of protection against him. This otherwise brilliant engineer was then arrested eight times for violating these orders, but repeated psychiatric examinations found no mental condition interfering with his routine handling by the criminal law.

That December, he wrote her a bloodcurdling letter from jail, describing in exquisite detail the physical harm he anticipated inflicting upon her. He was brought to trial for aggravated harassment, a misdemeanor, because of the letter. In May 1978, in court, he threatened to kill her and even lunged at her to assault her. The judge then decided, apparently assisted by the District Attorney, that Berwid needed "treatment not prosecution." Declaring Berwid "incompetent to stand trial," he sent him into the mental health system as a patient, despite the disagreement of the two senior members of the three-psychiatrist panel examining him at the time.

In April 1979, Berwid escaped from Pilgrim where he was a civil patient, since criminal charges on accused misdemeanants are dropped after 90 days of hospitalization. He broke into Ewa's home and cut the telephone wires. The District Attorney's office had warned most vividly about Berwid's dangerousness when he had been made a patient in May 1978, and that warning was resurrected on *Newsday's* front page after he killed her in December 1979. But that April, after Berwid had feloniously broken into his ex-wife's home, the District Attorney's office assented to his merely being transferred - still on civil status - to a higher-security mental hospital. The question of legal status is important: on civil status Berwid had to be released as soon as he had recovered, while on criminal order he would then have had to be returned for trial.

Berwid had thus tried out his psychiatric hunting license, which the District Attorney's inaction had validated. He was thus apparently encouraged to believe that the "license" might help him quite literally to "get away with murder." The District Attorney's office confirmed the existence of that hunting license - the belief that his being a patient removed any responsibility from him for criminal acts he committed. In February 1982, Assistant District Attorney Barry Grennan was asked why no indictment had been obtained against Berwid in April 1979. He replied that "a felony indictment was not obtained because Berwid was in a mental institution and under their custody" [17]. The psychiatric hunting license was further confirmed by Grennan's characterization of Berwid at that time as "incompetent," despite his well-planned criminal behavior.

Responsibility for the subsequent murder was placed squarely on the office of the District Attorney by Abraham L. Halpern, president of the American Academy of Law and Psychiatry, and one of the country's most distinguished forensic psychiatrists. In February 1982 he wrote to Mr. Dillon that [18].

> ... it was a result of your staff's not taking appropriate legal action that Mrs. Berwid came to her untimely and horrible death ... The gross negligence of the law enforcement officials on that occasion prevented the state from ensuring his clutchability in the only way then feasible: that is, through the authority of the Criminal Procedure Law".

Six months after being sent to the more secure facility after the break-in, Berwid, having behaved well in the interim, was returned to Pilgrim for release. After 3 weeks of good behavior there, he was given on off-grounds pass for 6 hours. During that period, he premeditatedly slaughtered his ex-wife. Berwid's pass was given him by Irving J. Blumenthal, a veteran of 40 years of psychiatric practice, who had not seen him prior to his readmission to Pilgrim 3 weeks earlier. Berwid had obviously fooled him.

Dr. Blumenthal was publicly criticized in all the media, as was his administrative superior, the much younger T. T. Loo, who had had no clinical responsibility in the case whatsoever. The District Attorney threatened them both with criminal charges, including homicide; on advice of counsel, they therefore refused to make public statements defending themselves. But their attorneys did not defend them either against the media attacks launched upon them. The media criticism and private harassment suffered by Dr. Loo - exactly as described by Adolf Hitler - almost drove him to suicide within 2 weeks of the murder [19]. This author, who met him then for the first time, had never seen anyone outside a psychiatric hospital as agitated as Dr. Loo was then.

The fact that Dr. Blumenthal was Jewish, and that Berwid had "proclaimed" through *Newsday*" to the people of Nassau County" that he had killed his ex-wife "in the name of Jesus Christ" [20] - the traditional cry of Jew-killing crusaders -

suggested a possible anti-Semitic element. The local representative of the B'nai B'rith Anti-Defamation League dismissed that possibility out of hand, however; to him, Dr. Loo's involvement clearly ruled out anti-Semitism.

While this Jewish defense organization categorically denied the subtle but vicious psychological attack on the people it was charged with protecting, many psychiatrists, particularly in the state hospital system, keenly recognized that this assault on two of their finest colleagues threatened them all. A few of them fought back, and eventually won; Drs. Loo and Blumenthal were exonerated and Berwid was convicted of murder. The American Psychiatric Association, on the other hand, helped little and obstructed much, with Dr. Talbott playing a central blocking role in preventing the profession's communications media from bringing the facts and the fight-back to the specialty's attention.

A medical staff meeting at Pilgrim Psychiatric Center some 6 weeks after the murder demonstrated the intimidation and demoralization of the psychiatrists which the case had caused. The nurses in the hospital were refusing to obey doctors' orders - the Director of the hospital is a nurse (!) - and the physicians were pleading that the nurses should not disobey or ignore such orders without first discussing the proposed disobedience with their own *nursing* supervisors! And at Nassau County Medical Center - not a state facility - Stephen L. Rachlin, the Director of Psychiatry, reported that his medical staff suffered for months from "Berwid fever": fear of releasing patients without his specific consent also, as Director, lest they be blamed individually should the patient misbehave [21].

Three years elapsed between Berwid's slaughtering his ex-wife and his conviction for her murder. During that period, the political currents and crosscurrents within and outside psychiatry concerning the case were veritably Machiavellian. Pitting one psychiatrist against another was only one small aspect of a much larger and more vicious picture. But one specific example of psychiatric prostitution warrants presentation here.

At the New York State Assembly Hearing on the Berwid case on 18 December 1979, the state Mental Health Department deliberately lied about the meaning of a Berwid chart entry, in order to place false blame on Blumenthal and Loo. Since they were not present to defend themselves, and their attorneys were not there either, the media credulously accepted these lies as true.

At a State Senate Hearing early the next month on the case, this author met John Iafrate, who had been Pilgrim's Director and who then was Long Island Regional Director and Deputy Commissioner in the Department. He had assisted and supported the earlier testimony. This author has known Dr. Iafrate long and amicably, but not well, and had always thought rather highly of him. "John, how could you do this to your colleagues?" Iafrate was asked. He looked down at his shoes and replied, embarrassed, "I got my orders." Speak of the banality of evil: Adolf Eichmann said the same.

Summary

The prostitution of the German psychiatric profession into a Nazi inquisitional tool was a major factor producing the total degradation of German medicine and morality. Its low point was its psychiatrists killing the patients they were sworn to care for, and its other physicians performing inhuman experiments on patients they were pledged to treat.

In America also, psychiatry has been performing some of the functions of an Inquisition: injuring innocents, both patients and dissenters, and exculpating criminals, terrorists especially.

Innocents are being injured both in and out of psychiatric hospitals. The increased fragmentation of care, the augmentation of its discontinuities, and assigning the responsibility for organizing it to non-medical managers are some of the factors worsening the treatment results of our hospitals. Wrongful deaths, due largely to the specialty's intoxication with drugs while ignoring the importance of common human decency, have become a national scandal.

Hitler described in 1925 the systematic "breaking" of individuals' "nerves," and the process has been occurring since. Eternal vigilance, against these and other dangerous occurrences, once considered the price of liberty, is now seen as the hallmark of paranoia. Individuals seeking psychiatric assistance because of distress caused by current harassment often find that physicians grossly minimize the persecution. This undercuts the validity of the victims' perceptions and their ability to combat these external dangers. Treatment focuses upon what the victims have allegedly done to "cause" that persecution, with change within them being seen as the way to stop the harassment. Political castration is a frequent consequence.

Should such individuals still wish to defend themselves, despite psychiatrists' primary concern with their "intrapsychic realities," these victims may be labeled as "paranoid" and "beyond help", rather than being assisted with difficult problems in the real, external world.

The Hinckley case is only the most vivid of many in which psychiatry has exculpated, condoned or mitigated deliberate criminality. Future terrorism may be encouraged, as it was in Germany, by thus minimizing the punishment terrorists would otherwise expect. Only by correcting the American psychiatric profession's refusal to face

1. Mistreatment in mental hospitals
2. Persecution of dissenting individuals
3. Its own systematic condonation of criminality

may we perhaps reverse the specialty's current thrust: the active fostering of statist tyranny.

References

1. Lehrman NS (1980) Psychiatric power and responsibility: abuse and abdication. The Humanist 40: 9–13, 58
2. Alexander FG, Selesnick ST (1966) The History of Psychiatry, Harper and Row, New York, (Jung and the national socialists) pp 407–409
3. Lehrman NS (1982) Effective psychotherapy of chronic schizophrenia. Am J Psychoanalysis 42: 121–132; see also Lehrman NS (1961) Follow-up of brief and prolonged psychiatric hospitalization. Comprehensive Psychiatry 2: 227–240 and Lehrman NS (1960) A state hospital population five years after admission: a yardstick for evaluative comparison of follow-up studies. Psychiatric Quarterly 34: 658–681
4. Sheehan S (1982) Is there no place on earth for me? Houghton-Mifflin, New York
5. New York State Commission on the Quality of Care for the Mentally Disabled (1982) Report: in the matter of "Janice Sherman," February 1982; Arnold Diaz, WCBS-TV (Channel 2) 6 pm News, 23 March 1982
6. Smothers R (1983) Death of a psychiatric patient is attributed to undue force, The New York Times, 6 February 1983, p 38
7. Hitler A (1943) Mein Kampf (trans. Manheim), Houghton-Mifflin, New York p 43
8. Lehrman NS (1981) Report on panel, American Academy of Psychoanalysis Academy Forum 25 (1): 7
9. The New York Times, February 5 1983, p 1
10. Anti-Semitic caller freed, Newsday February 4, 1983, p 32
11. Wertham F (1949) The show of violence, New York
12. Duffy KT (1982) Opinion and order. In: *Boudin* v. *Thomas et al.*, 81 Civ. 7190 (KTD), 7 January 1982
13. McNeil DG Jr (1979) Youth acquitted as insane in L.I. abortion clinic fire. The New York Times, October 31, 1979, p 5
14. Robitscher J (1980) The powers of psychiatry. Houghton-Mifflin, Boston p 22
15. The New York Times, 15 March 1980, pp 1,23; 17 March, p B-1; 10 February 1981, p B-8
16. Gunther J (1938) Inside Europe. Harper, New York, p 47
17. Grennan B, Assistant District Attorney, Nassau County, telephone conversation with author 25 February 1982
18. Halpern AL, letter to DE Dillon, District Attorney, Nassau County, 22 February 1982
19. Kessler RE (1981) A doctor's struggle to heal his wounds. Newsday, 8 December 1981, pp 6, 23
20. Killing the only way "to protect my kids." Newsday, 15 December 1979, p 7
21. Rachlin SL (1981) Report to workshop, Lessons of the Pilgrim-Berwid-Blumenthal witch-hunt, Annual meeting of the American Psychiatric Association, New Orleans, 14 May 1981

The Role of Social Energy for Man

G. Ammon

The concept of psychic energy has always been discussed in the field of science. Freud discusses psychic energy in connection with his notion of libido, which is closely linked up with his concept of man as being primarily directed by instincts. Such a concept of psychic energy, or rather the underlying concept of man, not only has effects on a theoretical level, it also affects all fields where man is concerned with practical matters and where human beings are concerned, such as education and therapy and also the field of law and the system of penal institutions. The theoretical consequences of this concept of man are the concept of endogenetics and the instinct model. On a practical level, it means regimentation, locking people away, punishing - deterrence rather than understanding, counterviolence rather than empathetic confrontation and therapy.

Our observations of the development of healthy children within their families and of group dynamic processes among healthy people and our clinical experience have led us more and more to the following proposition that psychic energy is

1. hot a biological-physical entity with corresponding characteristics,
2. and must always be seen as linked with groups and individuals.

Generally speaking, I understand social energy to be energy which is given to the individual by his environment. Social energy is mediated through human relations [4, 7, 8, 12].

Through social energy the individual develops the whole of his personality, his physicality, his character, his behavior. What fundamentally sets apart the notion of social energy from the traditional psychological and psychoanalytical concepts of energy is the fact that human development is primarily conceived of as being caused by social, interhuman processes and not, as the hypothesis of endogenetics says, by way of intrapsychic biological regularities which have nothing to do with each other.

So this concept of social energy has consequences on various levels:

- On the metaphorical level [183].
- On the theoretical level, in general and in particular.
- On the level of group dynamic treatment,
- On the level of therapeutic work (cf. [4, 6, 9, 10, 13]).

The notion of social energy allows us to evaluate interhuman relations qualitatively. The relation between the individual man and the group and also between the individual man and society can be described economically, dynamically, and energetically. This has important implications also for the handling of people who appear before the court, of those who are in prison, and of those who are on probation. It has implications also, one step earlier, for legislation, for the awarding of punishment, and for ethical considerations regarding law as a science.

Looking at the formation and the development of the theory of dynamic psychiatry, it is apparent that the notion of social energy has been developed by me as a consistent conclusion of my concept of narcissism (cf. [11, 20]). Social energy is to be seen in connection with reciprocal interhuman relations which bring about change and growth in all the people involved. Social energy is the strength and the power which human beings can give to each other and which manifests itself in all spheres of the ego structure. Social energy can be constructive, destructive, or deficient, depending on the group dynamic context in which the human contact takes place. This is the most recent stage of our theoretical thinking. Social energy is determined by the group dynamic context in which human beings confront each other and approve of each other; I have coined the phrase "social energetic field" in order to characterize this group dynamic context (cf. [4]). This social energetic field can be characterized by constructive, destructive, or deficient dynamics, and it will always have elements of all of these dynamics, if to a varying extent.

So the controversial concept of endogenetics of traditional psychiatry has given way to the concept of social energy; in the same way the controversial instinct theory of traditional psychoanalysis has given way to the concept of social energy. Because of this, it is possible to work in the field of the prevention of mental illness as well as the prevention of criminal offenses, which I regard as a special form of mental illness (cf. [15, 16]).

No doubt you will have experienced yourself how on encounter with a particular person has made a deep impression on you and given you a good feeling, how vitalizing such an encounter can be, and how it inspires your thinking and your feelings. The feeling of being taken notice of, of being understood, and of taking notice of and understanding the other person may well also entail a dispute, a dialectical, critical argument. The one person sees himself in the other person, he experiences how the other person sees him, and this gives him the feeling of being taken seriously, of being meaningful, Constructive social energy is set free through encounters which are felt to be meaningful; such encounters influence the development of the personality from early childhood onward.

The characteristic feature of constructive social energy is that confrontation leads to the development of the personality, to its growth, to the change of the personality and the ego structure. Constructive social energy, among other things, is marked by the fact that relations may be strained and yet they do not break up. This means that the people concerned are also able to face up to feelings of anxiety and aggression, and that such negative feelings are not shut out but made a part of the relationship. I would like to call this the interdependence of social energy, of the ability to make contact, and of the ability to tolerate anxiety. The more somebody is able to tolerate anxiety, the greater is his ability to make contacts and the higher is the level of social energy. I understand social energy to be the motive force and the impetus behind any kind of human structural development and human change in a constructive, destructive, and deficient sense.

Deficient social energy is insufficient social energy or, in other words, it means being deprived of social energy, being ignored. One of the worst punishments of parents is the so-called withdrawal of love from their children. We say that somebody lacks social energy if he is deprived of all affection, of all interest, of all meaningful contacts in a conscious or unconscious way. Also bodily contact is extraordinarily important for the building up of social energy. People who have never been caressed and who have never experienced bodily contact have been deprived of social energy in a way which deeply affects their personality, and their personality structure is therefore deficient (cf. [4, 8, 14]).

The dynamics of deficient social energy manifests itself in a lack of interest in the other person and in a lack of affection, even though the person concerned is being taken care of on a formal level. What is missing is the understanding of the person, of his specific personality traits; there is no arguing-out of conflicting standpoints and views. This is a typical feature of the life-stories of neglected people who commit criminal offenses because of their structurally deficient personality, and who then give themselves up to the police. They do so in order to experience, by way of making claims for their needs within the framework of a prison, a border situation or a meaningful encounter. Border situations and meaningful encounters are characterized by the fact that they affect man's central ego, i. e., his unconscious; because of this they are able to have a social energetic effect. Thus out of helpless desperation the delinquents create for themselves by force a border situation which they have not experienced through personal contact in their lives so far.

In contrast, destructive social energy is characterized by open destructiveness toward other people, by prohibitions, by the restriction of activities, by punishments, by abuse, and by compulsion of various kinds. Extreme forms of destructive social energy include child maltreatment and the venting of one's destructive and aggressive feelings on other people and also on material objects in general (cf. [3]).

The dynamics of constructive, destructive, and deficient social energy can have many different forms; it manifests itself in many different ways in the changing ego structure of the individual. As far as the extreme group of people who have committed criminal offenses is concerned, we see that they have been decisively influenced by correspondingly extreme social energetic experiences, as has recently been shown by my co-worker Ulrike Harlander, who analyzed the life histories of murderers [21].

The whole atmosphere of the group surrounding the individual is reflected as if by a mirror in the ego structure of the developing person. The ego structure can be understood as manifested social energy. Group dynamics plays a decisive role in the development of the ego structure: it can encourage, interfere with, or even arrest ego structural development (cf. [2, 11]). On it depend both the constructive development and the deficient development of various ego structures and of the identity as a whole. Social energy is passed on between mother, child, and the group primarily unconsciously, and the younger the child is, the more this is so.

Identity and the group cannot be separated, because only when one experiences one's own personality in the mirror of other people and, on the other hand, takes notice of, takes seriously, and understands the other people in the group can ego and identity development take place. Identity is a constant factor of human personality, yet at the same time it is not static. Identity is a process, a perpetual effort, a continual development.

There is no definite moment or definite phase in life when the identity of a person is established for good. Rather, identity is something which has to be found anew again and again. So identity means asking questions: asking other people who they are, and asking yourself who you are. Man is a being who is involved in a life-long process of development and change. This fact implies the opportunity of constructive development; it also implies the possibility of bringing about, through social energetic intervention, change within the system of the penal institutions (cf. [7, 11]).

Ego development has to be understood as a chain of meaningful events or border situations in an atmosphere of continuity and reliability. This, however, does not exclude the possibility that one specific meaningful event in a border situation may have a decisive impact on the further life of the person concerned and his identity.

From this perspective, we have to regard the criminal offense, the ensuing arrest, the appearance before the court, and the possible imprisonment as border situation which the delinquent has brought about by force. They provide an opportunity to change his personality through constructive social energetic processes. Such a constructive development is excluded from the very beginning if the legislation is based on principles such as atonement and deterrence. How ineffective these principles are in the field of law is illustrated by the situation after the abolition of capital punishment, as well as after the abolition in various countries of the laws against homosexuality.

As to legislation, the concept of social energy implies a number of conclusions and demands which have to be elaborated by teams of experts in the field of law and dynamic psychiatry (cf. [16, 26]). This necessitates research projects which deal with the problems at the most concrete level. From a transcultural or transsocietal point of view, it is necessary to compare the different and conflicting laws of different nations and different cultural spheres. Special foci of interest are: the laws concerning so-called "sexual offenses"; the positions of women, children, and men in legislation; the attitude to abortion; and matrimonial law.

The constructive possibility which the border situation principally offers will not be made use of if, for example, the judge presiding over a court action denies because of orthodox views the possibility of change and positive development in the defendant. This becomes obvious, particularly when he has to assess the penal responsibility of the defendant. Again, this is linked up with ethical and moral questions.

In my opinion, basic psychological and group dynamic training, including participation in self-awareness groups, must be part and parcel of the university education of all people who are going to work in the field of law. They must be enabled to take over responsibility, in the way of leading the trial as well as regarding the awarding of punishment, and moreover, they must learn that doing their work responsibly also means keeping in personal contact with the convicted person after the trial, as well as doing supervisory work in the penal institutions.

In my theory of the human structure I distinguish between three ego spheres. In each of these ego spheres I distinguish further between the ego functions: the primary ego, with its biological and neurophysiological ego functions; the central ego, with its unconscious ego functions; and the secondary ego, which means the skills, abilities, and manifest behavior. My hypothesis is that social energy influences the ego structural growth of the ego functions of all three spheres (cf. [4, 8]).

This is most evident when we look at the secondary ego, i.e., the ego of behavior.

The giving of social energy in this sphere means approving of somebody and criticizing somebody on a rational level. Modes of behavior, skills, and abilities develop depending on how much they are taken notice of and how much they are encouraged by the surrounding group – provided there are no unconscious motives rooted in the overall group dynamics which impede this development. This is not to say, however, that I deny factors such as intelligence, talents, and special aptitudes. These factors set a limit to the development which is possible in and through the group.

The central ego consists of ego functions which become manifest in the behavior in various ways and forms. The exchange of social energy on the level of the central ego depends especially on the group dynamics of the social energetic field. This means that not only what is manifestly happening in the group and what is openly talked about is important, but also the unconscious group dynamics. To put it another way: not only the spoken words and the manifest behavior are important, but also the attitudes and unconscious messages which are expressed through facial expression, gestures, and body language in general, and above all the attitudes, expectations, fears, and wishes of the people concerned. The interplay of all these dynamic factors of a group determines the social energetic field of the group. This field energetically affects the central ego of each member of the group and determines the central ego functions.

Turning to the sphere of the primary ego it must be said that there is a lot of research still to be done in terms of analyzing the role of social energy in the process of the development of the primary ego functions. The functions pertaining to this sphere must still be defined and, in particular, the relations must be established between neurophysiological brain activity, human existence and behavior, and the concept of social energy.

It is a fact that the human brain to a large degree develops after birth, and it is also a fact that out of the immeasurably great number of possible synaptic links in the brain, in actual fact only a small number are established. Which synaptic links are established? To what degree and how is the potential of the brain put to use? All this, I suggest, depends on the social energetic influence. The findings of modern research on the hemispheres of the brain allow us to draw further conclusions (cf. [22, 25]); likewise, the theory of the functional system of Anochin (cf. [17, 24]) in connection with the theory of human structure leads us to new perspectives of research.

My hypothesis is that social energy is an agent of development also in the biological-physical sphere of man, and especially that social energy determines the functioning of the neurphysiological structures (cf. [5]). With this background of a concept of man – I call it the "holistic" principle of dynamic psychiatry (cf. [8, 23]), the therapeutic work with mentally ill people, among whom I generally speaking include criminal offenders, gets a widened perspective. It provides an opportunity to reconsider the ethical side of the problem and it has implications for the practical treatment which I have described as ego structural work.

In order to establish a social energetic field, ego structural work with archaically ego sick or narcissistically ill patients requires a careful regulation of narcissistic approval on the one hand and of social energetic confrontation on the other (cf. Ammon et al. 1981). The social energetic field is the precondition for trust and thus the basis for dealing with the deficient and destructive components of the personality. A social energetic field is characterized not only by safety and trust, but also by "delimitation" and confrontation. By way of confrontation the disturbed patient has to face up to the sick aspects of his personality so that he can dissociate himself from them, i. e., experience these components as alien to his ego. Through the methodical principle of delimination by the therapist, the patient's own ego function of delimination is supported on the one hand against the overflowing flood of the irrational and on the other hand against the world of reality. Social energetic confrontation means taking the whole man seriously – which is different from reacting in a concrete way to every action and every word of the patient (cf. [4].

In confronting the patient, it is necessary for the therapist to make clear to him how he time and again makes himself unhappy and isolated, how he again and again is his own stumbling block, how he unconsciously destroys not only his own life but also the lives of others. Therefore, in the penal institutions it is necessary, from a dynamic point of view, to allow the imprisoned person to have contact with a group which is constructively structured as a social energetic field or, to begin with, to allow him to have such a contact with one person. The aim of this is (as opposed to groups with pathological dynamics, which such people always try to find again) to enable the prisoner to develop his ego structure and to enable personality growth to take place – a process which I have called "the overcoming of a backlogged ego development."

I coined the term "social energy" relatively recently. Yet also in the past the mentally ill have received help, and there has been what I call a social energetic field. The reason for this is, I think, that such fields were created by intuition, thus making the treatment efficacious. Another important point is that to establish such a constructive social energetic field much more than theoretical knowledge is necessary: it requires personality and stamina on the part of the one who works in this way. This especially applies to all people who work in penal institutions.

The system of the penal institutions should be turned into a system of social therapy, and so-called crime should be seen from a psychopathological point of view and should be dealt with accordingly. This calls above all for specific psychological and group dynamic training for all people working in penal institutions, linked with a sufficient amount of experience in self-awareness groups.

Man is a being who, from the very beginning, seeks contact and warmth, who tries to understand the other person and wants to be understood by him; he is a being who wants to enter into a critical dialogue with his environment. He is able to behave in this humane way only if he himself, in his development, has gathered positive experience. Man, from the very beginning, is also a being who wants to be active, who wants to realize himself in his groups. People who have become delinquent have been denied the opportunity to do this throughout their lives until they reach the point when they do not know any other way. They are driven by unconscious motives, and seek to destroy everything in relation to themselves as well as to others. To turn the court trial into a border situation and to turn the penal institutions into a system of therapy is, to my mind, not only the necessary conclusion from what I have said above, but also the answer to the ethical and moral question of how society treats those outcasts.

I conclude by expressing my conviction that our research is inseparably linked with the endeavor to bring about humanity, peace, and justice.

References

1. Ammon G (1970) Gruppendynamik der Aggression. Pinel-Publikationen, Berlin, 1973, Kindler, Munich, 1981
2. Ammon G (1979) Gruppendynamisches Prinzip. In: Ammon Günter (ed) Handbuch der Dynamischen Psychiatrie, vol 1. Reinhardt, Munich
3. Ammon G (1979) Kindesmißhandlung. Kindler, Munich
4. Ammon G (1982) Das sozialenergetische Prinzip in der Dynamischen Psychiatrie. In: Ammon Günter (ed) Handbuch der Dynamischen Psychiatrie, vol 2. Reinhardt, Munich
5. Ammon G (1982) Hirnstrukturen, Unbewußtes und Ich-Strukturologie. In: Ammon Günter (ed) Handbuch der Dynamischen Psychiatrie, vol 2. Reinhardt, Munich
6. Ammon G (1982) Behandlungsmethodik und Widerstand von der traditionellen Psychoanalyse zur Dynamischen Psychiatrie. In: Ammon Günter (ed) Handbuch der Dynamischen Psychiatrie, vol 2. Reinhard, Munich
7. Ammon G (1982) Identität - ein Geschehen an der Grenze von Raum und Zeit. Zum Prinzip der Sozialenergie. In: Dynamische Psychiatrie/Dynamic Psychiatry 15: 114-128
8. Ammon G (1983) Das Prinzip der Sozialenergie im holistischen Denken der Dynamischen Psychiatrie. In: Dynamische Psychiatrie/Dynamic Psychiatry 16: 169-191
9. Ammon G (1983) Ego-structural conception of art therapy. In: Japanese Bulletin of Art Therapy 14
10. Ammon G (1984) Dynamische Psychiatrie - Human-Strukturologie. In: Toman W, Egg R (eds) Handbuch der Psychotherapie. Kohlhammer, Stuttgart
11. Ammon G, Ammon G, Griepenstoh D (1979) Entwurf eines Dynamisch Psychiatrischen Ich-Strukturkonzepts. Zur Integration von funktional-struktureller Ich-Psychologie, analytischer Gruppendynamik und Narzißmus-Theorie. In: Ammon Günter (ed) Handbuch der Dynamischen Psychiatrie, vol 1. Reinhardt, Munich
12. Ammon G, Ammon G, Griepenstroh, D (1981) Das Prinzip von Sozialenergie - gleitendes Spektrum und Regulation. In: Dynamische Psychiatrie/Dynamic Psychiatry 14: 1-15
13. Ammon G, Ammon G, Griepenstroh D (1981) Psychoanalytische Aspekte des Widerstandes. In: Petzold H (ed) Widerstand - ein strittiges Konzept in der Psychotherapie. Junfermann, Paderborn
14. Ammon G, Ammon-Schibalski K, Herold J, Finke G (1984) Psychodynamics and ego-structure in skin disease. In: Clinics in Dermatology. Saunders: Philadelphia
15. Ammon G (1979) Präventive Maßnahmen - psychoanalytische Kindergärten und psychoanalytische Pädagogik. In: Handbuch der Dynamischen Psychiatrie, vol 1. Reinhardt, Munich
16. Ammon G (1983) Die Suche nach Identität von Kindern und Jugendlichen in der Hortarbeit. In: Dynamische Psychiatrie/Dynamic Psychiatry 16: 276-294
17. Anochin PK (1978) Beiträge zur allgemeinen Theorie des funktionellen Systems. In: Bures BJ et al (eds) Abhandlungen aus dem Gebiet der Hirnforschung und Verhaltensphysiologie, vol 8. Fischer, Jena
18. Bassin FV, Rotenberg VS, Smirnov IN (1983) On Günter Ammon's principle of social energy: analysis of the methodological basis. In: Dynamische Psychiatrie/Dynamic Psychiatry 16: 14-47
19. Carmi A (1983) The role of social energy in prison. In: Dynamische Psychiatrie/Dynamic Psychiatry 16: 383-406
20. Griepenstroh D, von Wallenberg Pachaly A (1979) Das energetische Prinzip bei Freud und Ammon. In: Ammon G (ed) Handbuch der dynamischen Psychiatrie, vol 1. Reinhardt, Munich
21. Harlander U (1983) Destruktive Sozialenergie in den Lebensgeschichten von Mördern. In: Dynamische Psychiatrie/Dynamic Psychiatry 16: 192-220
22. Marsen B (1982) Neurophysiologische Aspekte der dynamischen Psychiatrie. In: Ammon G (ed) Handbuch der dynamischen Psychiatrie, vol 2. Reinhardt, Munich
23. Mönnich H (1983) Ammon und Jantsch - Pioniere eines neuen wissenschaftlichen Paradigmas. 2nd World congress of the World Association for Dynamic Psychiatry, December 1983, Munich
24. Peschke V (1982) Neuropsychische funktionelle Systeme und Ich-Struktur. In: Ammon G (ed) Handbuch der dynamischen Psychiatrie, vol 2 Reinhardt, Munich

25. Rotenberg V (1982) Funktionale Dichotomie der Gehirnhemisphären und die Bedeutung der Suchaktivität für physiologische und psychopathologische Prozesse. In: Ammon G (ed) Handbuch der dynamischen Psychiatrie, vol 2. Reinhardt, Munich
26. Schmidts R (1982) Psychodynamische Aspekte in der forensischen Psychiatrie. In: Dynamische Psychiatrie/Dynamic Psychiatry 15: 43-53
27. Walter B (1983) Gedanken zu Günter Ammon: 'Das sozialenergetische Prinzip in der Dynamischen Psychiatrie'. In: Dynamische Psychiatrie/Dynamic Psychiatry 16: 429-441

III. Psychiatry and Law

A. General

Some Psychiatric Phenomena in Ancient Law

H. H. Cohn

All law must take its lead from the phenomena of life: the factual data on which legal norms are fashioned are but the result of common and long-standing observations of human nature, and more particularly human frailties. This paper will discuss phenomena of mental diseases and disorders observed and recorded in antiquity, most of which are reflected, in some way or other, in the various systems of ancient law. However, I shall restrict myself to the phenomena and their descriptions and etymologies, without going into details of the legal norms and provisions to which they may have given rise. I shall use the comparative method, drawing on biblical, talmudic, Greek, and Roman sources – and I hope to furnish the reader with yet another proof of the theory first enunciated by Auguste Comta and recently restated and brilliantly elaborated by Karl Jaspers, to the effect that the evolution of ideas and knowledge proceeded in cycles, leaving similar or identical traces wherever the human spirit was at work.

Of King Saul it is related that one day the spirit of God rested upon him and he began to prophesy with the prophets [1]. This distinction appears to have been rather transitory, for a few chapters later we are told that that spirit of the Lord departed from Saul, and an evil spirit from the Lord started to torment him [2]. Note that both the good spirit which invested him with the gift of prophesy and the evil spirit which tormented him came from the Lord. (By the way, the medication prescribed to the King by his servants, namely listening to music, is there reported to have had the desired effect that "the evil spirit departed from him" [3]). We do not know whether this evil spirit departed for good or took leave only when and for as long as the musical medication was administered. There are some indications to the effect that the King was permanently diseased – as witness not only his attempts on the life of David but also, and even more so, his own eventual suicide [4]. But we find the King yet once more blessed with the good spirit of the Lord and prophesying with the prophets [5] – and lo and behold! "he stripped off his clothes also . . . and lay down naked all that day and all that night" [6]. There is no escaping the connection between prophesying and exhibiting clear symptoms of insanity. The word "also," which occurs in this verse twice, indicates that it was not only the King who stripped himself naked but that all the other prophets had done the same; the symptom of insanity attached not so much to Saul personally as to the prophets, on all of whom rested the spirit of the Lord. Indeed, it would appear from a passage in Jeremiah that it was such madmen as pretended to be prophets who were dangerous enough to need incarceration [7]. The verb to prophesy *(hitnabbei)* occurs in biblical parlance also to describe ecstatic or convulsive behavior [8].

We know from Greek sources that *ekstasis* was a state of trance in which the soul had entered into a special relationship, or had become united, with a deity [9]. The ecstatic was possessed by a god, and so long as the *ekstasis* continued, there was a temporary *alienatio mortis* which was regarded as *hieromania,* meaning sacred madness. "The soul is now in and with the god, in the condition of the *enthousiasmos:* those who are possessed are the *entheoi* – they are completely in the power of the god, they live and have their being in the god, the god speaks and acts through him" [10]. In the same vein we find Plato putting these words into the mouth of Socrates: madness is not simply an evil, "there is also a madness which is a divine gift, and the source of the chiefest blessings granted to man. For prophecy is a madness. The prophets ... when out of their senses have conferred great benefits on Hellas, both in public and private life, but when in their senses few or none" [11]. He then goes on to distinguish madness "produced by human infirmity" from the divine madness, and subdivides the divine madness into four different categories: prophetic madness, whose patron god is Apollo; telestic or ritual madness, whose patron god is Dionysus; poetic madness, inspired by the Muses; and erotic madness, inspired by the goddesses Aphrodite and Eros – and this last kind of madness is "said to be the best" [12]. In another place, Plato reiterated that no man can attain prophetic inspiration "when in his wits: but when he receives the inspired word, either his intelligence is enthralled in sleep, or he is demented. ... While he continues demented, he cannot judge of the vision which he sees or the words which he utters" [13].

The Platonic alternative between sleep and dementia as breeding grounds of prophecy reminds one of the "deep sleep" which fell upon Abraham "When the sun was going down," and "a horror of great darkness fell upon him" [14] before God spoke to him. The Septuagint translates the "deep sleep" *(tardeimah)* by *ekstasis* – as the same word is rendered also in another context, namely the "deep sleep" which fell upon Adam by way of anesthesia before the divine extrication of one of his ribs for the creation of woman [15]. I wonder whether the scholars were right who held that Adam's ecstasy really had nothing to do with prophecy [16]. The same ecstatic sleep occurs again in Isaiah, there connoting both prophecy and madness: "Act stupid and be stupified! Act blind and be blinded! For the Lord has spread over you a spirit of deep sleep, and has shut your eyes, you prophets, and covered your heads, you seers" [17]. The "spirit of deep sleep" *(ruah tardeimah)* here befalls the false prophets, God making use of it to close their eyes and stupefy their wits – not unlike the use God made of his evil spirit to torment King Saul. Indeed, the *ekstasis* is defined by Philo Judaeus – whose description of biblical traditions and institutions was, of course, decisively influenced by the Greek philosophers – as appearing in three different forms. One is a mad frenzy leading to stupefaction and caused by senility, depression, organic disorders, or sudden vehement frights; the second is a state of serene tranquility where the spirit is at rest; and the third and best is the divine emotion and possession of the prophet [18]. All of these are phenomena of the same ecstasy: madness, frenzy, stupor, serenity, inspiration – all under one and the same phenomenological heading.

We find this connection between madness and prophecy also in rabbinic literature. The terms "the deceived and the deceiver" occurring in Job [19] are defined by one rabbi as meaning the prophets and their prophecies, and by another as connoting madmen and their nonsensical utterances [20]. The "deep sleep" we have encountered as *ekstasis* is interpreted by some rabbis as insanity [21]. And Rabbi Yohanan, the great third century teacher, assures us that from the day of the destruction of the temple, prophetic inspiration was taken away from the prophets and given to children and madmen [22]; the insinuation of any madness to our prophets of old bordering, of course, on the blasphemous. And Maimonides, who was a medical man, found that when prophesying "their limbs tremble, their physical strength fails them, their thoughts become confused" [23]. And the *enthousiasmos* which we found characterizing the Greek prophets we find again described as the characteristic of Hebrew prophets by Flavius Josephus, who calls them *entheoi* rather than ecstatics [24].

It may seem fortunate, in view of that sacred madness by which they excelled, that the Hebrew prophets were not aware, or at any rate did not make use, of the very wide legislative competencies retrospectively conferred on them by talmudic law: the *ekstasis* and the *enthousiasmos* which proved so effective in producing the most brilliant and lofty of prophesies might not necessarily prove the best of tools in the legislative process.

Whether it was that David, the young musician called to please and pacify King Saul with his harp-playing, was fascinated by the symptoms of insanity displayed by the King, or that feigning mental disorder was already in those early times a common practice with the purpose of escaping recognition or responsibility, at any rate we find David deciding to deceive the King of Gatt and his men into believing that he was raving mad [25]. It is said there that David was very much afraid of that King [26], and it seems that by simulating madness he hoped to avoid identification and to make good his departure. Nor was he wrong in his calculations: the King is reported to have instructed his courtiers not to bring David before him: "Do I lack madmen that you brought this fellow to rave for me?" [27].

The simulations chosen by David for his purpose, which were so eminently successful, were that he "scratched marks on the doors of the gate, and let his saliva run down his beard" [28]. Why the scratching (or, according to the King James Version, the scrabbling; or, according to the Septuagint, the thumping or bumping) on the doors of the gate should be a mark of insanity we do not know; maybe it was the way he did it that disclosed his derangement, or the things or signs that he scratched on the doors [29]. But letting his saliva run down his beard will sound more familiar we find the same symptom of insanity in Greek poetry [30], especially coming together as it does with two general remarks, namely that he changed his bearing and that he raved.

The simulation of insanity (or, as it is called in Israeli military slang, "artistics") presents, of course, a legal problem of some magnitude, and has done so apparently throughout legal history. It is one of the phenomena to which we men of the law are eternally indebted, for were it not so much in evidence, I am afraid we would have had to forego much of the benefit – not to speak of the pleasure – which we derive from our acquaintance with, and the opinions of, the psychiatrists. The knowledge of how old this strategem is, and how widespread it was even in antiquity, may perhaps contribute to our understanding of the great demand for, and of the indispensability of, psychiatrists in our time. According to historical records, these simulations were inordinately successful – whether for the reason that, as at the court of the King of Gatt, madmen were anyway in plentiful supply and anybody displaying symptoms of insanity was immediately shunned, or for the contrary reason that, as we hear from some Greek historians, insane persons were often regarded with a respect amounting to awe: their utterances were received with a certain reverence, and so far as they were intelligible were taken as prophetic predictions [31]. A good example of a simulation successful for this latter reason is provided by Solon, the great lawgiver. When a law was passed in Athens prohibiting, on penalty of death, political agitation for the conquest of the Isle of Salamis, Solon

> "... could not bear this open shame, and seeing the most part of the lustiest youths desirous still of war, though their tongues were tied for fear of the law, he feigned himself to be out of his wits, and caused it be given out that Solon was become a madman. ... So one day he ran suddenly out of his house with a garland on his head and got to the market-place, where the people straight swarmed like bees about him ... [32]".

Plutarch goes on to relate that instead of addressing the people as a normal orator would have done, he started to recite an elegy of a hundred verses which were "excellently well written" and which so impressed the people that they insisted that the law be revoked [33]. You may think that speaking in verses instead of in prose is a rather innocent and rather uncommon demonstration of mental deficiency, but it may well be, of course, that the simulations of insanity, such as running wildly through the streets with a garland for a headdress, were, after having been successful in gaining him access to the marketplace podium, intended to be neutralized and disproved by such display of poetic prowess. Be that as it may, we have here, it seems, the earliest instance of a successful evasion of capital punishment by feigned insanity.

I cannot leave David's simulation without letting you in on a beautiful dialogue which took place, according to ancient legend [34], between David and God Almighty.

Said David:

> Master of the Universe, everything you have created in your world is perfect, and wisdom is the best of all perfections – but why did you create insanity? What is good about the madman who wanders around the streets and tears his clothes and is a laughing-stock to people, and children run after him? Is that your sense of beauty?

And God Almighty is reported to have answered him: "You contest the beauty of insanity? By your life, you shall have need of it!" And when David had indeed found out how useful insanity – albeit feigned – could be, he is said to have exclaimed, "I will bless the Lord at all times" [35] – at times of sanity and at times of insanity; and when "God saw everything that he had made and found that it was very good" [36] – "everything must have included insanity, too."

In the same vein we find King Solomon, the wisest of men, giving his heart and mind not only to wisdom and knowledge, but also to madness and folly and the vexation of the spirit. To his mind they all alike were but the pursuit of wind [37], but the one should be pursued no less than the other.

This is not to delude you into thinking that insanity was, except in legend, ever regarded in Jewish tradition as a desirable or beautiful phenomenon. On the contrary: madness is one of the curses with which transgressors of God's laws are threatened, along with blindness and numbness of heart [38], and the worst that can strike you is to be driven mad by what your eyes behold [39].

To judge from biblical records, however, the punishment of madness was not the one to enjoy divine preference. Apart from King Saul, there is not a single instance of true insanity reported in the Bible [40], although transgressors of God's laws have abounded at all times. But the fact that insanity was quite widespread among ancient Jews is testified to in the New Testament. There we find records of people possessed by demons *(daimoniyomenoi),* or of evil spirits displaying clear symptoms of insanity - such as going around naked [41], screaming, and cutting themselves with stones [42], and being fierce, dangerous, and aggressive [43]. The commonest symptom, however, appears to be spending time in, and coming out of, burial caves and cemeteries [44]. The question why the insane are so well represented in the New Testament and so neglected in the Old already perplexed the Church Fathers. Why, asks Anastasius, should Christians have more demoniacs among them than Jews or barbarians [45]? The question in this form is, of course, misconceived. The *daimoniyomenoi* of the New Testament are all Jews, however quickly they may have adopted Christianity after their miraculous cure. The simple answer to the question is that the Gospels relate the miracles by which Jesus excelled, and none of these patients would have been regarded worthy of any mention, were it not for having been healed by Jesus. There appears to me to be no merit in any of the other theories which have been propounded: for instance, that the marked religious excitement at that time produced increased insanity, or that an epidemic of mental illness developed from the belief in demons and evil spirits, or that mental diseases multiplied because at that time there no longer existed "a strong naive public religion," paganism having ceased and Christianity not having taken over as yet [46].

The fact that the New Testament *daimoniyomenoi* were, indeed, good Jewish lunatics, is attested to by the symptoms reported of them. I have already mentioned the rather peculiar but almost universally recorded symptom of roaming about in cemeteries, of all places. Now the talmudic definition of a madman - which is really an enumeration of symptoms rather than a legal definition - is as follows: "He who goes out at night alone, and stays overnight in a graveyard, and tears his garments, and destroys everything that is given him" [47]. This frequentation of cemeteries and graveyards, especially at night, must have been the favorite pastime of Jewish madmen. Some scholars believe that they were attracted there by the spirits and demons with whom they intended to do some conjuring or magical business [48], but then the belief in such spirits and demons with headquarters in cemeteries was shared by great and enlightened scholars [49], and people associating and negotiating with them, or attempting to do so, were sternly rebuked, but not necessarily regarded as insane. We even find staying overnight in a graveyard decried as a capital risk, along with such innocent and eminently sane if trifling indiscretions as eating peeled garlic or peeled onion or drinking beverages which had been left open overnight [50]. The reason given there is that the spirit of impurity prevailing among the cemetery demons endangers human life. Even if the message intended to be conveyed was that persons deliberately endangering their lives were to be considered insane, it would appear rather odd to choose the overnight stay in a graveyard as the model type of dangerous action. I think there is no escaping the simple conclusion that this phenomenon of frequenting cemeteries at night was in fact observed time and again with insane people, and was in the event elevated to the rank of a typical symptom of the disease. As people sought to define insanity by an enumeration of symptoms, the question arose whether the disease presupposed all those symptoms to be present cumulatively, or whether any one of the symptoms could separately constitute the disease. As both possible answers to this question were propounded by equally authoritative scholars, a compromise was found to the effect that as these symptoms in themselves proved nothing unless they were displayed in an insane manner, any one symptom so displayed would be sufficient, while all of them together would be insufficient without the framework of apparent insanity [51]. It comes to this, then, that the definition is practically useless. What you really have to look at is not so much the particular symptom but rather the general bearing and behavior. And if from observing the general bearing and behavior you conclude a diagnosis of insanity, then it will not matter very much whether this or the other symptom enumerated in the definition is present. I would submit to you that rather than a list of symptoms serving as elements of a legal definition, what you have here is a description of psychotic phenomena which were probably the most common at that time.

One of the talmudic sources [52] gives the Greek terms for the diseases exemplified by the symptoms described in the definition. He who goes out alone at night is a *katnotrokos,* or suffering from an illness of that name; he who tears his clothes is a *kollykos;* and he who destroys everything he is given is a *kodaikos*. The very mention of these Greek names is some indication not only of the prevalence of these or similar diseases in the Hellenic world, but also of the existence of some kind of primitive international psychiatry. It is significant that no Greek term is given for the nightly frequentation of graveyards: this as we said, seems to be a disease reserved for Jews only.

Looking now at the Greek terms and trying to decipher them, we encounter great difficulties. There are no such terms in ancient Greek. As regards *katnotrokos,* talmudic etymologists have done their best to find the proper meaning by emending the Greek word. The *katnotrokos* has been authoritatively identified as *kanantropos* [53]. This is supposed to be combination of *canis,* dog, and *anthrspos,* man, and to mean a person infected by a dog and suffering from rabies. Why persons suffering from this disease should want to go out at night alone, and why this should be its most characteristic symptom, is certainly not for legal historians to say. It may, however, be of interest that the English term rabies is in reality a Latin word, derived from the verb *rabire* which means to rave or to rage (and I may perhaps remind you in this context of Cicero's famous warning, *nihil rabiose facere* – do nothing in rage). The adjective *rabidus* is used to describe raving dogs and ferocious animals, while the corresponding term used for human beings who are raving is *furiosus.*

As far as *kollykos* is concerned, it is assumed that this is a corrupted version of the Greek *cholera* – which originally signified only the common nausea and did not yet connote the disease we call by that name. Still, in the same way as we use the adjective "choleric" to describe an irritable or bilious disposition, not necessarily connected with cholera proper, so may the ancients have used this term to denote a certain form of mental disorder. While tearing one's clothes may perhaps under certain circumstances amount to a demonstration of choleric anger – even today, here too, I think, the talmudic jurists could not be expected to provide us with a medically accurate symptomatology.

Finally, there is the term *kodaikos* for the wanton destructionist. The Greek *kodeia* means poppyhead – but while even in ancient times the *kodeia* may have been used for the extraction of opium or other drugs, it seems a little farfetched to bring these destructive urges home to the possible consumption of drugs. The next best would be to relate the *kodaikos*, or *kydaikos*, to some derivation from *kydos*, which stands for glorious fame (hence the English word "kudos"), if it is not too farfetched, again, to associate this mental derangement with possible hallucinations of glory.

Let me conclude by presenting you with a gem from the moral rather than the clinical phenomenology of insanity. There is an ancient Jewish tradition to the effect that no man ever commits a transgression unless a spirit of derangement has entered into him [54]. The scholar who first enunciated this dictum based it on hermeneutics, in good talmudic fashion. The verb used to describe the offense of the adultress is derived from the same root which connotes insanity [55]; hence the – however bold – conclusion that some insanity must be at the root of all criminality. The purpose of enunciating this rule cannot have been to mitigate or reduce in any way the criminal responsibility and punishability of transgressors: we have from the mouth of the same purist (Resh Lakish) many dicta in the fields of criminal law and penology which make it very clear that in his view, notwithstanding the presumed derangement, responsibility and punishability are in no way affected or diminished. On the other hand, we do not find him dissenting from the rule that mentally deranged persons are not criminally responsible. They may well perform the criminal acts, but they can never form a criminal intent [56]. Hence it is irrelevant in Jewish law – in contradistinction to modern legal systems – whether any causal connection can be established between the disease and the offense: once insanity is shown, responsibility is excluded. You may, then, draw this logic out *ad absurdum:* while the general state of insanity is highly relevant and will exclude responsibility, the relation of the particular offense to some latent insanity causing or underlying it is wholly irrelevant and will never diminish responsibility. The purpose of relating the offense back to some presumed mental derangement cannot, therefore, be a legal one. The law takes no cognizance of the underlying derangement, as it takes no cognizance of underlying motives – and on the other hand, the law will take no cognizance of the offense where the offender is patently and generally insane. What then may the purpose have been behind this presumption of mental derangement underlying all offenses? I would submit that it was intended to have a deterrent effect. Ever since biblical times, transgressors have been denounced as evil and wicked, and this kind of stigma did little or nothing to reduce sinfulness. It appears that the many stubborn people who had decided to disobey God and his laws were quite prepared to be so stigmatized – the more so as God himself had in primordial times come to the conclusion that the wickedness of man was great and the thoughts of his heart were only evil all his days [57]. Moreover, the malignity of the criminal was brought home to all and sundry by the punishment inflicted on him in public, even by the (mostly capital) punishment with which he was threatened by the hand of God or by the hand of man. All this had proved to be of no avail; maybe the diagnosis of insanity might do the trick? If people were told by the highest authority that criminal behavior was a sure symptom of mental disease, maybe they could be terrified into keeping the law? It is not only the fear of the disease itself that may be a potent deterrent, but more particularly the almost certain prospect of being shunned and ostracized, as deranged people were in ancient societies (and often still are today). Not that this ingenuous attempt at deterring from crime proved to be more effective than the traditional ones, but the assumption of pathological causes of crime went into the history of ideas to stay and take root, eventually to be put on its Lombrosian pedestal and then to be discarded again.

We have it on the authority of the Roman orator Quintilianus that the view according to which a man is wicked and criminal only when insane *(stultus)* "is held not only by philosophers but widespread also among laymen" [58]. Indeed, many philosophers propounded that view even long before the days of Resh Lakish.

May I quote again from Plato:

> No man is voluntarily bad: the bad becomes bad by reason of an ill disposition of the body ... and in the case of pain the soul suffers much evil from the body. For where the acid and briny phlegm and other bitter and bilious humours wander about in the body and find no exit or escape but are pent up within and mingle their own vapours with the emotions of the soul and are blended with them, they produce all sorts of diseases ... creating infinite varieties of ill-temper and melancholy, rashness and cowardice, forgetfulness and stupidity ... thus all of us who are bad have become bad from causes which are entirely beyond our control [59].

Or again through the mouth of Socrates:

> What makes a man a good physician? Clearly the knowledge of the art of healing the sick. Now, who becomes a bad physician? Clearly he who is in the first place a physician: as he may become a good one, so he may become a bad one. But none of us unskilled individuals can by any amount of doing ill become physicians, any more than we can become carpenters; and he who by doing ill cannot become a physician at all, clearly cannot become a bad physician. In like manner the good man may become deteriorated by time or toil or disease or other accident; but the bad man will never *become* bad, because by nature he is not good [60].

The subtle distinction between the man who was good and has "deteriorated" by reason of disease, and the bad man whose disease is inbred or constitutional and apparently incurable, may roughly correspond to the distinction between the casual criminal and the professional or recidivist. What they have in common is that their criminality is beyond their control or volition.

We find the same idea in Horace's satires: *Ergo ubi prava, stultitia, hic summa est insania, qui sceleratus est furiosus erit* (Where there is wickedness, there is derangement – this worst of insanities; and whoever is a criminal, is insane) [61].

Here and in Greek philosophy, the deterrent purpose which we traced in the talmudic sources appears to be absent: what we have here is perhaps a grossly unmedical but an eminently ethical diagnosis of criminality. Quite contrary to the divine pessimism which found expression in Genesis, the approach of philosophers and poets here stems from an invincible belief in the inherent goodness of man – a goodness which is thought to be incompatible with any deliberately wicked disposition or tendency. The manifest fact that there are wicked people all around is easily explained away by the no less manifest fact that there are sick people all around – and the sickness of the soul and of the mind will easily explain asocial aberrations in behavior. A good man would not of his own volition choose a life of crime, and as all men are good – or at least all healthy men are good – it must be that those who chose a life of crime did not do so of their own volition at all. You may think that these are idealizations which render the ethics behind them utterly impracticable. So I would like to refer by way of conclusion, to a variation on the same theme, in which these ethics are translated into more practicable, and for us moderns, much more appealing, sentiments. I quote from the meditations of Marcus Aurelius, the great humanist Emperor of Rome:

> Only a human being is capable to love even those who do him wrong. And this can happen only if when the wrong is done to you, you remember they are human too, and wrong you only because their mental predisposition or condition prevented them from abstaining. Anyhow soon both of you will die; and you being so fortunate as being sane and sound, the wrongdoer can really do you no harm, while you can do him only good [62].

A similar reflection may lie at the root of the Christian doctrine of the love of one's enemies: one can have compassion on them, notwithstanding their hostility, if one can attribute their ferocity to some derangement beyond their control. And in talmudic law, it is the choice of the most humanitarian mode of execution of condemned felons which is proclaimed as the best and truest fulfillment of God's command: Love thy neighbour like yourself [63].

We know of many early, so-called primitive civilizations in which all insane people are treated as criminals: they are believed to house a demon within their body, and the demon would never have chosen the body of that particular man for his seat were it not for his wickedness and blameworthiness. For them insanity is conclusive proof of criminal disposition - and insane people are punished or exterminated or expelled not for their criminal acts but for their insanity. It was Nietzsche who first asserted that the time had come to turn the scales.

> Are we not finally ripe for the contrary view? Ought we not to say: every criminal is insane, instead of: every insane man is criminal? It seems that that hour has not yet come. ... We lack above all physicians for whom that science which is called applied morals *(praktische Moral)* has become a medical art, a medical science; we still lack that hungry interest in these matters that might resemble the *Sturm und Drang* of ancient religious ecstasies ... [64].

References

1. 1 Samuel 10: 10
2. 1 Samuel 16: 14
3. 1 Samuel 16: 23
4. 1 Samuel 31: 4
5. 1 Samuel 19: 23
6. 1 Samuel 19: 24
7. Jeremiah 29: 26
8. E.g., Numbers 11: 25-27
9. Rohde (1925) Die Psyche, vol 2. Berlin, pp 311ff
10. Ibid, pp 19ff
11. Plato, Phaedrus 244 (Translation by Jowett, Random House, New York, 1937, vol 1, p 249)
12. Ibid, 265 (p 269)
13. Plato, Timaeus 71-72 (Translation by Jowett, Random House, New York, 1937, vol 2, p 50)
14. Genesis 15: 12
15. Genesis 2: 21
16. Heschel A (1962) The prophets. Philadelphia, p 336, note 9
17. Isaiah 29: 11, as translated in: The prophets, a new translation of the Holy Scriptures. Philadelphia, 1978, p 415

18. Philo Judaeus, Quis rerum divinarum heres, 249
19. Job 12: 16
20. Midrash Tehillim 7,3 (Buber ed., 1891, p 32)
21. Genesis Rabba 17,5 (Levin-Epstein ed., 1922, p 32)
22. Babylonian Talmud (hereafter BT), Bava Batra 12b
23. Maimonides Mishneh Torah, Hilkhot Yessodei HaTorah 7: 2
24. Josephus F, Antiquitates Judaicae VI 56, 76; VIII 346; IX 35
25. 1 Samuel 21: 14
26. 1 Samuel 21: 13
27. 1 Samuel 21: 16
28. 1 Samuel 21: 14
29. David Kimḥi (Redak) *ad loc* 1 Samuel 21: 14
30. Euripides, Heracles 935
31. Dodds (1963) The Greeks and the irrational. Los Angeles, pp 68, 85
32. Plutarch, Solon (translation by North, Heritage, New York, 1941, p 237)
33. Ibid, p 238
34. Midrash Tehillim 34,1 (Buber ed., 1891, p 123)
35. Psalms 34: 2
36. Genesis 1: 31
37. Ecclesiastes 1: 17
38. Deuteronomy 28: 28
39. Deuteronomy 28: 34
40. Except perhaps for the Babylonian King Nebuchadnezzar: Daniel 4: 29
41. Luke 8: 27
42. Mark 5: 5
43. Matthew 8: 26, Mark 5: 4, Acts 19: 16
44. Matthew 8: 28, Mark 5: 2, Luke 8: 27
45. Anastasius Sinaita, Quaestiones 40 (Lugdunam edn IX 1677)
46. Cf. Preuss (1978) Biblical and talmudic medicine. New York, p 315
47. BT Hagigah 2b, Tossefta Terumot 1: 3, Palestinian Talmud Gittin 7: 1
48. Preuss, *loc cit*, p 317
49. Such as Rabbi Akiba: BT Sanhedrin 65b
50. BT Niddah 17a
51. BT Hagigah 3b
52. Palestinian Talmud Terumot 1: 1
53. Sefer HeArukh, by Nathan ben Yehiel of Rome (11th century), edited by Kohut (Vienna, 1891), vol 7, p 137
54. BT Sotah 3a
55. *tissteh* from the root *sth*. Cf. Numbers 5: 12
56. Mishnah Makhshirin 3: 8, 6: 1
57. Genesis 6: 5
58. Institutio Oratoria 12a4 (edited by Meister, 1886, p 465)
59. Plato, Timaeus 86-87 (Random House, New York, 1937, vol 2, p 63)
60. Plato, Protagoras 345 (Random House, New York, 1937, vol 1, p 114)
61. Horace, Satirae II 3, 220-223
62. Marcus Aurelius, Meditationes VII 22 (Translation by Long, reprinted in: Edman (ed) (1945) Marcus Aurelius and his times. New York, p 71)
63. BT Sanhedrin 45a
64. Nietzsche FW, Morgenroethe 202 (Musarion, 1924, vol 10, p 186)

The Evolutionary Relationship Between Psychiatry and the Law

S. B. Cohen

The opportunity to address this distinguished gathering concerned with psychiatry, law, and ethics is a great privilege which carries with it much responsibility for the author's being so bold as to think that he has something to contribute to these topics. Having rewritten the paper a number of times, I am tempted to retitle it "The Evolution of a Paper", but I trust that some of the fossils in the abstract may be seen as precursors of the creature fleshed out today.

One of the major arenas which lawyers and psychiatrists enter together is the attempt to determine mental capacity and hence criminal responsibility. With the changing attitudes of society toward the insanity plea, there may well be a significant diminution in the expenditure of psychiatric man hours devoted to such determination. To this author, forensic psychiatry has always appeared to devote a disproportionate amount of its time to this more glamorous issue of the insanity defense, neglecting the opportunity to focus our expertise and talents on the possible prevention of more ordinary, much less spectacular crime.

The roles and scope of our two professions, law and psychiatry, must always be seen as a reflection of what goes on in the overall society. Henry Sigerist, the medical historian, discussing the roles of physicians and the scope of medical practice, has noted that this is dependent on "the general civilization of the time and largely determined by the cultural conditions of that time" ([3], p. 24).

Viewing the relationship of the two professions, one can see an evolution having taken place in three stages. The first was the era in which society noted that some behavior was so abnormal that it stemmed from a disordered mind and, therefore, this particular "criminal" was placed in the hands of the psychiatric profession. The M'Naghten rule, formulated almost a century and a half ago, stated that if the individual did not know right from wrong and could not appreciate the consequences of his action, then he was considered insane and the law would wash its hands of the matter, with psychiatry having the responsibility of taking care of that person. What became implicit in the instructions from society was that this individual should remain incarcerated indefinitely, in many instances for the remainder of his life. This system worked well for quite some time, its success being directly proportional to and dependent upon psychiatrists keeping these deranged individuals locked up. In other words, as long as such individuals were out of sight, incapable of further mischief to the public at large, society was content with this arrangement.

The second stage was the age of expanding knowledge of human behavior. We learned much about how people functioned and about unconscious mental processes and developed a science of psychodynamics. At this point, society gave psychiatry an additional job and the legal profession was happy to have psychiatrists take on this role. Essentially, the psychiatrist was told, "You have learned so much and we have such faith in you that if you will give us your revered and refined judgment about the mind of the criminal, we can proceed in a much more modern, scientific manner." This was the era of enlightenment, and I remember well that my professors were pleased with the rulings such as those of Judge David Bazelon of the Fifth District Court of Appeals in the United States when he formulated the Durham rule, which stated that if an act is a product of a disordered mind, then the person is not guilty by reason of insanity. There were many variations on this rule with an attempt by various groups to come up with the ideal that would allow us to find that these people were indeed sick individuals.

The third era is upon us. This is the era of disenchantment. Society is confused and unhappy with psychiatry. Lawyers have many opinions about psychiatrists but practical opinions of the lawyers are twofold. The defense attorney noted that his clients were locked up for prolonged periods of time and were deprived of their rights. Further, that if his client had simply pleaded guilty and gone to trial, he would have been released much sooner, and that therefore the psychiatrist was at fault for prolonging incarceration. Consequently, there were many suits to release those individuals in mental hospitals because they were originally adjudged "not guilty by reason of insanity" but no longer met the criteria for insanity. At the other end of the spectrum are those, primarily prosecutors, who say that we discover insanity one day, examine the patient the next day and find him sane, and consequently release him. They question whether insanity resides within the patient, the psychiatrist, or the system.

At the extreme, the insanity defense is used as a ploy by an attorney. For example, a woman has been provoked beyond reason by her husband, shoots him in a fit of rage, pleads not guilty by reason of insanity, and is hospitalized. It is soon apparent to the hospital staff that this is a person without the stigmata of major mental illness who has been overcome by rage, and that she is not psychotic, delusional, or hallucinatory, and she is released. The public wonders, and it cannot be blamed. Society asks, "Can't you psychiatrists agree on anything?" They see the battle of the experts. One does not have to be reminded of Arthur Brenner, Sirhan Sirhan, and more recently, John Hinckley. Although society recognizes honest differences of opinion between experts, they look for much more consistency than we display. We physicians know that in all fields the practice of medicine is neither simple nor uncontroversial. For example, experts do not agree upon how the early hypertensive should be treated, whether he should receive drugs, and if so, what kind. Therefore, it is simple and naive for the public to think that we can have such unanimity of opinion or that we can all know the answers, but this is what is asked of us. The public views the matter much like "The whole array of practitioners . . . looking at one another and at the spectators, as if nobody had ever heard that all over England the name in which they were assembled was a bitter jest . . . that little short of a miracle could bring any good out of it to anyone" ([4], p. 263). It is more than coincidence that Charles Dickens began penning the words of *Bleak House* 8 years after the M'Naghten rule was put into effect. Although he was talking about the English Chancery Court, his words seem hauntingly relevant to the public's perception of the courtroom testimony of psychiatrists.

Ermutulu [2] has recently sketched out some of the current views about the insanity defense, noting revolutionary changes being made by psychiatrists, lawyers, and legislatures. Before lamenting what may well be our diminished role in this aspect of forensic psychiatry, we may look upon it as an opportunity to shift some of our energies into the study, understanding, and prevention of a ubiquitous form of disordered human behavior, i.e., the garden variety of crime involving burglaries, robberies, muggings, and their all too frequent accompaniment, drug abuse. We can use our knowledge to look at the system of crime and to elucidate those factors that initiate, encourage, and perpetuate crime. With this knowledge we may be able to intervene effectively in the cycle of criminal behavior. Again, through no fault of our own, we are asked only to look at and evaluate the end product of the system, the apprehended criminal. However, by the time this individual comes to the attention of the adult criminal justice system, there has been so much positive reinforcement for a career in crime that often there is little we can do besides temporarily removing this person from society.

We have been much concerned with whether a crime is a product of a mental illness, but I would ask that we seriously examine the converse, i.e., the possibility that the milieu of crime and drug abuse may lead to widespread emotional distress. This may be something that we cursorily acknowledge but rarely subject to serious scrutiny. Though many would say that this is far too much for the mental health field to consider and that human nature is unchangeable, I would like to give an example of a major crime whose incidence could be markedly reduced by simple, inexpensive measures that would harm no one and deprive no individual of constitutional rights.

The example I should like to sketch out is the prevention of automobile theft by the use of vehicular identification numbers (VINs) [1]. One might ask what this has to do with psychiatry, law, and ethics. In the United States each year one million cars are stolen, having a value of $ 4000000000. This means that one million people will suddenly be deprived of their major means of transportation. Most of the automobiles will not be recovered, and if they are, they will be so damaged and mutilated that the owners will always, whenever driving the recovered car, have feelings of unease. You may well ask, "What does this have to do with the theme of this conference? Why should psychiatrists worry about car theft?" Many of us would probably see this as simply a job for the police and think that this conference has more important matters to discuss, such as the rights of the mentally ill, questions of confidentiality, and predictions of dangerousness.

However, we should look upon automobile theft as more than just the loss of a major possession. You should understand that in the United States it may be the major possession of those of modest means and their only transportation to work. The automobile is the determinant of status. I would further remind the audience of the practical and emotional significance of transportation in the United States. Not too long ago, the punishment for horse thievery was hanging for the lucky. For the unfortunate, it was hamstringing, the process of cutting the large tendons in the back of the leg, leaving the individual helpless in getting about, just as the thief had done to the rider whose horse he had taken. One must understand the major emotional significance of the automobile. We should remember, too, that many victims of car theft are injured or killed as an unfortunate side effect of the theft.

The ethical dilemna is that this is a crime that experts tell us is 90% preventable by simple, relatively inexpensive means which harm no one and which infringe on the rights of no one. The technique is simplicity itself: stamping identification numbers on all parts of the vehicle. As is well known, in the case of a stolen automobile the sum of the parts is worth much more than the whole automobile. Each part is quite valuable for resale and a major illicit business enterprise has developed with the theft, dismantling of cars, and resale of parts. Although a few cars are stolen for joyriding, automobile thievery in the 1980s is virtually a purely criminal activity pursued by highly skilled, intelligent people who know a good business, albeit illegitimate, when they see it. This is one area where the poverty factor is scarcely applicable because few poor people possess the skills or resources to become competent car thieves, chop men, etc. The insanity defense is rarely raised any more than it is in intricate stock fraud schemes.

The reason why the use of VINs would be effective in preventing car theft is that thieves are not psychotic or grossly neurotic, and recognize that they cannot dispose of marked car parts, and the whole enterprise would then no longer be viable. If this were accomplished in the United States and one million people did not have their cars stolen in one year (as in 1983), it would substantially reduce a source of emotional tension. It would promote a positive feeling of well-being, a feeling that something could be done. Having fewer car thieves to pursue, the police, courts, and the rest of the criminal justice system would have reduced pressure and more time and manpower to be applied to other areas.

I have gone into considerable detail about VINs simply as a paradigm for those areas where the application of psychiatric knowledge to criminal behavior could pay rich rewards to a society overburdened by crime.

Typically, behavioral scientists make many observations about human behavior, studying it in the usual unfettered course of activities over a period of time or via controlled experimental conditions. However, serendipitous circumstances may present us with unexpected opportunities. The concept of VINs undoubtedly came from pragmatic observations by “nonscientists,” who observed that marked and easily identifiable items are much less likely to be stolen. This rests upon the solid psychological basis that individuals, be they honest or thieves, will not engage in nonproductive and at times self-destructive behavior, such as accumulating a supply of automobile parts which cannot be sold. Despite the fact that we “scientists” did not originate the concept, and it does not call upon us to utilize all of our clinical skills, nonetheless we should use our energies, as individuals and organizations, in a constructive fashion for the universal adoption of this disarmingly simple but quite effective weapon in our forensic armamentarium. We should also look for, develop, and exploit other similar techniques.

Rapid technical, social, and economic changes in recent decades have produced criminal behavior that threatens to overwhelm our system of criminal justice, producing an epidemic of emotional distress. However, our twin disciplines of law and psychiatry acting together can be responsive to the needs of society. To do this we will have to evolve not only refinements of the existing techniques but entirely new ways of viewing our interactive, complementary roles.

References

1. Anon (1983) Automobile theft. Atlanta Journal-Constitution. 13 February 1983
2. Ermutulu I (1983) Guilty but mentally ill – in search of a perspective. Journal of Medical Association of Georgia 72: 345–349
3. Marti-Ibanez F (ed) (1960) Henry E. Sigerist on the History of Medicine. The Publications, New York
4. Zabel M (ed) (1956) Bleak House, Charles Dickens. Houghton-Mifflin, Boston

The Ideology of Entitlement: The Contemporary Function of Law and Its Application to Psychiatry

L. Gostin

The legal approach to psychiatry – the application of a formal body of procedural and substantive rules to shape and control mental health services and practices – is now well established in a number of modern Western societies. This paper will describe and explain the function of law in relation to psychiatry in two areas: the contribution of law to the provision of health and social services, and the use of law in defining the parameters of psychiatric decision-making and practices. The ideology of entitlement, on the face of it, appears to be an ill-conceived philosophy on the basis of which to promote the interests of any socially impoverished group of people. The law has traditionally been perceived as concerned more with maintaining and enforcing the social order than with the provision of services or the meeting of social needs. This paper will present a case for a legislative planning approach and will critically examine the "judicial moralism" apparent in the United States.

Historical Overview

Social historians have sometimes characterized the process of reform of mental health legislation as a pendulum swinging between two opposing schools of thought – legalism and professional discretion. The influence of law in mental health was firmly established in England and Wales by the Lunacy Act 1890. The Lunacy Laws required certification of lunacy and magistrates' approval as a prerequisite to both voluntary and compulsory hospital admissions. This legislation, devised in the late Victorian era, was seen in conventional historical assessments as an obstacle to early and effective treatment of mentally disordered people. The Mental Health Act 1959 (England and Wales), which had a striking influence on mental health legislation in North America and the Commonwealth, was thought of as a negation of, and reaction to, legal formalism. Its approach was effectively to make access to treatment and care a matter for medical discretion. Review of medical decision-making was limited to a small minority of cases; the system of review was to be *de facto* and exercised by an administrative tribunal with a medical component.

A reemergence of a legal approach to psychiatry has taken place in the United States in the last decade. A notable characteristic of American federalism is that domestic policy has been substantially determined by the courts; the judiciary has introduced its own social morality, based largely upon constitutional construction, to try to ensure reasonable access to services and protection from the unjustified use of compulsion for those designated as mentally ill and handicapped.

Recent decisions by the United States Supreme Court may have marked the end of an era where judicial solutions were to be offered for such complex sociomedical issues as voluntary admission of children to institutions *(Parham* v. *J. R.);* the minimum standards of treatment or habilitation to be provided in hospital (see, e.g., *O'Connor* v. *Donaldson*); consent to treatment *(Rogers* v. *Okin);* and the transfer of people and resources from institutions to the community *(Pennhurst State School and Hospital* v. *Halderman).* In each of these contexts the Supreme Court has taken perceptible, albeit inconclusive, steps to transfer decision-making from the judiciary to mental health professionals and planners.

Following the emergence of a legal approach to psychiatry in the United States, and perhaps unaware of the signs of its descendency, the British Parliament enacted the Mental Health Act 1983. Its main provisions are concerned primarily with furthering legal safeguards available to patients. Ironically, the Act was, in part, imposed upon the Government of the United Kingdom by a ruling of the European Court of Human Rights that the Mental Health Act 1959 had violated article 5(4) of the European Convention. The Court held that patients detained on the basis of "unsoundness of mind" had the right to periodic access to a court of law to determine the substantive justification for confinement (*X* v. *the United Kingdom,* judgment given 5 November 1981; [1]).

Legal Justifications for an Entitlement Philosophy

The concept that the law can have an important function in relation to the availability, organization, and delivery of services is a relatively recent development. The premise of the ideology of entitlement is that access to health and social services should not be based upon charitable or professional discretion, but upon enforceable rights. The rules of equity and fairness are deeply entrenched principles of law. From an international legal perspective, a government is not obliged to provide health and social services. However, once it chooses to provide services it cannot arbitrarily exclude or deprive certain individuals or client groups. If there is an unreasonable denial of a service the remedy is, or should be, provided by the law.

The right to a service, of course, does not emanate from intangible jurisprudential or moral philosophy but from statute and, in some jurisdictions, a written constitution. In countries which provide a nationalized health and social service there is a wide-ranging body of legislation which provides a general entitlement to treatment, care, housing, and social services. In these jurisdictions the provision of services is, from its origin, integrally associated with law. Improvements in the quality or nature of that service lie, at least in part, in enforcement of the law or in its reform. It should be observed that this approach relies upon "open-textured" or "enabling" legislation, which must be supported by adequate financing, efficient management, and good practice. However, the law can, and sometimes does, place specific statutory duties on central or local government authorities which can be enforced through the courts or by administrative remedies. The objective of the ideology of entitlement is to establish the right to a service which can be enforced at the behest of a client group or an individual. This draws the attention of the relevant authorities to their legal and social obligations to particularly underprivileged client groups and draws public attention to underprovision and underresourcing in areas of concern. It may be helpful to examine some of the specific legal strategies utilized in Great Britain and the United States in order to assess their impact.

Great Britain

The Mental Health Act 1983 introduced two specific measures which promote an entitlement philosophy: a mandatory duty of the local authority to provide community aftercare services for detained patients once they are discharged and the right of the patient to publicly financed legal representation, together with public finance for independent psychiatric and social work reports at Mental Health Review Tribunals. The "aftercare" amendment specifies a continuing duty to provide housing and health and social services in the community. The parliamentary debates repeatedly emphasized the chronic underprovision of community resources, the fact that aftercare services would prevent prolonged institutionalization of mentally disordered people in hospital, and the fact that they would be both invasive of individual liberty and uneconomic.

In addition to the theme of a legal entitlement to health and social services, a persistent feature of the parliamentary debates was the attempt, ultimately successful, to provide patients appearing before Mental Health Review Tribunals with an entitlement to public funding for their legal representation. The effectiveness of Mental Health Review Tribunals is only to a limited extent dependent upon their procedures and powers. Far more important is the availability and quality of representation. The effects of institutionalization, the patient's mental illness or handicap, his deference to medical authority, and the effects of major tranquillizers make self-advocacy invariably difficult and sometimes impossible. Further, the unrepresented patient is frequently denied the full details of the case against him, including medical and social inquiry reports, which provide the rationale for detention.

One of the central criticisms of the legal formalism of the old Lunacy Laws was that the review by a magistrate presented formal procedural barriers to access to care, but was not a reliable safeguard against medical discretion exercised without sufficient cause or justification; magistrates' review became a highly routinized confirmation of medical authority [2]. A trained representative is needed to put the legal, medical, and social aspects of the case to the tribunal. The availability of representation, moreover, should not be a matter which is dependent upon the ability of the patient to pay. Mental Health Review Tribunals are the only tribunals where the outcome of the hearing affects a person's liberty. It is very much a part of the legal approach in mental health to ensure that there is public financing for representation to enable the patient to know and critically examine the reasons for detention, to seek independent professional advice, and to explore community alternatives to hospital care.

The arguments in Parliament for the right to state-aided representation were advanced primarily by lawyers who emphasized the importance of effective legal controls on matters involving individual liberty. An application, *Collins* v. *the United Kingdom*, was lodged with the European Commission of Human Rights alleging that article 5(4) of the Convention required contracting parties to grant public financing to their nationals for representation at mental health hearings. The Collins application is awaiting a decision of the Commission. It should be observed, however, that the organs of the Convention have repeatedly emphasized the need for effective legal assistance as part of the "special procedural guarantees" required in mental health cases. Further, in *Airey* v. *Republic of Ireland*, the Court considered that the right of a person to appear in the High Court without representation would not be "effective in the sense of whether [he] was able to present [his] case properly and satisfactorily." The Court concluded that publicly funded representation was required so that a person's rights under the Convention were not "theoretical or illusory" but "practical and effective." The Government of the United Kingdom has now agreed to make legal aid available for representation before Mental Health Review Tribunals.

The European Commission of Human Rights has also begun to place duties on member states to provide minimal programs of treatment and conditions of adequate hygiene and safety in mental hospitals. Most of the cases have emanated from article 3 of the European Convention of Human Rights, which prohibits inhumane and degrading treatment or punishment. In *Smith* v. *the United Kingdom,* the Commission held admissible a complaint that treatment and rehabilitation must accompany detention for unsoundness of mind and that hospital conditions must provide protection from harm and humane sanitary facilities. The Commission sent a fact-finding delegation to Broadmoor Hospital in England. Thereafter, a £120-million allocation was made by the British Government to improve facilities and staff ratios. In *Clarke* v. *the United Kingdom,* the Commission presided over a friendly settlement between the applicant and the British Government which established minimal guidelines in the use of seclusion.

There is currently a "second generation" of cases before the European Commission on a variety of mental health issues, including the right of patients to have unimpeded access to courts; the right of nondangerous patients to be transferred from maximum security institutions; and the right to procedural safeguards before Mental Health Review Tribunals *(Ashingdane* v. *the United Kingdom; Kynaston* v. *the United Kingdom).*

The United States

The legal profession in the United States has had a profound effect on the mental health system. Any attempt at charting the course of legal activity would result in oversimplification, and I propose only to trace the landmarks and general trends. A series of cases from the late 1960s onward criticized the very existence of psychiatric institutions. The constitutional parameters of these cases were complex and diverse, but broadly relied upon the fact that patients were involuntarily detained. If the Government was to deprive individuals of their liberty, the argument went, it was bound to provide (and here the judicial prescriptions varied) some minimal treatment or habilitation *(O'Connor* v. *Donaldson).*

Two conceptual obstacles have impeded a major shift in resources from institutions to the community. First, as stated above, the basis of the constitutional claims rested largely upon the legal status of patients; voluntary patients or people in the community were, therefore, not entitled to equivalent constitutional protection. Subsequent cases have sought to circumvent this obstacle by, for example, proclaiming a constitutional right to protection from harm *(New York State Association for Retarded Children* v. *Carey).* However, this constitutional path has never firmly established itself. The second conceptual obstacle was to be the pivotal factor; the success of this strategy was to be an important measure of the success of the legal approach itself. It involved the power and willingness of the judiciary to compel Government to provide community-based alternatives to institutional care. The concept of affirmative action found its most complete expression in a Federal District Court case: "Constitutional rights are hollow if there are in fact no alternatives to institutionalisation. The State may not circumvent the Constitution simply by refusing to create any alternatives to incarceration; it must act affirmatively to foster such alternatives" *(Morales* v. *Tutman).*

One should be reminded of the radical nature of such judicial pronouncements. The United States has never sought to enshrine in its law any comprehensive right to health or social services, although federal legislation has been enacted providing an incentive to states to develop community-based psychiatric and social services. The United States Supreme Court recently refused to uphold any constitutional or statutory right to care in the community *(Pennhurst State School and Hospital* v. *Halderman).* Although the Supreme Court has not conclusively decided that there is not a constitutional right, it will now be difficult for the legal profession to pursue such a course in the courts.

It would be clearly wrong to be overcritical of judicial intervention in the United States, particularly since it has come in the wake of chronic legislative and executive neglect of the needs of people suffering from mental distress. Nonetheless, it is regrettable that important policy decisions have been taken within the narrow context of litigation. The disadvantages of this judicial approach are that the courts are limited by the particular facts and issues raised in the immediate case and they are able only to set minimal standards based upon nonspecific constitutional principles; they are unfamiliar with the range and appropriateness of treatment approaches and facilities; and they are ill-equipped to assure long-term compliance with, and implementation of, their judgments.

Limitations on the Practice of Psychiatry

Psychiatry is a profession with a traditional affinity to humanism; its *raison d'être* is to care for people with deep emotional and human distress. It is, moreover, a specialism of medicine which has well-established traditions of healing the sick and which is guided by scrupulous ethical principles. When one examines the caring traditions and benevolent principles underlying the profession, it is curious that it has been so closely associated with power and its abuse.

The principal concern of those who advocate a legal approach is that psychiatrists have gone much further than simply caring for people who are thought by themselves and others to be suffering from mental distress. Psychiatrists, according to the legal approach, should be required to state the grounds for their decisions in terms which are open to examination by others. The confrontation should then be on the question of the adequacy of the grounds advanced and not on the basis of presumed expertise. This is the area of disagreement at the interface of law and psychiatry. The legal approach does not accept unsupported claims of knowledge in areas of diagnosis, behavior prediction, or treatment. In each context the law requires some observable evidence to support professional judgments.

There is a sense of contradiction in the way that contemporary psychiatry presents itself. Psychiatry purports to be a specialism of medicine; it strives toward objectivity and has an affinity with the natural sciences. The psychiatric journals bristle with research to establish the empirical efficacy of somatic treatments. At the same time, psychiatry asks not to be held to account for its views in an objective and scientific way. It asks, rather, to operate under the ambiguous parameters of "clinical judgment," which relies not upon an empiricist view but upon unspoken areas of personal judgment. Medical thought concerning the propriety of allowing those designated as mentally ill to exercise judgment in respect of admission or treatment decisions appears to be this: Mental patients are to be detained in hospital because they are considered a danger to themselves or others and/or they are unable to make reasonably informed judgments concerning the need for treatment. Members of the medical profession are delegated the task of determining those who are dangerous or lacking competence, and then substituting their judgment for that of the person concerned. It is the benefit that is said to accrue to the patient which is thought to justify the deprivation of his or her ordinary right to self-determination. It follows that society operates on the assumption that psychiatrists can reliably and validly diagnose particular forms of mental disorder, that psychiatrists have an ability to predict future behavior in cases where the lay person could not, that psychiatric treatments with reasonably established efficacy exist, and that psychiatrists can make reasonably consistent and objective judgments concerning the need for a treatment response to a particular medical condition. The evidence to support each of these assumptions is highly equivocal, and needs to be established before it would be logical to remove legal criteria and procedures from psychiatric activity and decision-making.

Conclusion

As I have indicated, it is curious that psychiatry, a profession steeped in the traditions of humanism, is now sometimes publicly perceived as a profession concerned with the use of compulsion over individuals and the misuse of its authority. It is perhaps a greater irony that the law is now seeking to influence medicine toward a new humanism - with greater compassion and freedom for the individual.

The formalistic and mechanistic approach of the law may not be entirely suited to a field of human endeavor which is, by its nature, highly individualistic and unpredictable. Yet it is in the interests of both psychiatry and law to lay down societal and ethical boundaries in the pursuit of an activity which concerns not only compassionate ideals but also limitations on personal autonomy.

References

Statutes

The Lunacy Act 1890, 53 and 54 Vict., chap 5
The Mental Health Act 1959, 7 and 8 Eliz. 2, chap 72
The Mental Health Act 1983, chap 20

Cases

X v. *the United Kingdom,* application number 6998/75, European Court of Human Rights, judgment given 5 November 1981

Rogers v. *Okin,* 478 F. Supp. 1342 (D. Mass. 1979), aff'd in part, rev'd in part, vacated in part and remanded 634 F.2d 650 (1st Cir. 1980), vacated and remanded *sub nom. Mills* v. *Rogers,* 102 S.Ct. 2442 (1982)

Parham v. *J. R.,* 442 U.S. 584 (1979)

O'Connor v. *Donaldson,* 422 U.S. 563 (1975)

Pennhurst State School and Hospital v. *Halderman,* 453 U.S. 1 (1981)

Collins v. *the United Kingdom,* European Commission of Human Rights, application number 9729/82

Airey v. *Republic of Ireland,* European Court of Human Rights, judgment given 9 October 1979, at para 24

Smith v. *the United Kingdom,* application number 6870/75, decision of the European Commission of Human Rights adopted on 7 October 1981

Ashingdane v. *the United Kingdom,* application number 8225/78, European Commission of Human Rights

Kynaston v. *the United Kingdom,* application number 9480/81, European Commission of Human Rights

O'Connor v. *Donaldson,* 422 U.S. 563 (1975)

New York State Association for Retarded Children v. *Carey,* 393 F. Supp. 1975

Morales v. *Tutman,* 383 F. Supp. 53 (1974)

Articles

1. Gostin L (1982) Human rights, judicial review and the mentally disordered offender. Criminal Law Review, pp 779–783
2. Gostin L (1983) Contemporary social historical perspectives on mental health law. J Law and Society 10 (1): 47–70

Psychiatrist and Lawyer - Total Incompatibility?

C. P. Seager and T. M. Napier

Introduction

This paper derives from many discussions, sometimes verging on arguments, between a psychiatrist and a lawyer - the two authors. Perhaps we are being naive in raising the issue of why psychiatrists and lawyers are so often at loggerheads, whether behind the scenes or in court, over the best way to help the person they both agree is the object of their concern. After all, psychiatrists and lawyers have apparently common aims - to direct their respective abilities in the best interests of their clients. Yet when both are involved with the same client, such well-intended intervention often results in professional conflict.

This paper examines the way the two professional disciplines look at their respective roles, using as an example the case of *X* v. *The United Kingdom,* decided by the European Court of Human Rights in November 1981. The case involved the recall of X to Broadmoor. A psychiatric colleague who had been responsible for his care prior to the time of return, but who had no actual involvement in the decision to recall, has expressed anxiety over the complaint made to the Court that this recall was hasty and unjustified. His anxiety was not mollified even though the European Court rejected this part of X's complaint. The Court said that on the facts there was sufficient reason for the Home Secretary to have considered that X's continued liberty constituted a danger to the public, having regard to his history of psychiatric troubles, so that his recall as an emergency measure for a short duration was justified.

Equally, the lawyer coauthor of this paper would be hurt at any suggestion that the effect of his efforts on behalf of X was damaging to X himself and to X's family. He recognized that as a lawyer it was his duty to respond to X's request that available legal methods be used, if possible, to challenge his recall.

The Case

Looking at X from the point of view of a psychiatrist first, it needs to be said that he suffered from a long-standing mental disorder, having received treatment from 1965 onward, when he was aged 31 years (Appendix A). He was always looked upon as a potentially violent, irascible, and unpredictable individual. On one occasion he attended the outpatient clinic carrying a gun. He had been in the local psychiatric inpatient unit on one short occasion and had been maintained on antipsychotic drugs as an outpatient. He was under the care of the former professor of psychiatry until an incident in which he caused grievous bodily harm to a workmate with a wrench.

At his trial X was found to be suffering from mental illness and was admitted to

Broadmoor Special Hospital for treatment. He remained in hospital for nearly 3 years and was then discharged on license, subject to the condition that he remain under supervision by a probation officer and a local psychiatrist. X lived in the community for 3 years, and during that period saw the supervising psychiatrist 11 times, the last occasion being 6 months before the recall. He also saw his general practitioner nine times during the same period, the last occasion being 7 weeks before recall. Throughout, the psychiatrist remained concerned about X's mental state without feeling that it was necessary to take any formal action.

One day, X's wife visited the probation officer and told him that for a long time X's condition had not been as she had described in progress reports. On the contrary, she said that he remained deluded and threatening, using obscene language, accusing her of loose morals, and drinking quite heavily. She told the probation officer that she had reached the end of her endurance and intended to leave X the following day, but was afraid to stay in the house with him that night. The probation officer alerted the responsible medical officer at Broadmoor, who, knowing X's previous history and continuing psychiatric reports, referred the matter to the Home Secretary, who exercised his absolute discretion to recall X to Broadmoor immediately.

X complained to his lawyer that he had not been given reasons for the recall, that the recall was not justified, and that he had no effective means of challenging his continued detention in Broadmoor. Mr. Napier saw X in the police cell in Sheffield just before the escort took him to Broadmoor. Instructions were received from X to apply for a Mental Health Review Tribunal under the Mental Health Act 1959 and to apply to the High Court in London for a writ of *habeas corpus*. Legal aid was obtained and some 7 weeks later the *habeas corpus* application came for hearing. The hearing was adjourned for Mr. Napier to try and discover more about the reasons for the recall. Affidavit evidence was obtained from the psychiatrist and the general practitioner regarding X's recent mental history, and further evidence was obtained from his workmates. At the adjourned hearing of the *habeas corpus* application some 11 weeks after the actual date of recall, the Court decided that it could not interfere, since technically X's recall was legally justified. A few weeks later, X lodged a complaint to the European Court. Approximately 2 years after his recall he was again discharged following a Mental Health Review Tribunal. Two and a half years after this discharge he was found dead in an hotel bedroom. A note contemplating suicide was found in the bedroom, but the pathologist found that death was due to a heart attack and the coroner recorded a verdict of death by natural causes.

Although X's case was initially lodged with the European Court because of his complaint about the circumstances of his recall, it achieved wider significance, being taken by the Court as the lead case in a group of other applications asking the Court to look at article 5 of the European Convention of Human Rights as it related to mental patients.

X complained of a breach of article 5 (2) of the Convention because he had not been given reasons for his arrest. Although the European Commission of Human Rights found a breach of this article, the Court decided that it was not necessary to make a ruling on the question. X's complaint under article 3 that he had been subjected to inhuman and degrading treatment was rejected by the Court. His complaint under article 5 (1) that there was no justification for his deprivation of liberty by way of recall was also rejected by the Court.

However, the Court unanimously found that there had been a breach of article 5 (4). The limited scope of judicial review available in *habeas corpus* proceedings did not satisfy the rights guaranteed to mental patients by article 5 (4). Further, a Mental Health Review Tribunal did not constitute a competent court within the meaning of article 5 (4), because it exercises an advisory function to the Home Secretary only.

From the point of view of the lawyer, this case achieved noteworthy success. It resulted in the Home Secretary issuing to Special Hospitals instructions that when a patient was returned, it was important that he should be informed clearly and immediately of the reason for readmission. More generally, as a result of this case the Mental Health Amendment Act 1982 includes major reforms concerning the discharge of restricted patients, their rights of application to Mental Health Review Tribunals, and the powers of these Tribunals.

With the background of this case, it is interesting to look at the views of the psychiatrist and the lawyer in an area of obvious possible conflict. The psychiatrist has the problem of looking after disturbed and potentially dangerous patient living in the community, perhaps with their families. He is concerned about the well-being of the individual and what is best for him, but cannot afford to close his eyes to the effect that such an individual has on the people around him. He has to make a clinical judgment concerning the point at which freedom becomes risky because of a looming potential disaster. There are considerable arguments about the diagnosis of dangerousness and I do not propose to go into these now. All I can say is that doctors are not able to prophesy the future any more than lawyers can. You may say that because X was returned to hospital, but was discharged fairly soon afterward, the lawyer's role is vindicated. Nevertheless, while X was in hospital for 22 months he did receive further treatment.

Who can say the extent to which, if at all, X's contemplation of suicide may have been influenced by one or other, or a combination, of the actions of his wife, his parents, the probation officer, the responsible medical officer, the Home Secretary, the lawyer, and the courts. Mr. Napier, who saw X from time to during the 5-year period between his recall and death, is of the view that the legal process which X initiated had no influence on his demise. X was of the opinion that he was right to feel aggrieved about what had happened to him, and in the view of Mr. Napier he was entitled to make use of whatever legal remedies were available to have his grievance satisfied. On the other hand, the psychiatrist is convinced that the stress and delay of the European Court hearing did play a part in what he has no doubt was a suicide act, in spite of the coroner's verdict. It is ironic that the satisfaction eventually given by the European Court of Human Rights came over 2 years after X's death, but with the result that many restricted patients in X's position will have less room for grievance than he had.

Conclusion

A psychiatrist endeavors to help his patient in the best way that he sees fit. It is his aim to look at the well-being of the patient in the broadest context. Sometimes by insisting on admission to hospital he acts against what the patient himself may see as his best interests. The psychiatrist also has to recognize that the man does not live in an isolated environment, but with family, friends, workmates, and neighbors. It may be in the patient's interests to take away his liberty because he runs the risk of losing the regard and support of people around him if he remains in the community, and may even suffer physical damage as a result of his behavior. It seems to me that the psychiatrist is able to take and perhaps should take a broader view of the best interests of his patients, adopting a paternalistic role which he may well have to defend but should be able to defend on the basis of acting on his best judgment, without malice, and with the overall interests of his patient at heart.

The lawyer's approach is necessarily different, although no less well intentioned. It is his duty to advise his client on the remedies which the law may offer and to advance whatever reasonable arguments may offer themselves in seeking those remedies. Although it is the lawyer's duty to act in the best interests of his client, it is not for the lawyer to prejudge the matter if the best interests legally do not coincide with the best interests psychiatrically. So long as he acts honestly and professionally throughout, making use of the available legal process, he should have a clear conscience, in just the same way as the psychiatrist's conscience should be clear if he decides to admit a patient against his will but in his own interests.

Is it even necessary to try and reconcile these two attitudes? The psychiatrist will argue that an attempt must be made to reconcile them, because of the risk that the patient may suffer as a result of the legal procedures which he has himself invoked using the assistance of the lawyer in their pursuit. Psychiatrists took the general view that the Mental Health Acts of 1959 and 1960 were important steps away from legal procedures. Prior to these Acts patients were certified insane by a magistrate. The Mental Health Acts allowed doctors to treat psychiatric patients in a manner similar to someone found unconscious in the street and admitted to hospital for treatment. In latter years the effects of the Acts have been criticized, and now we are moving to a legalistic view-point.

The Mental Health Amendment Act 1982 introduces major reforms and we have yet to see its practical effects. It is to be hoped that it will not require doctors to spend excessive amounts of time appearing before tribunals to defend their actions when they have, throughout, acted in good faith. On the other hand, Mr. Napier argues that to ensure that the system of detention is fair to the patient it is essential that there should be an adequate periodical method of enquiry, and that the psychiatrist should not be oversensitive about his duty to participate in such an enquiry, particularly because it relates to the rights of liberty of the individual, which are just as important to the mental patient as to any other citizen.

Appendix Life History of X

19 January 1934	Birth of X
7 October 1965	First outpatient appointment following onset of illness in 1963; sexual preoccupations; separation from wife
2 December 1965	New letter of referral; refusal of admission
20 September 1966	Voluntary admission
20 October 1968	Attack on workmate
7 November 1968	Admission to Broadmoor Hospital
23 August 1971	Conditional discharge from Broadmoor
8 October 1973	Last of 11 outpatient attendances
5 April 1974	Report to Home Secretary
6 April 1974	Return to Broadmoor
9 February 1976	Conditional discharge from Broadmoor to live with parents
17 November 1978	Departure from parent's home
1979	Death in an hotel bedroom

Post-Divorce Family Psychopathology: An Empirical Report

G. Zlotnik

Introduction

As the divorce rate in Western industrialized societies rises [5], so does the amount of attention given to the child psychiatric aspects of the divorce process. As the number of unresolved custody and access cases increases, so does the reliance of the judiciary upon expert opinion [18]. Thus a growing amount of professional literature deals with the emotional processes which encompass family members before, during, and after divorce, whether the divorce is "civilized" [9] or contested. Divorce studies examine the legal-psychiatric problems [16] and evaluate the "children of divorce" and their vulnerability [1], response to the divorce stress [10], symptomatology [14], coping and adaption [17], and future development [13]. Some studies focus on techniques of assessment [3] and intervention [6]. Others discuss the role of the mental health professional [8], while some devise strategy [11] and guidelines [2]. A few deal with the custody contest *per se* [12].

This paper draws attention to a specific clinical picture that emerges in the course of a child psychiatric assessment procedure in custody and/or access cases. The symptomatology denotes an emotional reaction and a personality change of such magnitude and depth that it borders on character deviation.

The Background and Setting

In Denmark the matrimonial law specifically states that the welfare of the child is the deciding factor in contested cases of custody and visiting rights. In 25% of divorce cases in Denmark the parents cannot agree on the question of the child's legal and practical placement, and some of these cases are subsequently resolved by a court decision based, among other things, on a written opinion from a specially appointed child psychiatrist [4]. In most cases the court of the county pays all the expenses.

In the period 1974–1981 the author evaluated 23 custody cases referred by the civil courts and nine access cases referred by the social authorities. In the 32 families involved there were, besides the 32 parental pairs, 45 "contested" children (25 boys and 20 girls), 15 "uncontested" siblings, and 46 steprelatives (18 stepfathers, eight stepmothers, and 20 stepsiblings). The assessment procedure was ambulatory and took place in the hospital setting, employing semistructural interview techniques. The frame of the exploration was family-oriented with the aim of shedding light on the psychodynamics of both the original and postdivorce family constellations. Accordingly, several conjoint/family interviews were conducted. The child in question was always seen alone at least once. As a minimal condition the contested child was in all cases seen together with the custodial and noncustodial parent alternately. No direct attempt was made at therapeutic intervention (still, three cases were settled out of court following the child psychiatric engagement). The resulting written opinion was sent to both parents through their respective advocates. Some parents demanded and obtained extra sessions after that. In 75% of the cases the courts and the social authorities followed the advice of the child psychiatrist.

The Clinical Picture

The pattern that emerged had the following central elements:

The Parents

Twenty-seven of the contesting parents were diagnosed prior to the actual investigation as suffering from a psychiatric condition (indeed, that was often the reason for the referral to the child psychiatrist). Six parents were labeled as psychotics, six as alcoholics, five as having a personality disorder of the antisocial type, and 12 as neurotics. Regardless of that, they were essentially no different from the "normal" parents in terms of manifesting the typical symptomatology. Indeed, the aforementioned psychiatric diagnoses became secondary. Furthermore, psychiatric diagnosis, sex, age, social class, and intelligence notwithstanding, all the parents manifested the behavioral symptoms in the same almost indistinguishable manner. The following pattern unfolded.

In the Interview Setting

1. At the meeting well-dressed, trim, and made-up.
2. Appearing friendly, smiling, and at the start undemanding.
3. Trying innocuously to "seduce" the child psychiatrist.
4. Maintaining a tolerant and nondominant attitude toward the child.
5. Making discreet and subliminal suggestions about the adversary parent.
6. Enhancing own image as the best guardian of the child.
7. Presenting a diametrically different view of family events from that of the other parent.

Add to that the behavior pattern outside the interview setting.

Outside the Interview Setting

1. Telling the psychiatrist by letter and telephone of occurrences that had taken place since the last meeting and things which if true, must be very detrimental to the other parent.
2. Influencing, indoctrinating, and "preparing" the child before the meetings.

3. Mobilizing other persons in order to pressurize the decision makers.
4. Sacrificing position, job, dwelling, or money in a win-at-all-costs attitude.
5. Attempting in a desperate and sometimes illegal way to force a fovorable decision by way of a *fait accompli* (kidnapping or withholding the child) and by protracted legal fights.

The Step parents

Twenty-six stepparents took part in some of the sessions. Their contribution was characterized by:

1. A superficial attempt to appear neutral, unconcerned, and uninfluential.
2. A seemingly secure belief in their powers of conciliation and observation.
3. An exaggerated and sometimes unrealistic loyalty to their new spouse.

Additionally, some of the stepparents manifested certain of the above-mentioned parental traits (in extreme cases, as partners in crime).

The Children

Apart from the better-known symptoms that one associates with the divorce situation [14], one could note that, not surprisingly, the children's loyalty conflict was most prominent. Their attempts at coping were marked by a chameleon-like emotional color change in harmony with the parent in place. Only during the individual sessions (comprising play and/or interview and/or psychological testing, depending on age and intelligence) did the children function more naturally, freely, and trustingly.

The Psychiatrist

As the human drama unfolds before him, the psychiatrist can easily be sucked into the divorce turbulence by its centripetal emotional forces. This creates a pronounced countertransference, first and foremost in relation to the child in question (in a positive and identificational sense), and secondly in response to the parents and their spouses (in a negative and rejectional way). Maintaining a position of objectivity becomes difficult if not impossible. A child psychiatrist is neither able nor trained to uncover the truth in a legal sense. The courts expect him to have the wisdom of a Solomon. The families involved invest him with great powers of observation, decision, influence, and infallibility. Needless to say, this is an illusion that the psychiatrist must cope with.

Discussion

Cases referred to child psychiatric assessment are, because of various selection factors, not representative of a divorce population. Furthermore, they are in many ways hard-core cases. The clinical analysis and conclusion is therefore limited to this special life situation. At the same time it offers an insight into a critical emotional process. When all the above-mentioned symptoms were analyzed in the light of the obtained psychiatric data (particularly the parent's premorbid personality structure), one was struck by the marked contrast between past and present behavior and reactions. The degree of aggression, malice, rigidity, and narcissism, coupled with antisocial impulsivity, could not have been predicted on the basis of earlier patterns. A possible explanation for this can be found if one sees it as an emotional crisis [7] and as an exacerbation of the unresolved marital conflict. The after effects of a wrecked marriage are revived and intensified, the period of dissolution is lived through, the threat to a previously damaged self-respect is renewed, the danger of one again loosing one's child is acute, and the feeling of impotence and helplessness is overpowering. No wonder then, that the methods used and the personality changes undergone are of a magnitude reflecting a fight for survival.

The same problems, fears, and latent hostility were evident in a group of ex-spouses whose children were in residential treatment because of adjustment difficulties. This group of 32 pairs of divorced parents showed, during exploratory interviews, a tendency to develop the same clinical picture. The noncustodial parents were especially vulnerable in this respect. One is therefore tempted to hypothesize that the combination of external pressure (the custody/access procedure) and internal tensions (a latent divorce complex) develops into the personality change described. In addition, one must speculate on whether crisis intervention techniques [15] show themselves to be most suitable in dealing with the situation. This could offer a field for future research.

References

1. Anthony EJ, Koupernik C (eds) (1974) The child in his family: children at psychiatric risk. Wiley, New York
2. Benedek EP, Benedek RS (1972) New child custody laws: making them do what they say. Am J Orthopsychiat 42: 825–834
3. Bentovim A, Gilmour L (1981) A family therapy interactional approach to decision making in child care, access and custody cases. J Family Therapy 3: 65–77
4. Brun G (1964) The children of divorce in Denmark. Bull Menninger Clin 28: 3–10
5. Derdeyn AP (1976) Child custody contests in historical perspective. Am J Psychiat 133: 1369–1376
6. Derdeyn AP (1977) Children in divorce: intervention in the phase of separation. Pediatrics 60: 20–26
7. Dohrenwend BS, Dohrenwend BP (eds) (1974) Stressful life events: their nature and effects. Wiley Interscience, New York
8. Fine S (1981) Children in divorce, custody and access situations: the contribution of the mental health professional. J Child Psychol Psychiat 21: 353–361
9. Futterman EH (1980) Child psychiatry perspectives: after the "civilized" divorce. J Am Acad Child Psychiat 19: 525–530

10. Gardner RA (1978) Social, legal, and therapeutic changes that should lessen the traumatic effects of divorce on children. J Am Acad Psychoanal 6: 231-247
11. Goldstein J, Freud A, Solnit AJ (1973) Beyond the best interests of the child. Free Press, New York
12. Krell R (1978) This child is mine. The battle cry for custody. Can Psychiat Ass J 23: 433-439
13. Rutter M (1981) Stress, coping and development: some issues and some questions. J Child Psychol Psychiat 22: 323-356
14. Schoettle UC, Cantwell DP (1980) Children of divorce: demographic variables, symptoms, and diagnoses. J Am Acad Child Psychiat 19: 453-475
15. Schwartz SL (1971) A review of crisis intervention programs. Psychiat Quart 45: 498-508
16. Slovenko R (1980) Law and psychiatry. In: Kaplan HI, Freedman AM, Sadock BJ (eds) Comprehensive textbook of psychiatry, vol 3. Williams and Wilkins, Baltimore, pp 3063-3065
17. Wallerstein JS, Kelly JB (1980) Surviving the break up: how children and parents cope with divorce. Basic Books, New York
18. Westman JC (1971) The psychiatrist and child custody contests. Am J Psychiat 127: 123-124

B. Patients Rights

Indexing Civil Commitment Criteria in Psychiatric Emergency Rooms[1]

S. P. Segal, M. A. Watson, and L. S. Nelson

The civil commitment of the mentally ill is a major dilemma for mental health professionals throughout the United States and the world. Given persistent ambiguities in commitment statutes and the difficulty inherent in predicting behavior, clinicians must make commitment decisions which may, on the one hand, violate individual rights or, on the other, result in the neglect of community safety or of individuals who need care. While it is generally agreed that commitment is necessary in some cases, there is widespread concern that the commitment process is irrational, arbitrary, and discriminatory [4, 14]. Further, is has been seriously questioned by the courts [3, 9, 15].

Most efforts to prevent the improper use of commitment have focused on procedural safeguards to insure the protections of due process [6]. Due process implies the existence of a standard which is thoroughly and consistently applied in all cases. To date, the courts and legislatures have left the assessment of the substance of commitment criteria to professional discretion. They have assumed that in the absence of predictive accuracy there are professional standards to be consistently applied. In view of this assumption, it is surprising to find that few studies [2, 7, 19] have examined clinical reasons for admission decisions and that none of these attempted to describe the clinical application of legal or statutory criteria.

According to Schwitzgebel [17], most states in the United States specify two or three criteria for involuntary commitment. Criteria of danger to self or others or likelihood of serious harm to self or others are usually combined with a criterion similar to California's grave disability standard. While state statutes vary in the degree of restrictiveness implied by their wording, "the trend has been to narrow the population of those who may be committed" [10, p. 84]. As the California statute was a harbinger of this trend when first implemented in 1969, information about its application by clinicians may be presumed also to be relevant to most other states and countries with similar laws or conditions.

Criteria for civil commitment in California were established by the Lanterman-Petris-Short Act (LPS), but the low provides very little definition of these standards. The commitment process begins with a 72-hour emergency detention for observation and treatment. While a variety of mental health and law enforcement officials

[1] Research supported by NCHSR Grant # HSO4564, NIMH Grant # MH37310-01, and the University of California Berkeley Campus Committee on Research

are authorized to begin this process, the critical decision about hospitalization is made by personnel in the psychiatric emergency rooms of general hospitals. There are no data to indicate how these clinicians apply legal commitment criteria.

According to LPS, involuntary hospitalization requires that

- due to a mental disorder for which the facility can offer treatment, the person must be
- dangerous to himself, dangerous to others, or gravely disabled, and that
- the person must be unable or unwilling to agree to the necessary treatment.

Thus the law requires that three separate assessments be made with almost no statutory guidance. In failing to specify the meaning of these criteria, the legislature clearly intended that these determinations be guided by clinical judgment.

The criteria that have been the focus of greatest concern are those of dangerousness and grave disability. In a statewide evaluation of California involuntary treatment procedures, Schwitzgebel and Swenson [18, pp. 38–39] noted that there is:

> Need for clarification of the criteria to be used in the detention of patients under the three LPS standards.... Consistently applied interpretations have been lacking. Facility staff members frequently seem to want information or suggestions about the detention or commitment criteria. Ambiguity of interpretation allows an unnecessary and unintended abuse of liberties. The preparation of regulations or guidelines describing involuntary detention criteria might, with suitable inservice training, reduce considerably the present diversity in the application of LPS standards.

Uncertainty among clinicians about how the involuntary commitment law should be interpreted and corresponding inconsistency in its application do not refute the assumption of a body of relevant clinical opinion, nor do they tell us in what particulars and to what extent its application is inconsistent. Moreover, most previous studies of determinants of admission decisions are seriously flawed. The conclusions of these studies are valid only to the extent that all significant variables that influence the admission decision were included in the analysis. Studies of the environmental determinants of admission decisions [5, 11, 16] have not considered the influence of legal commitment criteria as they are clinically construed. Indeed, only one study [8] included as an independent variable a clinical assessment of the state of the patient with regard to a legal criterion for commitment.

In short, it is too soon to conclude that mental health professionals need administrative guidelines in order to achieve substantial agreement and consistency in applying involuntary admission criteria. Further effort is warranted to establish (a) the extent to which there is already agreement among clinicians as to the meaning of the criteria, and (b) the extent to which there is consistency in their application. Note that the question being addressed here is not the predictive validity of emergency psychiatric assessments, but rather the prior question whether clinicians respond to similar cases with similar judgments. In this chapter we report the preliminary results of the development of a tool to reflect the application of legal commitment criteria in psychiatric emergency rooms.

Method

In an attempt to reflect the way clinicians in psychiatric emergency rooms interpret and apply the legal criteria of dangerousness and grave disability, we developed a prototype index entitled "Three Ratings of Involuntary Admissibility" (TRIAD). The instrument was developed through an iterative process which included literature review, observation of actual cases, and debriefing of clinicians. This iterative process resulted in the identification and ranking of patterns of behavior and circumstance more and less likely to lead to a determination that a patient is involuntarily admissible by LPS standards.

We theorized that through professional training and experience clinicians are sensitized to clusters or patterns of behavior and circumstance that are associated with danger of self, danger to others, and grave disability, and that they internalize scales by which they weigh or rank these patterns. (Several patterns are of equivalent rank.) Thus clinicians will react to some patterns as unambiguously dangerous or not dangerous, and they will consistently respond to these patterns with decisions that a person is admissible or not admissible under commitment criteria. Admission decisions will therefore be highly consistent in cases involving these unambiguous patterns. Other patterns will be experienced as more ambiguous, and this ambiguity will lead to a greater variation in the outcome of the decision-making process.

Expecting that many patients would present complaints or behavior related to more than one of the legal criteria, we further hypothesized that an ambiguous presentation on any one criterion would be more likely to lead to a decision that the person was admissible if it was accompanied by at least a low-level presentation on another criterion. For example, a person who presented some moderate threat to the safety of others would be more likely to be judged admissible if he also seemed to present a moderate or mild potential for harming himself. Thus we expected that in these cases a total score across all three criteria on TRIAD would also predict the clinician's judgment.

Observations

After creating the first draft of TRIAD, we observed evaluation interviews in the Psychiatric Emergency Service (PES) of San Francisco General Hospital and Highland General Hospital, Oakland. These are the major emergency evaluation units for the two largest San Francisco Bay Area counties. Eighty-nine patients were chosen on the basis of their availability at a time when an observer was free to follow a new case. Observers followed a patient and the assigned clinician as long as the patient remained in the PES, usually for a period of several hours. TRIAD was scored when a disposition decision had been reached. The clinician handling the case was not involved in the scoring process.

Description of TRIAD

The result was an easily scored instrument consisting of three scales. The three scales, organized as checklists, consist of a total of 84 numbered items which can be combined to yield 146 patterns of behavior and circumstance relevant to the clinical prediction of violence and suicide and the assessment of grave disability. On each of the scales, a number of patterns are assigned to the highest score, a number are assigned to the next highest score, and so on.

No pattern combines more than nine items, and most involve two, three, or four items. For example, "threatened to harm another" is one item which, by itself, scores at a low level (=1) on the danger to others scale. However, such a threat may yield the highest score (=4) if it occurs in combination with three other particular items. The first additional item has to do with provocation or lack thereof. The others involve indications of having a concrete plan and/or weapon, and/or being in a volatile or unpredictable or enraged state, and/or having a history of assault. According to our hypothesis, if such a presenting picture is accompanied by a mental disorder, the evaluating clinician will determine than the patient is clearly admissible by LPS standards. In order to prevent hospitalization, he may attempt to bring about some change in the picture through crisis intervention or medication in the emergency room, but if these efforts fail, admission will follow. If the efforts succeed, the danger to others score will be lower than it would have been otherwise. Other patterns seem equally clear, but some are more ambiguous and yield intermediate scores.

TRIAD is scored at the time of disposition by simply checking off items applicable at that time and finding the standard pattern that includes the numbers of the checked items and yields the highest score.

Results

Inter Rater Reliability

Three pairs of observers rated ten cases each and achieved interrater reliability coefficients (Pearson's r) of 0.94, danger to self score; 0.89, danger to others score; 0.77, grave disability score; and 0.89, total admissibility score. The results demonstrate that it is possible to use this instrument reliably to rate psychiatric emergency cases.

Patient Characteristics

Table 1 summarizes some of the demographic and diagnostic characteristics of the sample of 89 patients observed in both hospital emergency rooms. On the basis of data for most of the sample we are able to describe what we believe to be the "typical" patient. This typical patient was a white male, aged 26–44, born in the United States, and fluent in English. The patient had never been married, had had 10–12 years of education, and was out of the job market as a result of disability, for which he was receiving Supplemental Security Income. He was more likely to receive a diagnosis of psychosis than a non psychotic diagnosis.

Table 1. Patient characteristics (%, adjusted for missing data) ($n = 89$)

Sex	
Male	69.3
Female	30.7
Age (years)	
14–25	12
26–44	65
45–87	23
Ethnicity	
White	61.7
Black	24.7
Spanish surname	8.6
Other	4.9
Birthplace	
United States	86.5
Other	13.5
Marital status	
Single	46.6
Married	25.9
Divorced/separated	25.8
Widowed	1.7
Education	
< 10 years	16.7
10–12 years	62.5
13–17 years	21
Employment	
Full- or part-time	5.6
Unemployed	8.5
NA/disabled	70.4
Other	15.4
Source of income	
None	10.5
Family/friends	12.3
Employment	10.5
Disability	54.4
Other	12.4
Living arrangements	
No address	30
Alone	23
With others	32
Sheltered care	8
Other	7
No. of previous PES visits	
None	52.9
1–5	24.2
> 6 or unclear	22.9
No. of previous hospitalizations	
None	14.3
Multiple (no. unknown)	49.2
1–5	25.4
7–13	11.2

Table 1. (continued)

Previous diagnoses	
Major affective disorder ± schiz.	44.2
Schiz. ± substance abuse	27.9
Substance abuse only	11.6
Organic psychosis	4.7
Acute or atypical psychosis	4.7
Adjustment, reactive or anxiety disorder	7
Current diagnosis (Axis I)	
Psychotic	
Schiz. or schiz. affective disorder	33
Major affective disorder	19
Organic psychotic disorder	6
Other psychotic disorder	8
Nonpsychotic	
Adjustment or anxiety disorder	13
Acute organic/substance abuse disorder	6
Other	8
No MDO or deferred	7

Fifty-five percent of the cases were evaluated by psychiatrists, 18% by nurses, 18% by social workers, and 7.5% by other professionals, paraprofessionals, or unlicensed professionals in training. Clinical experience of evaluators ranged from 2 to 23 years, and the emergency psychiatric experience of the clinicians ranged from less than 6 months to 13 years. Of the patients observed, 93% were examined by clinicians with 2 years of PES experience or more.

The number of patients evaluated in the emergency service on the day of our observations ranged from 14 to 32, and in most cases was 20–26. If admitted to a ward following the emergency evaluation, the patient was most likely to remain for 7–9 days (30%) or for 15–17 days (25%). Average occupancy rates for the inpatient wards at the two hospitals during the study period were 94% and 91%.

Severity of Presenting Problem

Our observations led us to believe that when a patient comes into the emergency room the clinician focuses his assessment on the area suggested by the patient's major presenting behavioral problem. For example, a suicide threat will lead to an assessment of danger to self rather than grave disability or danger to others. These areas will be explored secondarily, as a result of information that comes to light in the assessment of danger to self. If the patient does not present a strong picture of admissibility on any one criterion, the overall picture becomes most relevant to the disposition. In our analysis, therefore, we attended not only to the patient's presentation on individual criteria but also to the overall presentation. Table 2 shows how scores are combined at different severity levels given a range of 0–4 on the danger to self (DSS) and danger to others (DOS) scales and a range of 0–3 on the grave disability (GDS) scale. The distribution of the 89 patients we observed across severity levels was: 69.7% at the highest severity level, 4; 2.2% at level 3; 10.1% at level 2; and 18.0% at level 1, the lowest level.

Disposition

Disposition was consistent with TRIAD severity scores in 82% of the cases (gamma = 0.82; see Table 2), and agreement was roughly equivalent for both hospitals. After the initial evaluation 58 patients were retained.

Table 2. Disposition of case by severity level ($n = 89$)

Severity level	Released	Retained voluntarily	Retained involuntarily	Totals
1 (DSS, DOS, GDS = 0 or 1; total = 3 or less)	13 (81%)	0	3 (19%)	16 (100%)
2 (DSS, DOS, GDS = 2; total = 2)	7 (78%)	0	2 (22%)	9 (100%)
3 (DSS, DOS, GDS = 2); total = 3)	1 (50%)	0	1 (50%)	2 (100%)
4 (DSS, DOS, GDS = 3 or 4 or total = 4 or more)	10 (16%)	4 (7%)	48 (77%)	62 (100%)

As expected, the most and least severe presentations were most predictive of disposition (84% and 81% predictions respectively). The high scorers who were retained and the low scorers who were released are the true positives and true negatives. False positives and false negatives are identified by heavily lined boxes in Table 2. False negatives are patients who scored low on TRIAD but were retained by the clinician; false positives are the high scorers who were released by the clinician.

Severity levels 2 and 3 represent the hypothesized ambiguous range on TRIAD. However, severity level 2 also turned out to be quite discriminating, with 78% of patients being released. At severity level 2, the picture presented by the patients was ambiguous, but at this level of severity clinicians were inclined to let the patient go. The least predictive score configuration represents the situation in which the patient presents only a moderate degree of concern on any one criterion but raises one other issue at a low level (severity = 3). With only two cases at this level, the figure of 50% released and 50% admitted is far from conclusive. However, the difference between severity levels 2 and 3 does suggest that the index is capable of representing salient dimensions of the decision-making process at a fine level. Future observations will be necessary to test our hypothesis that severity level 3 represents more ambiguous situations that provide wider latitude for clinical discretion.

Most (69.7%) of the 89 patients scored at the highest level of severity. Table 3 describes the disposition of patients at severity level 4 according to whether their high score resulted from danger to self (8%), danger to others (35%), grave disability (38%), or a combination (2%). Thirteen percent ($n = 12$) scored at the highest level on two scales.

Table 3. Disposition of cases at severity level 4[a] by scale/Total score

Score qualifying case for severity level 4	Released	Retained voluntarily	Retained involuntarily	Totals
Danger to self = 3 or 4	5 (71%)	0	2 (29%)	7 (100%)
Danger to others = 3 or 4	4 (13%)	2 (6%)	25 (81%)	31 (100%)
Grave disability = 3	1 (3%)	2 (6%)	31 (91%)	34 (100%)
Total score = 4 or more but no scale score = 3 or	0	0	2 (100%)	2 (100%)

[a] $n = 62$ (12 cases scored at highest level on two scales)

Of the patients whose scores on danger to others and grave disability but them into the highest severity level, 87% and 97% respectively were retained. Of those who attained the highest severity level by reason of a high danger to self score, 71.4% were released, contrary to our expectation, and 28.6 were retained.

Diagnosis

Disposition may legitimately be influenced by legal and clinical considerations in addition to dangerousness and grave disability. The presence or absence of a mental disorder and the severity of the disorder are major criteria. To the extent that the presence or absence of psychosis captures these concerns, we are able to report their influence on disposition.

To facilitate analysis, DSM-III [1] Axis- I diagnoses were categorized as psychotic and nonpsychotic. While the presence of psychosis was moderately related to severity of presentation on TRIAD (gamma = 0.53), it was strongly related to disposition (gamma = 0.79), although not as strongly as TRIAD severity (gamma = 0.82). Thus it appears that severity of dangerousness and disability, on the one hand, and presence or absence of psychosis, on the other, make partially independent contributions to the explanation of disposition. Not surprisingly, the relationship between disposition and TRIAD severity was stronger for nonpsychotic patients (gamma = 0.89) than for psychotic patients (gamma = 0.74). Presence or absence of psychosis is helpful in explaining dispositions that differ from those predicted by the TRIAD score.

Discrepant Cases

It appears that the best explanation for the discrepancy between TRIAD scores and disposition in the false positive cases is the clinician's judgment in each case that admission was not clinically indicated – i.e., slight degree of mental disorder (insofar as it is reflected by diagnosis), the availability of treatment alternatives, and the judgment that patients would not benefit from hospital care appear to have been the critical factors. At least two cases appear, however, to have been influenced by obviously non clinical considerations – one case a false positive and the other a false negative.

Comment

The results of this study strongly suggest that psychiatric emergency room clinicians employ shared constructs of danger to self, danger to others, and grave disability; that these constructs are reliably applied in actual cases; and that most involuntary admissions are predictable from the severity of the patient's status with respect to these criteria. Further, it seems that these shared constructs can be operationalized to provide a behavioral description of how a patient comes to be seen as admissible under one or more involuntary admission standards.

The study provides a test of TRIAD as an instrument which describes the process and content of clinicians' judgments as to whether a patient meets legal standards for involuntary admission. In this instance, the concurrent measure was disposition. By this criterion, the construct validity of the DOS and GDS was supported. Also supported was the validity of the total TRIAD score as a measure of the construct "involuntary admissibility." However, the validity of the DSS has yet to be established.

While disposition proved a useful concurrent measure of the construct validity of TRIAD, it is obviously limited by the fact that variables beyond the clinician's assessment of dangerousness and disability appropriately influence these decisions. We are currently proceeding with other ways to test the validity of TRIAD as a measure of clinicians's constructs of danger to self and others and grave disability.

If these procedures establish that TRIAD reflects the way clinicians interpret and apply legal criteria in most instances, and if, in addition, TRIAD predicts disposition, the discussion of emergency involuntary commitment criteria and procedures should be greatly facilitated. TRIAD could then provide a very useful description of the state of patients being held involuntarily, as well as assurance that legal criteria are applied consistently and equitably.

References

1. American Psychiatric Association (1980) Diagnostic and statistical manual of mental disorders, 3rd ed. APA Washington DC
2. Baxter S, Chordorkoff B, Underhill R (1968) Psychiatric emergencies: dispositional determinants and the validity of the decision to admit. American Journal of Psychiatry 124: 1542–1546
3. Doe v. Gallinot (1979) 486 F. Supplement 983
4. Ennis BJ, Litwack TR (1974) Psychiatry and the presumption of expertise: flipping coins in the courtroom. California Law Review 62: 693–752
5. Feigelson EB, et al. (1978) The decision to hospitalize. American Journal of Psychiatry 135 (3): 354–357
6. Friedman PR, Yohalem JB (1978) The rights of the chronic mental patient. In: Talbott JA (ed) The chronic mental patient. American Psychiatric Association, Washington DC

7. Hanson GD, Babigian HM (1974) Reasons for hospitalization from a psychiatric emergency service. Psychiatric Quarterly 3: 336–351
8. Kirstein L, Prusoff B, Weissman M, Dressler DM (1975) Utilization review of treatment for suicide attempts, American Journal of Psychiatry 132 (1): 22–27
9. Lessard v. Schmidt (1964) 349 F. Supplement 1078 (E.D. Wisc. 1972); vacated and remanded, 94 S. Ct. 713
10. Lipsitt PD (1981) Emergency admission of civil involuntary patients to mental hospitals following statutory modification. In: McGarry A, et al. (eds) Civil commitment and social policy: on evaluation of the Massachusetts Mental Health Reform Act of 1970. Center for Studies of Crime and Delinquency Rockville
11. Mendel WM, Rapport S (1969) Determinants of the decision for psychiatric hospitalization. Archives of General Psychiatry 20: 321–328
12. Monahan J (1978) Prediction research and the emergency commitment of dangerous mentally ill persons: a reconsideration, American Journal of Psychiatry 135 (2): 198–201
13. Monahan J (1981) Predicting violent behavior: an assessment of clinical techniques. Sage, Beverly Hills
14. Morse SJ (1982) A preference for liberty: the case against involuntary commitment of the mentally disordered. California Law Review 70 (54): 54–106
15. O'Connor v. Donaldson 422 U.S. 563, 95 S. Ct. 2486, 1975
16. Scheff TJ (1964) The societal reaction to deviance: ascriptive elements in the psychiatric screening of mental patients in a midwestern state. Social Problems 11 (4): 401–413
17. Schwitzgebel RK (1981) Survey of civil commitment statutes. In: McGarry A et al. Civil commitment and social policy: on evaluation of the Massachusetts Mental Health Reform Act of 1970. Center for Studies of Crime and Delinquency Rockville
18. Schwitzgebel RK, Swenson EW (1981) Evaluation of involuntary care and treatment under the Lanterman-Petris-Short Act. California State Department of Mental Health, Sacramento
19. Tischler B (1966) Decision-making processes in the emergency room. Archives of General Psychiatry 14: 69–78

The Rights of a Psychiatric Patient in a Mental Hospital

R. R. Mayer

This paper will examine the personal and civil rights of a patient following his being interned, possibly even against his will, in a closed psychiatric hospital.

Pinel initiated the transformation of the keeping units of "mad" people into mental hospitals [15]. He and his followers, Esquirol [5], and the psychiatrists of the romantic period [15] discovered that the mental patient is a person; an individual, who has changed his living style, because he could not master his personal problems, in a way which is acceptable to society.

Today we understand more and more that John Stuart Mills' [10] concept of the freedom of man applies also to mental patients, even if they have to be closed temporarily in a hospital ward. Enclosure may be necessary for the patient's own safety or that of his surroundings: but we do not cease to see him as a human being. We may quiet him down by chemical means, but the essential treatment cannot succeed as long as we do not help him to face his real problems. We must understand him in order to give him back his feeling of human dignity.

Part of this process is the consideration of his human and legal rights. The struggle for these rights began in the U.S.A. in the form of a series of legal claims against treating doctors [6].

In Israel, the forced seclusion of a mentally ill person is the obligation of the regional psychiatrist [6], when he is convinced that the patient is dangerous to himself or others.

The rights of these patients can be seen in two directions:

1. The psychiatrist has to make sure, by all available means, that the presumption of dangerousness is convincing [12]. The justifications should be specified in the interment order. There also should be a second psychiatric examination when the patient is admitted into the hospital.
2. The patient has to be informed about his means of appeal [7].

There should be a thorough discussion of what we consider as "dangerousness." In my opinion, this is mainly a medical-psychiatric question and not only a problem of forensic definition. It should be made clear whether only acute physical violence, as opposed to also neglecting children or squandering money, should be included in the definition of the word "endanger".

It is important that the regional psychiatrist have enough competent personnel in order to perform all the necessary examinations in a thorough way. The patient has, above all, the right to get competent treatment, and considerate and respectful care.

I think that the right for treatment begins even before the reception of the patient into the hospital. This point seems to be neglected in many of the libertine approaches, which stand on every legalistic and formal point, while giving no consideration whatsoever to the idea that many patients are not aware of being ill. Patients often oppose psychiatric treatment against their best interests. But they too have the right to get this treatment in due time, and even when they are not dangerous, society has to find a way to bring them to treatment. I see this as one of the mental patient's rights. The decision in each case is, of course, a medical one, and it should be in the power of the regional psychiatrist. The appointment of a guardian should not be necessary for most cases.

The patient has the right to get enough information about his illness and the treatment that he will undergo, so that he may give informed consent. There are of course patients who may not have sufficient understanding as a result of their mental illness, and they must be helped by a guardian. But even when these patients are unable to make a decision, they should get the information due to them [4, 13, 12]. The giving of information itself is, in my opinion, part of the treatment, and an excellent opportunity for creating a relationship, and showing understanding and devotion to the patient. It may even be part of the diagnostic process.

The giving of information to a mental patient may be even more difficult than with a somatic patient. Information may cause anxiety or other unwanted reactions. The psychiatrist needs a great deal of intuition and sensitivity in order to find the right statements and, to use it as part of the therapeutic process.

There are many cases where the rights of a patient may conflict. We saw that refusal of treatment [2, 3] or even giving information may endanger the treatment process. The doctor has to weight one right against another very thoroughly for the benefit of the patient.

One word about the doctor's attitude: We often feel very superior to the patient. Many of us have this "paternal attitude". I believe that we have the duty to hear and understand and even to reach, to as great an extent as possible, a consensus with the patient. This is one way to allow him his dignity. This is connected with extending him another right - the right to privacy. But too much privacy once again may conflict with the treatment process. Once again the psychiatrist has to judge the optimal path for treatment.

As long as the patient has not been declared incompetent, he has the right to receive and to spend money. Upon the admission of the patient into the hospital, the admittine doctor fills in a declaration whether or not the patient is fit to manage his affairs. If unable, the public guardian looks after his monetary affairs; but he is not the guardian of the patient's body. The patient should have his right to settle his monetary affairs restored whenever the is able. Unfortunately, the changing of the initial declaration of his inability to manage his own monetary affairs is usually forgotten. Generally, we have attempted to use this rule in order to protect the patients and their families' interests. But if the doctor or social worker do not follow up this situation, the right of the patient may become a nuisance. Rules may lose their true purpose if they are not observed in a spirit of real understanding and watchful helpfulness [6].

A patient has, even during hospital treatment, the right to marry or divorce. This, as long as he is able to understand the full meaning of the act; and even when he may be in a short remission of his illness.

A question arises concerning the patient's rights over his own body? He can refuse treatment, for instance, of a pending operation. But does a patient, who is already in a state of good remission, but still under hospital treatment, have the right to engage of his own free will in intimate relations?

Case: A male nurse was present, when a maniformic, schizophrenic female patient was admitted into a government psychiatric hospital. She suffered for years from her illness. After the first "wave" she married, after the second one she divorced. She came to this country alone. After a short time she had a new, maniformic attack with overactivity, vagabondage, and some hallucinations. She was hospitalized with the help of the police. Under treatment, the patient quieted down very quickly, and some weeks later, she was in good remission. The head nurse of the hospital even invited her to visit her in the evening in her flat, outside the hospital.

During this period the male nurse, who knew her from the time of her reception into the hospital, became friendly with her. She finally agreed to have initimate relations with him. It is of course highly unethical and forbidden for a male nurse to have intercourse with a female patient. But there arises another question: Has the women the right to give her consent to a proposition such as this? (for the male nurse the difference in law may be between statuatory rape or an error in judgment!).

Here we once more have to balance between two rights of the patient: The right to be protected against exploitation and the right over her own body. The question may be rather hypothetical, but it shows once more the complexity of our problem.

All this strengthens my opinion that the answer should not consist mainly of legal hairsplitting. The rights of the patient should be understood more or less as his rights as a human being under hospital conditions. His freedom is a considerably larger question, over and above this right or that one. Freedom cannot be contained by laws only, but by a growing process. Freedom means taking up responsibility. We must use the rights of the patient during the treatment process in order to make him able to take up his responsibility. One of our tools is that the treating personnel employ every means to bring the patient to use his freedom in order to return to society and to an acceptable life style. The use of the patient's rights seen in this light, seems to be a very important therapeutic tool. We have to create a therapeutic atmosphere in the hospital by utilizing the rights of the patient in the right direction.

There must be legal norms. But they have to grow out of this therapeutic spirit. Psychiatry is, even in this mechanistic world, an art. Using the rights of the patient in the way shown here is part of an artistic activity.

Together with my idealistic interpretation of the weighing up of the patient's rights and the proposal to see in the patient's rights a therapeutic tool, I propose that every psychiatric hospital and mental health unit develop legal services. There should be the possibility of legal advice for the patient and his family. These services should be regarded in a spirit similar to the psychological and social services, which have already been developed. Also the legal service should be adjusted to the general therapeutic atmosphere of the hospital.

Conclusions

In a world which proclaims more and more the freedom of man (John Stuart Mill) we have tried to investigate which human rights a psychiatric patient preserves after being interned in a closed hospital and how we should use these in the course of the treatment process.

The first right is that the hospitalization order will be given only after the regional psychiatrist, on the grounds of examination of the medical and social circumstances as thoroughly as possible, is convinced that there is no alternative to interment in a hospital. The reasons for internment are dangerousness, but also may include the fulfilment of the patient's right for treatment. The patient has to be informed about his right to appeal. In the hospital, he has the right to get considerate and competent treatment, which includes the right to be informed about the treatment that he gets. He has the right for privacy.

The different rights in many cases conflict may with each other. One of the doctor's duties is to weigh up one right against another and to decide what is best for the patient.

It is pointed out that these decisions, which are medical in principle, would become an important tool in the treatment process. When used in the frame work of a therapeutic hospital atmosphere. This leads to the opinion that we should not ensure the freedom of the patient in a formal way by hairsplitting concerning this right or the other one. Freedom of the patient cannot be ensured by legal formality only. It must be stimulated by a dynamic treatment process, which will make the patient able to take up his responsibility in a society and to find a living style which enables him to return to society. In the frame work of a therapeutic atmosphere, we use these rights in order to give him the opportunity of exercising his rights in a responsible way.

Legal norms must be observed, but they must grow out of the therapeutic spirit mentioned above. Psychiatric hospitals and mental health units should develop legal counseling services in a similar fashion, as they have developed psychological and social services.

References

1. Alexander FG, Selesnik ET (1969) The history of Psychiatry
2. Appelbaum PS, Gutheil TG (1980) Drug refusal: a study of psychiatric inpatients. Am J Psych 37: 340–348
3. Appelbaum PS, Gutheil TG (1980) The Boston State Hospital case. Am J Psych 137: 720–728
4. Dix GE (1981) Realism and drug refusal. Am Acad Psychiatr Law 9/3: 180–198
5. Esquirol JE (1838) Les maladies mentales, considerées sous les rapports médicales hygieniques et médico-legales, Paris
6. Gutheil TG (1980) In search of true freedom. Drug refusal and rotting with with your rights on. Am J Psych 137: 327–328
7. Herr S, Wallace RE, Arens S (1982) Legal rights and mental health care. Lexington, Lexington
8. Israel Ministry of Health, Dept. of Mental Health (1981) Form 154 B. The rights of a mental patient in a mental hospital
9. Israel Law for the Treatment of the mentally Ill (1956) Paragraph 5, 6, 7
10. Mill JS (1980) On liberty, Oxford, Clarendon

11. Mill JS (1977) In Reiser ST (ed) Liberty in ethics in medicine. Historical perspectives and contemporatory concerns. M.I.T. Press, Cambridge
12. Rappeport JR (1967) The clinical evaluation of the dangerousness of the mentally ill. Thomas, Springfield
13. Roger vs Okin (1975) The Boston State Hospital case. Civil action, 75 - 1610 CD - Mass.
16. Zihlborg G (1941) A history of medical psychology. Norton, New York, pp 424–425

Involuntary Psychiatric Hospitalization and Civil Liberties – The Case of Israel

U. Aviram and D. Shnit

Unlike other countries, where there has been a surge of legislative reforms in the mental commitment laws during the last two decades, there has been no substantial modification to the Israeli mental health law, which was enacted in 1955. The fact that the law has remained unchanged does not mean that there is satisfaction with the legal situation and the administrative arrangements with respect to involuntary hospitalization of the mentally ill. Every so often the matter comes up in the news media, and at such times the law's shortcomings are openly decried [1]. Not long ago, the Supreme Court voiced its own criticism of the law. In his verdict, the Chief Justice wrote that:

> "The provision of the law is vague as well as being superficial . . . and also [that] the law should be thoroughly amended and clarified" [2].

The purpose of this chapter is to show how the Israeli model of involuntary hospitalization, which is based completely on the medical model, creates a situation by which the civil liberties of hospitalized people may be violated (reported in more detail in [3]).

Models of Involuntary Hospitalization

Although society has made great strides in handling issues involving the treatment of the mentally ill, there nevertheless remains, many problems of a moral, legal, and medical nature which are unsolved. Among the reasons for the difficulties encountered are the fact that there are a number of different conceptual approaches to, and definitions of, mental illness and mental health [4], inadequate and incomprehensive knowledge, and low levels of diagnostic and prognostic reliability [5].

Aside from these problems, society is confronted with the basic dilemma: How it is possible to strive toward goals which are at variance or even, at times, opposed to each other – to protect society from those who pose a threat to its safety; to ensure necessary treatment for those who may be incapable of recognizing the need for it; to ensure that treatment will in fact be provided for those for whom it has been ordered; and to protect the basic liberties of these involuntarily hospitalized individuals.

The source of the dilemma lies in the set of values and ideologies which guide policies regarding the mentally disordered. One (the paternalistic) ideology stresses the duty of society to care for its weak and needy and to provide treatment and services for the individual's own good [6]. The second ideology is based on the idea that society must be protected from individuals whose disordered behavior poses a danger to society. The third approach stresses the freedom of the individual to conduct his life free from outside interference, as long as his conduct is not harmful to others [7]. The different approaches have been reflected in legislation and judiciary decision. Among the variety of legislation and policies one can distinguish between two opposing models: the medical-psychiatric model and the libertarian-legalistic one. The former maintains that mental disorders are within the domain of medicine and that treatment and care of the mentally ill must be put in the hands of medical experts. It is they who, on the basis of their professional judgment, should decide when an individual is in need of treatment and when he should be committed against his will to a mental hospital. Those who believe in this approach feel that the doctor possesses the knowledge to determine a person's need for hospitalization and that his ethical commitment guards the individual from any abuse of his rights or unnecessary hospitalization. They feel that interference from legal or any outside nonmedical body may be injurious to treatment and that irreparable damage to the individual's health may occur [8]. Contrary to the medical model, the libertarian-legalistic approach puts civil liberties at the forefront and opposes paternalistic reasons for forcing treatment and hospitalization on individuals [9]. Those who adhere to this approach stress that in order to guard the liberty and autonomy of the individual, clear statutory standards and strict procedural safeguards must be established in relation to involuntary hospitalization, and that decisions about these must rest with social institutions such as the legislature and the courts [10].

Israeli legislators have clearly preferred the medical approach and have given the medical system the autonomy to decide when commitment of the mentally ill is called for. To this end the Treatment of the Mentally Ill Law (1955) [11] made the District Psychiatrist the medical authority in these matters, and his authority is based on purely medical considerations. This was recently reaffirmed by remarks of the Israeli Supreme Court [12].

The Israeli legislators were apparently aware of the need for safeguards to protect the liberty of people hospitalized against their will. The law has some checks and balances, however, relying mainly on the medical system. Although in all cases but emergencies there must be a physician's certificate recommending hospitalization, the District Psychiatrist is the one required by the law to be convinced of the need of hospitalization, and he must issue a commitment order. However, once the person is brought to the hospital it is within the discretion of the director of the hospital whether to continue with hospitalization or release him. On the basis of his professional judgment he may release him immediately. Perhaps those who prepared the law thought that this triangle of the physician. District Psychiatrist, and director of the hospital would create checks and balances within the system, to assure treatment and prevent abuse of liberty.

Aside from the Psychiatric Committee, which serves as the first appeal level regarding commitment and includes one nonmedical person, there are three social elements external to the medical system which were given by the law some responsibility regarding the civil involuntary hospitalization in Israel:

- The Public Guardian,
- The Attorney General,
- The Administration of the Ministry of Health.

The District Psychiatrist is required by the law to inform the Public Guardian if he is convinced that a patient is not able to handle his own affairs. The District Psychiatrist must send a copy of the hospitalization order to the Attorney General. The law allows the Minister of Health to issue regulations requiring directors of hospitals to provide him with reports on the patients hospitalized and the arrangements made in hospitals for treating patients.

Study

A sample of more than 1300 hospitalization cases, representative of the total number of hospitalizations effected in 1 year, was taken. In addition, interviews were conducted with those individuals who were active participants in the civil commitment process. The study includes an analysis of the law and the regulations for treatment of the mentally ill, as well as observations on commitment procedures [13]. The study was completed in the late 1970s. As there have been no changes in the law or regulations since that time and no new findings have been assembled, we are confident that the data remain valid and are more or less representative of the situation at the present time.

The central question posed by the study were:

1. How did those responsible for commitment view this power and how did they perceive the reasons for commitment as defined by law?
2. To what extent does the position of the patient, his family, or others in the community affect the decision to commit?
3. Who participates in the procedures leading up to commitment of the mentally ill, and to what extent do they affect the decision to commit?
4. What are the hospitalization procedures used by the hospitalizing institutions and others involved?
5. What measures have been taken by the system to ensure proper control and supervision and how is this carried out?

Findings

The study [14] has revealed ambiguities in the law itself, and that the law has been interpreted in different ways by the various people in the field, which has led to non-uniformity in the commitment process. It was found that in most commitment cases the provisions of the law are not adhered to. It was learned that the existing arrangement in Israel – according to which the medical authorities have the right to decide on commitment on the basis of their professional judgment – is far from satisfactory. And finally, it was quite apparent that there is no reliable reporting system and efficient form of control and supervision.

Issuance of Commitment Orders

On the basis of the sample used in the study, the estimated number of involuntary hospitalizations per year nationwide is 3000, i. e., 25% of all psychiatric hospitalizations in the country. According to estimates, 1000 commitment orders are issued annually. Of this number, approximately 400 (38%) should not have been issued because they were issued on individuals who did not refuse hospitalization. On the other hand, however, no commitment orders were issued for almost 2400 civil involuntary mental hospitalizations, i. e., 79% of all cases. It seems that the commitment order was used in the main as a writ of delivery in cases where documents had to be furnished in order to transfer unwilling patients to the hospital. Patients are brought to the hospitals under a variety of circumstances, and when they refuse to be hospitalized, contrary to the law, no commitment order is issued. It would appear that in many instances the patient's wishes are not taken into consideration at all.

In more than three-quarters of all involuntary hospitalizations the commitment order was not issued, nor was it possible to check whether or not the patient, who might have been admitted in an emergency, was released after 5 days as required by section 7 (c) of the Treatment of the Mentally Ill Law. Most patients who were involuntarily hospitalized were not reported on to the Attorney General, who is supposed to receive a copy of all commitment orders. When the copies were sent to the Attorney General, he took no action on them.

Family Influence

We have learned that the attitude of the family has an overwhelming influence in the matter of civil commitment. Analysis of the regulations [15] has revealed that once a patient has been brought to the hospital – by any means – a commitment order is no longer required in order to have him committed, and the hospital fulfills its obligation by having a relative of the patient sign the standard hospitalization request form. This state of affairs allows a family to apply pressure for hospitalization, while at the same time the will of the patient and his position on the matter are given no real consideration. By the same token, a family's opposition to hospitalization is used at times as the basis for not hospitalizing an individual, even though this step is called for by the patient's condition in the judgment of his own physician.

The Interest of the Patient

Despite the fact that in 66% of the cases it was determined and reported that the patient was unable to handle is own affairs, a sampling done at the Public Guardian's offices revealed that in only 3.5% of all cases reported to these offices was any action taken to protect the patient's property interests. And what is more, the idea or initiative for action did not originate in the Public Guardian's office, but came rather from outside, from individuals or agencies interested or concerned with patient's property or other affairs. Even if the Public Guardian was interested and able to take action in some of the cases it might have proved to be too late. It was found that in about half (53%) of the cases, 3 weeks had passed between admission to the hospital and receipt of information about it by the Public Guardian.

Appeals

According to the law the first level of appeal against involuntary hospitalization is the Psychiatric Committee. This Committee is appointed by the Minister of Health, and is composed of three members, two of whom are physicians. Procedures of deliberation of the Psychiatric Committee were left pretty much to the discretion of the Committee. The right to appeal to the Psychiatric Committee requesting that the civil commitment order be cancelled on the grounds that it is illegal or unjust is almost never exercised. In three out of the five districts studied there were practically no appeals submitted over a period of 1 year. Also, the system by which appeals are handled – i. e., through the Psychiatric Committee – was found to be inefficient and unreliable [16].

The District Psychiatrist

The law places the District Psychiatrist in a central position in the commitment process as well as in the control and supervision of the system. However, the state does not provide staff and facilities for adequate execution of his duties. District psychiatrists are appointed to this position in addition to another position which they already hold, e. g., director of a mental hospital, director of mental health clinic. Apart from a secretary, they are not provided with additional staff.

The study revealed that the lack of experienced office personnel at the disposal of the District Psychiatrist prevented him from fulfilling his duties properly, and he was often dependent on other individuals or offices within the system. Due to the fact funds are so limited, the District Psychiatrist will often request that the patient in question be brought to his office or to the hospital for examination and evaluation, and this is often too heavy a burden for the family or whoever else may have charge of the patient. Findings pointed to the fact that if and when one individual holds the two positions of District Psychiatrist and hospital director, the number of commitment orders goes up. The rate of issuance of commitment orders by hospital directors who are also district psychiatrists is more than twice the rate of issuance by those who do not fill both positions. Rates of commitment also vary with respect to the different parts of the country. In the central area and in Jerusalem, hospitals are readily available and close at hand. Here the rate of issuance of commitment orders varies between 7.5% and 10%. In areas where the possibilities for hospitalization are more limited, however, the rate of issuance of commitment orders drops to between 1.6% and 3.5%.

Interviews of the district psychiatrists revealed that there is a great deal of unclarity and a lack of uniformity in their perception of their duties. There is a diversity of interpretations of the provisions and concepts in the law, such as "dangerousness" or what it meant by law stating that the District Psychiatrist must be convinced that a person may be dangerous to himself or others. Even if this is interpreted to mean that the District Psychiatrist must examine the patient himself rather than relying on evidence provided by others, he would not be able to do this because of lack of time and personnel.

The District Psychiatrist is required by a regulation issued by the Minister of Health to report on admissions [17]. The copy of this report which is to be returned to the hospital allows the District Psychiatrist to certify the hospitalization or use it to order a commitment. Our findings indicate that in most cases these forms are signed without further examination. Furthermore, according to the law, a copy of this form cannot replace the commitment order. This is not only because it does not include all the information which is included on the regular form of commitment order, but also because a copy of it is not sent to the Attorney General, as required by law for commitment orders. And in any case, more than 50% of them were signed beyond the 5-day limit within which a commitment order must be issued for involuntary cases who were admitted in an emergency without an order.

The Reporting System

A reliable reporting system is a necessary condition for effective supervision of the commitment procedure. Without such reporting the District Psychiatrist and others required to assure quality of service and safeguards of civil liberties cannot do their job. Findings indicate that the reporting system was not a reliable one.

This was attributed to the following factors:

1. Unclarity in the law and regulations.
2. Lack of uniformity among policy makers and practitioners in the interpretation of the reporting requirements.
3. Lack of technical reporting measures and trained personnel.
4. Lack of regulations and nonadherence to them by those required to report.

It was not clear what was meant by the concept "dangerous" or what the psychiatrist must do in order to be "convinced" that a person presents a danger to himseld and others. Also, the law required that a copy of the commitment order must be sent "immediately" to the Attorney General. This word was interpreted differently and it was actually left to the discretion of the District Psychiatrist as to how soon he should act.

Until the end of 1976, the official form used by hospitals to report to the District Psychiatrist on admissions made it possible to check whether the patient was admitted voluntarily or against his will. This allowed the District Psychiatrist to follow up cases that were admitted in an emergency against their will without a commitment order. Such patients had to be released from the hospital within 5 days of admission unless a commitment order was issued. However, as of 1977 the Mental Health Services introduced another form in which the hospital reporting admission could indicate only whether it was a voluntary admission or an admission by a hospitalization order, thus not providing the possibility of reporting the accurate legal status of those hospitalized involuntarily in an emergency without a commitment order. This type of form made it impossible for the District Psychiatrist to fulfill his duty even if he wanted to do so. Only recently, in late 1982, as a result of criticism, was this form changed again to allow more accurate reporting.

Supervision and Control

From all that has been described, it can be seen that the various systems designed for supervision and control did not do this at all. Contrary to the spirit of the law, the involuntary hospitalizations and the activities at the hospital in his district are not actually supervised by the District Psychiatrist. The faulty reporting systems and the absence of a separate, independently run office with its own staff has been found to have a deleterious effect on the power of the District Psychiatrist to fullfil the duties of supervision and control which have been entrusted to him. It was also found that the Mental Health Services central administrative office did not have an efficient system of control and supervision, or a reliable reporting network.

Discussion

The Treatment of the Mentally Ill Law in Israel is based on the medical model. The legislators, who were probably aware of the sensitivity and importance of the issues of the liberty of hospitalized patients, provided same procedural safeguards in the law. However, they relied heavily on the medical system. It was, perhaps, thought that the independent medical judgments of the community physician who first certifies the need for hospitalization, the District Psychiatrist who makes the commitment order, and the hospital director authorized to decide whether the committed person needed to continue to be hospitalized or could be released would provide built-in checks and balances within the system. The Attorney General and the Public Guardian were additional societal components which were expected to safeguard the system. Analysis of the law indicates ambiguity and a lack of clarity. A great deal of variation was found in the interpretation of the law and regulations. It was found that legal requirements attending involuntary hospitalization were not fulfilled nor was there a satisfactory system of reporting, evaluation, and supervision. It was observed that administrative arrangements set up by the state did not coincide even with the original intention of the legislation of 1955, when the law was enacted, and did not create a system of checks and balances regarding involuntary hospitalization. Current arrangements and programs impede the possibility of running a balances system which provides treatment and care while observing the civil liberties of users of the system.

The fact that the position of the District Psychiatrist was not an independent position and that it was held in addition to another appointment in the system was (though not illegal) contrary to the spirit of the law. This created a situation in which the same person has three roles: a quasi-judiciary role, an executive role, and a supervisory role. How could anyone expect the District Psychiatrist to supervise his own actions when he is also the director of a hospital? However, this double position could become functional if he used his power and staff as a hospital director to help him perform his duties as a District Psychiatrist.

The state does not provide the District Psychiatrist with professional and administrative staff to allow him to carry out his duties. He has to rely on other components of the mental health system, at times at the expense of patients and putting extra burden on families or the community. There is no doubt that if the Public Guardian's office or the Attorney General's offices wanted to perform their duties according to the spirit of the law, they would have to be provided with additional resources.

Most of the district psychiatrists and their deputies who were interviewed during the research expressed dissatisfaction with the fact that the District Psychiatrist did not have an independent position but that it was held in addition to another position in the system. They were critical of the fact that the District Psychiatrist was not provided with a well-staffed office and a budget to be able to perform his role adequately. Some even commented that this state of affairs was "absurd" or "immoral." Yet they did not resign and hardly put up a fight to change the situation, nor did the medical professional association or the psychiatrists association put pressure on the state to change the situation on ethical and practical grounds.

It seems that the approach taken by the state bureaucracy was to save money and simplify matters. The issue of a form which allowed the District Psychiatrist to return a copy of it to the hospital for approval of hospitalization (should anyone opposed it) or for commitment (should the hospitalization be against the person's will) was not in accordance with the law. It allowed what was merely the rubber-stamping of a previous decision. The District Psychiatrist signed the "approval" without hearing the objection to hospitalization and in fact without even knowing if anyone objected to hospitalization at all. Using the same signature to commit the person was not only illegal (as a copy of the commitment order was not sent to the Attorney General) but also administratively in bad taste. Even the criticism of this practice by the State Comptroller did not lead the administration of the Ministry of Health to change its instructions and regulations [18]. For some years the District Psychiatrist was not able even to find out if people admitted in an energency were admitted against their will without a commitment order. The form reporting admission did not allow this to be reported. One would have expected that the central administration of the Mental Health Services would collect information and use it to supervise the system. However, information collected was used for other purposes than evaluation and supervision of the involuntary hospitalization system's operations. The fact that the central office of the Mental Health Services did not receive a copy of the commitment order did not allow it to supervise the system even if it would at some point have decided to do so.

Conclusion

It seems to us that the state perhaps failed to assume its regulatory and supervisory role because it had accepted the claims of the medical model that its expertise and ethics assure service in the best interests of the individual and shield him from a violation of his liberties. The state provided the medical profession with a monopoly of the involuntary hospitalization system and saw no justification for the spending of resources on supervision and the provision of checks and balances.

The fact that administrative arrangements of this type have continued to exist for such a long time may indicate that it was in the interests of the state and the profession to maintain it. Unless the citizens' groups and legislators apply pressure, we doubt whether any meaningful change can take place. It may be that a continued use of a system based so completely on the medical model leaves little hope that the system can be corrected through the provision of more resources and administrative mechanisms for supervision. It may be that the only possibility is to reform the system and structure it on a different model. This model should include in the commitment process social mechanisms (such as the courts), independent of the medical system. A reform should create a balanced system designed to ensure the rights of the mentally ill, and at the same time it should preclude rigid procedural barriers liable to deter caregivers from offering vital treatment.

Acknowledgment. The authors wish to acknowledge support for the research provided by the Association for Mental Health Affiliation with Israel and by the School of Social Work, Tel-Aviv University, and the cooperation of the Israel Mental Health Services.

References

1. For example, see articles in Yediot Aharonot, 22 and 29 September 1978, and Ha'aretz, 6, 21, 22, 23 January 1980 (Hebrew).
2. *Yarmilowitz and the State of Israel* v. *Hovav,* C.A. 219/79, Piskei Din (Law Reporter of the Israeli Supreme Court, hereinafter "P.D.") 35 (3) 766 (Hebrew)
3. Aviram U, Shnit D (1981) Psychiatric treatment and civil liberties: the involuntary hospitalization of the mentally ill in Israel. Z'mora, Bitan, Modan, Tel Aviv (Hebrew)
4. On the different definitions and concepts and limited knowledge see discussion in Mechanic D (1980) Mental health and social policy, 2nd edn. Prentice Hall, Englewood Cliffs, New Jersey
5. Ennis BJ, Litwack TR (1974) Psychiatry and the presumption of expertise; flipping coins in the courtroom. California Law Review 62: 693-752; Temerlin MK (1968) Suggestion effects in psychiatric diagnosis. Journal of Nervous and Mental Disease 147 (4): 349-353; Rosensweig et al. (1961) A study of the reliability of the mental status examination. American Journal of Psychiatry 117: 1102-1108; Cocozza JL, Steadman HJ (1978) Prediction in psychiatry: an example of misplaced confidence in experts. Social Problems 25: 265-276
6. See, for example, Hart HLA (1962) Law liberty and morality. Oxford University Press, Oxford, pp 32-33
7. See, for example, the argument of Mill in Mill JS (1946) On liberty. McCallom, London
8. Hart HLA (1962) Law, liberty and morality. Oxford University Press, Oxford, pp 23, 33
9. Szasz T (1963) Law liberty and psychiatry. MacMillan, New York
10. Brooks AD (1979) The impact of law on psychiatric hospitalization: onslaught or imperative reform? In: Halleck SL (ed) Coping with the legal onslaught. New Directions for Mental Health Services 4. Jossey Bass, San Francisco, pp 13-25
11. For a thorough discussion of the Israeli Civil Commitment Law see: Bazak J (1969) Procedures of hospitalization and release of the mentally ill in Israel. Hapraklit 25: 666-681 (Hebrew); Bazak J (1979) Involuntary civil hospitalization of the mentally ill in Israel. In: Miller L, Pollak H, Berman H (eds) Social psychiatry in Israel. Jerusalem Academic Press, Jerusalem, p 81 (Hebrew); Shnit D (1981) Civil hospitalization of the mentally ill in Israel. In: Aviram U, Levav I (eds) Community mental health in Israel. Cherikover, Tel Aviv; Aviram U, Shnit D (1981) Psychiatric treatment and civil liberties: the involuntary hospitalization of the mentally ill in Israel. z'mora, Bitan, Modan, Tel Aviv (Hebrew)
12. See Judge Cohen's remarks in Supreme Court ruling 603/76, *Roth* v. *State of Israel.* P.D. 31 (2) 757, 761. Also, see Judge Cohen's remarks in Supreme Court ruling C.A. 219/79, P.D. 35 (3), p 781 (Hebrew)

13. For more details on the method see Aviram U, Shnit D (1981) Appendix A (see [3])
14. For detailed description of findings see Aviram U, Shnit D (1981) (see [3])
15. Kovetz Takanot (K.T.) 3750, 17 August 1977, p 2418, s 7b (Hebrew)
16. Aviram U, Shnit D (1981) pp 179–180, 214–223 (see [3])
17. Section 4, Regulations on the Treatment of the Mentally Ill – 1959. K.T. 908, p 1372, 1959
18. Israel; State Comptroller, Annual Report No. 25. Government Printer, Jerusalem, 1974, p 261

Civil Commitment Under Israeli Law

Y. Ginath, Y. Bar-El, and D. A. Frenkel

Historical Background

Civil commitment of mental patients is a rather delicate issue and might serve as a gauge of the value system of a society. It constitutes a compromise between the needs and rights of society and those of the sick individual, as well as a safeguard of the rights of patients.

The history of psychiatric treatment for mental patients is relatively short. In the medieval period, violent mental patients were put in prisons or exiled from society in a variety of ways (e.g., the "ship of fools"). The fifteenth century witnessed the erection of the *hospicium,* which served as a shelter for various kinds of people in need, including mental patients [5].

Mental illness was regarded at that time as a punishment, or as effected by an evil spirit. Following the French Revolution and the developments in science and medicine in the early nineteenth century, mental disorder slowly came to be looked upon as an illness. This change, among other things, led to the transferal of the treatment of mental patients into the hands of the medical profession.

The medical model helped to change considerably the image of the crazy person or lunatic to that of a sick person, a patient. It relieved the sufferer from the responsibility, the guilt, and some of the shame of his condition, and introduced a "scientific" approach to psychiatry. It provided the patient with treatment instead of seclusion, custodial care, or punishment.

However, there are some inherent differences between medical and mental patients. The latter, more often than the former, exhibit an impairment of judgment, lack insight into their illness, or behave in a way that might endanger thenselves or others. They may avoid seeking treatment when it is needed, and become violent, suicidal, negligent, troublesome, or frightening. In short, they may need treatment without their cooperation or without consent and, in extreme conditions, even against their will.

In the last generation one can observe, in most countries, an increasing trend to make the medical profession responsible for compulsory treatment, thus replacing "administrative" compulsory hospitalization (by mayors, chiefs of police, etc.) by medical commitment [15]. T. Szasz, known for his consistent criticism of the psychiatric system, defined commitment thus: "Commitment is a compulsory or involuntary detention of a person in a mental hospital. Like imprisonment in jail, commitment entails the loss of basic civil liberties. Unlike imprisonment, commitment serves a medical-therapeutic, rather than a judicial-punitive, purpose" [17]. From a standpoint of psychiatrists having legal responsibilities, but also aware of civil liberties, we want to adopt this definition.

Needless to say, in the democracies compulsory medical certification of mental patients is one of the very few cases within the framework of the legal system in which a person's liberty may be violated without actually breaking the law and, in many countries, even without going through any court procedure.

Police and Paternal Powers

The state uses psychiatry to execute both its police and paternal powers. The police power refers to the dangerousness to others of mental patients. Recently, the common belief in the dangerousness of mental patients has been seriously challanged [12]. This category has too often been extended to include "anyone . . . we would . . . prefer not to encounter on the street," as put succintly in one case (*Cross* v. *Harris*, cited in [15]).

In exercising its paternal power, with respect to mental patients, the state assumes that it has the power to take care of patients who might act in a way that constitutes a "danger to self." This right is much less widely agreed upon and has been the subject of hot debates. An early critic of this right, the philosopher J. S. Mill, stated: "The only purpose for which power can be rightfully excercised over any member of a civilized community against his will is to prevent damage to others. His own good, either physical or moral, is not a sufficient warrant" [9]. Legislation in most countries does not agree with this statement, and includes dangerousness to self among the indications for civil commitment. Psychiatrists, by undertaking the dual role of medical professionals and representatives of the state, have put themselves in a conflicting and an almost impossible position. Many would readily relieve themselves of this "social control" function. Many psychiatrists believe, however, that there is no better system at present, and that no other professional group is better equipped for this task.

Recently, the traditional medical model, to which psychiatry adhered for many years, has been challanged by behavioral scientists. The behavioral-social model views mental disorder not as an illness, but rather as a special kind of behavioral deviance [16]. This model inevitably denies the right of psychiatrists, as medical professionals, to execute compulsory measures against these deviants. Even though the law has not adopted this view, it has had a considerable effect on the thinking and approach of many psychiatrists.

Israeli Legislation

The Israeli Treatment of Mentally Sick Persons Law 5715–1955 [18] replaced the Ottoman Act of 1892 (Asylum for the Insane Act), which was in force until then. It emerged against the background of the immense immigration into the country in the early 1950s, and the shortage of facilities to take care of the increasing number of the mentally sick, many of whom were survivors of the Holocaust. Reviewing the debate in the *Knesset*, it strikes one that members of the Israeli Parliament were mostly concerned that the Act should ensure enough facilities to hospitalize all patients in need. Other issues, such as the protection of the civil rights of patients, were never mentioned by the participants [4].

Dealing with civil commitment, the Israeli legislator chose to grant this power to the medical profession rather than to the judiciary system or any administrative authority. This approach was, at that time, shared by both jurists and psychiatrists. According to this act, district psychiatrists, who are appointed by the Minister of Health, have the sole legal authority to execute commitments, as well as to supervise psychiatric institutions. It should be noted here that this concept is unique to the Israeli legal system.

The main section dealing with compulsory medical hospitalization, section 5, states: "Where a district psychiatrist is satisfied that a (mentally) sick person is likely to endanger himself or another person, he shall direct, in writing, that he be admitted to a hospital" [8]. This directive is termed a "hospitalization direction."

This laconic statement has led to a wealth of divergent interpretations, mainly in regard to three key issues:

1. "Is satisfied": it was never specified what procedures the district psychiatrist should follow in order to be "satisfied." Should he personally examine the patient in question? Should he content himself with an indirect testimony, such as a medical letter from another psychiatrist, from any physician, or from another mental health professional, or is it sufficient to rely on testimony from relatives? Should this evidence be "beyond resonable doubt" or of the nature of "clear and convincing proof"? Obviously, the 1955 law left it open for the district psychiatrist to decide what kind of evidence, by whom, and how convincing it must be in order for him to be "satisfied."

2. "Sick person": this term was defined in section 1 of the same law as "a person who suffers from a mental sickness." Mental sickness, however, was not defined in this law. Did the legislator use this term to refer to psychotic patients only, as some would believe, or might it, under specific conditions, also include neurotics, drug addicts, or others? In 1976 [8] a list of mental illnesses was compiled and included in another set of regulations dealing with information to be supplied to the authorities with regard to military service. The use of this list was not limited to use in these regulations. It was not meant to constitute a complete list, but all the conditions included in it were considered to be mental illnesses. Should this list guide the District Psychiatrist in executing commitments?

3. "Is likely to endanger himself or another person": it is extremely difficult to predict a potential danger. Furthermore, what danger did the legislator have in mind? A strict interpretation would include only an immediate physical danger. A broader interpretation might also include serious disturbances of public order or behavior that might cause adverse negative consequences to the patient or others in the future. Again, this point was left vague.

Remarkably, the Israeli law does not contain any other justification for civil commitment besides dangerousness to self or others. However, most legal systems contain a third category which refers to people who, due to mental disorder, are "gravely disabled" and "unable or unwilling to agree to the necessary treatment" [6], or uses similar phrasing [7]. Other legal systems go even further and mention loose definitions such as "mental disorders which justify urgent therapeutic intervention" as a reason for civil commitment [1]. The lack of such a category has led some district psychiatrists to stretch the term "dangerous" to include the gravely disabled, while others are more cautious, using a strict interpratation, and avoid committing these patients. Once satisfied that the necessary conditions do exist, the District Psychiatrist must order hospitalization: it is not left to his discretion.

Criticism of the Sefeguards of Civil Rights

The Israeli Treatment of Mentally Sick Persons Law: 5715 – 1955 contains three important safeguards of civil rights:

1. The power given to the director of the hospital to discharge a patient hospitalized under a hospitalization order at his discretion (section 16)
2. The right of any person to appeal against compulsory medical hospitalization before a Regional Psychiatric Board (section 11)
3. The penalties prescribed by law against "a person who knowingly causes the admission of a patient to a hospital unnecessarily or unlawfully" (section 29).

It should be noted that copies of all hospitalization orders issued by district psychiatrists are sent, by law, to the Attorney General and to the Minister of Health (in practice, to the Mental Health Services). All these safeguards have been widely criticized by a variety of critics [2, 3, 21]. Bazak [3] states: "The Treatment of the Mentally Ill Act 1955 does not provide sufficient safeguards for the protection of the patients' civil rights." Aviram and Shnit [2] very meticulously analyze these safeguards and come to the conclusion that they are far from satisfactory.

The professional committee which prepared the Act did, in fact recommend that a "District Psychiatrist's office" be established and staffed, so as to enable him to examine thoroughly any request for compulsory hospitalization. Because of financial restrictions this proposal was rejected [20]. As a result of this, as well as for other reasons, many of the positions of district psychiatrists and their deputies are held by directors or associate directors of the hospitals into which the patients are committed. Thus their decisions are not supervised by another senior professional.

> The other two safeguards mentioned were criticised by the former Supreme Court President, Judge Landau, as follows [22]: . . . Nor do I see in the right of appeal to the Psychiatric Board a sufficient barrier against these dangers. Not everybody has friends or relatives who could act for him and appeal to the Board. And as for the hospitalized person himself, there is no provision in the law by which he must be informed of his right to appeal, and in any case, with his hospitalization he enters a new world in which he no longer acts as a free and independent person, if only because of the drugs he is being treated with or because of the environment in which he finds himself. The criminal sanction against wrongful and malicious hospitalization also operates only after the event and is no substitute for legal provisions aimed at preventing grave mishaps beforehand. It is worthwhile to stress that all three safeguards share the same disadvantage of being *a posteriori* provisions.

To realize that this is the case one has only to remind oneself that, since 1955, there have been only a handful of appeals per year to the Psychiatric Board, and even fewer cases have been dealt with by the courts [2, 3].

The Supreme Court's Critisicm of Section 5

Recently, the issue of medical commitment was dealt with by the Supreme Court [22]. The judges (President M. Landau, Judges H. Cohen and M. Ben-Porat) used the opportunity to interpret and criticize the Act, as well as its execution by the district psychiatrists. Judge Ben-Porat tended to take the phrasing of the law at face value:

> Section 5 is very widely drafted. The only condition for issuing a hospitalization order is that the District Psychiatrist should be "satisfied" that the person suffers from a mental disease and is likely to endanger himself or others. Once he is satisfied – and the legislature does not determine how and why he is to satisfy himself – he is under obligation to ("shall") order hospitalization. The question what the material may be on the strength of which he may be satisfied is a complex medical question of fact. Whoever alleges that a hospitalization order was negligently made has to prove, by psychiatric expertise, that the data on the strength of which it was made did not afford a reasonable basis for the conclusion reached.

The same judge was of the opinion that the safeguards against violating patients' rights are sufficient [22]:

> I am not sure, even after having read the opinion of President Landau, that the legislature did indeed go too far in vesting such wide powers in district psychiatrists. The aim to prevent great harm to a patient or by a patient sometimes forces speedy action by a qualified person. This consideration overrides even the basic right of the freedom of the individual. So long as the patient, though in need of hospitalization, is not dangerous, he may not, of course, be deprived of his liberty against his will and may be hospitalized only with his consent. The situation is entirely differnet where he constitutes a danger: in that event the legislature chose to rely on the skill and honesty of district psychiatrists to perform their duties with due care and in a professional and ethical way . . . The two channels – one judicial, by way of appeal, and the other administrative, through the hospital director – appear to me to provide sufficient (thought not absolute) safeguards to ensure that no person should stay hospitalized, under a hospitalization order or a court order, longer than is necessary for the protection of himself or the public. There is always the possibility of a mishap, but I am not sure that can be avoided: that, too, is first and foremost a question for the psychiatrists, and it is not for me to express an opinion which system is the better one, ours or the English or the American.

The court also, concerned itself with the nature of the evidence used by district psychiatrists, and with the amount of proof needed in order for the District Psychiatrist to be satisfied. Said President Landau [22]:

> The provisions of the law on this important subject matter of the liberty of the person and his compulsory confinement in a mental asylum are vague and abstruse . . . What is the nature of the medical evidence which has to come before district psychiatrists so as to enable them to exercise their powers under section 5? Must there be one medical opinion only and no more? Can any doctor give the opinion, or must be be a psychiatrist? Must the District Psychiatrist himself examine the person before giving his directive, or may he have him examined by another psychiatrist of his choice? Under what circumstances and at what stages may district psychiatrists direct the compulsory examination or hospitalization of a person suspected of being mentally ill and endangering himself or others? What is the District Psychiatrist to do when satisfied that there is an immediate danger of grave violence, and how is he to satisfy himself that such a danger indeed exists?

These ideas were shared and extended by Judge H. Cohen, who stated [22]:

> The Israeli legislature - unlike, for instance, the American - chose to invest not the courts nor any quasijudicial or administrative organ, but district psychiatrists, with the power to make compulsory hospitalization orders. The clear legislative intent is manifested that hospitalizations should be ordered only upon psychiatric considerations and tests. The question whether the District Psychiatrist possesses such data as are sufficient to justify or necessitate a hospitalization order as regards both quantity and quality, is a medicopsychiatric question, and neither the rules of evidence observed by the courts nor the principles of justice observed by administrative agencies provide any standards for determining the validity, the weight, or the reliability of such data. It is a matter of common knowledge, for instance, that the anamneses which serve doctors as a basis for their medical considerations always contain second-hand reports and hearsay: the fact that any such tales are inadmissible (as yet) as evidence in court does not disqualify them at all from being used by doctors for their clinical purposes . . . The same considerations apply to the prior examination of the patient and his right to be heard: the question whether any such examination or hearing is or is not required is a medicopsychiatric question only. If from the medicopsychiatric point of view they are not required, and a psychiatrist may well conclude that a person is mentally ill and endangers himself or others even without first hearing and examining him, then the hospitalization order is perfectly in order, although a court or a quasi-judicial or even an administrative authority would never be allowed to do without a hearing.

Judge H. Cohen went further to suggest the following [22]:

> A detailed legislative enumeration of the data or findings which district psychiatrists are required to possess in order that they may be able to satisfy themselves that a person ought to be compulsorily hospitalized is needed, not only for the protection of the citizen, so that he may know beforehand on what conditions he can be deprived of his liberty for psychiatric treatment, but also for the protection of district psychiatrists, so that they may not be suspected of unlawful harassments and may not be exposed to actions like the present.

This thorough review of section 5: may be summed up by President Landau's concluding statement: "the law needs thoroughly to be overhauled and amended in respect of the procedure for making hospitalization orders, and the sooner the better" [22]. A similar conclusion, i.e. that the 1955 Act needs amendments in respect of involuntary civil commitment procedures, was shared by other critics [2, 3] as well as by the district psychiatrists themselves.

Possible Courses of Action in Order to Increase Protection of Civil Rights

What courses of action can be taken in order to amend the procedures of involuntary civil commitment and provide better safeguards for patient's civil liberties?

1. The addition of a legal procedure to the medical process was recommended by Bazak, who states "The Treatment of the Mentally Ill Act 1955 should be amended to state that commitment orders are to be issued by the magistrates' court on a written application by the District Psychiatrist" [3, p. 141]. This suggestion is sugmented by a few additional proposals:

- The justifications for a commitment order should be set out specifically and clearly.
- Due notice of the reasons for hospitalization should be given in writing.
- The patient should be present at the legal procedure.
- The patient should be provided with legal representation [3, pp. 139–144].

This approach, which had been supported mainly by jurists, has advantages as well as disadvantages [2, 3, 11, 14, 19]. The Israeli legislator, as well as most psychiatrists in Israel, views civil commitment as a psychiatric rather than a legal procedure. The Supreme Court decision cited above also accepted this approach and proposed amendments within its framework.

2. Changes in procedures have been proposed by a variety of authorities [2, 22; personal communications with district psychiatrists]. We would like to mention three such changes:

- The provision of both patients and their families with information regarding their legal rights. A major step was taken recently in this direction by the Mental Health Services at the Ministry of Health by introducing the "rights and obligation form" for patients hospitalized within the mental health system and for their families [10].
- Use of the state's right to appeal on behalf or patients before the Regional Psychiatric Board in each case in which a patient has been hospitalized for the first time under a hospitalization order. This came into effect as of January 1983 and compels the district psychiatrists to defend the hospitalization orders issued by them.
- Introduction of guidelines regarding the nature of the "data or findings required to be in the hands of district psychiatrists in order that they may be able to satisfy themselves that a person ought to be compulsorily hospitalized" [29].

3. The third line of action involves changes in the law regarding redefinition of key issues such as "mentally ill" and "is likely to endanger himself or another person." Most professionals agree upon the existence of mental illness, and would define the people who suffer from it as "mentally ill." It is unnecessary to list the difficulties of psychiatric diagnosis [21] and the evaluation of mental status. It must be stressed, however, that this law deals with people who are likely to endanger themselves or others because they are mentally ill. This, of course, limits the application of this law to patients whose judgment and reality testing are impaired to a considerable degree – namely, patients who suffer from various psychogenic psychoses or some organic and toxic psychotic conditions, and only rarely people with other diagnoses. The crucial element is the mental state of the person at the time of the psychiatric evaluation, rather than the formal diagnosis he has been ascribed. Most psychiatrists do believe that it is futile as well as too limiting to provide a list of diagnoses instead of a sound professional evaluation concentrating mainly on the reality testing and judgment of the person under examination.

The phrase "is likely to endanger himself or another person" poses another problem to the District Psychiatrist. It seems almost impossible to define the level of likelihood sufficient for this purpose, and how this likelihood is to be decided from the behavior or oral expressions of the person. Three levels of certainty are used in legal procedures: (a) something may be true "beyond reasonable doubt," (b) there may exist "clear and convincing proof" that it is true, or (c) it may be indicated by the "preponderance of the evidence." When dangerousness is being evaluated, the two upper levels are only seldom attainable. Even the third may not be achieved, in view of the risks at stake. Another unresolved problem is: Do the two dangers, namely to another person and to oneself, have the same weight in this regard? We feel unable to answer these questions.

A Proposal for a New Section on Civil Commitment

One area which might be easier to define is the differentiation of various degress of the anticipated danger, placing immediate and physical danger in one category, and less severe dangers (danger to property, public order, reputation, etc.) in a second. A third category of patients who might be in need of compulsory treatment are people who, though not "dangerous" in the strict sense of the term, cannot take care of themselves (e.g., patients who are confused or depressed to the extent of self-neglect or inability to function). Often this state is exacerbated by the absence of relatives or other support systems or their unwillingness to cope with the patients. Most countries have thus added a third category to "dangerousness to self" and "dangerousness to others," which is defined as "gravely disabled" or "in need of care and treatment," or by a similar phrase. In our view the inclusion of some version of this category is necessary, even though different procedures have to be adopted for people included in it.

As mentioned before, a point that constitutes a major difficulty for the district psychiatrists under the current law is the existence of only one kind of hospitalization order, which has to be applied to all patients. It is suggested here that the law will differentiate "levels of illness" and "degrees of dangerousness." A preliminary version of the following suggestions was presented before the Ministry of Health in 1981 by one of the authors (YB).

In the following version, the current section 5 will be replaced by a number of sections, each dealing with a different level of illness and degree of dangerousness. The first of these will be applied to the most sick and most dangerous patients and will read thus:

> Where a District Psychiatrist is satisfied that a person who is mentally ill to the extent of suffering severe impairment of judgment or reality testing is likely to endanger himself or others, and the nature of this likely danger is physical and immediate, and the person is unable or unwilling to agree to the necessary treatment, he shall direct such a person to be hospitalized.

The next section will deal with commitment of patients whose degree of dangerousness is less severe and will read thus:

> The District Psychiatrist may order a person to be hospitalized provided he is satisfied that all of the following conditions have been fulfilled:
>
> 1. The person is mentally ill.
> 2. a) As result of his illness he behaves in a way that might endanger himself or others, but the danger is not physical and immediate.
>   b) As a result of his illness he is gravely disabled and in need of care and treatment.
> 3. a) The person is unable or unwilling to agree to the necessary treatment.
>   b) There is no appropriate treatment available outside of a psychiatric institution.

The next section will authorize a District Psychiatrist to order a person to receive ambulatory psychiatric treatment. It will read as follows:

> The District Psychiatrist may direct a person to receive ambulatory treatment provided the following conditions have been fulfilled:
>
> 1. The person is mentally ill.
> 2. Past experience contains evidence that
>   - compliance with such treatment is related to a reasonable remission, and
>   - lack of such treatment is related to an exacerbation of the person's illness to a degree which might qualify him for a hospitalization order.
> 3. The person is unwilling to comply with the suggested treatment.
>
> This order will be put into effect in the same way as a hospitalization order.

This section has to be reserved for patients who, for example, benefit from being treated by long-acting antipsychotic medications or lithium salts. It is hoped that the use of this section will decrease the number of civil commitments and prevent hospitalizations. It also provides a "least restrictive environment" for many patients.

Another difficulty unattended in the current law stems from the unwillingness of many "candidates" for a hospitalization order (e.g., the combative paranoid) to subject themselves to a psychiatric examination. The District Psychiatrist is then compelled either to avoid hospitalizing the patient or to issue a hospitalization order without examining him, relying on indirect evidence which, too often, comes from laymen or is circumstantial. There is thus a need for a provision in the law which will authorize the District Psychiatrist to compel a person to be examined when mental illness such a decision. Such a provision might be as follows:

> The District Psychiatrist is authorized to direct a person to be brought before him to undergo a psychiatric examination if *prima facie* evidence has been brought to his attention which, if found to be correct, would justify the issuing of a hospitalization order. A District Psychiatrist should not use this power unless the person refuses to come and be examined, or the circumstances bear witness to a probable refusal.

It is worthwhile to mention that one version of such a provision was put before the *Knesset* a few years ago (1980), but did not get beyond the preliminary stages of the legislative process [13].

Another provision should state that no patient will be hospitalized in a psychiatric institution without being examined by a qualified psychiatrist.

The right of a patient to appeal before the Regional Psychiatric Board and demand his discharge from the hospital will be retained, but will apply only to the very sick and very dangerous person, whose appeal will not prevent the execution of the order. In all other cases such an appeal will prevent the order from being put into effect until after the appeal has been brought before the Psychiatric Board, and the order will then either be carried out or cancelled, depending on the Board's decision.

It should be pointed out that the current Israeli law does not differentiate between a "voluntary" and an "involuntary" status of hospitalized patients (i.e., patients who came to the hospital of their own free will and patients who were hospitalized under a hospitalization order). Once having been admitted to the hospital, both depend for their discharge on the decision of the medical director of the hospital (Section 16). Thus the "hospitalization order" is, in fact, no more than an order to bring the patient to the hospital. Once he is admitted it expires and has no more effect.

Conclusions

Almost 30 years have elapsed since the *Treatment of Mentally Sick Persons Law 5715-1955* was passed in the *Knesset*. This period has witnessed a major change in the approach toward mental illness and mental patients. Also, extensive experience has accumulated through the execution of this act. These processes justify a review and probably a change in the sections dealing with civil commitment. These changes may amend the shortcomings pointed out by the Supreme Court, as well as by civil rights proponents and district psychiatrists. We would like to conclude this paper by presenting the proposed sections 5 and 11, compared to the current sections.

1. Current Section 5
Where a District Psychiatrist is satisfied that a sick person is likely to endanger himself or another person, he shall order, in writing, that he be admitted to a hospital.

2. Current Section 11
Any person may submit to a Psychiatrict Board an objection to the admission of a sick person to a hospital other than under a court order.

3. Proposed Section 5
a) A District Psychiatrist shall direct, in writing, that a person be admitted to a hospital where he is satisfied that:

- A person who is mentally ill to the extent of suffering from a severe impairment of judgement or reality testing is likely to endanger himself or others.
- The nature of the likely danger is physical and immediate.
- The person is unable or unwilling to agree to the necessary treatment.

b) The District Psychiatrist may direct, in writing, that a person be admitted to a hospital, provided he is satisfied that all of the following conditions have been fulfilled:

- The person is mentally ill
- As a result of his illness he either behaves in a way that might endanger himself or others, but the danger is not physical and immediate, or he is gravely disabled and in need of care and treatment.
- The person is unable or unwilling to agree to the necessary treatment, or there is no appropriate treatment available outside of a psychiatric institution.

c) The District Psychiatrist may, in writing, order a person who is unwilling to comply with ambulatory treatment to be in such a way provided he is satisfied that the person is mentally ill and past experience contains evidence that compliance with such a treatment is related to a reasonable remission, and lack of such treatment is related to an exacerbation of his illness to a degree which might qualify him for a hospitalization order.

This order will be excuted in the same way as a hospitalization order.

d) The District Psychiatrist is authorized to direct a person to be brought before him to undergo a psychiatric examination if *prima facie* evidence has been brought to his attention which, if found to be correct, would justify the issuing of a hospitalization order. A District Psychiatrist should not use this power unless the person refuses to come and be examined, or unless the circumstances bear witness to a probable refusal.

4. Proposed Sections 11

Add to the current section the following paragraph" ... When the admission is in virtue of section 5, the execution of the hospitalization order will be withheld until after this objection has been brought before the Psychiatric Board and will be dependent on its desision. For the purposes of this section, "admission of a sick person" shall include ambulatory treatment as directed in virtue of section 5 (see 2.c).

References

1. Aceretament: e trattamenti sanitari voluntari e obbligatori. A legge 180, 16/5/1978
2. Aviram U, Shnit D (1981) Psychiatric treatment and civil liberties: the involuntary hospitalization of the mentally ill in Israel. Zmora-Bitan-Modan, Tel Aviv (Hebrew)
3. Bazak J (1979) Involuntary civil commitment of mental patients in Israel and the protection of civil rights. International Journal of Medicine and Law 1: 129–146
4. Divrei Ha'Knesset (1955) 21: 1576–1584 (Hebrew)
5. Foucault M (1971) Madness and civilization: a history of insanity in the age of reason. New American Library, New-York
6. Lanterman-Petris-Short Act (1969) California, Community Mental Health Services Act
7. Massachusetts Mental Health Reform Act 1970
8. Military Service Regulations (Disclosure of Information Regarding Mental Illnesses) 5738–1976 (Israel)
9. Mill JS (1961) On liberty. In: Cohen M (ed) The philosophy of J. S. Mill. The Modern Library, Newport
10. Rights and obligations form for persons hospitalized in psychiatric facilities (1983) A form issued by the Ministry of Health, State of Israel
11. Roth LH (1980) Mental health commitment: the state of the debate, 1980. Hospital and Community Psychiatry 31: 385–396
12. Shah SA (1975) Dangerousness and civil commitment of the mentally ill: some public policy considerations. Am J Psychiatry 132: 501–505
13. Stern-Katan S (1980) Private bill to amend the Treatment of Mentally Sick Persons Law, submitted to the Israeli Knesset 17 March 1980
14. Stone AA (1975) Overview: the right to treatment – comment on the law and its impact. Am J Psychiatry 132: 1125–1134
15. Stone AA (1976) Mental health and law: a system in transition. Jason Aronson, New York
16. Szasz T (1961) The myth of mental illness. Dell, New York
17. Szasz T (1963) Law, liberty and psychiatry. MacMillan, New York
18. Treatment of Mentally Sick Persons Law 5715–1955 (Israel)
19. Winnik HZ (1979) Comments on Prof. Bazak's article involuntary civil commitment of mental patients in Israel. In: Miller L, Pollak H, Berman H (eds) Contributions to community psychiatry in Israel. Kedmi, Jerusalem
20. Winnik HZ (1981) personal communication
21. Wooton B (1980) Psychiatry, ethics and the criminal law. Brit J Psychiatry 136: 525–532
22. *Yarmulovitz and the State of Israel* v. *Hovav* (1980) Civil Appeal 219/79 P. D. 35 (3), 766, at 775

Two Different Levels of Patient Autonomy

U. Lowental

Introduction

Autonomy, literally the use of one's own law, is the quality or state of being independent, free, and self-directing, and employing "the sovereignty of reason, self-determination and self-legislation in the realm of morals" *(Webster's)*. Implied here is a social-interpersonal milieu wherein other-directed behavior is the counterpoise of autonomy. However, these general definitions are inadequate for the question of autonomy in doctor-patient interactions. Take, for example, a case of "simple" influenza. The doctor may prescribe prophylactic antibiotics and forbid next month's scheduled business trip, out of concern for its possible effects upon his patient's cardiac condition and for the danger of a secondary infection. The patient refuses to comply, having always succeeded through unflagging work, while ignoring what he calls his "minor heart problem." At what point would the doctor's respect for his patient's autonomy become a medical blunder?

Such highly charged alternatives are generated by the bimodal nature of patient autonomy, with two different sets of parameters which are not always equal or parallel. On one level we find the individual's sense of inner harmony, the coordination of drive tension with moral regulation leading to initiative and decisions over manifest behavior. The other level concerns the person's conduct in his social surroundings, and this level is close to the general definition cited above.

Disease and Individual Autonomy

Psychological Aspects

Regarded from the first level, that of intrapsychic harmony, falling ill often reveals a concealed motivation, some strange need of one single aberrant part of the personality evoked by a certain developmental setting, life stress, etc. Temporarily, this need comes to prevail over other, hedonistic needs. At these times, an aberrant portion of the psychosocial unit called "individuum" looks forward to disease and the pain and suffering involved, even to agony and death. The terms "choice of illness" and "primary or secondary gains" denote these tendencies.

Depression is a notorious example. Overt depression is always the outcome of guilt, a derogatory judgment of one's wishes and actions, with autopunitive drives, a sad slowing down, and feelings of hopelessness or thoughts of suicide. The condition itself seems to be the execution of the sentence and, untreated, it lasts until the punishment is felt to be enough.

These dynamics may call forth symptoms of a "masked depression" in the cardio-vascular, musculoskeletal, or endocrine systems or elsewhere [11]. Quite often we get a glimps of patients' pathological trends which are held in check by expiation, in the form of ill health or, again, as a sort of payment for illusory crimes; and indeed depressive suffering is a lesser evil than the alternative "solutions," such as death by suicide [12].

Another type of outcome is psychosomatic impairment. The key factor here is disharmony, which restricts the emotional support usually provided by social transactions; in addition, there is a clash between the patient's needs and drives (e.g., the striving for a directorship of a great company alongside the need for love and support). Disharmony creates unbearable tension which threatens the person's integration, unless it becomes centered on one bodily organ or system, which is sacrificed, so to speak, in order to maintain overall health. Such mechanisms operate with duodenal ulcer, bronchial asthma, and other "classical" psychosomatoses.

Similar factors are etiological in many other "psychogenic" diseases [13]. Very often there is an unconscious dread involved, as when the fear of sex leads to the (now uncommon) "honeymoon cystitis" in newly wed women – a painful condition which prevents further sexual relations. This example illustrates that illness almost never provides a constructive solution, and the underlying conflicts remain unaltered. However, when considered from a deterministic point of view, these clinical data bespeak some from of autonomous coping and the choice of a "solution." The same holds true for the teleological orientation: all symptoms may be regarded as achievements or "primary gains." There are also "secondary gains", various beneficial sequelae or consequences, such as the exemption from duties or obligations.

Secondary gain can also consists of rest, with nurses' comforting words or with more concrete compensations. Therefore, committees assigned to examine disabled persons and decide on the extent of their invalidism often see subjects who fight for an appreciation of their disease, not their health. Hypochondriac patients are known to seek such advantages, and similar observations have been reported in medical and surgical wards where some (recovered) patients plead against discharge [6]. Physicians and scientists, too, may actually welcome illness at times [18], for when confined to bed they cannot attend committee meetings, see patients, or entertain visitors; this secondary gain consists of a freedom from the ordinary chores of life and it provides the ideal conditions for creative work.

It becomes clear that rhe concept of autonomy must be widened in order to be applicable to these various gains. These are inconstant and changeable, turning patient autonomy into a dynamic variable, to be estimated anew at every medical examination. Furthermore, since these intrapsychic changes are only one part of the picture, one must turn to examine the other, the interpersonal, the social aspects of illness.

Socio Cultural Aspects

The new biopsychosocial medical model [5] is based on modern sytems theory. Man and society belong to one hierarchially arranged continuum of system; each one is at the same time a component of a higher system: system cell is a component of system tissue, organ, person, family, community, and so forth. But how does this relate to the problem of individual disease and autonomy?

The answer is that each symptom acquires a full meaning only in the light of sociocultural variations; otherwise it remains a plain sign. For example, Kleinman [9] saw cardiac complaints as a very common somatization in Chinese patients. Among them the language of the heart provides the socially appropriate idioms for articulating loss or personal tragedy, and thereby receiving attention and care.

Thus each individual's autonomy is affected both by the private psychology and by the affiliation to an ethnocultural group. Groups vary in the specifity of their medical complaints. For example, first-generation Italians tended to present diverse medical complaints related to various organ systems, while Irish patients presented far fewer and more limited symptoms. Groups vary in their style of medical complaining. For example, Jewish and Italian patients alike were observed to express their suffering openly and dramatically, while Irish patients deny their symptoms, and Old American patients suffer quietly and try to view their pain with detachment. The groups also vary in the nature of their anxiety about the meaning of the symptoms. Protestants seemed most concerned about symptoms that are incapacitating; Jews were most anxious about the implications of symptoms as indicators of serious disease; Italians were most concerned with pain itself [7].

Each individual has internalized the norms of his group. Therefore, concepts such as freedom and destiny [15] or personal identity and autonomy take on a different meaning, influenced by such norms as whether people are allowed a direct expression of emotional misery or are trained to use somatization. Related to this is the well-known effect of religious affiliation: the more frequently people engage in religious activities of all types, the less likely they are to report emotional distress [16].

In view of such social forces, we must shift the emphasis from individual freedom to the autonomy of the group vis-à-vis ill health. Furthermore, certain societies seem to be losing their distinctive group characteristics with the passing of each generation [8].

Medical Treatment and Patient Autonomy

Patient autonomy is one of the central issues of medical ethics. The fourth of the seven principles of medical ethics adopted by the American Medical Association is: "A physician shall respect the rights of patients, of colleagues, and of other health professionals, and shall safeguard patient confidences within the constraints of the law" [23].

Some limitations on patient autonomy are well known: a patient may not withhold information, must endure discomfort and pain, and must repress all shame while he displays private parts of body and mind. Despite his basic right to medical treatment he has no right to determine this treatment, since the state has assumed the paternal role *(parens patria)* – sometimes to an absolute degree. Thus manuals of military medicine state that soldiers with over 75% burns should be given no treatment other than fluids and sedatives because they will not survive. Psychotic patients are given drugs without their consent. Does this disregard their autonomy? Only to a certain extent. One must remember that it was the advent of just these psychotropic drugs which reduced the number of inpatients in the United States from

559000 in 1955 to less than 200000 in 1979; on the whole, therefore, thanks to drugs administered without their consent, patients now have greater freedom [22].

The attitude of nonphysicians to the question of patient autonomy is usually quite critical. For example, parents might object to a certain measure required for their child's treatment, or might disagree with each other, thereby creating an insoluble dilemma [21]. A direct outcome of this kind of attitude is the charge of medical paternalism (cf. [2]). Medical practitioners themselves speak rather apologetically about the conflicting demands of the profession on this score, as in the case of a cancer patient who has the right to receive complete, accurate information, yet also the right to be spared the truth.

The dilemma of decisions over life and death brings the individual's autonomy into sharp focus. Medical intervention such as euthanasia, abortion, or infanticide in cases of congenital defects raise an outcry, with "society imposing a confusing and contradictory set of obligations on medicine" [17, p. 167]. Cases of terminal illness or irreversible vegetative existence, such as the famous sad case of Karen Quinlan, have provided no solution.

Cassel [3] once stated: "The function of medicine is to preserve autonomy, and the preservation of life is subservient to the primary goal." This strikes me as an excessive generalization. True, every human being has, at least in theory, the right to life and a similar right to death. The Natural Death Acts of California and Oregon, like some other ones throughout the world, are based on this premise. It is intended to ensure that upon the patient's signing a "living will," in the event of malignant disease or other severe disablement, no life-saving measure will be undertaken, nor any resuscitation attempted. But now let us imagine that an unconscious accident victim has been rushed in, profusely bleeding from the stump of an amputated arm, while in his one remaining fist is clamped a signed statement that a missing arm will be a severe disablement as mentioned. Must not the surgeon ignore any such suicidal autonomous "self-determination"?

There are people who retain their autonomy even in life-threatening situations [4, 20]. Each patient responds with a characteristic coping style, each with his peculiar degree of defensiveness and a typical attempt at personal control [19]. He might, for example, choose to be treated by a folk healer but be forced eventually to enter a modern hospital. Here the physician must ascertain what amount the treatment he is prepared to agree to. Would the patient rather risk death later from the disease or immediate death from surgery? In other words: can be distinguish between the dangers of omission and those of commission [1]?

Disease may reinforce a person's unswerving adherence to his sociocultural standards, but it also induces certain infantile expectations of succor. A patient may lose his open-minded capacity for constructive reasoning when agonized or terrified; applying for treatment and becoming a patient involves an emotional regression with increased dependency. If he sacrifices some of his autonomy for the sake of cure, he does so in his own best interests.

Patient Autonomy and Modern Medicine

The two different levels of autonomy seem to come even further apart in our era of rapidly advancing scientific discoveries, when lay people may be offered unexpected, new therapeutic measures by a skilled, highly specialized professional. Thus a young couple coming for genetic counseling might consider eugenic abortion a crime, whereas the medical specialist believes that this pain will ultimately spare the couple the far greater pain of very sick children. Newer techniques, such as artificial insemination from sperm banks and "test-tube" babies, also have adverse effects on patient autonomy. Notwithstanding the great therapeutic assistance rendered by these techniques, the fact that the donor's identity is never revealed by the doctor limits the recipient's autonomy.

Methods of gene transduction and organ transplantation, sex change operations, and new measures to prolong life all augment the already enormous power of scientists and practitioners. These experts can transform the entire biopsychological system, the very core of individual autonomy, by buttressing and strengthening it or by disavowing and almost wrecking it. Government decisions on health policy from the opposite point of view, e.g., medical cost containment or reduction, call for a careful protection of patient autonomy with regard to informed consent an other ethical topics [14].

Conclusions

Two clinical vignettes will illustrate the bimodal reflection of patient autonomy. A wounded prisoner-of-war was returned home, and he was happy even though orthopedic surgeons now had him chained and suspended in a plaster cast. His relief seemed to hinge on the restored inner harmony and on the normal therapeutic transactions rather than on observable "freedom." The second example is that of a 14-year-old Nigerian boy who was observed to submit to circumcision, performed during an initiation rite without any chemical anesthesia, only the trance-inducing sound of the tom-tom. On the first level of autonomy, these are problems of personal harmony, especially of those mental structures concerned with pain control and tolerance. On the second level, that of social interaction, it is a question of identity, or of the moral principle of holding on to the norms of one's tribe or country.

When autonomy changes are being assessed in medical patients, attention must be paid simultaneously to both levels reflecting that change. This measure facilitates a comprehension of the two sometimes opposite-directed effects of most therapeutic interventions. By and large, however, patient autonomy must yield to some extent, temporarily at least, to the necessities of medical care and cure.

References

1. Bret A (1981) Hidden ethical issues in clinical decision analysis. New England Journal of Medicine 305: 1150–1152
2. Buchanan A (1978) Medical paternalism. Philosophy and Public Affairs 7: 370–390
3. Cassel EJ (1977) The function of medicine. Hastings Center Report 7: 16–19
4. Clarke JR, Sorenson JH, Hare JE (1980) The limits of paternalism in emergency care. Hastings Center Report 10: 20–22
5. Engel GL (1977) The need for a new medical model: a challenge for biomedicine. Science 196: 126–136
6. Glickman LS (1980) Psychiatric consultation in the general hospital. Marcel Dekker, New York
7. Good BJ, Good-Delvecchio M (1980) The meaning of symptoms: a cultural hermeneutic model for clinical practice. In: Eisenberg L, Kleinman A (eds) The relevance of social science for medicine. Reidel, Dordrecht, pp 165–196
8. Greenbaum J (1974) Medical and health orientations of American Jews: a case of diminishing distinctiveness. Social Science and Medicine 8: 127–134
9. Kleinman A (1977) Depression, somatization and the "new cross cultural psychiatry." Social Science and Medicine 11: 3–10
10. Leventhal H, Meyer D, Nerenz D (1980) The commonsense representation of illness danger. In: Rachman S (ed) Medical psychology, vol 2. Pergamon, New York, pp 7–30
11. Lesse S (ed) (1974) Masked depression. Jason Aronson, New York
12. Lowental U (to be published) Mood versus mental illness. Journal of the Israel Medical Association *in press*
13. Lowental U (1981) Psychosomatic diagnosis: nosological considerations. Journal of the Israel Medical Association 101: 10–12
14. Mahler DM, Veatch RM, Sidel VW (1982) Ethical issues in informed consent. Research on medical cost containment. JAMA 247: 481–485
15. May R (1981) Freedom and destiny. Norton, New York
16. Ness RC (1980) The impact of indigenous healing activity: an empirical study of two fundamentalist churches. Social Science and Medicine 14B: 167–180
17. Pellegrino ED, Thomasma DC (1981) A philosophical basis of medical practice. Oxford University Press, New York
18. Pickering GW (1974) Creative malady. Oxford University Press, New York
19. Ray C, Lindop J, Gibson S (1982) The concept of coping Psychological Medicine 12: 385–395
20. Siegler M (1977) Critical illness: the limits of autonomy. Hastings Center Report 7: 12–15
21. Thomasma DC, Mauer AM (1982) Ethical complications of clinical therapeutic research on children. Social Science and Medicine 16: 913–919
22. Varga AC (1980) The main issues of bioethics. Pulist Press, Ramsey, p 123
23. Veatch RM (1981) Ethics. JAMA 245: 2187–2189

The Rights of the Mental Patient Under Israeli Law

A. Levy and S. Davidson

The current Israeli legislation on the treatment of the mentally ill was passed in 1955 [1] and has been amended several times (1972, 1974, 1975, 1977, 1978) [2–6]. Likewise, a number of regulations have been added in the course of the years (1957, 1959, 1972, 1977) [7–11].

A discussion of the rights of mental patients can, in our estimation, take place mainly on two levels:

1. Rights in the narrow sense of the word, as opposed to rights in the broad sense
2. Rights from a psychiatric point of view, as opposed to a legal viewpoint.

The 1955 law is a compromise between the psychiatric viewpoint and the legal one. We shall discuss briefly the rights of mental patients under this law and in the regulations of 1959 and 1972, and in a number of amendments suggested in recent years. Our discussion will mainly reflect a psychiatric point of view.

Rights of Mental Patients in Israel at Present

The rights of mental patients in Israel at present may be discussed under the following points.

1. Rights of patients concerning contacts with the outside world, confidentiality, and privacy. These are the rights of patients in the narrow sense of the word. The law makes provision for them all, except for the right of privacy.

2. Rights of patients concerning suitable arrangements for hospitalization, discharge, transfer, and leave of absence from hospital. From here on we are dealing with the rights of patients in the wider sense of the word. A considerable part of the Act is devoted to details of these procedures.

3. Rights of patients as to treatment. The patient has the right to refuse electroconvulsive therapy, but may not object to any other form of treatment or therapy, even exceptional courses of treatment. Furthermore, the law does not define the patient's right to receive proper treatment.

4. Rights of patients concerning forced restraint and limitation of freedom.
   The choice of treatment which is less restrictive is not mentioned at all. Limitations of the patient's freedom of movement within the hospital – observation, special supervision, and use of restrictive measures – are clearly defined in the 1977 regulations.

5. Rights of patients concerning the representation of their interests during the period of their hospitalization.
   The law deals only briefly with the question of representation of the patient while he is hospitalized and after his release. The law gives the public guardian the right to intervene in legal processes which cannot be deferred with regard to the patient's property, but his day-to-day material interests are nowhere dealt with. With respect to the patient's treatment, the law authorizes the patient's personal guardian to object to electroconvulsive therapy, but to no other kind of treatment.

Patients' Rights in Several Proposals for Reform

We have briefly outlined the patient's rights, in the narrow and in the broad sense of the word, under the 1955 law and in the 1959 and 1977 regulations. In recent years, perhaps as a result of social change, there has been growing dissatisfaction with the law and the regulations. This dissatisfaction finds its expression, in our opinion, in the relatively large number of amendments that have been proposed in recent years. We shall review patients' rights as they find their expression in these amendments.

Proposal of the Forensic Committee of the Ministry of Health

The proposal of the Forensic Committee of the Ministry of Health 1977 [12] deals chiefly with regulations concerning hospitalization, discharge, transfer, and leave of absence, and partly with treatment and representation of patients' interests. The main changes proposed are as follows.

Hospitalization and Discharge

The authority of the hospital director can be delegated to a head of a psychiatric department (including one in a general hospital) and to a psychiatrist to whom the director has delegated power. In the event of objection to the hospitalization of a voluntary patient by family members or other interested parties, the request for delay in hospitalization will not prevent the admission of the patient to the hospital for 3 days. During this 3-day period, the request will be considered by the District Psychiatrist, who will then decide whether or not the patient should remain in the hospital after the 3 days.

Reasons for nonvoluntary hospitalization due to dangerous behavior will also include the danger of causing severe damage to property. This can be carried out by the District Psychiatrist even if there is only a "reasonable likelihood" of such behavior taking place. In this case, the District Psychiatrist may examine the likelihood by a clarification of the necessary material or by an examination of the patient. The hospitalization order issued by the District Psychiatrist will expire within 5 days (instead of 15). There will be a difference between a hospitalization order (under paragraph 5) and a compulsory hospitalization order (under paragraph 7). There will be no obligation to inform the State Attorney of a compulsory hospitalization order. However, the District Psychiatrist will inform the body issuing the compulsory hospitalization order (the court or the physician issuing the certificate) of the execution or nonexecution of the order.

The patient may appeal to the court against hospitalization without a court order. The District Psychiatrist will provide the patient with a copy of the hospitalization order and inform him of his right of appeal. (This is in the recommendation of Judge Bazak. The other committee members opposed this recommendation.)

The hospital director can impose upon a patient who has been discharged, either finally or temporarily, the obligation of follow-up care and, if need be, can order the patient's return to hospital if he was conditionally released. The patient can appeal to the Psychiatric Committee against the decision of the director. The Committee will be authorized to enforce follow-up care on a patient who was hospitalized by court order. The District Psychiatrist will be obliged to bring for discussion before the Committee the case of any patient who has been hospitalized by court order and who has not come up for discussion by the Committee for a period of 2 years.

Treatment

Both the District Psychiatrist and the Court are authorized to order compulsory ambulatory treatment. In this case, the therapist will deliver a report as to the progress of the treatment every 3 months.

Representation of the Patient's Interests

The director will immediately advise the patient's next of kin or guardian about the hospitalization, unless he was accompanied by one of them when hospitalized.

Minority Recommendation of Justice Bazak

The minority recommendation of Justice Bazak tended much more toward the legal model. It included a transferal of the responsibility for issuing hospitalization orders to the court. Hospitalization against the patient's wishes will only be carried out by a hospitalization order which will be issued only in case of danger. The District Psychiatrist will be authorized to issue a temporary hospitalization order (in the likelihood of dangerous behavior, including danger to property). Such an order will remain in force for up to 7 days. Should anyone, other than the patient, oppose the hospitalization, the patient will not be hospitalized without the agreement of the District Psychiatrist.

Should the District Psychiatrist consider the patient to be a source of danger, he will take the necessary legal steps to have the patient hospitalized. However, should he refuse to issue a hospitalization order, he will inform the referring party of his refusal and of their right of appeal to the Psychiatric Committee.

The proceedings before the judge can take place in the hospital. A hospitalization order issued by a judge will be in force for up to a year and may be extended beyond this period. The judge has an obligation to hear the case for the patient - delivered by the patient and his counsel - prior to issuing the hospitalization order. The request for the issue of such an order will be delivered in writing by the District Psychiatrist. However, should the judge be convinced of the urgency of the case due to the danger involved, he may issue a hospitalization order without hearing the case for the patient, if there is no reasonable opportunity of a hearing in the presence of the patient.

Only if, in the light of the evidence of two physicians, the judge is convinced of the impossibility of a hearing in the presence of the patient will the hearing take place in his absence. A hospitalization order which has been issued in the absence of a patient will be enforced for a period of up to 90 days each time, unless a guardian has been appointed for the patient. A hearing in the presence of the patient's guardian is regarded as the same as a hearing in the presence of the patient.

The Shtern-Katan Recommendations of 1981

The Shtern-Katan recommendations of 1981 [13] refer mainly to the need for a compulsory examination of the patient, and include the appointment of a "committee for the examination of mental health" in every district, which will consist of the District Psychiatrist, a lawyer, and a social worker. In the case of "an individual behaving in a manner having an extremely adverse effect on his family" - mental harm or damage to property - "and [whose] unreasonable behavior would seem to indicate that he is in need of treatment", the committee can authorize his examination (even in his home) to ascertain whether he is ill or not.

The committee will act in such a way only if it has been asked to do so by two relatives and a social worker, or a social worker and a physician, and with suitable depositions and certificates. The District Psychiatrist will fix the type and place of examination. The person may appeal against the decision of this committee before the District Psychiatric Committee and the order will not be carried out until the appeal is decided. The Shtern-Katan proposal emphasizes the adverse effect on the family - and not necessarily on other individuals - as justification for compulsory examination.

The Bar-el (Breiter) Proposal of 1981

The Bar-el (Breiter) proposal of 1981 [14] comprises comprehensive suggestions which take into account the draft prepared in the past by various forensic committees.

Hospitalization, Discharge, Transfer, and Leave of Absence

The main changes are as follows. Hospitalization will be effected only after a psychiatric examination, and if the patient agrees to be hospitalized, he must give his agreement in writing. The District Psychiatrist is empowered to order an examination if he considers that the patient has caused severe suffering, mental or material, to himself or to his environment as a result of his illness - but only after receiving direct evidence from a public servant. Likewise, he is empowered to issue a compulsory hospitalization order on the grounds of a psychiatric examination as well as compulsory outpatient care. The court has similar powers. A hospitalization order will be valid for a period of up to 2 weeks from the day of hospitalization and can be extended only for a period of up to another 15 days. A hospitalization order that was based on a court order (but not on a medical certificate) empowers the District Psychiatrist to order a compulsory examination.

A patient who has been referred for examination will immediately receive a copy of the decision, including notice of the means of appeal, and will be informed of his rights. Such a document will be posted in a prominent place in the hospital for study. If the patient leaves the hospital without permission or is found to be missing, he will be returned to the hospital by the police if he was hospitalized by a court order; by the District Psychiatrist if he was hospitalized by a hospitalization order; and by the hospital if he agreed to voluntary hospitalization. Under these circumstances, a hospitalization order is not just an order to bring a patient to the hospital, but also defines ways of returning him to the hospital should he leave.

Treatment

A patient who was voluntarily hospitalized will express his agreement to treatment in writing. The District Psychiatrist is empowered to order compulsory ambulatory treatment. The extent of the authority of the District Psychiatrist for supervision in the hospital includes the possibility of appointing an inquiry commission.

Means of Restraint and Limitation of Freedom

The use of a straightjacket has been reauthorized.

Representation of the Interests of Hospitalized Patients

In the case of a patient who has been hospitalized, or is to be examined by order of the District Psychiatrist, his family or guardian, should they accompany him, will be given a copy of the order including notice of the means of appeal. In every case the patient and his relatives "must be given at the earliest opportunity" a copy of the decision.

Contact with the Outside World and Confidentiality

The patient's rights have been increased by 1955 Mental Health Act. The Bar-el recommendations would appear to increase the rights of patients both in the narrow sense and with resepct to the procedures of hospitalization, discharge, and treatment.

The Aviram-Shnit Recommendations of 1981

The Aviram-Shnit recommendations are the result of considerable research and have been published in book form. The authors make severe criticisms of the various sections of the Act and of the way it is implemented. They concern themselves chiefly with the question of enforced hospitalization and suggest that there should be a clear definition of its justification.

They propose that there should be a differentiation between:

1. The patient who is severely dangerous to other people
2. The patient who is dangerous to himself
3. The patient who is severely limited in his ability to understand and make decisions considering his affairs.

The authors suggest further:

1. The abolition of compulsory hospitalization of unlimited duration.
2. Change in the status of the hospitalized person during the period of hospitalization: a person who has been voluntarily hospitalized and subsequently changes his mind will continue to be hospitalized only after a psychiatric assessment of the need for continued hospitalization.
3. The establishment of a time limit on compulsory hospitalization and the adaptation of procedures of compulsory hospitalization for the different types of patients and according to the purpose of hospitalization. Compulsory hospitalization will be carried out only with those patients who are dangerous or who are of severely limited capacity.

The proposed types of compulsory hospitalization are the following:

1. Hospitalization for the purpose of evaluation, diagnosis, and emergency treatment.
2. Compulsory hospitalization for the purpose of intensive care. This will be for a period of up to 30 days.
3. Compulsory hospitalization for the purpose of continued care of dangerous patients. This is intended for extremely dangerous patients only. The hearing of the request of the District Psychiatrist will take place before a Justice of the Peace, who can appoint an expert to act for him and can issue hospitalization orders for a period of up to 6 months for those patients who are a danger to other people, and up to 2 months for patients who are dangerous to themselves.
4. Compulsory hospitalization to include treatment and prolonged supervision for patients of severely limited capacity. Patients who are unable to take care of their

basic needs may need continued hospitalization, consequent on the appointment of a guardian and on the subsequent agreement of the guardian to further hospitalization.

5. Continued hospitalization of patients requesting a discharge. Clear procedures must be established so that a patient who has undergone voluntary hospitalization can be released should he rescind his agreement, unless there is a justification for enforced hospitalization and the necessary procedures have been carried out.

The authors, who call their approach the "balanced approach," sum up their proposals as follows. The creation of:

1. a definition of the justification of compulsory hospitalization
2. The establishment of clear procedures of hospitalization and their adaptation to different goals (as detailed)
3. The establishment of a strong and independent office of the District Psychiatrist, including the placing of necessary means at his disposal
4. The inclusion of various helping bodies for the realization of the patient's rights
   - Every patient will be informed of his rights.
   - Reliable and independent persons will be appointed to clarify to the patient his rights and represent him before the authorities (advocacy).
5. The evaluation of the ability of the patient to understand and to be responsible for his interests, which will be carried out at every stage of hospitalization
6. The establishment of a reliable system of report, supervision, and control.

With regard to the rights of patients in other fields, the Aviram-Shnit recommendations deal mainly with suitable arrangements and procedures for compulsory hospitalization, but these recommendations also deal with the rights of patients regarding treatment and representation of interests as detailed.

Discussion

We have reviewed the rights of patients as expressed in the Mental Health Act, its regulations, and a number of suggested amendments. These suggested amendments represent the rights of the patients in both the narrow and the broad sense of the word. The view that they take is a mixed one. The recommendations of the 1977 Ministry of Health Forensic Committee move slightly toward the legal model, but still maintain by and large the psychiatric viewpoint.

The 1981 Shtern-Katan recommendations are mainly of a social nature. The 1981 Bar-el recommendations are psychiatric, but enlarge the legalistic component. In the 1981 Aviram-Shnit recommendations, there is a shift toward the legalistic model. These aroused considerable opposition among most psychiatrists in Israel when they were published. The most extreme "legalistic" recommendations are those of Judge Bazak in his minority report of the 1977 Forensic Committee.

It must be admitted that every model has its advantages and disadvantages. The advantages of the medical or psychiatric model are that the emphasis is placed on the needs of the patient first and foremost and there is heavy reliance on the integrity and professional standards of the individual physician. This model regards the legalistic viewpoint as cumbersome, lacking in appreciation of clinical reality, and placing unrealistic demands on the therapeutic staff [16]. This point of view also regards the cumbersome legalistic steps as a further means of social stigmatization of the patient, which adds to that already connected with psychiatric treatment and hospitalization. As opposed to this, the legalistic viewpoint stresses the need to respect, as far as possible, the various rights of patients, even in those cases where the treatment is complicated or compulsory, and also when the patient is a source of danger. From this viewpoint, the psychiatrists are neither trained nor qualified to protect the patient's rights. These must be clearly defined by the law, and their enforcement must be supervised.

In this paper we have presented impressions based on our experience of this subject over the course of many years. Furthermore, we have taken into account the opinions of many of our colleagues. It is clear that psychiatrists in Israel are predominantly opposed to a change in the Mental Health Act in the direction of the legalistic model, for reasons we have stated.

It is our impression that there is only a small minority of psychiatrists who tend toward the legalistic viewpoint, but it is possible that this minority is growing. It would be interesting to attempt to provide a statistical basis for these impressions. In our opinion, public and legal pressure in Israel will cause a change in the law in the forseeable future, and the Israeli psychiatrists would be well advised to prepare for this eventuality in good time.

A step in this direction was taken in January 1983, with the publication of the directives of the State Attorney [17]. In these directives, the State Attorney has instructed that an appeal be automatically made on each and every hospitalization order issued by the District Psychiatrist which is not a court order, where this involves a first psychiatric hospitalization.

Another step is the publication of the duty to explain to the newly admitted patient his rights and obligations, including his signature on a special document [18]. As far as we know, the first information on these steps was brought to the attention of psychiatrists in Israel (including directors of mental hospitals and apparently also district psychiatrists) by the media. The trend, so it seems, is toward more legalistic procedures.

References

1. The Israeli Mental Health Act (1955) Law Book 187: 121
2. Law Book 662: 126 (1972)
3. Law Book 747: 8 (1974)
4. Law Book 763: 97 (1975)
5. Law Book 876: 24 (1977)
6. Law Book 883: 65 (1978)
7. Regulation for treatment of the mentally ill – appeal before the District Court. (1957) Regulation Collection 707: 1482
8. Regulations for treatment of the mentally ill (1959) Regulation Collection 908: 1372
9. Regulations for treatment of the mentally ill (1972) Regulation Collection 2920: 126
10. Regulations for treatment of the mentally ill (1972) Regulation Collection 2915: 80
11. Regulations for treatment of the mentally ill (1977) Regulation Collection 3750: 2418

12. Memorandum – A suggested law for treatment of the mentally ill (amendment) (1977) Ministry of Health
13. Shtern-Katan S (1981) Mental Health Act (amendment no 6). A proposition to the Labour Committee of the Knesset
14. Bar-el Y (1981) Mental Health Act – First Draft. Jerusalem
15. Aviram U, Shnit D (1981) Psychiatric treatment and individual liberties: a compulsory hospitalization of mental patients in Israel. Zmora Bitan Modan, Tel Aviv
16. Wijsenbeek H (1981) The family physician 10: 351
17. The general attorney instructions: the Mental Health Act 1955 – an appeal at a compulsory hospitalization of a mental patient, no 21,064, Jerusalem 1983
18. See Ginat Y, Porat S, Bar-el in this volume

Mental Health and Human Rights: Illegal Detention in Japan

E. Totsuka, T. Mitsuishi, and Y. Kitamura

Are the human rights of the mentally ill properly protected in Japan? Regrettably, our investigation shows that they are not. The mentally ill in Japan are unnecessarily detained for lengthy periods. This state of affairs and the legal criteria for detention violate the International Covenant on Civil and Political Rights (Treaty number 7, proclaimed in August 1979), which prohibits arbitrary detention. In addition, the current legal system does not provide a review procedure for the mentally ill, which is guaranteed by the Covenant.

In 1970 a prominent journalist, Mr. Kazuo Okuma, revealed appalling mistreatment and abuse of mental patients by medical staff in his newspaper report "Japanese Mental Hospitals" [18]. More than a decade has passed since the publication of this report, but has the situation actually changed? To find out how well the human rights of patients are protected, we examined the rights to personal liberty and security.

We first examined whether there was any breach of clause 1 of article 9 of the Covenant. While the Japanese Mental Health Act contains no provision for voluntary or informal admission, it has three main provisions that allow the detention of persons suffering from mental disorders.

As indicated in the appended (Appendix A) translation of the Mental Health Act [10], these are:

- Article 29: compulsory admission by the governor
- Article 33: compulsory admission with the consent of the person responsible for care
- Article 34: provisional compulsory admission.

Most of the patients are detained indefinitely under articles 29 and 33.

As Table 1 shows, the scale of the problem is enormous. There were over 300 000 patients in mental hospitals and mental wards in 1978. Just how many of the 300 000 were being compulsorily detained we do not know with certainty, but the following estimates can be made.

Table 1. Numbers of patients and beds in mental hospitals and mental wards in Japan as at 30 June 1973 and 30 June 1978 [1]

	Beds	Patients
1973	265 904	273 814
1978	292 720	301 245

Firstly, Table 2 shows that during 1978, of the 213558 newly admitted patients over 80% – i.e., about 170000 – were detained compulsorily under one of the three provisions mentioned above. If we assume that those who are committed compulsorily stay longer than patients admitted voluntarily, then we can estimate that over 80% of all mental hospital patients are being compulsorily detained.

Further evidence is provided by Dr. Isoo Hirota, who has produced figures showing that only 20% of Japanese mental hospitals were practising open-system therapy [9, p. 124]. These two figures suggest that well over 80%, that is 240000 patients, were being forcibly detained in locked wards in 1978 [3, p. 18]. This figure is all the more startling when one considers that only 50000 people were being detained in prisons in Japan at the same time [15, p. 197].

Another way to evaluate this figure of 240000 is to compare it with United Kingdom figures. Table 3 shows that in the United Kingdom only 7033, namely 5·2%, of the 134618 patients in mental hospitals were being compulsorily detained in 1978. The United Kingdom experience suggests that most of the 240000 or more Japanese detainees could have been treated in open wards. This means that the most of the patients in Japanese mental hospitals are being arbitrarily and unnecessarily detained.

What, then, does the future hold for patients in Japanese mental hospitals? Table 4 shows that the average length of stay is increasing. About 55000 patients detained under article 29 had spent, on average, 6½ years in psychiatric hospitals [1, p. 170].

Figure 1 vividly illustrates the rapid growth of the number of patients in Japanese mental hospitals. Japan should be called the "land of asylums." What is more frightening is that the situation could become even worse.

Table 2. Admission to mental hospitals and mental wards in Japan in 1968 and 1978 (16, pp. 47, 99, 103)

	All admissions (including voluntary)	Compulsory admissions by governors [11]	Compulsory admissions with the consent of the person responsible for care [12] and provisional admissions [13]
1968	191677 (100%)	18831 (7.3%)	149149 (77.8%)
1978	213558 (100%)	6393 (3%)	165493 (77.5%)

Table 3. Comparison of the numbers of hospitalized mental patients and of prisoners in Japan and the United Kingdom

	Residents in mental hospitals and mental wards (1978)		Prisoners
	All admissions	Compulsory admissions	
Japan	301245 (100%)	>240000 (>80%)	50596 (1980)
UK	134618 (100%) [4, p. 24]	7033 (5.2%) [4, p. 24]	45500 (1982) [19]

Table 4. Average periods of stay in mental hospitals and mental wards in Japan in 1968 and 1978

	Average of all beds (days) [5, p. 214]	Average of compulsory admissions by governors (days) [14]
1968	460.3 (1.3 years)	1533 (4.2 years)
1978	520.8 (1.4 years)	2396 (6.6 years)

What are the causes of this tragedy? In our opinion, the major cause is a profit-orientated mental health industry. In Japan, 85% of the beds for the mentally ill are owned by private institutions [1, p. 56]. Dr. D. H. Clarke, consultant on Mental Health for WHO, politely criticized Japanese mental hospitals in his WHO report in 1968 [2]. In this report he said, "These problems are particularly bad ... where the proprietor, anxious for a return on his investment, is putting pressure on the medical staff to increase income by overcrowding the institution [2, p. 16]. It is common knowledge that mental hospitals are one of the most successful industries in Japan [17].

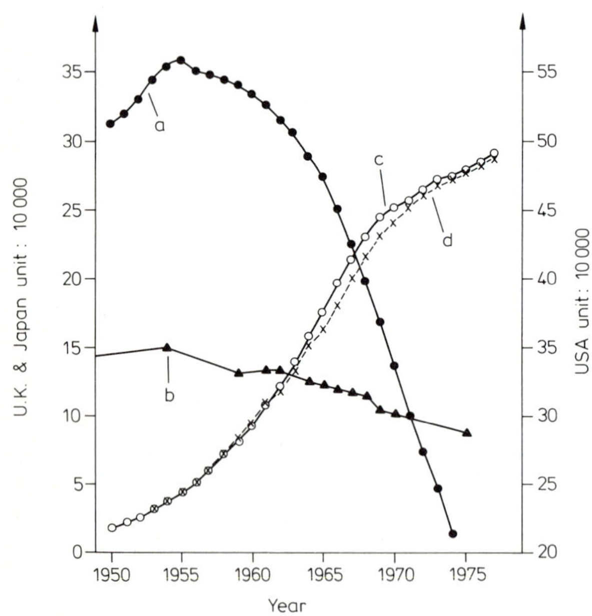

Fig. 1. Residents in mental hospitals and mental wards in Japan, the United Kingdom and the United States 9, p. 172

a = Psychiatric Services and the Changing Institutional Scene, 1950–1985. NIMH Series B. No. 12, NIMH, 1977
b = K. Jones: A History of the Mental Health Services, 238: 1061, 1978
c = Japan Residents
d = Japan Beds

Moreover, Japanese society has tacitly accepted the situation. In Japan, there was said to be a folk tradition of abandoning old people in the mountains and leaving them there to die [8]. In modern Japan, mental hospitals are used as a dumping ground for people who are considered unable to contribute to industry and become a burden on families and society because of their mental disorder. Having once been committed to a mental hospital, they carry the stigma of incompetence. This could possibly be one of the secrets of Japanese success in industry and one of the causes of the trade imbalance! Do the provisions of the Mental Health Act offer adequate safeguards against arbitrary detention?

Article 33 of the Act is especially important in this regard, since it accounts for four-fifths of the patients compulsorily detained. Under this article, provided that the person responsible for care consents, the administrator of the mental hospital can detain the person without any independent psychiatric diagnosis. The European Court of Human Rights stated in its judgment of 24 October 1979 three minimum conditions which have to be satisfied in order for the "detention of persons of unsound mind" to be lawful within the meaning of article 5, clause 1 (e) of the European Convention on Human Rights. One of the three is that a true mental disorder must be established before a competent authority on the basis of objective medical expertise [7]. As article 33 obviously lacks this provison and article 9, clause 1 of the International Covenant makes the same provision as that of the European Convention, the Japanese Mental Health Act is in breach of the International Covenant.

In assessing whether procedures for releasing patients from arbitrary detention are adequate or not, it is useful to consider article 9, clause 4 of the International Covenant. Article 9 clause 4 of the Covenant states: "Anyone who is deprived of his liberty by arrest or detention shall be entitled to take proceedings before a court, in order that the court decide without delay on the lawfulness of his detention and order his release if the detention is not lawful." The current Mental Health Act in Japan, however, provides no independent review body equivalent to "a court" as stated, nor does it provide any review procedure.

Ordinary court procedures are not effective in the case of mental patients, and we know of no precedents of this kind. It may be claimed that the release of patients is already possible through proceedings under the Habeas Corpus Law. However, despite the existence of habeas corpus legislation, on 5 November 1981 the European Court of Human Rights unanimously ruled that a restricted patient who had been detained indefinitely under the British compulsory committal system had been held in breach of article 5, clause 4 of the European Convention, as the system lacked an automatic periodic review of a judicial character or a review before a court at reasonable intervals [6, 20]. The previously mentioned article 9, clause 4 of the International Covenant contains the same provisions as the article of the European Convention, and Japanese habeas corpus legislation is no better than the British habeas corpus legislation as regards a safeguard. Since the European Court judgment can validly be applied to interpret article 9, clause 4 of the International Covenant, the Japanese Mental Health Act, which lacks the necessary judicial procedures, can be said to be in breach of the International Covenant.

We believe that the following urgent measures are required to reform the Japanese mental health system [3, p. 19]:

1. Reform of article 33 of the Act, which allows detention without any independent psychiatric diagnosis
2. Establishment of the review procedure which is required by article 9, clause 4 of the International Covenant
3. Guarantee of the right to be informed of the reason for detention, the rights provided by safeguard procedures, the right to free communication, and the right to receive freely lawyers, family, and friends who can defend the person detained.

Guaranteeing the rights stated in 3. above is of particular importance, since current laws do not guarantee these rights, meaning, in effect, that detained persons cannot take legal proceedings.

Regrettably, however, the Japanese Government is very reluctant to undertake reforms of this kind. Concern and research by our international colleagues could make a substantial difference in persuading the Government to reconsider this attitude. We earnestly seek international assistance in relieving the plight of a great many people arbitrarily detained in Japanese mental hospitals.

Appendix Translation of the Japanese Mental Health Act (law no. 123 of 1 May 1950)

Measures relating to committal to hospital by the Prefectural Governor.
Article 29.

1. A Prefectural Governor may, where he deems as a result of a medical examination undertaken under the provisions of article 27 that the person who underwent the medical examination is mentally disordered, and is liable to injure himself or others owing to his mental disorder if he is not committed to hospital for treatment and care, commit the person to a state or prefectural mental hospital or other designated hospital.

2. In order for the Prefectural Governor to commit the person concerned to hospital as described in the preceding clause, the results of examinations by each of two or more certified mental health practitioners shall agree with the diagnosis that the person is mentally disordered and is liable to injure himself or others owing to his mental disorder if he is not committed to hospital for treatment and care.

3. The administrator of the state or prefectural hospital or other designated hospital shall admit the mentally disordered person under the preceding clause, except in cases where there is no reserved bed for him (i.e., a bed in a hospital a section of which has been designated under article 5) owing to the committal of patients under the provisions of clause 1 above or clause 1 of the following article.

4. Persons already admitted to hospital in accordance with the provisions of the Mental Hospitals Law (law no. 25 of 1919) at the time of enactment of this Law shall be deemed to have been committed in accordance with the provisions of clause 1.

Committal with the consent of the person responsible for care. *Article 33.*

The administrator of a mental hospital may, with respect to a person who has been diagnosed as mentally disordered as the result of medical examination, in cases where he deems the committal to hospital of the person in question to be necessary for the purpose of medical treatment and care, commit that person to hospital without his or her consent if the person responsible for his or her care consents thereto.

Provisional committal. *Article 34.*

The administrator of a mental hospital may, in cases where he deems as a result of medical examination that a considerable period of time is necessary for diagnosis, provisionally commit a person suspected of being mentally disordered, to hospital for a period of not more than 3 weeks without his consent, if the guardian, spouse, person who is exercising parental authority, or person responsible for his support consents thereto.

References

1. Bureau of Mental Health, Department of Public Health, Ministry of Health and Welfare (1981) Mental health handbook (in Japanese). Kosei Mondai Kenkyukai
2. Clarke DH (1968) Assignment report Nov 1967–Feb 1968
3. Daini Tokyo Bar Association, Committee on Human Rights (1981) Interim report on mental health and human rights (in Japanese)
4. Department of Health and Social Security, Home Office, Welsh Office and Lord Chancellor's Department (1981) Reform of mental health legislation, Cmnd 8405. Her Majesty's Stationary Office
5. Department of Statistics and Information, Office of Minister of Health and Welfare (1981) Survey on medical care institutions and hospital report (in Japanese). Kosei Tokei Kyokai
6. European Court of Human Rights, Judgment on *X* v *the United Kingdom*, 5 November 1981
7. European Court of Human Rights, judgment on *Winterwerp*, 24 October 1979
8. Fukazawa S (1964) *Narayama-bushi Kō* (in Japanese). Shincho-sha
9. Hirota I (1981) Mental hospitals: philosophy and practice (in Japanese). Iwasaki Gakujutsu Shuppan-sha
10. Mental Health Act (1950) (1 May 1950, law no 123)
11. Mental Health Act, article 29
12. Mental Health Act, article 33 (compulsory admission with the consent of the person responsible for care)
13. Mental Health Act article 34 (provisional compulsory admission). There are said to be few provisional compulsory admissions.
14. Ministry of Health and Welfare (1981) Material delivered at the Conference of certified mental health practitioners in 1981
15. Ministry of Justice (1981) White paper on crime (in Japanese)
16. National Institute of Mental Health (1980) Annual report on mental health (1979, 80/no 24) (in Japanese)
17. Okuma K (1973) Japanese mental hospitals (in Japanese). Asahi Shimbun-sha
18. Okuma K (1970) Japanese mental hospitals (in Japanese) Serialized in the Asahi Shimbun from 5 March 1970
19. The Times, 9 September 1982
20. Totsuka E, Mitsuishi T, Kitamura Y (1982) European Court of Human Rights judgment and the rights of the mentally disordered (in Japanese). Jurist, No 779, Dec 1982, p 47

Clinical Perplexities in the Treatment of Treatment-Refusing Forensic Patients

P. Rodenhauser

For many, the right to refuse treatment in a forensic hospital is a contradiction in terms. Court systems require maximum security hospitals for the protection of society from the committed, psychiatrically ill individual whose rights to privacy and autonomy are thereby modified, yet the involuntary "patient's" rights to privacy and autonomy are upheld by the courts in defense of treatment refusal. Court-committed patients are met on admission by a patient advocate who explains the treatment authorization form for signature – before the patient has contact with the admitting psychiatrist. Although the courts accept recommendations of competency to stand trial contingent upon continuation of antipsychotic medication [1], the same medications have been considered mind controlling [2] in support of the right to refuse treatment. The invasive nature of psychoses [2] has not been conceded by the legal system.

Through the eyes of a forensic hospital psychiatrist, contradictions are abundant. Management of the drug-refusing patient often requires physical restraint as an alternative to medication. Not infrequently, restraint takes the form of "four-point seclusion," i.e., the patient's ankles and wrists are cuffed and tethered to the posts of a metal bed positioned in the middle of a locked, barren room. Is not rights consciousness in some respects pushing back the clock to medieval methods of patient management?

The purpose of this paper is twofold:

1. To illuminate the implications of patient's rights to refuse treatment in a forensic setting
2. To elaborate the clinical responsibilities of forensic psychiatrists.

Clinical impressions are drawn from a 12-month experience as a part-time staff psychiatrist for a 16-bed treatment ward at the Dayton (Ohio) Mental Health Center Forensic Unit, one of the regional forensic hospitals built in response to the *Davis* v. *Watkins* decision [3].

Designed to treat forensic patients, the Dayton Forensic Unit was created out of the same federal court decision [3] as ordered due process hearings at Lima (Ohio) State Hospital for drug-refusing patients. The absence of a complicated legal or hospital mechanism for management of treatment refusal at the Dayton Forensic Unit, however, provides for dramatic contrast in styles of psychiatric practice at the two institutions [4]. Supported by multidisciplinary teams, Dayton Forensic Unit psychiatrists are privileged to manage by clinical methods independent of legal mandates.

Despite modern efforts to soften the effects, a maximum security hospital has the ambiance of a human compression chamber in which the external world becomes a series of projections promoting further regression. The workings of the patients' internal systems cannot be ignored, nor can the influences of the legal and psychiatric professions on patients and on each other (Fig. 1).

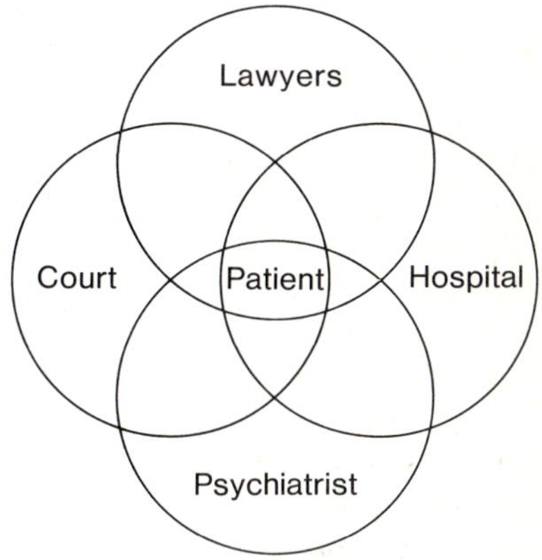

Fig. 1. Influence of the legal and psychiatric systems on patients and on each other

Awareness of the divergent purposes and inherent weaknesses of these two powerful systems – psychiatry and the law – has generated recommendations for solutions based on the development of a superimposed system – administration [5]. While a strong administrative campaign might redefine and redirect working relationships, the question will persist: can any but a clinical discipline design and establish fundamentals of treatment and implement specific plans?

In a psychiatric hospital setting, a hierarchy of categories of privileges, earned on the basis of appropriate behaviors, is considered an important milieu component of treatment. In a forensic setting, the range of "privileges" is from unsupervised off-ward hallway passage through seclusion with four-point restraints (Fig. 2). Guided by a staff of trained mental health professionals, activity therapies are strongly encouraged when privileges permit. This spectrum of therapies, identified by the courts as noninvasive, is "available" to all patients. Authorization has not become an issue in regard to the psychosocial forms of treatment. Once he is clinically

- Off-ward, unsupervised hallway passage
- Confinement to ward
  - with supervised off-ward activities
  - with supervised on-ward activities only
  - with wrist-to-waist restraints
    - with added ankle restraints
- Seclusion
  - with "four-point" restraints

Fig. 2. Forensic hospital "privilege" hierarchy

considered ready for a less restrictive environment, however, the committed forensic patient's treatment presents coloration of a different ilk. In such instances, restriction of lack of it becomes very much a "treatment" issue, while rationalization blends the interests of an absolute clinical approach with the interests of a society in need of protection.

In conjunction with researching three broad categories of reasons for drug refusal, Appelbaum and Gutheil postulated clinical grouping of drug refusers based on behaviors [6]. Half the refusers in the Dayton Forensic Unit ward sample were young, acutely ill, grandiose, delusional – and persistently uncooperative with drug treatment – "symptomatic refusers" [6]. Three out of the seven symptomatic refusers manifested refusal attitudes on admission before being interviewed by the psychiatrist. Altogether, one out of four patients refused attempted drug treatment at least once. When first treated for reasons of an emergency nature, however, several of the drug refusers reversed their refusals for periods of time which sometimes lengthened with repeated need for emergency drug interventions. In the absence of emergency circumstances or determinations of incompetency to refuse, persistent refusers remain drug free and their condition often deteriorates [2], while denial of illness intensifies. In this sample population, denial of illness was observed to be the predominant cause of drug refusal.

As in the general population, predicting probable forensic hospital violence is difficult [7]. Considerations of demographic data and criminal/psychiatric histories may be related to the likelihood of violence [8]. Not only are forensic hospital patients thereby representative of a violence-prone population [9], they are participants in a violence-producing situation. For some patients, institutionalization has a quieting effect: absence of troublesome relationships and other external stimuli, absence of alcohol and drugs, and provision of boundaries and basic needs result at least in temporary improvement. For some, internal stimuli in association with real or imaginary external conditions render them and others victims of volcanic violence. In a forensic hospital, there can be absence of danger only when there is an absence of patients.

A comprehensive view of the system and its vital signs is critical. Patients' rights to safety and effective treatment depend on environmental balance and predictability [10], and even subtle disturbances of the milieu can spiral to infringe heavily on the rights of other patients and staff [11]. Ethical, legal, and clinical principles become amalgamated, particularly at the point of forcibly medicating a patient considered harmful to others. Is this treatment? Or is the psychiatrist clearly an agent of social control at this juncture? Who will benefit from the emergency intervention? The physician's primary reason for treating a patient who is disrupting the milieu is supposedly one of concern for repercussions harmful to the patient, not others. The individual's fusion with his environment, especially in a locked ward, illuminates one of the issues of conflicting rights [12]. In that clues to potentials for behavioral disruptions are sometimes derived from frequent patient-staff interaction, the team approach to treatment provides assistance with the need for broad-based information from which the psychiatrist can derive the support and means to manage clinical complexities [4].

Among the resources for persevering forensic psychiatrists is the application for a judicial ruling on the treatment-refusing patient's competence [13]. A declaration of incompetence at the initial commitment hearing would seemingly facilitate the desired medical and social end [14]. The use of legal guardianship offers the promise of a solution to the problem [15], yet the cumbersome and time-consuming process of appointment, the tendency for legislation to authorize "limited guardianship" [16], and problems inherent in inclusion of a third party into the doctor-patient relationship are reportedly prohibitive of efficient treatment [15]. Due process hearings, hospital based but legally imposed, are part of clinical procedures in some institutions [3]. Reviews in nonemergencies by the clinical director or opinions from another consultant might be useful, as ordered in the *Rennie* v. Klein decision [17].

Yet the aforementioned procedures have in common multiple obstacles to the efficient delivery of mental health services, especially in a resource-limited, closed forensic hospital ward in which there is a conflict of rights. From a systems point of view, the right to treatment and the right to refuse treatment can become one - a milieu momentarily a melee, wherein "increasing one person's rights decreases freedom and safety of others" [11]. Especially if rehabilitation is the mission of forensic hospitals, then all patients require access to treatment unclouded by psychopathological, institutional, or legal mechanisms leading to denial.

References

1. Feldman HS (1976) Psychopharmacology and the law: a forensic psychiatrist's viewpoint. J Clin Pharmacol 16: 577-580
2. Gutheil TG (1980) In search of true freedom: drug refusal, involuntary medication, and "rotting with your rights on." Am J Psychiatry 137: 327-328
3. Heller A (1979) Impact of *Davis* v. *Watkins* on Ohio forensic hospital practice. Bull Am Acad Psychiatry Law 7: 39-62
4. Rodenhauser P, Heller A (to be published) Management of forensic patients who refuse treatment - two scenarios. J Forensic Sci
5. Wood Sir J (1982) The impact of legal modes of thought upon the practice of psychiatry. Br J Psychiatry 140: 551-557
6. Appelbaum PS, Gutheil TG (1980) Drug refusal: a study of psychiatric inpatients. Am J Psychiatry 137: 340-346
7. Dietz PE, Rada RT (1982) Battery incidents and batterers in a maximum security hospital. Arch Gen Psychiatry 39: 31-34
8. Monahan J (1982) Clinical prediction of violent behavior. Psychiatric Ann 12: 509-513
9. Rofman ES, Askinazi C, Fant E (1980) The prediction of dangerous behavior in emergency civil commitment. Am J Psychiatry 137: 1061-1064
10. Wilkerson CD, O'Connor WA (1982) Human ecology and mental illness. Am J Psychiatry 139: 985-990
11. Zusman J (1979) Against the right to refuse treatment. Adv Now 5: 12-16
12. Ford MD (1980) The psychiatrist's double bind: the right to refuse medication. Am J Psychiatry 137: 332-339
13. Appelbaum PS, Roth LH (1981) Clinical issues in the assessment of competency. Am J Psychiatry 138: 1462-1467
14. Roth LH, Meisel A, Lidz CW (1977) Tests of competency to consent to treatment. Am J Psychiatry 134: 279-284
15. Gutheil TG, Shapiro R, St Clair RL (1980) Legal guardianship in drug refusal: an illusory solution. Am J Psychiatry 137: 347-352
16. Appelbaum PS (1982) Limitations on guardianship of the mentally disabled. Law and Psychiatry 33: 183-184
17. Bryne G (1981) Conference report: refusing treatment in mental health institutions: values in conflict. Hosp Community Psychiatry 12: 255-258

C. Psychiatry and Criminal Law

Sentencing Offenders with Mental Disorders

J. Bazak

One of the most perplexing problems facing penologists is the determination of the proper punishment for grave offenses which were committed as a result of mental disturbances not amounting to mental illness proper (psychosis). Quite a number of such offenses are committed by people suffering from psychosexual disorders or disorders of impulse control. It should be noted that in many cases of offenses committed under the influence of such disorders the actual damage caused is not great, as in cases of exhibitionism, voyeurism, fetishism, kleptomania, etc. [1]. There are cases, however, where the offenses can be quite serious and cause considerable harm, such as pyromania or pathological gambling, which sometimes leads to offenses of fraud, forgery, and embezzlement. Cases of psychosexual disorder can also sometimes lead to serious offenses causing grave damage to the victim and the victim's family.

In considering the proper punishment for offenses committed because of such mental disorders, one cannot morally ignore the fact that the defendant acted under the influence of mental disorders which were almost, if not completely, beyond his control. On the other hand, the very fact that the defendant suffers from such mental disturbances makes him much more dangerous to society, and hence gives society the right and the duty to defend itself against him by, among other means, inflicting much more serious forms of punishment than are usually imposed for such offenses.

Another consideration is to what extent, if any, the defendant can be cured of his deviance. The better the chances of treatment are, the less it will be necessary, in the determination of his punishment, to take into consideration his future dangerousness. In most legal systems such offenders, i. e., persons suffering from mental disorders not amounting to mental illness, are held to be responsible for their actions. At the same time, however, some leniency in punishment is allowed, though not a significant amount.

The English law regarding provocation is a good example in this context. The defense of provocation is limited to the offense of murder. A person who committed murder under provocation will be charged with manslaughter only. English law has consistently held that the test in such cases should be an objective one, i. e., the test of the reasonable man, and that no account should be taken of individual mental disorders peculiar to that specific defendant [2]. Thus, for instance, the defense of provocation will not be granted simply because the specific defendant was exceedingly impulsive and hot tempered, and not even if he was neurotic or otherwise mentally disturbed. This doctrine was changed in the Model Penal Code of the

American Law Institute [3], which stipulated that the test for provocation should be a subjective one, i.e., it should take into account mental disorders of specific defendants. The English Homicide Act of 1957 also stated that mental disorders not amounting to mental illness might justify a conviction for manslaughter instead of murder [4]. We can thus see that the trend in modern law is to take into consideration mental disorders not amounting to mental illness, but this consideration is limited to mitigating factors only, and never leads to complete absolution from criminal liability.

We shall now turn to an analysis of this attitude of the law, and to an examination of its justifications. In order to simplify the discussion, we shall start by describing summarily two concrete cases that were recently dealt with in the Israeli courts. The first one relates to a compulsive gambler, the second one to a pyromaniac.

The Compulsive Gambler

The defendant, aged 44, was a senior clerk in a certain bank in Tel Aviv. In 1978 he started to commit a series of acts of theft and forgery in the bank. Within 1 year he had obtained from the bank, by false and forged documents, a total sum of about half a million dollars. On these offenses he was charged in the Tel Aviv District Court. The Court was told that he had lost all the embezzled money in gambling. In recent years he had left home almost every evening to spend whole nights gambling. During the day he functioned normally. A psychiatrist testified that the defendant had developed an infantile neurosis and that he was a compulsive gambler and in need of psychotherapy. The Court found the defendant criminally responsible for his acts and sentenced him to 6 years' imprisonment, stating that, although the defendant acted under the influence of mental disorder, this fact in itself could not be a decisive factor in determining the defendant's sentence. In approving the sentence, the Supreme Court [5] stated that both legally and morally the defendant should be judged like any other person committing an offense. In the same way, according to the Supreme Court's argument, as the court will not mitigate the sentence of a thief just because he acted out of a strong greed for money that he could not overcome, in the same way as we are not allowed to be lenient in sentencing a person convicted of sexual attack just because he was unable to overcome his sexual desire, so it is not a mitigating factor that the appellant in this case acted out of a compulsion for gambling. "Society, concluded the Court, is entitled to defend itself against him by sentencing him to imprisonment. The psychological treatment he needs he can also get in prison." The sentence of 6 year's imprisonment was upheld and the appeal disallowed.

The Pyromaniacal Captain

The second case relates to a captain of the Israel Defense Forces aged 32, married with three children, who was in charge of a squad of firemen in one of the biggest Israeli Air Force camps. In the course of 1 year he had committed 12 acts of arson in the camp, setting fire to various buildings and to huge quantities of ammunition and supplies. The damage he caused amounted to $ 1 million. The acts of arson were committed once or twice a month. The defendant would arrive at the place using his military car, and would then set fire to an object according to a prearranged plan. He would immediately return home or to the fire station, where he would await an alarm call to which he would quickly respond, bringing in his fire brigade to extinguish the fire, a task he would accomplish with much devotion and skill.

At last he was apprehended and brought to trial before a military court. Both prosecution and defense called psychiatric experts, who were unanimous in the opinion that the defendant was a pyromaniac. They differed, however, as to whether or not he acted under a completely irresistible impulse. The defendant was born in Rumania of a poor family who lived with four children in one room. When he was 10 years old his family moved to Israel. His self-image during most of his childhood years was very negative. He remembered himself as a thin, ragged, dirty child, despised by his friends. At the age of 16 he had joined the fire brigade scouts, where he had found great satisfaction. When he was conscripted into the army he made every effort to join the military fire brigade. When he finally succeeded, he devoted himself completely and compulsively to his job. Nothing but his work in the fire brigade was important to him. He was extremely pedantic and tough, and did not rely on anybody else, insisting on being personally involved in every activity. During the last year, so he told the psychiatrist, he had felt very tense and had suffered from internal stress. He used to calm himself by driving, and began to feel an urge to light fires. In the evening he would sit at home waiting until his wife fell asleep, and then leave home and quietly set fire to the preplanned objects. During the setting of the fire he would feel completely relaxed. When busy afterward extinguishing the fire he acted calmly, professionally, and with no feeling of excitement or tension whatsoever. Only the next morning would he have feelings of remorse, fear of punishment, and anxiety about what would become of his career. He understood that his conduct was immoral, but neither logic nor conscience could prevent him from committing arson. The military court found him guilty and sentenced him to imprisonment for 12 years. On appeal [6] his sentence was reduced to 9 years. The court explained that were it not for the defendant's mental disturbances, they would have inflicted the maximum penalty, which would have amounted, in the circumstances, to some 30 years' imprisonment.

Discussion

Cases of criminal acts committed on the grounds of mental disorder not amounting to mental illness present most difficult penological problems. On the one hand it is clear that in such cases there is no complete correlation between the moral blameworthiness and the actual damage done. In cases of a criminal act committed by a mentally ill person, as, for instance, by a schizophrenic, it is commonly agreed that no moral blame whatsoever exists, the reason being that a mentally ill person acts under the influence of an illness which completely dominates him and disturbs his mental faculties.

On the other hand, in cases of criminal offenses committed under the influence of mental disorders such as pyromania or compulsive gambling, it is generally agreed that there is some degree of moral blame, though this is considerably diminished because of the mental disorder.

The legal approach in cases of criminal acts committed because of mental disorders can theoretically be one of the following:

1. To absolve the defendant completely from any criminal sanction whatsoever, because it was a product of mental disorder
2. To ignore the factor of the mental disorder as long as it has not reached the degree of real mental illness, i.e., psychosis, and to fix the punishment in accordance with the actual damage done
3. As a compromise between these two extremes
   - to give decisive weight to the factor of mental disorder, or
   - to give decisive weight to the factor of the actual damage done.

The second approach, i.e., fixing the punishment proportionately to the actual damage done, is proposed by proponents of the retributive school in penology, which in recent years has gradually gained more and more supporters among scholars of various faculties. Thus, for instance, David Fogel [7] recommends a system of criminal law that will fix the precise punishment which the court will impose on each crime, allowing very little room for the discretion of the judge on account of extenuating circumstances relating to the offender or to the offense.

A similar approach is recommended by Andrew von Hirsch [8]. These scholars and their followers demand a penological approach which is decisively retributive with no pretence of correctional aims, simply fixing the punishment in accordance with the severity of the actual crime committed.

It should be noted, however, that this system has already been practiced in the past when, under the influence of classified penology, the French Code Pénal of 1891 fixed very detailed and inflexible punishments for all kinds and degrees of offenses [9], the main reason being to prevent disparity of the punishments inflicted by various courts on various defendants. This system, as is very well known, completely failed, because it was soon discovered that the outcome was in many cases very harsh, and that the deficiencies of such a system strongly outweigh its advantages.

The approach which appeals to us as being most just is based on the principle expressed most profoundly by H. L. A. Hart in his now classic essay, "Prolegomenon to the Principles of Punishment" [10]. In this essay Hart has shown that criminal punishment can never be founded on only one of the four common justifications for punishment: retribution, deterrence, prevention, and rehabilitation. In most cases, punishment is inflicted for the achievement of more than one of the abovementioned goals - goals which quite frequently contradict each other. The final decision in each case is a compromise between these conflicting goals with more weight given to one or another aim, according to the particular circumstances of the case and of the person in question:

> In dealing with these and other questions concerning punishment we should bear in mind that in this, as in most other social institutions, the pursuit of one aim may be qualified by . . . the pursuit of others. Till we have developed this sense of the complexity of punishment . . . we shall be in no fit state to assess the extent to which the whole institution has been eroded by, or needs to be adapted to, new beliefs about the human mind . . . Justice requires that those who have special difficulties to face in keeping the law which they have broken should be punished less [10].

The sentencing of a defendant who acted under the influence of a grave mental disorder not amounting to mental illness must be done by taking into consideration the following two main purposes, which, in the present case, conflict with each other. From a mere moralistic retributive point of view, the punishment could have been a light one because of the major part of the mental disturbance involved. There is, however, the deterrent aim of punishment, which the law cannot ignore. There are sometimes circumstances which minimize to a large extent the immorality of a specific criminal act, and yet there is no possibility of waiving punishment completely because of deterrent considerations. When a person steals bread and milk from a grocery because he and his family suffer from hunger, few people would despise his conduct morally, yet there is no alternative but to punish him for this act; otherwise it would mean that there was a general license to steal in similar circumstances. This principle was very concisely and clearly expressed in the following verse in Proverbs (6:30):

> Men do not despise a thief
> if he steals to satisfy his soul when he is hungry.
> But if he be found
> he must restore sevenfold.
> He must give all the substance of his house.

The same holds true regarding offenses committed as a result of mental disturbances. Such mental disturbance considerably diminishes the immorality of the act, but it still does not completely annul it. That is why there is some justification for leniency in the sentencing of a pyromaniac or of a compulsive gambler. But such leniency cannot go too far, otherwise it could be interpreted as a general permit to a pyromaniac to set fire to buildings, and to a compulsive gambler to embezzle and cheat.

The same argument does not apply, however, to cases of criminal acts committed by people subject to mental illness, not only because mental illness is much more dramatic and far-reaching than mere mental disorders, but also because in most countries mental illness in itself does not absolve one from criminal liability unless it has produced such a state of mind that te defendant could not understand what he did or that it was wrong, or unless he was subject to an irresistible impulse. In all such cases there is a complete disorganization of the personality and a gross misinterpretation of reality, so that the patient is not at all influenced by the law's attitude to his offense.

On the other hand, in cases of mental disorders such as pyromania and compulsive gambling, the defendant is very well aware of what the law has to say regarding his conduct. Telling a pyromaniac in advance that he is not criminally liable for his acts might only encourage him to proceed and carry on with further acts of arson without trying to seek psychiatric help.

This is the justification for the legal approach to criminal acts committed under the influence of mental disorder not amounting to mental illness: on the one hand, not absolving a person from criminal liability for his actions, while on the other hand taking such mental disorders into consideration as a mitigating factor.

References

1. Reese JT (1979) Obsessive compulsive behavior: the nuisance offender. Polygraph: 8 (3): 258-270
2. Williams G (1954) Provocation and the reasonable man. Crim L Rev 740
3. MPCS (1962) 210.3 (1) (b)
4. Homicide Act 1957. See also: Fletcher G (1978) Rethinking criminal law. Little, Brown, Boston, p 250
5. Israel Supreme Court judgments, Cr A 292/81
6. Military appeals 440/8
7. Fogel D (1975) We are the living proof: the justice model of corrections. Anderson, Cincinnati
8. Von Hirsch A (1976) Doing justice - the choice of punishments. Report of the Committee for the Study of Incarceration Hill and Wang, New York. See also: Task Force on Criminal Sentencing (1976) Fair and certain punishment - report of the Twentieth Century Fund, McGraw-Hill, New York
9. Radzinowicz L (1966) Ideology and crime. New York, Columbia University Press, chap 2
10. Hart HLA (1968) Prolegomenon to the principles of punishment. In: Punishment and responsibility. Oxford University Press, London chap 1, pp 1-27

Psychiatric Evaluation of Criminal Accused

Y. Z. Zadik

Introduction

Sir John Wood, in the 55th Maudsley Lecture, discusses the impact of legal modes of thought upon the practice of psychiatry, and he notes that "the criminal process has turned increasingly to psychiatry to help to solve some of its own intractable problems" [7, p. 552]. The main topics concern issues of volition, free will, criminal responsibility, and competency to stand trial. These highly important philosophical and social issues are beyond the scope of this paper [8]. While these issues remain under debate, a system has been built for referring people accused of criminal acts for psychiatric evaluation. The description of this procedure and the characteristics of those involved is the topic of this paper.

Lately, John Hinckley's acquittal as not guilty of the attempted assassination of President Reagan has focused puplic opinion on the use of psychiatric evaluations during trial. Time magazine even published an article named: "Is the System Guilty? - A Stunning Verdict Puts the Insanity Defense on Trial" [6].

What is the procedure for referring people accused or suspected of criminal acts for psychiatric evaluation in Israel? Section 6 D of the Treatment of Mental Patients Law 1955 enables the court to refer defendants for medical evaluation, with hospitalization if necessary. Section 6A, B enables the court to send someone under detention for medical examination, and the District Psychiatrist can order his hospitalization for observation. After the court's decision, the person involved (either charged or in detention) is taken by police to the District Psychiatrist, where a psychiatrist examines him. If the psychiatric status is clear to the examiner, a medical report is sent to the court. If the psychiatric status is not clear, the person accused is sent for observation in a psychiatric hospital. The length of the observation is determined by the court, but the hospital can ask (and sometimes does) for more days of observation. According to the medical report the court decides whether to proceed with the detention or trial, or to order the forced hospitalization of the person concerned (section 6A or 6B). This is the procedure in principle, but many questions arise. Who are these people, and do they have some common demographic characteristics (regarding their sex, age, education, religion, place of birth, marital status)? Is there a typical person, or can they be divided into several clearly defined groups? Are they under detention or have they been charged? Who prompts this referral for psychiatric evaluation: the accused, his lawyer (if he has one), the police, or the court itself? Are these people sent by the magistrates court or by the district court? Do some judges send more accused people for psychiatric evaluation than others? What types of offenses are they accused of? What questions are asked by the court and what answers are given by the hospital's staff? Do the accused sent for observation have previous criminal records? Had they been sent for such an evaluation by

courts in the past? Had they been hospitalized before in a psychiatric hospital or ward? What is the diagnosis given at the end of the evaluation or hospitalization? Are the accused people diagnosed mainly as psychopaths or as psychotics? How many of them are later hospitalized under court order because they were found to be incompetent to stand trial or not criminally responsible?

The data presented here are based on the case records of 120 consecutive cases referred to the Tirat-Carmel Psychiatric Hospital from 1979 to 1982, by court orders for psychiatric observations and evaluation. This analysis is important and can lead to important conclusions. Nevertheless, it must be mentioned that the hospital records might not include all relevant information. For instance, if the accused had a previous criminal record dating back some years and in another region, it might not have been reported to the hospital. There were a number of cases in which the same person had been sent for psychiatric observation to the hospital more than once, sometimes on a new charge. There are two possible means of avoiding statistical problems in this respect. Bluestone et al. [1] decided to eliminate this group and to analyze these cases in a separate paper, as they assumed that those who were repeatedly sent for competency examinations represented a more problematic group. In the present study it was decided to include these cases within the sample, but to consider only their first referral from the court for psychiatric observation in the hospital.

Results

The demographic characteristics of the simple are summarized in Table 1. The level of education was surprisingly low: only 13.3% were high school graduates and only 3.3% had a college degree.

Table 1. Demographic variables

Sex		
Male	110 (91.6%)	
Female	10 (8.3%)	
Age (years)		
16–19	5 (4.1%)	Average 32
20–29	63 (52.5%)	
30–39	25 (20.8%)	
40–49	14 (11.6%)	
50–59	9 (7.5%)	
60–69	3 (2.5%)	
70–79	0	
80	1 (0.8%)	
Marital status		
Single	75 (62.5%)	
Married	30 (25%)	
Divorced	10 (8.3%)	
Widowed	5 (4.1%)	
Ethnic group		
Jewish	104 (86.6%)	
Sephardic	67 (64.4%)	
Ashkenazi	37 (35.5%)	

Table 1. Demographic variables *(continued)*

Arab	11 (9.1%)
Druze	4 (3.3%)
Other	1 (0.8%)
Place of birth	
Israel	66 (55%)
Years of formal education	
0–8	59 (49.1%)
9–12	31 (25.8%)
13–	10 (8.3%)
Unknown	10 (8.3%)

The legal variables are summarized in Table 2; while the psychiatric variables are summarized in Table 3. Half of the referred (52.5%) had previously been in a psychiatric hospital not for evaluation for the court but for treatment. For 15% of the referred, it was not the first time they had been sent by courts for psychiatric observation within a hospital setting. For 40% of the referred this hospitalization was the first and only contact, up until now, with the psychiatric hospital system.

With respect to the type of offenses, 39.1% of the referred were accused of offenses against body and 26.6% were accused of offenses against property. There was a very narrow overlap, with only 4.1% accused both of offenses against people and against property. Of the 11 cases of sex offenses, three of the accused were found to be psychotic, six to have personality disorders, and two to be mentally retarded.

Only in 24% of those detained but not yet charged was a criminal charge presented while they were under observation in the hospital (19 out of 58 + 19). While 94% of those detained but not yet charged were sent by the magistrates' court, 75%

Table 2. Legal variables

Source of referral	
Magistrates court	83 (69.1%)
District court	37 (30.8%)
Legal status while under observation	
Under detention	58 (48.3%)
Detained and later charged	19 (15.8%)
Charged at beginning	43 (35.8%)
Previous forensic psychiatric observation	18 (15%)
Previous criminal record	39 (32.5%)
Type of offense	
Against body	47 (39.1%)
Against property	32 (26.6%)
Against morals (fraud)	8 (6.6%)
Sex	11 (9.1%)
Drugs	10 (8.3%)
Against national security	3 (2.5%)
Against humans and property	5 (4.1%)
Against morals and security	1 (0.8%)
Against property and morals	3 (2.5%)

of those hospitalized with a criminal charge were sent by the district court ($x^2 = 60.31$, df = 1, $p < 0.001$).
It seems that most of those referred for psychiatric observation were brought by the police to the magistrates court, and there a magistrate decided to send them for psychiatric observation. During their stay in hospital they were legally in detention. Only in 20% of the cases was the name of the magistrate written clearly. For this reason, and also because most referrals were made by the magistrate on duty, the question of whether some magistrates were more keen than others on psychiatric evaluation cannot be answered. The details of the discussions in court were very difficult to read (as they were written by hand). Only in 6.6% of the referrals were specific questions asked by the court. Most of the referrals required a general report of the accused's mental state.

Table 3. Psychiatric variables

Previous nonforensic psychiatric hospitalization	63 (52.5%)
Hospital diagnosis at end of observation	
Schizophrenic psychosis	37 (30.8%)
Depressive psychosis	3 (2.5%)
Paranoid psychosis	5 (4.1%)
Organic psychosis	1 (0.8%)
Psychotic episode	4 (3.3%)
Neurosis	0 (0%)
Reactive anxiety	2 (1.6%)
Posttraumatic disorder	1 (0.8%)
Personality disorder	57 (47.5%)
Mental retardation	9 (7.5%)
No diagnosis	1 (0.8%)

The "answers" of the hospital's psychiatrists were varied, and a thorough content analysis of them needs a separate presentation. Generally, most medical reports discussed the issues of competency to stand trial and of criminal responsibility, and some of them included a psychiatric diagnosis. It seems that the psychiatrists knew what specific questions the court wanted answered, even though the court's referral seldom contained specific questions.

While under observation, 23.3% of the accused were referred for psychodiagnostic testing. The main psychiatric diagnosis for these people were as follows: 30.8% were diagnosed as schizophrenics (mostly paranoid schizophrenics), five were diagnosed as paranoid psychotics, three as depressive psychotics, one as an organic psychotic, and none as manic. Taken together, 41.6% of the sample were considered psychotic. Almost half of the sample (47.5%) were diagnosed as having personality disorders, most of them antisocial. No correlation was found between diagnosis and crime category.

No information concerning the verdicts on those found competent to stand trial and criminally responsible was available in hospital records. However, 18.3% of the sample were referred again by the court, not for observation but for forced hospitalization after having been pronounced incompetent to stand trial or not criminally responsible.

To sum up, the typical person referred for psychiatric observation within a hospital setting is male, aged between 20 and 40, single, Jewish, and of Sephardic origin, and has a low level of education. He is sent by the magistrates court while under detention but before being charged.

Discussion

Several surveys have been conducted in the United States regarding referrals by courts for psychiatric evaluation. Contrary to the case in Israel, special centers have been organized for this purpose. According to Cooke et al. [3], all competency evaluations in the state of Michigan are, by law, conducted by the Center for Forensic Psychiatry. Henn et al. [4] describe the Forensic Service at the St. Louis City Hospital. In Israel, the psychiatric evaluations are done within regular closed wards. A question worth considering is whether it is appropriate to put people under detention and not yet charged (some maybe mistakenly arrested) with psychiatric patients.

A review of 22 years of the Forensic Service in St. Louis [4] shows considerable changes over the years in the distribution of demographic variables and in the types of offenses. Several other studies [3] show a lot of inconsistency concerning the types of offenses of the referred in various states. It seems that a very important variable is the difference between states in how often certain crimes occur. The present survey should be compared to findings in other regions of Israel, or in other hospitals. It is also important to see if these results remain stable over certain periods of time.

Much research has been done concerning the differences in diagnostic practices between countries and among hospitals. These differences probably also affect the distribution of diagnoses among the accused referred for psychiatric observation. Contrary to expectation, there is considerable consistency in several surveys. Cooke et al. [3] review seven such surveys, and they conclude that these studies generally indicate that most patients referred for competency evaluations are not psychotic. The studies cited vary as to the percentage of patients classified as psychotic (ranging from 10% to 47%). Most of the patients fall into the character disorder category, with most studies reporting only a few patients classified as other than psychotic or having a character disorder. The results of the present study are very similar: 41% were considered psychotic, and only 10.9% neither were psychotic nor had personality disorders.

Attention should be directed to the difference between the percentage of diagnoses of psychosis (41.6%) and the percentage of cases sent for forced hospitalization by the court because incompetency to stand trial or being not criminally responsible (18.3%). While most of those hospitalized by court order for treatment were diagnosed as psychotics (95.0%) (mostly schizophrenia), more than half of those who were diagnosed as belonging to the psychotic spectrum were sent back to court. The reason seems to lie in the episodic nature of many psychoses. Someone may have been responsible at the time of the alleged crime even though he had been psychotic in the past and hospitalized many times. It should also be noted that competency to stand trial is not always a stable feature. One can commit an offense while responsible for one's acts, then develop a psychotic state after arrest, but be competent to stand trial after a short period of intensive drug treatment. The survey indicates that someone can be regarded as a schizophrenic and still be held responsible for his deeds and be considered competent to stand trial.

Some studies have found a lot of mental patients inside prisons [5]. Some studies describe a trend of diverting the mentally ill into the criminal justice system [2]. The present study suggests that some psychiatric patients may end up in jail not because of disregard of their diagnoses but in spite of them. They were diagnosed as psychiatric patients, but yet found competent to stand trial and criminally responsible.

What about those referred more than once for psychiatric observation, comprising 15% of the sample? A special analysis of their diagnoses revealed almost identical distribution with the whole sample.

A closer analysis revealed three types of accused persons who were reffered more than once:

1. Those whose mental status changed as a result of the natural episodic nature of their illness, or as a result of treatment
2. Hard-core criminals who were referred every time they were arrested for a new crime
3. Persons referred for mandatory observation immediately after they had been observed in another hospital, although no new offense had been committed. These were cases of very severe crimes, where the court wanted the accused observed in more than one hospital. The impression is that the psychiatrists are seldom called for questioning and cross-examination, and instead the accused is sent to another hospital for yet another set of tests, inquiries, and interviews.

Conclusion

The process of referring people accused of criminal acts for mandatory psychiatric observation has been described in detail, and some characteristics of those involved have been examined. Some questions remain unanswered. As the present study is based on hospital case records, there are some important links missing.

It is very important to examine the efficiency of the District Psychiatrist's office in preventing unneccessary commitment for observation, by making the psychiatric observation ambulatorily. In view of the low percentage of people found to be incompetent to stand trial or not criminally responsible (only 18% of the sample were later hospitalized for these reasons), methods should be devised for making the observation within an outpatient facility. This is important not only because hospitalization is very costly, but especially because a psychiatric hospitalization can damage the accused's potential for social rehabilitation. It should be noted that many people in detention are never charged. This might lead to a situation where a person was mistakenly arrested, then sent for psychiatric observation in a closed ward, found competent to stand trial, and sent back to the police, only to be released because there was no evidence against him. He would carry the stigma of being hospitalized in a psychiatric hospital and the unpleasant memory of having been committed to a closed ward. Such cases can be minimized if an effort is made to refer an accused only after a criminal charge has been presented.

As mentioned, the verdicts of the court are unknown to the hospital. Such information would be helpful feedback for the hospital's staff. It is interesting and highly important to check the use or misuse of the medical report made by the court and all the participants in the criminal justice system - how well it is understood and how it affects the decisions of the court.

References

1. Bluestone H, Melella J, Baskin D (1981) A study of criminal defendants referred for multiple psychiatric examinations (regarding their competency to stand tria). Journal of Forensic Sciences 26 (2): 416-423
2. Bonovitz JC, Bonovitz JS (1981) Diversion of the mentally ill into the criminal justice system: the police intervention perspective. American Journal of Psychiatry 138 (7): 973-976
3. Cooke G, Johnston N, Pogany E (1973) Factors affecting referral to determine competency to stand trial. American Journal of Psychiatry 130 (8): 870-875
4. Henn FA, Herjanic M, Vanderpearl RH (1977) Forensic psychiatry: anatomy of a service. Comprehensive Psychiatry 18 (4): 337-345
5. Lamb HR, Grant RW (1982) The mentally ill in an urban county jail. Archives of General Psychiatry 39: 17-22
6. Leo S (1982) Is the system guilty. (A stunning verdict puts the insanity defense on trial). Time, 5 July, pp 25-26)
7. Wood J (1982) The impact of legal modes of thought upon the practice of psychiatry. British Journal of Psychiatry 140: 551-557
8. Wootton B (1980) Psychiatry, ethics and the criminal law. British Journal of Psychiatry 136: 525-532

Criminal Liability: Psychiatric Evaluation vs. Legal Tests

A. Elizur and M. Moser

In the course of a criminal trial, there are several stages at which a court may resort to psychiatric opinion as to the mental state of the accused. First, the psychiatrist may be called upon at the commencement of preliminary proceedings, and henceforth at any later stage, to present his professional opinion as to the defendant's competency to stand trial. Here the question concerns the present mental state of the accused at the time of the proceedings, and whether he is able to undergo such proceedings.

The job of the psychiatrist is to evaluate the mental status of the patient in at least three areas:

1. Clarity of consciousness and orientation.
2. Cognitive capacity to understand the process of the trial; and in addition.
3. Ability to assist the counsel provided for the defense.

It should be noted that an opinion determining the incompetency of the accused to stand trial due to mental illness has no bearing whatsoever either on the nature of the relationship between the criminal act and existing mental disturbances, or on the extent to which the accused was criminally responsible and what state of mind can be attributed to him at the time that the offense was committed.

At the second stage, the defendant having been found competent to stand trial, the psychiatrist may be asked during the defense pleadings to testify to the degree of criminal responsibility which may be attributed to the accused. Israeli law, unlike American and European legal systems, limits the discussion to two possible extremes: the accused must either be found fully responsible for his act(s), or be totally absolved of any responsibility for their perpetration.

Exoneration from criminal responsibility due to mental illness is based on one of two factors, according to the law:

1. Lack of "knowledge" [1], according to which the accused lacks the intellectual ability to understand the nature of his act(s). This may be based on either of the following findings:
   - Failure of the mind to grasp the meaning of the physical nature and illegality of the act
   - Lack of such moral judgment as is necessary in order to be able to tell right from wrong
2. The "irresistible impulse": here it must be determined that the defendant, at the time of the act, suffered from an impulse he could not control and which brought him to commit the said act [23].

In both of the above, such a defense can only be applied if a direct connection is proved between the mental illness and the act the time of its perpetration. Mental illness is strictly defined, and includes only psychosis.

There are no provisions in Israeli law for partial or diminshed responsibility due to mental deficiency, notwithstanding the recognized existence of many varied mental disorders which impair the mental facilities, and which extend far beyond the two above-mentioned legal criteria. The relationship between behavior of a criminal type and the underlying mental disorder is a very complex one. Each type of behavior may be facilitated or inhibited by many factors. Some of the facilitating factors are: drive, impulse, temptation, wish, motivation, intentions, expectation, and goal. Some of the factors that may inhibit, control, modify, or sublimate the behavior are: cognitive factors (intellect, reality testing, learning ability, etc.), affective factors (emotional involvement, ability to use anxiety as internal signal for control, etc.), moral factors (shame, guilt, moral judgment, etc.), volition, and level of consciousness (orientation, awareness). Thus the question of irresponsibility should be extended in view of our broad understanding of aberrant human behavior.

Stage three comes after the verdict, when, prior to sentencing, a psychiatric evaluation of the accused's capacity to undergo punishment may be submitted. The purpose of this psychiatric evaluation is to give an opinion on how to fit the punishment, not to the crime, but to the personality of the accused, and in particular to his mental state. An additional purpose is to indicate how much of a threat is posed by the accused, both to himself and to society, which may be related also to his ability to express feelings of guilt and repentance. The third purpose is to evaluate the accused as to his potential for future education and reform through therapeutic intervention.

Israeli law, as mentioned above, does not officially recognize diminished or partial responsibility. In reality, there are many cases where it is possible for the courts to reach a clear decision, as required, in the matter of criminal liability. Such a dilemma can often be noted in the psychiatric evaluations submitted. Courts, being limited to an either/or decision, resort to various alternative decisions in such cases. These solutions differ and, being merely substitutes for a proper solution, are often inappropriate for the situation that they are called to deal with. We will demonstrate, with reference to several criminal cases, what difficulties arise when a defendant in a criminal prosecution who suffers from mental disorders cannot be said to fall into either of the present categories.

The first two cases are of patients suffering from schizophrenia. They had both been committed to hospitals several times in an acute state of their illness. There is no doubt that both of them suffered from severe psychotic illnesses. The course of their illness was intermittent. During the remission time, they suffered only from the residual symptoms of their illnesses, mainly impoverishment of affect and poor judgment. Both were sent by court order for psychiatric evaluation, after having been caught committing an indecent act against a minor. In each case, the act was committed during a remission period. Thus, according to the M'Naghten rule, they could not be considered legally irreresponsible for their criminal acts.

In the first patient, psychiatric examination showed the accused to be aware of his behavior. He was able to grasp the significance and moral nature of the offense. This patient also planned his act with all due care and deliberation, so as to escape detection. However, it was evident to us that the deed resulted from impaired judgment and affect due to the chronic illness. We recommended that he be declared fit to stand trial and responsible for his acts, but that because of his illness, partial responsibility should be considered. We recommended that a suitable punishment be found, involving psychiatric treatment, instead of his being sent to jail. Nevertheless, the court, upon finding him guilty, sentenced him to jail. The end result was that his mental state eventually deteriorated and he was finally sent to hospital.

The second patient gave the clinical impression of having committed an unplanned, unpremeditated, and silly act. The inevitable conclusion was that his behavior was a result of a severe impairment of judgment. Thus he was found by psychiatry not to be responsible for his act. Nevertheless, according to legal criteria the examination failed to show that the accused was incapable of understanding what he had done, nor did it show that the patient had fallen victim to an irresistible impulse. Thus, contrary to our recommendation, the judge did not find him irresponsible. He decided on hospitalization only because the accused was unable to stand trial, and did not deal at all with the problem of criminal responsibility, presumably because of the impossibility of applying the existing strict legal criteria to such a situation. The consequence of such a decision for the patient was a grave one. According to Israeli law, such a patient can be released from hospital only by decision of a Psychiatric Board, and must then face a criminal indictment, still pending, subject to decision by the Attorney General on whether to reactivate proceedings. But because he committed his criminal act while he was in the chronic and not in the acute stage of his illness, he will never in his life be allowed to be discharged from hospital.

The other two patients whom we will describe suffered from one of a typical group of mental disorders named "disorders of impulse control" [4, 5]. Their criminal act was a symptom of pyromania, which involves a failure to resist an impulse to set fire to things, where this irresistible impulse is not due to psychotic illness. The following are the essential features of the DSM III description of pyromania [6].

1. The individual fails to resist an impulse, drive, or temptation to set fires that are harmful to himself or to others.
   - There may or may not be conscious resistance to the impulse.
   - The act may or may not be premeditated or planned.
2. He suffers an increasing sense of tension before setting the fire.
3. He experiences either pleasure, gratification, or release at the time of committing the act. The act is ego-syntonic, in that it is consonant with the immediate conscious wish of the individual. Immediately following the act there may or may not be genuine regret, self-reproach, or guilt.
4. There is no logical motivation, such as monetary gain or sociopolitical ideology, for setting fires.
5. It is not due to an organic brain syndrome, schizophrenia, or antisocial personality disorder.

The first patient did not present any mental symptoms until the 1973 war, when he underwent a traumatic battle experience and witnessed tanks burning and many casualties. At the climax of his excitation, he felt relaxed by masturbation. From then onward he started to set fires, compulsively driven by the reexperience of the traumatic episode, again culminating in masturbation. The only motivation for this criminal act was unconscious and was related to his traumatic experience. It was obvious that there was no benefit-seeking behavior on his part. Despite an evaluation by the psychiatric consultant to this effect, his plea of an irresistible impulse was rejected, because his state was not diagnosed as a "psychotic illness" but as a lack of impulse control due to pyromania. The judge, instead, ruled him unable to stand trial at the time. After successful treatment in our hospital, his condition improved; he was cured of his pyromanic symptoms. He was able to be discharged and to become a fully functioning member of the community. Despite this recommendation of the psychiatric consultant, the Psychiatric Board decided that he must retain the status of a patient "on leave" from the hospital. He has to wait from one psychiatric board to the next, and a criminal indictment is still pending.

The second patient also suffered from pyromania. He was the head of a fire-extinguishing department. His impulse to set fires started a year before he was finally caught. His premorbid personality can be described as being characterized by a schizotypal disorder. He was an unwanted and emotionally neglected child. During the examination, it became clear that he had failed several times to resist an impulse to set a fire. He experienced an increased sense of tension before committing the act and gratification and release at the time of committing it. All these factors fit the definition of pyromania. However, it was consciously premeditated and carefully planned. He was also motivated by the expectation of gain. The judge found the defendant fully responsible, despite his illness. He took no account of the severe mental problems of the accused and their probable contribution to the commission of the criminal act. The severe sentence was reduced only on appeal.

These cases illustrate two aspects of the difficulties in the interface between psychiatry and the law which arise in the defense of the criminal patient. In the first two cases, despite the accused's severe psychosis, the psychiatrist was not able to prove that the act was due to the illness, nor that the patient was incapable of "knowing" what he was doing. Thus, even if the "criminal acts" were due to a severe impairment of judgment and affective involvement on the part of the patients, the latter could not be considered largely irresponsible according to the strict legal criteria.

In the second two cases the criminal acts were due to an irresistible impulse, a symptom of pyromania [4]. This definite mental disorder is not regarded as a psychotic disorder. In previous American and international classifications it was categorized as a compulsive neurosis. Today, it is classified as a personality disorder [5]. Thus the patients cannot be exempted from criminal responsibility. However, this symptomatic behavior is a result of many factors and determinants based on emotional conflicts. This should be explored and carefully evaluated. The patient has to be assessed according to all dynamic factors involved in his past history and present behavior. Our patients illustrate that even in cases with the same diagnosis, the psychiatric recommendations can be different.

These cases also illustrate that even if Israeli law does not adopt the law of diminished responsibility, the psychiatrists and the judges take the psychological problems into account in the trial process. However, these attempts to apply the present law in the face of the diversity of mental problems are only marginally successful and often heavy-handed and inappropriate, and may be harmful to the patient.

We believe that the concept of partial responsibility should be applied to cases in which abnormality of the mind of any etiology substantially impaired the accused's mental responsibility. It should be stated clearly that those of us who believe in the concept of partial responsibility do not intend all psychopaths to be set free. We also believe that punishment, in those cases where partial responsibility is recognized to exist, should be adapted to each special case, and that alternative and suitable psychiatric treatment should be considered.

The conventional system, under which there is no provision for partial responsibility and no special treatment is given to those who are partially responsible, has proved itself wrong - the percentage of recidivism is almost 80% in Israel. Society should not abandon the belief that things can and should be done better.

Therefore, we should like to join the Israeli Supreme Court in its recommendation for a reform in the system of punishment that will give the courts and society tools with which to treat those who are partially responsible. The Israeli Supreme Court said in the case of *Ladani* v. *the State of Israel:* "Courts should be given rightful tools of punishment for those cases worthy of consideration in which the mental state or other specific circumstances place them in the category of partial responsibility" [8].

However, the problem is not only one of new laws, but also of how to explore and find ways to implement the law and punishment for those who need psychiatric care. Punishment in these cases should go hand in hand with treatment, so that in the long run results will be vastly improved.

References

1. Daniel M'Naghten's case 1843. 8 Eng Rep 722–723
2. Mandelbrot V (1953) Attorny General Criminal A 118/53 Supreme Court Judgments, vol 10, p 181
3. Mesan V (1955) Attorney General Criminal A 186/55 Supreme Court Judgments, vol 11, p 769
4. Lewis NDC, Yarnell H (1951) Pathological firesetting, nervous and mental diseases. New York
5. Winer JA, Pollock GH (1980) Disorders of impulse control. In: Kaplan HI, Freedman AM, Sadock BJ (eds) Comprehensive textbook of psychiatry, 3rd edn Williams and Wilkins, Baltimore, pp 1817–1829
6. Diagnostic and statistical manual of mental disorders, 3rd edn (1980) American Psychiatric Association
7. International classification of diseases, 9th revision. Clinical modification, ICD-9-CM (1980) US Department of Health and Human Services
8. Ladani V, State of Israel, Criminal A 870/80, Supreme Court Judgments, vol 36 I, p 29 (38)

The Insanity Defense: Current Law and Reform Options

G. Ferguson

Introduction

The issue of the proper scope of the insanity defense – and whether such a defense should even exist – has been hotly debated for at least the past 150 years. The longevity of the debate is testimony to its intractibility. As one commentator has observed, "Rivers of ink, mountains of printer's lead, forests of paper have been expended on this issue" [1]. Yet in spite of all this effort, no obvious solution has emerged.

In Canada, as part of its Criminal Code Review Project the Department of Justice is studying the need for legislative changes to current laws dealing with the mentally disordered accused. This review includes topics such as psychiatric remands, privilege against self-incrimination and confidentiality arising out of psychiatric evaluations, fitness to stand trial, disposition and release of mentally disordered offenders and, of course, the insanity defense. As a consultant in this review process, I have been asked to advise the Department of Justice on one of these topics, namely, "what changes, if any, should be made to the current law governing the insanity defence". In my opinion, an answer to that question requires an analysis of three other questions:

1. What is the current law?
2. What are the problems with the current law?
3. What alternatives exist and what are their advantages and disadvantages?

In this chapter, I will try to summarize very briefly the more extensive work which I have done on these three questions for the Department of Justice.

Current Law

The current Canadian insanity test was enacted in 1892 and is a slightly modified M'Naghten test [2]. Section 16 of the Canadian Criminal Code states that a person is insane "when he has a disease of the mind to an extent that renders him incapable of appreciating the nature and quality of an act or omission or of knowing that an act or omission is wrong" [3]. The principal Canadian gloss on the M'Naghten rules is the substitution of the word "appreciate" in the Canadian test for the word "know" in the M'Naghten rules. But does this substitution really make a difference?

In 1956, a Royal Commission on the Law of Insanity in Canada, investigating possible reform of the insanity defense, concluded that the Canadian test was not in need of reform since it was much wider than the M'Naghten test [4]. In particular, the Commission contended that although the word "wrong" in the M'Naghten test may only have meant "legally wrong," the word "wrong" in the Canadian test included both legally and morally wrong. Secondly, the Commission contended that although the word "know" in the M'Naghten test restricted the insanity test to a mere cognitive test, the expression "incapable of appreciating" in the Canadian test was much wider and went far beyond the mere cognitive nature of the M'Naghten test. Unfortunately, the Royal Commission's views have not been confirmed by recent Supreme Court of Canada decisions.

In 1976, in a five to four decision, the Supreme Court held in *Schwartz* v. *The Queen* [5] that "wrong" means legally wrong and does not include morally wrong. In 1980, in the twin cases of *Cooper* [6] and *Barnier* [7], the Supreme Court held that the expressions "know" and "appreciate" are not synonymous, that "appreciate" is wider in meaning than "know," and that it involves emotional as well as intellectual awareness of the impact and consequences of an act and an analysis of knowledge and experience. But in the subsequent cases of *Kjeldsen* [8] and *Abbey* [9], the Supreme Court effectively undercut its own broad interpretation of "appreciate." In *Kjeldsen,* the Supreme Court effectively excluded severe psychopathy from the scope of the insanity defense by holding that the word "appreciate" only requires that the accused know the nature of his act and its physical consequences. The emotional component of "appreciate" was dispensed with. In *Abbey,* the "physical consequences" test was further restricted. In addition, the *Abbey* case even casts doubts on whether foresight and understanding of the physical consequences must be reality-based. The Supreme Court held that Abbey was improperly acquitted on account of insanity on a charge of importing cocaine from Peru, even though he had delusional beliefs that he was protected from apprehension, conviction, and punishment by some "outside force" and that he had astrotravel fled from Peru to Canada.

In summary, the recent judicial interpretations of the insanity test in Canada have transmogrified what the Royal Commission thought was a unique Canadian test into little more than the old M'Naghten rule. In addition, it should be noted that Canadian courts have refused to recognize irresistible impulse as part of the insanity defense [10], and the Canadian test does not have a volitional component such as the United States' Model Penal Code test of "substantial capacity to conform his conduct to the requirements of the law" [11].

In Canada, the Crown prosecutor can impose the insanity defense on an unwilling accused [12]. In addition, if the accused decides to raise the insanity defense himself, he must prove it on a balance of probabilities [13]. If the insanity defense is proven, the judge or jury *must* return a special verdict of "not guilty on account of insanity" [14]. Once this verdict is returned, the court *must* automatically order that the accused be kept in strict custody until the Lieutenant Governor of the province decides to release him [15]. The Lieutenant Governor has unfettered discretion as to release. He does not have to grant the person a hearing or give reasons for his decision. His decisions are not subject to judicial review. In the light of these draconian provisions and the narrow M'Naghten-like test for insanity, it is not surprising that there have been many calls for reform.

Problems and criticisms of the insanity test

Some of the following criticisms relate to the insanity defense in general and others relate only to the specifics of the current Canadian test. I will deal with the general criticisms first.

1. Confusion exists as to the theoretical basis for the insanity defense. This confusion is in part due to the conflicting notions in criminal law between theories of subjective moral culpability and utilitarian concepts of social protection and deterrence.

2. The insanity defense is based on the assumption that human behavior is generally a product of free will, thereby eschewing theories of determinism and other modern insights into human behavior. The ability to reason is paramount. Other determinantes of behavior (e.g., heredity, social and cultural influences) are irrelevant except to the extent that they are seen as leading to "mental illnesses" that "affect the ability to reason."

3. The insanity defense is neither logical nor fair. If the law is going to recognize mental disorder which impairs free will as a defense, then why should not other factors (e.g., heredity, poverty, cultural deprivation) which may equally impair free will be recognized as defenses? The fear of jumping onto the slippery slope of determinism, pragmatic concerns about weakening social controls, and real problems with proof and evidence have been the main reasons for not allowing these other factors to act as defenses to crime.

4. It can be argued that the insanity defense is antitherapeutic. It encourages an accused to see himself as a helpless victim of his own sickness rather than encouraging him to be autonomous and to accept responsibility for his deviant behavior.

5. The state of mind of the accused is not susceptible to hard scientific evaluation in the same fashion as bloodstains, fingerprints, and other types of physical evidence. As the Hinckley case demonstrates, regardless of the intensity of the investigation no one, including the best-trained psychiatrists and psychologists, really knows for sure what was going on in the accused's head, what inner forces drove him, and to what extent he could have resisted those forces if he had only tried harder.

6. In spite of the uncertainty of psychiatric evaluations, some psychiatrists testify about an accused's mental state as if their testimony were authoritative, reliable, scientific fact, rather than educated guesswork. This can sometimes cause judges and juries to place too much reliance on expert opinion and thereby allow the finding of criminal responsibility to be converted into a medical decision rather than treating responsibility as the legal, moral, and social determination which it actually is.

7. Because of the uncertainty in determining who is sane and who is not, the insanity defense is essentially arbitrary. Some are acquitted, others are not, with no appar-

ent consistency. The insanity defense secretly ratifies discretion without guidelines. It is a guilt-avoidance mechanism which is selectively used for empathetic accused persons. The type of accused and victim, the nature of the crime, and other social factors have more to do with the outcome of an insanity trial than the legal test for insanity.

8. The public have a very poor opinion of the insanity defense, and this weakens their respect for the law. The public perceive that the insanity defense is an unwarranted guilt-avoidance mechanism in most cases, successfully raised in too many cases, and a danger to society since insanity acquittees are thought to be released back into the community too early. Though these beliefs about the insanity defense may be pure myth, they are destructive of public confidence in the criminal justice system.

9. The Canadian insanity test is too narrow. It only includes cognitive impairment, not volitional or emotional impairment. Incapacity to know that one's acts are morally wrong, caused by a disease of the mind, is not included within the insanity defense. The Canadian insanity test does not expressly recognize that substantial rather than total incapacity is sufficient.

10. The Canadian insanity test is supposedly based on cognitive impairment, but the test does not make it clear that rationality and ordinary perception of reality are prerequisites. *Mens rea* in the form of intent, knowledge, and purpose may exist both in a rational and in an irrational, delusional mind.

11. The Canadian test is so narrow that many seriously mentally disordered persons are convicted and sentenced to prison, where often they do not receive necessary psychiatric treatment.

12. The Canadian test contains archaic language, such as "natural imbecility," "disease of the mind," and "insane." In addition, the test contains vague or ill-defined expressions such as "capacity to appreciate" and "disease of the mind."

13. The stark choice between sanity and insanity does not adequately recognize degrees of responsibility and fault, nor does a doctrine of diminished responsibility currently exist to assist in this regard.

14. Disposition following an insanity plea is too rigid and lacks necessary safeguards such as due process and the right to appeal. Because insanity dispositions are so rigid and draconian, concerns about disposition tend to control the substance and scope of the insanity defense.

15. Requiring the accused to prove insanity on a balance of probabilities is an historical anomoly which is unnecessary and unfair. Likewise, allowing the Crown to impose the insanity defense on an unwilling accused is an unfair invasion into the accused's right to direct his own defense.

16. Experts testifying as to mental disorder should not be entitled to usurp the function of judge and jury by offering an opinion on the ultimate legal issue.

Alternatives and Options

Abolition

A call for abolition of the insanity defense is an understandable reaction to the long list of criticisms which I have briefly summarized. Abolition has been advocated by a number of prominent and thoughtful commentators [16]. Their reasons for advocating abolition and their alternatives to it are not identical. Thus abolition is not simply one option. It has several variations. Wootton suggests the abolition of notions of criminal responsibility and, with it, the insanity defense [17]. Goldstein and Katz recommended abolition of the insanity defense but would allow evidence of mental disorder as proof that the necessary mental element of a crime was missing [18]. A New York proposal, contained in a 1978 Report to the Governor, recommended abolition of the insanity defense but its replacement with a diminished capacity or diminished responsibility test [19]. Recently, some jurisdictions have enacted a "Guilty but Mentally Ill" law either as an alternative verdict to an insanity plea or as a complete replacement for the insanity defense [20].

There is not space in this article closely to examine the advantages and disadvantages of each of these abolition proposals. Suffice it to say that I reject all abolition proposals. The insanity defense (like many other excusing, justifying, or exempting conditions) is essential if our system of criminal law is to be considered moral. Punishment is only moral if it is deserved and it is only deserved if there is some minimal capacity to understand and to choose right from wrong. What constitutes "minimal capacity" is, of course, a vexed question, but what is clear is that calls for the total abolition of the insanity defense must be rejected as fundamentally immoral. It is immoral to punish those who do not have the capacity to reason or to choose right from wrong.

The proposal to abandon the insanity defense and rely solely on the absence of *mens rea* as a defense must also be rejected as essentially immoral, since it would result in the conviction and punishment of some persons who could not reason or choose right from wrong. An insane person, particularly a psychotic person who has delusions, may have *mens rea* in the strict sense, for example, an intent to kill. But it is a *mens rea* concocted in an irrational or crazy mind. The normal controls, the beliefs and the perceptions of reality which influence the right-minded citizen, are absent or impaired. Thus the capacity to reason or choose are impaired even though *mens rea* in the narrow sense exists.

The vexed question of what constitutes minimal capacity must be addressed. Obviously, if there is no capacity there can be no responsibility. Total incapacity excuses totally. But what ought to be done when there is substantial impairment of cognitive or volitional faculties? Is it just or moral to punish in those circumstances? We must answer that question by posing another question. Can we fairly or justly have expected that person to resist the illegal and to conform his behavior to the law? That question is a moral, philosophic, social, and legal question more than a medical one. Hence the current role of mental health professionals in resolving that question must be closely examined.

It is clear that an insanity defense of some scope must be recognized. However, the public expectation that citizens must in general take personal responsibility for their conduct is an important value which is essential to the continued preservation of peace and order in our society. This public expectation must not be destroyed by setting the minimal capacity for responsibility too high, thereby allowing a large number of persons to escape this general expectation.

Since the insanity defense results in total exemption from criminal liability, the level of impairment warranting a finding of insanity ought to be set at a level where it is unreasonable to attribute any blame to the accused for failing to conform to the requirements of the law. For lesser impairments, where it is not unreasonable to attribute some blame to the accused (though not total blame), a system of diminished responsibility may be more appropriate.

M'Naghten-Type Test

The Canadian test is in essence a M'Naghten-type test. I have already listed the substantial disadvantages of that type of test. In the light of its exclusive reliance on cognitive impairment, its medical obsolescence, and its unpopularity with lawyers and psychiatrists for all the reasons previously listed, this type of test should not be adopted or maintained.

Durham Test

Instituted in 1954 by Judge Bazelon [21], the Durham test (no criminal responsibility if "the unlawful act was the product of mental disease or defect") has been widely described, studied, and criticized. Due to limitations of space, I will not review that literature here. Suffice it to say that in 1973, in *U.S.* v. *Brawner* [22], Judge Bazelon and the rest of the District of Washington Court, which invented the Durham test, abandoned it out of frustration since it had not solved the problems it was supposed to solve. According to Judge Bazelon, in practice the Durham test did not produce the expansion of the inquiry into the accused's mind and behavior which had been anticipated. Instead, experts continued to speak "in conclusory terms which inevitably included but concealed their underlying value judgments, and their own views as to the appropriate legal outcome" [23]. As Goldstein has noted:

> In short, *Durham* had travelled a remarkably circuitous path toward the conclusion that the jury needed some guidance, that words like "mental disease" and "product" were inadequate, and that the standard would have to incorporate a description of the sorts of effects of disease somehow that were relevant to compliance with the criminal law. Those effects, inevitably, were very much like the ones which were central to the broadened *M'Naghten* and "control" tests [24].

Leaving the issue of responsibility to the jury without any guidelines is undesirable because juries will not form consistent rules or produce consistent decisions; since they do not form a continuous body, reasons are not given and thus precedents do not develop, and there is no supreme jury to correct or systematize other jury decisions. In addition, the "product" test, if accurately applied, does not escape the criticism of considering the mind as compartmentalized rather than integrated. Some have argued that the Durham test is too wide, thus detracting from deterrence and public confidence in law enforcement.

A test which lays down no legal standard for criminal responsibility and permits the ultimate issues to be decided by psychiatrists, as if the issues were medical in nature, rather than recognizing that the issues are really social and moral and nature and leaving them to the jury to decide, should not be adopted elsewhere. It was a bold experiment which failed. Its failure provides valuable lessons for future reform.

Justly Responsible Test

The Royal Commission on Capital Punishment 1949–1953 in Great Britain recommended the abrogation of the M'Naghten test and its replacement with a formula which does not define the relationship of insanity to criminal responsibility but rather leaves the decision on insanity to the common sense of the jury in the light of all the evidence given in each case. The Commission recommended that the jury be left "to determine whether at the time of the act the accused was suffering from disease of the mind (or mental deficiency) to such a degree that he ought not to be held responsible" [25].

In *Brawner,* Chief Justice Bazelon, dissenting, recommended the adoption of the following "justly responsible" test: Our instruction to the jury should provide that a defendant is not responsible if at the time of his unlawful conduct his mental or emotional processes or behaviour controls were impaired to such an extent that he cannot justly be held responsible for his act [26]. This test was designed to discourage the jury from basing its decision solely on the medical evidence and to encourage them to recognize that the issue is a moral one for them, not a medical one for experts.

The disadvantages are as follows:

1. The Bazelon formulation is a nontest which exposes accused persons to arbitrary and unequal jury decisions in which each jury formulates its own legal rule and standard of justice. See also in this context a similar criticism made in regard to the Durham test. The concept of justice is abstract and imprecise and thus will depend on personal criteria of each juror [27]. Traditionally, the establishment of legal rules has been left to judges and legislators, not juries.
2. The secrecy of jury deliberations prevents the accused from obtaining an appellate court's review of the equality of their treatment [27].
3. The American Law Institute's (ALI) justly responsible test runs a greater risk than the official ALI test of individual jurors setting up their own individual standards of justice and thus denying equal treatment to all accused.
4. Bazelon's formulation lacks a number of jury guidelines which are present in both of the ALI tests.

It may be concluded that Bazelon's formulation is too lacking in guidelines and direction to the jury, and thus should not be adopted.

Butler Committee Test

In the Report of the Committee on Mentally Abnormal Offenders (1975) (Lord Butler, Chairman) [28], a new test to replace the M'Naghten test was recommended. The new test has two distinct branches.

It is designed to determine whether there is

1. Mental disorder negating the requisite *mens rea* (i. e., intention, foresight, knowledge, etc.), or
2. Severe mental disorder or severe subnormality notwithstanding technical proof of *mens rea*.

The two branches are defined and described in detail in the Butler Report. The Butler Committee argued that in some mental disorders "the patient's beliefs are so bizarre or his change of mood is so profound and inexplicable, or he is so changed in manner and conduct, that his condition can only be described as alien, or mad" [29], yet he may know what he is doing and that it is wrong (i. e., unlawful). The Committee noted that there is general agreement in civilized countries that such persons should not be held criminally responsible. The challenge is to find a test which exempts them. The Butler Committee believed that the second branch of their test achieves this purpose.

There are several advantages to the Butler test and these are dealt with in their report. However, there are a number of disadvantages that warrant mentioning.

1. Some criticism can be directed at the total abolition in the second branch of the test of a causal connection between the mental disorder and the unlawful conduct.
2. The second branch of the test, according to the Butler Committee, "necessarily turns over the test of criminal responsibility to medical opinion" [30]. This may be unwise. It is quite arguable that medical testimony will not only be conclusory but also so influential (since the test is in detailed medical terms) as virtually to usurp the jury's function of deciding on criminal responsiblity.

Since this test is untried, and has been the subject of little comment, very extensive consultations should be held with legal and medical experts on this proposal in an effort to judge its practicality and desirability. It has sufficient positive features to warrant such consultation. Consideration should be given to conducting a pilot project using this test with judges and juries in mock trials.

The American Law Institute's Model Penal Code Test

In 1955, 1 year after *Durham* but before its subsequent judicial clarification, a new insanity test was proposed in a Tentative Draft which with very minor changes found its way into the 1962 Official Draft. In addition, two alternative tests were put forward for consideration. The test in the Official Draft is as follows:

> Section 4.01. Mental Disease or Defect Excluding Responsibility.
> 1. A person is not responsible for criminal conduct if at the time of such conduct as a result of mental disease or defect he lacks substantial capacity either to appreciate the criminality [wrongfulness] of his conduct or to conform his conduct to the requirements of law.
> 2. As used in this Article, the terms "mental disease or defect" do not include an abnormality manifested only by repeated criminal or otherwise anti-social conduct.

The word "wrongfulness" in brackets indicates that there is an option in word choice between it and the word "criminality." Subsection [2] is an express attempt to exclude most psychopaths from the scope of the insanity defense.

Advantages

1. Goldstein describes some advantages of the ALI test in the following words:

   > This test is a modernized and much improved rendition of *M'Naghten* and the "control" tests. It substitutes "appreciate" for "know," thereby indicating a preference for the view that a sane offender must be emotionally as well as intellectually aware of the significance of his conduct. And it uses the word "conform" instead of "control," while avoiding any reference to the misleading words "irresistible impulse." In addition, it requires only "substantial" incapacity, thereby eliminating the occasional reference in the older cases to "complete" or "total" destruction of the normal capacity of the defendant [31].

2. In adopting the ALI test in preference to the Durham test the Fourth Circuit Court of Appeals described its advantages as follows:

   > With appropriate balance between cognition and volition, it demands an unrestricted inquiry into the whole personality of the defendant . . . Its verbiage is understandable by psychiatrists; it imposes no limitation upon their testimony, and yet, to a substantial extent, it avoids a diagnostic approach and leaves the jury free to make its findings in terms of a standard which society prescribes and juries may apply [32].

3. As of 1980, 28 states and ten out of 11 federal circuit courts had adopted in substance the ALI test as the best and most functional insanity test [33, 34].
4. It is a reasonable compromise between the strictness of the M'Naghten test and the unstructured nature of the Durham test.

Disadvantages

1. The test includes recognition of volitional impairment and may therefore widen the insanity exemption beyond public tolerance.
2. The test of "conformity" suffers from the same problem as the "irresistible impulse" test – how is the jury to distinguish between incapacity to conform and will – ful or reckless failure to conform?

3. It is argued that the words "substantial" and "appreciate," which are not defined, are vague [34].
4. It has been argued that the words "as a result of" are subject to the same causality difficulties as the *Durham* court faced with the words "product of" [34].
5. It is argued that the term "mental disease or defect" in the ALI insanity test is "too entangled with the medical model - that is, mental disorder explained as illness - to be usable as a legal concept" [34]. This argument is based on a substantial scepticism about the validity of the medical model in insanity cases.

Conclusion

Although the ALI test is not without its faults, it is the best test to date, since it provides a reasonable and tested compromise between the extremes of *M'Naghten* and *Durham*. Minor variations can be made to the ALI test to improve it. For example, when the District of Washington adopted the ALI test in 1973, to replace the Durham test, they adopted it subject to the wide definition of mental disease or defect which they had earlier expressed in *McDonald* v. *U.S.* [35] and subject to the judge's instructions both to psychiatrists and the jury as to their respective functions and roles in insanity trials, which they had promulgated in the earlier case of *Washington* v. *U.S.* [36].

Another variation of the ALI test is the recent American Bar Association (ABA) Provisional Criminal Justice Mental Health Standards (1982). Unfortunately, in their final, approved Standards (April 1983), the ABA opted for a solely cognitive, M'Naghten-like test and rejected the ALI test. This reactionary approach was fuelled by the Hinckley insanity acquittal.

A Proposal

In my opinion, the best method for dealing with mental disorder and criminal responsibility is to take an aggregate approach, borrowing the best from various approaches. This aggregate approach would contain, in brief, the following components.

An InsanityDefense

There would be an insanity which recognized volitional, cognitive, and emotional impairment, as the ALI test does. However, since the insanity defense exempts the accused totally from any criminal responsibility, the impairment must not only be "substantial," but it must be so substantial that it is "unreasonable to attribute *any* blame to the accused for his conduct." If it is reasonable to attribute some blame or partial responsibility to the accused, then the defense of diminished responsibility should be used.

A Diminished Responsibility Test

The diminished responsibility test would cover cases where it was reasonable to assign some but not full blame to the accused for his conduct. This should apply to all offenses, not just murder as in England and Scotland. In addition, if successful, this defense should have the effect of statutorily reducing the level of the offense (e.g., robbery in the first degree to robbery in some lesser degree) and statutorily reducing the maximum punishment.

Defense of No Mens Rea

The defense that there was no *mens rea* because of a mental disorder which falls short of constituting the defense of insanity should remain a defense.

Automatism Defense

Automatism (unconscious, involuntary behavior) caused by factors other than mental disease should remain a separate and distinct defense from the defense of insanity.

Other Procedural and Evidentiary Reforms

1. Mandatory commitment following an insanity acquittal should be abolished and replaced by judicial discretion to commit or release. If release decisions are made by the executive, they should be subject to judicial review.
2. The persuasive burden of proof in regard to insanity, diminished responsibility, and automatism should remain on the prosecutor, as it does in regard to other criminal law defenses. In other words, if the evidence creates a reasonable possibility that the accused's actions were committed in a state of insanity, diminished responsibility, or automatism, the defense must succeed.
3. The prosecutor should not be entitled to introduce evidence of insanity if the accused is competent at his trial and has made a competent decision not to raise the insanity defense.
4. Limits and controls should be placed on the use of psychiatric and psychological evidence in insanity trials.

Conclusion

Clearly the current Canadian law in regard to the insanity defense is inadequate. However, there is a conservative wind blowing through the United States, especially in regard to limiting the scope of, and reliance on, the insanity defense. It is too early yet to determine whether this cold United States wind will have a chilling effect on needed insanity reforms in Canada.

References

1. Morris N (1968) Psychiatry and the dangerous criminal. S Calif Law Rev 41: 514, 516
2. The M'Naghten test requires that the accused be "labouring under such a defect of reason, from disease of the mind, as not to know the nature and quality of the act he was doing, or, if he did know it, that he did not know he was doing what was wrong." 10 Cl and F 200, 233 (1843)
3. Criminal Code, Revised Statutes of Canada, 1970, Chap C-34
4. Report of the Royal Commission on the Law of Insanity as a Defense in Criminal Cases (1956) (McRuer Report)
5. (1976) 29 CCC (2d) 1 (SCC)
6. (1980) 51 CCC (2d) 129 (SCC)
7. (1980) 51 CCC (2d) 193 (SCC)
8. (1981) 24 CR (3d) 289 (SCC)
9. (1982) 68 CCC (2d) 394 (SCC)
10. *Chartrand* v *The Queen* (1976), 26 CCC (2d) 417 (SCC)
11. American Law Institute, Model Penal Code, sect 4: 01 (Official Draft, 1962)
12. This is a qualified right. It must be done with leave of the judge and is permissible only if it is in the "interests of justice." *Regina* v *Simpson* (1977), 35 CCC (2d) 337 (Ont CA); *Regina* v *Saxell* (1980), 59 CCC (2d) 176 (Ont CA); *Regina* v *Dickie* (1982), 67 CCC (2d) 218 (Ont CA)
13. Criminal Code, sect 16; *Clark* (1921), 61 SCR 608; *Smythe* (1941], SCR 17
14. Criminal Code, sect 542 (1)
15. Criminal Code, sects 542 (2), 545
16. For a short list of abolitionists, see Brackel S, Rock R (eds) (1971) The mentally disabled and the law. University of Chicago Press, Chicago, p 378
17. Wootton B (1981) Crime and the criminal law, 2nd edn Stevens, London, especially Chap 3
18. Goldstein J, Katz J (1963) Abolish the 'insanity defence' - why not? Yale Law J 72: 853-876
19. Report to Governor Hugh L Carey (1978) The insanity defence in New York. New York State Department of Mental Hygiene, Albany, New York, pp 140-141
20. Mesritz G (1976) Guilty but mentally ill: an historical and constitutional analysis. J of Urban L 53: 471-496; Lauter D (1982) New verdict: guilty but mentally ill. The National Law Journal 4: 11-14; Sherman S (1981) Guilty but mentally ill: a retreat from the insanity defence. Am J of Law and Medicine 7: 237-264; Watkins C (1981) Guilty but mentally ill: a reasonable compromise for Pennsylvania. Dickinson L Rev 85: 289-319; Amarilio J (1979) Insanity - guilty but mentally ill - diminished capacity: an aggregate approach to madness. John Marshall J of Practice and Procedure 12: 351-381; Comment (1978) The constitutionality of Michigan's guilty but mentally ill verdict. Mich J L Reform 12: 188-196
21. *Durham* v *US*, 214 F 2d 862 (DC Cir 1954)
22. 471 F 2d 969 (DC Cir 1972)
23. 471 F 2d 1010-1011 (DC Cir 1972)
24. Goldstein AS (1983) The insanity defence. Yale University Press, New Haven, p 86
25. Cmnd 8932, p 116
26. 471 F 2d 1032 (DC Cir 1972)
27. Morris GH (1975) The insanity defence: a blueprint for legislative reform. Heath, Lexington, Massachusetts, pp 19-20
28. Cmnd 6244, pp 222-230
29. Cmnd 6244, p 218
30. Cmnd 6244, pp 229
31. Goldstein AS (1983) The insanity defence. Yale University Press, New Haven, p 87
32. *US* v *Chandler* 393 F 2d 920, 926 (1968)
33. Weiner B (1980) Not guilty by reason of insanity. Chicago Kent Law Rev 56: 1057, 1063, 1084, App A
34. Morris GH (1975) The insanity defence: a blueprint for legislative reform. Heath, Lexington, Massachusetts, p 17
35. 312 F 2d 847 (DC Cir 1962)
36. 390 F 2d 444 (DC Cir 1967)

The Insanity Defense Under Nigerian Law

A. A. Kuforiji

In Nigeria the defense of insanity is provided for in the Criminal and Penal Codes operating in the Southern and Northern States respectively.

Section 28 of the Criminal Code provides that:

> A person is not criminally responsible for an act or omission if at the time of doing the act or making the omission he is in such a state of mental disease or natural mental infirmity as to deprive him of capacity to understand what he is doing or of capacity to control his actions or of capacity to know that he ought not to do the act or make the omission.

Section 51 of the Penal Code reads thus:

> Nothing is an offence which is done by a person who at the time of doing it, by reason of unsoundness of mind, is incapable of knowing the nature of the act, or that he is doing what is either wrong or contrary to law.

The object of this chapter is not to examine what interpretations the courts in Nigeria have given to the wordings of the Codes or to determine whether the provisions are adequate to cover all aspects of mental deficiencies known to modern psychiatric science. Our aim is to justify the retention or make a case for the abolition of the insanity defense in the Nigerian law, having regard to the issue of determination of insanity at the trial of criminal cases and the consequences of a successful plea of insanity to the accused person and to the administration of justice in Nigeria.

Before we proceed on our study, a few preliminary points should be made. It should be noted that the insanity defense is raised at the trial of very serious offenses, mostly murder and rarely manslaughter, and has been upheld in very few of such cases. Under Nigerian law there exists the rule that every adult is presumed to be sane and to possess a sufficient degree of reason to be responsible for his acts [1]. Section 140 [3] (c) of the Evidence Act [2] also provides that the burden of proof of a defense of intoxication or insanity be on the accused.

From this presumption of sanity it follows that the onus is on the accused to prove that be was insane at the time he committed the offense [3]. However, the onus of proof on the defense in this regard is not the same as the onus on the prosecution in all criminal cases to prove its case beyond reasonable doubt [4].

From the foregoing it is clear that the burden of proof is discharged if it is established on balance of probability that the accused was insance when he committed the offense for which he is facing trial. Thus in an appeal from Nigeria the West African Court of Appeal in *R.* v. *Echem* [5] held "that the burden of proof which rests upon the person to establish the defence of insanity is not as heavy as that which rests upon the prosecution when proving its case against an accused person. It may be stated as not being higher than the burden which rests on a plaintiff or defendant in civil proceedings." [6] The Supreme Court recently restated this position in *State* v. *Inyang,* [7] when it held that the burden of proof on the defense is discharged if it is established on balance of probability that the accused was insane when he committed the offense.

We now come to the important question in this chapter. How is the issue of insanity determined by the courts? If the issue "unfitness to stand trial by reason of insanity" arises, it must be investigated, and it may arise at any stage of the trial, either before the accused pleads to the charge or after, and even after evidence has begun to be heard. As soon as the question is raised it must be investigated before the trial begins or continues. At this stage the judge will order that the person pleading insanity be sent to an asylum or psychiatric hospital for observation. The medical officer may detain him for such a period (not exceeding 1 month) as may be necessary to enable him to form an opinion as to the state of mind of the accused, and must forward a copy of his opinion in writing to the court. However, the issue of the unsoundness of mind of the accused must be resolved on evidence, for which purpose the certificate of the medical officer is admissible [8]. It is for the court to decide the question on the basis of its observation of the accused, whatever the opinion of the medical officer [9].

Where a trial is postponed under sections 223 and 224, the court may at any time begin the trial *de novo* and require the accused to appear or be brought to court as soon as he is fit to face trial. At the resumed trial the issue whether a person is insane or not for the purpose of criminal liability for the alleged offense is a question for the court to determine [10]. At the trial, expert evidence is taken from the medical officer who observed the accused, to determine the soundness of mind of the accused at the time of the alleged act constituting the charge. However, the court is not bound to accept the evidence of the expert and act on it in establishing the defense, no matter how eminent the expert may be in the field of psychiatry [11]. Thus it was held in *R.* v. *Madugba* [12] that it is for the judge to decide the question, for which purpose he may make use of his own observation of the accused, and he is not bound by the certificate of the medical officer, though great store ought to be attached to the medical opinion. The West African Court of Appeal held in *R.* v. *Inyang* [10] that medical evidence by an expert, though desirable, is not a necessity. The court rejected the medical evidence to the effect that the accused was sane [13].

In the recent case of *State* v. *Joshua Agboola* [14] the Oyo State High Court adopted the same position. The medical report was to the effect that the accused, who was charged with murder, was of sound mind. The court rejected this opinion and on the basis of the evidence adduced came to the conclusion that the accused was insane, and entered a verdict or guilty but insane [15].

The above raises some important questions. What is responsible for the judicial attitude, and how do the courts arrive at the conclusion that an accused is insane, having rejected the contrary opinion of the expert witness? It should be borne in mind that courts in Nigeria, like their counterparts all over the world, base their decisions on the evidence before them both in civil and criminal proceedings. This attitude cannot be different where the issue concerns the insanity defense. The fact that the relevant time for determination of insanity is the time of the commission of the alleged offense, coupled with the fact that an insane person does have moments of sanity (the lucid interval), makes the position of the psychiatrist an unenviable one. The psychiatrist is called upon to examine the accused person after the offense has been committed [16], and it may happen that at this time the accused is in his lucid interval. But having heard evidence of close relations to the effect that there is a history of insanity in the accused's family and that the accused had in the past, before the commission of the alleged offense, showed signs of mental illness and in some cases had been treated, the court is inclined to lean on such evidence [17]. Furthermore, absence of motive for the commission of the offense becomes a relevant and material factor indicative of insanity. Thus the West African Court of Appeal held that absence of motive by itself is not sufficient ground to infer mania. Where there is as much evidence indicative of insanity as of the opposite, as in that case, the absence of any evidence of motive may become relevant to the point at issue and material to it [10, 13]. In State *Joshua Agboola* [14], the accused was praying in the church with the prophet and others when, unknown to other worhsippers, he jumped out of the window and attacked his victims with a cutlass he had picked up somewhere on his way. All the victims were complete strangers to the accused. This and other evidence led the court to conclude that he was insane.

The above in a nutshell explains the judicial attitude to psychiatric opinion. However, it does not mean that psychiatric evidence does not assist the courts or that it is rejected in all cases. What the courts say is that expert opinion is just one of the kinds of evidence to be considered in any given case, but it is not intended to be the only evidence to be relied on. The issue of insanity is a peculiar one, and as long as the law seeks to know the state of mind of the accused person at the time of the commission of the alleged act, and as long as the insane has lucid intervals, the time is not in sight when law and psychiatry will see eye to eye, at least in Nigeria.

Lastly, we come to the most crucial aspect of this paper. On a successful plea of the insanity defense, the verdict of the court must be an acquittal on the grounds that at the time at which the accused is allged to have committed an offense he was by reason of unsoundness of mind incapable of knowing the nature of the alleged act as constituting the offense or that it was wrong or contrary to law; the finding must state specifically whether he committed the act or not [18]. By virtue of the provision Nigerian courts usually pronounce a verdict of "guilty but insane." The court will order such a person to be kept in safe custody in such place and manner as the court thinks fit and will report the case for the order of the Governor. The Governor may order him to be confined in a lunatic asylum, prison, or other suitable place of custody during the pleasure of the Governor or President [19].

Immediately the court gives the order, the convicted person is returned to the prison custody where he had been kept since his arrest (murder is not a bailable offense), pending the Governor's confirmation of the court's order. From that point the prison authorities take responsibility for the execution of the order [20]. In an interview with a senior official of the Agodi Prison in Ibadan, Oyo State [21]. I gathered that on receipt of the Governor's order, the prisoner is handed over to the prison's medical officer, who puts him under observation to determine whether to keep him in the prison or send him to a psychiatric hospital. The placement is determined by the degree of mental illness. If he is violent, the medical officer will send him to Aro Psychiatric Hospital [22], but the non violent are detained in a separate cell in the prison with a warder attached to it. The warder is required to keep a record of his daily observation of the detainee's behavior and general disposition. The chief warder is required to write a weekly report based on the entries in the warder's record book. This report is countersigned by the Superintendent. The prison's medical officer is supposed to visit the detainee for the purpose of examination two or three times a week. The weekly report and the doctor's treatment record should be in the detainee's file. The Superintendent must write a monthly report on the progress of the prisoner based on the medical treatment and the warder's observation [23].

At the end of every 4 years a Periodic Review Order, countersigned by the prison's medical officer, is required to be issued on the progress of the detainee. The purpose is to assist the authorities in the determination of his subsequent release. However, it is not clear if any detainee has ever been discharged in compliance with the provision of section 233 of the C. P. A. [24].

At Aro Psychiatric Hospital I had a more useful discussion, with one of the chief medical consultants [25]. According to him the hospital has contact with this category of patients at the trial and posttrial stages. The hospital has no problems at the first stage in view of the fact that the order from the court always specifies the period of observation. But the confinement order which the prison authorities deliver with the patient creates problems of no mean dimension to the hospital. The patient is admitted as an inpatient of the hospital immediately he is brought in. Unfortunately, when the patient is medically fit and reasonably capable of being reintegrated into society, nobody comes round to take him away.

The experience of the hospital is that the prison authorities show no interest, and do not contact the hospital after the patient has been brought in. In many cases, when the hospital takes the initiative to contact them on the discharge of such patients, it is discovered that the prison authorities can no longer trace their records.

The problem of inadequate hospital beds is worsened by these government patients. His experience is that such patients are forgotten in the hospital. Many of them have stayed in the hospital for periods ranging from 5 to 10 years; all of these would have been discharged had they been brought in by relations. He mentioned the case of a man who has been in the hospital since the 1950s. Hospital contact with the prison authorities yielded no fruitful result because they had no records of his case. The hospital has had to keep him because the "patient" informed the hospital he had nowhere to go. He has become, as it were, a permanent "member" of the hospital. He goes to work during the day and returns there as to his home.

The chief consultant informed me that he had personally been instrumental in the release of three of such patients by bypassing the bureaucratic system and contacting the governor directly. Even then it was a time-consuming exercise which the hospital is not prepared to undertake. He is of the opinion that confinement at the Governor's pleasure ties the hospital's hand from discharging a patient when he is medically fit after a course of treatment. While appreciating the anxiety of the authorities over the possible danger to society should a discharged mental patient relapse, he cannot understand the rationale for the guarantee or assurance demanded from the hospital that such persons will not fall ill again. He would like a situation whereby the government sets up a medical board to review the cases of such patients periodically and make recommendation to the state.

From the above, it is now necessary to make a few observations. As mentioned earlier, the insanity defense is raised in very few instances and rarely succeeds. Cases in which the plea fails go by unnoticed and leave no dent in the system. But it is the successful instances that call for concern, concern to lawyers, judges, psychiatrists, and probably the prison authorities. Nigerian society has not reached such a stage of development as to be aware of issues like the insanity defense and the consequences of a successful plea to the criminally insane and the administration of justice in Nigeria [26]. It is even doubtful whether many lawyers are aware of the problems involved. For if they were, they would be less eager or might even be very reluctant to "ask" their clients to put up the defense as they do at the moment. It is a common practice among counsel to put up the defense relying solely on the accused's statement that "his head turned" or that he did not know what he was doing at the time of the alleged act constituting the offense, or that "some voices told him to kill." [27]. Also, counsel tend to cling to the mere absence of motive for the commission of the offense [28]. This is sad, to say the least. According to a judge of the Federal Court of Appeal [29], very few counsel in Nigeria make any serious or conscious effort to elicit in cross-examination of prosecution witnesses such evidence of insanity as would enable the court to come to a conclusion that on balance of probability the accused is insane. In his experience, counsel hardly go out of their way to produce evidence, medical or otherwise, to establish the plea of insanity and rebut the presumption of law, and do not make any pretrial investigation with a view to finding out the antecedents, the mental history, or the family background of the accused.

We may ask now what benefit accrues to the person who successfully pleads insanity. The aim of the law is that an insane person should not be held criminally responsible for his actions [30]. Having found that the accused's action was unwilled, being the product of a diseased mind, the law says he needs help in the form of psychiatric treatment. In the Nigerian situation, one cannot seriously say that the accused receives such treatment, whether he is confined in prison under doubtful psychiatric treatment or in a psychiatric hospital where he is forgotten. In the latter case, the chances are that such persons, after medical treatment but without hope of being discharged, have a gloomy future to look forward to. This in itself may have a psychological effect on them and cause a relapse of their mental illness. In our view, the death sentence or a term of imprisonment for murder or attempted murder respectively is a far better deal for an accused person. The indefinite confinement as noted above contravenes the provision of fundamental rights by the country's constitution [31].

This situation exists and will continue to exist in Nigeria as long as there are no civil libertarians to fight the cause of these unfortunate citizens. Furthermore, the relations of such persons do not show the least interest in them because of the stigma society attaches to insanity. It is indeed very disturbing.

On the other hand, society does not benefit from a successful plea of insanity. Unfortunately, nobody seems to be aware of the cost of maintaining such inmates in the prisons in terms of manpower and finance. To keep such people indefinitely in psychiatric hospitals deprives other mentally ill people of the opportunity of receiving much-needed treatment [32].

In the light of the above, our conclusion is that if a successful plea of the insanity defense does not produce the desired result – that the insane be exculpated from criminal liability – as our study has shown, one may ask why we retain it in our codes. In our view the insanity defense should be abolished in Nigerian law. An accused person should be tried and insanity pleaded as an extenuating circumstance at the sentencing stage if he is found guilty. This, in our view, will serve the end of justice.

References

1. See section 27 of the Criminal Code. Although this presumption is not specifically mentioned in the Penal Code, it is obvious from a reading of the whole Code that liability under it is based upon that presumption. It has been held in India that the presumption exists: *Baswantrao Bajirao* v *Emp,* AIR 1949 Nagpur 66. The Penal Code is based on the Sudanese Penal Code, which is based on the Indian Penal Code. The courts in the Northern States have always been guided by the interpretation of the courts in India on similar provisions in the Nigerian Penal Code.
2. Chap 62, Laws of the Federation of Nigeria. The Evidence Act applies throughout the country
3. *Dim* v *R* (1952) 14 WACA 154; *R* v *Smith* (1910) 6 Cr App R 19
4. *R* v *Nasamu* (1940) 6 WACA 74; *R* v *Yayiye of Kadi Kadi* (1957) NRNLR 207 at 209 Section 137 (1) of the Evidence Act provides that the onus of proof of the commission of a criminal offense beyond reasonable doubt is on the prosecution.
5. (1952) 14 WACA 158 at 160
6. This decision was followed by the old Federal Supreme Court of Nigeria in *Onakpoya* v *The Queen* (1959) 4 FSC 150
7. (1972) 8/9 SC 283
8. *R* v *Ogor* (1961) 1 All NLR 70. See also *R* v *Podola* (1960) 1 QB 325
9. See sections 223 and 224 of the Criminal Procedure Act
10. *R* v *Inyang* (1946) 12 WACA 5
11. *R* v *Rivett* (1950) 34 Cr App R 87
12. (1959) 3 FSC 1
13. The decision was followed by the court in *R* v *Ashigifuwo* (1948) 12 WACA 389
14. Unreported suit no HIF/HC/75 of 2 April 1976
15. See also *The Queen* v *Bashiru Ayinde* (1963) WRNLR 27
16. Such examinations do not take place immediately after the commission of the offense. It takes weeks or months in most cases before the trial begins and it is at the trial that the issue of insanity is raised.
17. That was the position in *R* v *Inyang* and *R* v *Ashigifuwo*
18. Section 229 of the Criminal Procedure Act, here in after refered to as the CPA
19. Section 230 of the CPA
20. The Nigerian Prison Services is a Federal Government agency with prison locations all over the country. It has its own medical unit within each prison for on-the-spot care of the inmates.
21. The official has served in many prison locations throughout the country and has put in over 12 years service.
22. Aro Psychiatric Hospital in Abeokuta, Ogun State, is a World Health Organization Collaborating Center for research and training in mental health. It has for years served not only Nigeria but several African countries in the cure of the mentally sick.
23. It is, however, doubtful whether the regulations are strictly complied with.
24. This official and another I spoke with maintained that the rules and regulations provide what ought to be, but what obtains was a matter they could not discuss with an outsider. They could not produce any records, even though I had the Controller of Prisons' permission to go through such records. This attitude of keeping sealed lips where government regulations are not being complied with either because the government does not provide necessary facilities and personnel or because of other administrative laxity is the general pattern in all government offices in Nigeria.
25. I owe a lot of gratitude to Dr. Dele Sijuwola for sparing the time to discuss this with me and for being outspoken on the problems the hospital faces with regard to discharge of this category of patients.
26. The public furor generated by the acquittal of John Hinckley Jr., the man who shot at President Ronald Reagan's entourage, on grounds of insanity has led to a reconsideration of the insanity defense in the United States of America. For example, Delaware has passed a bill which allows

juries to find the defendant "guilty but mentally ill." Convicts under the new law (which is also in force in Michigan, Indiana, New Mexico, Georgia, and Illinois) can be treated in mental institutions until they recover, and will then be transferred to prisons to serve their terms.

27. See *Simeon Okoye* v *The state,* Appeal no FCA/1/12/79; *Onyendinefu* v *The State,* Appeal no FCA/1/117/78. Both are decisions of the Federal Court of Appeal.
28. See the view of the West African Court of Appeal in *R* v *Inyang* 10; *R* v *Ashigifuwo* 13
29. Hon Justice MMA Akanbi of the Ibadan Federal Court of Appeal was particularly helpful in my research. Hon Justice SO Agbaje-Williams, High Court of Oyo State, assisted me in no small measure. I am grateful to them.
30. Section 24 of the Criminal Code forms the basis of criminal responsibility under Nigerian law. The effect of the provision under this section is that a person is not criminally responsible for an act or omission which occurs independently of the exercise of his will.
31. Section 31 (1) (a) of the constitution of the Federal Republic of Nigeria provides that every individual is entitled to respect for the dignity of his person and accordingly no person shall be subjected to torture or to inhuman or degrading treatment.
32. It makes one sad if one bears in mind that Nigeria is a country where provision of adequate care for the sick is an acute problem, yet the available resources are not being judiciously utilized.

Victimology Without a Victim

P. Silfen

In September 1979, the Third International Symposium on Victimology took place in Münster, West Germany. One of the central issues at this symposium was the definition of the scope of victimology.

From the talks and discussions on this subject [1–4] it emerged that there are two main views:

1. The narrow definition restricts the practice and scope of victimology to dealings with the victims of criminal acts only
2. According to the wider definition, victimology concerns an the victims of human action (as distinct from victims of natural disasters, etc.).

Among the participants of the conference, most of whom were criminologists, many favored the wider approach. As far as they were concerned, victimology is not only concerned with victims of crime, but covers a larger field. This change of views about the definition of the scope of victimology should, in my opinion, be attributed to the disappointment of the professionals with care for criminals and crime prevention activities. This disappointment, I believe, leads them to attempt to engage in a different filed, which promises more successes and fewer disappointments and frustrations. That field is victimology. Among these criminologists, only a few professionals were engaged in the actual treatment of criminals, and I do not think that clinical criminologists with a good psychotherapeutic training share this feeling of disappointment.

The new, wider definition of victimology raises many basic questions and there is still a need to consolidate appropriate conceptions and theories. No consolidated concept of the wider approach emerged at the conference; it was mainly a matter of general declarations and individuals' attempts to feel their way. This chapter is the result of the impressions I gained at this conference and sums up the thoughts it evoked in me during and after the event.

I shall concentrate mainly on four subjects:

1. The competence of the potential victim
2. Relations between the state and the individual
3. Psychology and psychopathology of the victim
4. Compensation or rehabilitation of the victim.

The Competence of the Potential Victim

At the conference, many ideas and opinions about self-defense were voiced [5]. One argument presented was that, in view of the great extent of victimization of the population which we witness (according to the wider understanding of the term), the institutions of the state and society are no longer able to come to the aid of the citizen. It therefore becomes necessary to devise new ways and means of preventing victimization, and many of the duties of the state will devolve on the individual. One of the things for which the individual will become responsible will be his personal welfare. This subject of the transfer of responsibility for his own defense to the individual was mentioned at the conference in all seriousness, without any mention of the dangers involved.

If the state surrenders responsibility for the citizen's defence to the citizen himself, that amounts to a regression in human civilization, and such a regression is liable to be followed by a further regressive development: the natural transition from self-defense to private justice. In other words, this regression is liable to generate the abolition of one of the most important elements of a legal state and an orderly society: the abolition of the state's jurisdiction.

Today, when the legal system is vested in the state and the protection of the citizen's peace is the responsibility of government agencies, the issue of self-defense arises from time to time. Mostly, a plea of self-defense is an argument for a reduction of sentence or a change of indictment, but it is rare for charges against a citizen to be dismissed on grounds of self-defense. These facts show the difficulty of defining self-defense and especially the need for caution in legitimizing extreme means of self-defense.

There is a danger now that the latest development in theory may result in changes in the law and in an expansion of the citizen's right of self-defense in order to prevent his being victimized. In the wake of such a change, the problems already existing today in the age of public defense will increase in number and become more acute. These problems call for great caution in legislation and for a clear determination and definition of the ways and means of self-defense permitted to the citizen, and of the situation in which the citizen is entitled to use those ways and means.

This foreseeable change raises the questions: What will be the effect of the wider resort to self-defense on the individual and society? And will the society be prepared to accept this change of concept? Further questions which arise and call for thought are those of the limits of the legitimation, and of who will care for those citizens who are mentally or physically incapable of defending themselves, and of what will be the social reaction to citizens who, because of mental disturbance or a pathological mental structure, will be incapable of restraining themselves and observing the legitimate limits.

These questions indicate that extending the scope of self-defense beyond what is accepted today and transferring it to the individual will cause such serious and complex problems that there is no foreseeable way of solving them. The thought of the consequent anarchy and an increase in social unrest positively frightens me.

The Relation Between the State and the Individual

The social arrangement that exists at present in the Western democracies defines the fields of responsibility of the individual and of the state. With the development of the welfare state, these definitions and the division of powers and responsibilities have changed, with the state assuming responsibility for many fields which had been the responsibility of the private citizen. Thus care for the citizens' health, for his and his children's education, and for retirement, old age, and invalidity pensions have been transferred from the private to the public sphere. At the same time, though, with the increase in crime, terrorism, and violence the private citizen is called upon to apply more of his own efforts and resources to his own security and that of his property. The responsibility for the protection of the individual has been shifted in part from the state to the citizen.

At present, this responsibility is still confined to legitimate organized efforts, such as the Civil Guard, and to private security companies, janitors, etc. These measures are carried out directly at the citizen's private expense and are his direct right and responsibility (and are not charged for indirectly, by way of taxation). These formations partly enjoy a semi-official status recognized by the law and resemble, in the means available to them and in their organizational structure, the corresponding state formations such as the police and the military.

A further extension of self-defense would in effect amount to establishing a new relationship between the authorities and the individual. That is not only a matter of law, but a complex process with extensive social, political, and psychological implications; in fact, it would mean a fundamental change in the concept of the state and its functions, which one may well doubt whether the citizen would accept.

Would the citizen be prepared to assume the burden of protecting his person and property while being relieved of the responsibility for his health, his education, and the schooling of his children? I, for one, prefer the state to take care of the security of my person and property, leaving it to myself to see to my health and education and my children's schooling.

Psychology and Psychopathology of the Victim

In the course of therapeutic care for prisoners, one is very likely to gain the impression that crime is not a matter of unilateral action in which only the criminal takes part. Actually, it is a process which develops patently or latently, with both the criminal and the victim playing a part. The process is patent in cases of crimes against the person [6], but also exists, latently, when it is a matter of offenses against property. The excellent paper of Ben-David [4] on the interaction between the rapist and his victim, based on clinical experience in care for criminals, brings out the importance of the human relation between the two participants in this tragic meeting. Ben-David comes to the conclusion that the victim can change the relationship between the rapist and herself, with a reasonable chance of preventing the rape.

Ben-David's conclusions may be expanded, and one may assume that in other cases of crimes against the person there is a similar process at work in the criminal's mind – a process which she calls "the depersonalization of the victim." If the criminal is to develop a personal feeling toward the victim, which cancels out the operation of the depersonalization process, there is a need for purposive action on the part of the victim. The victim's ability to take such action in the situation of the confrontation with the criminal depends on the victim's mental, or rather on his psychopathological, condition. Anxious, obsessive, schizoid, or hysterical personalities will have difficulty developing the relation recommended by Ben-David and this will reduce their prospects of avoiding injury at the criminal's hands.

In my opinion, there is a need for psychological and psychopathological studies in the light of Ben-David's approach, with a view to determining the mental states in which a person is incapable of developing the interpersonal relationship necessary to prevent agression against him. Pinpointing these mental states or personality structure defects which obstruct the establishment of this human relationship will help to find ways of overcoming this particular disability.

In clinical work with criminals and in court, one often comes up against another aspect of the criminal-victim meeting which is equally related to the interpersonal relationship and the process of patent or latent interaction between the partners in the crime situation. In judgments, there is sometimes mention of provocative behavior on the part, of the victim, especially in cases of murder, assault, bodily harm, and sex offenses. It is my belief that this concept should be expanded beyond its legal meaning, and that stimulation should be viewed as a concept in terms of the psychopathology of the victim.

Stimulation is a mental phenomenon based on subconscious processes operating in the mind of the criminal. The criminal is not aware of these processes, which are activated by the victim's actions or even more by his apperance. But stimulation is no less a result of the psychopathology of the victim. As a result of the victim's mental disorders, there are processes at work in his mind which are as unconscious as those of the criminal, and their effect is to make the victim react a manner that leads to aggressive reactions on the part of the criminal. From this viewpoint, the difference between provocation and stimulation is that the former is a patent act on the part of the victim, on the conscious plane of his actions, while the latter results from subconscious processes in the victim's mind.

Study of the psychopathology of the victim and its expression in stimulation and provocation is thus no less important than study of the psychopathology of the criminal. If we are to prevent victimization, we must discover and treat stimulation in prospective victims; by this means it will be possible to reduce the criminogenic factor in offenses against the person.

Compensation or Rehabilitation of the Victim

In the course of the Third Symposium on Victimology, there was a great deal of talk about compensation of the victim by the criminal [8].

Some contributors even went so far as to propose that the attitude to the criminal and his victim after the crime is committed should focus on compensation. The idea of compensation has also attracted the attention of jurists and legislators.

The importance of compensating the victim for the treatment of the criminal is evident nowadays, but there are doubts as to whether, for the victim, compensation is a positive act. Psychiatry has by now a wealth of experience of the effect of compensation on victims in such fields as traffic and industrial accidents. That experience has taught us to distinguish the negative aspect of the effect of compensation, which takes the form of the development of aspirational neuroses. The aspiration to obtain compensation becomes, in people with a certain personality structure, the main content of their lives and leads to the perpetuation of the trauma situation and of the feeling of being a victim. The trauma of the injury as such can result in the development of a morbid mentality, and obtaining compensation is liable to increase or intensify that development, and in certain cases even to result in neuroticization of the victim.

In my opinion, we should stop acting for, and talking about, compensation of the victim and act for, and talk about, rehabilitation of the victim. Equally important, I think, is to stop using the term "victim," since the word carries negative connotations and elements favoring the development of mental disturbance. I propose that we should replace the term "victim" by "target person."

In my opinion, expanding the scope of the term "victim" to include those injured by occurrences not due to criminal action and establishing the requirement to compensate them will result in the neuroticization of many people. It will render the character of our society more pathological. The task of professionals and scientists, as I see it, is to reduce the pathology by all the means available to them, rather than cause it to spread. Using the term "target person" instead of "victim" may well become a postive step in the direction of reducing pathology in our society.

Conclusion

The paper discusses four aspects of victimology and attempts to propose new concepts and to present a theoretical and practical development of these new fields.

The first aspect considers recent developments in the Western World, involving the expansion of self-defense. In my view, the danger inherent in transferring self-defense to the individual is particularly great because of the social implication of this regression: the transfer of means of control from the state ot the individual.

The second aspect also deals with relations between the state and the individual. In the distribution of powers between the individual and the welfare state, the state has assumed responsibility for the health, education and civilization of its citizens, while making them responsible for their self-defense. In my opinion, it would be preferable to reverse this division of responsibilities, making the state responsible for protecting the citizen's life and property and the citizen himself for his health and for the education of his children.

Two other aspects concern the psychology of the victim. The first involves the contribution of the victim to the crime by way of the conscious mental process of provocation or the subconscious mental process of stimulation. Attention is also drawn to the victim's role in preventing the performance of a crime against him, while the concept of depersonalization (which was presented at Münster by Ben-David) is expanded.

The other aspect concerns the effect of compensation on the victim's mental processes. In my opinion, the aim should be rehabilitation, not compensation, of the victim, so as to contribute to his mental health rather than to aggravate the traumatic effect of the crime on the victim.

In view of the negative influence liable to result from defining a person as a "victim" and the negative connotations of this term, it should, in my opinion, be replaced by that of "target person." The latter term's meaning conforms better with the latest theoretical developments in the fields of criminology and victimology.

I hope that this paper, which reflects the first thoughts and attempts to present some new concepts and spheres of thinking in the field of victimology, will lead to discussion and research by theoreticians and practical workers alike. Hopefully, study of these aspects of victimology will contribute to our understanding of the processes by which a person becomes a "target person," and also to the examination of ways of preventing crimes against the person.

References

1. Wolfang E (1979) Basic concepts in victimology theory. In: Proceedings of the 3rd international symposium on victimology, Münster, West Germany
2. International trends in victimology (1979) Panel discussion. In: Preceedings of the 3rd international symposium on victimology, Münster, West Germany
3. Conceptual issues and dimensions of victimology (1979) Section I of Proceedings of the 3rd international symposium on victimology, Münster, West Germany
4. Victim treatment, restitution and prevention (1979) Section V of Proceedings of the 3rd international symposium of victimology, Münster, West Germany
5. Shoham S, Ben-David S, Rahav G (1975) Interaction in violence. Human Relations 27: 417–430
6. Ben-David S (1979) Interaction rapist-victim during rape. In: Proceedings of the 3rd international symposium on victimology, Münster, West Germany
7. Schneider HJ (1979) Victim's damages, victim compensation and victim treatment: preliminary remarks. In: Proceedings of the 3rd international symposium on victimology, Münster, West Germany
8. Viano E (1979) Victim-witness program. In: Proceedings of the 3rd international symposium on victimology, Münster, West Germany

Considerations Regarding the Legal Responsibilities of Schizophrenic Patients

I. Treves and A. Elizur

Psychiatrists who testify as expert witnesses in courts of law are presented with a complex and difficult task. They are asked to express an expert opinion regarding the mental state of an individual accused of a criminal act. An especially difficult aspect of this task is the expectation that the psychiatrist will be able to define the relationship between the mental disease as diagnosed in the accused and the criminal act itself.

The court wants to know whether the crime is the result of the disease. To enable this question to be answered, there are clearly defined legal tests. For example: Was the accused able to distinguish between right and wrong at the time of perpetration of the criminal act? Did he understand the criminal nature and quality of the act, or did he act as the result of an "irresistible" impulse? In a large proportion of the cases, it is impossible to provide unambiguous answers to these questions. The commonsense view that has persisted over many years, that a "mad man" is beyond reasoning and therefore innocent of intent to do harm, and consequently not legally responsible, still prevails today.

The question is put whether the accused, having been diagnosed as mentally ill, can be assumed automatically not to be legally responsible. In many cases, it is impossible to evaluate the mentally ill with such certainty. Under the Israeli legal system there is no concept of "diminished responsibility." As a result, there is a tendency to underestimate the ability of the mentally ill to make free choices in their actions. Similarly, the psychiatrist may find it difficult to translate the concept of legal responsibility into psychiatric language. It must also be remembered that one cannot determine the nature of past acts with any certainty. We can only try to infer the intent and mental state of the accused criminal at the time. In the present chapter, we wish to provide several examples of this difficult problem. In particular, we emphasize the difficulty of forging the connection between the criminal act and the mental illness.

Case 1. G., 22 years of age, unmarried, without occupational training, was brought for examination as a result of being accused of murder. He was described as having been an introverted child, un responsive to his environment. In kindergarten G. did not participate, stayed on the sidelines, and always appeared sad. At school G. was a poor student and restless; when he was disturbed by others, he reacted with anger, yelling and becoming violent. G. ended his studies at the age of 14, because he felt that he was unable to learn and understand. He became involved with a criminal subculture, where he dealt in drugs and committed other delinquent acts. He used various types of drugs and was first hospitalized at the age of 17 as a result of repeated suicide attempts. He was diagnosed as suffering from a schizophrenic illness.

Six months later he was rehospitalized on a court order as a result of having sadistically attacked a young man. He was released after 18 months and received psychiatric follow-up treatment. During this period there was no evidence of active psychosis, but he continued to carry out criminal acts. He was once more hospitalized for observation on a court order after having confessed to murdering, together with an accomplice, one of his friends, whom he suspected of having informed to the police. On the basis of his testimony, the murder seemed clearly premeditated and planned.

On psychiatric examination, disturbances in thought process and content were noted. He alleged hearing voices and found it difficult to reconstruct the act. There were many contradictions in his statements; he claimed he could not remember or that the police dictated his confession.

This case raises, in particular, the problem of intention. Intention is wholly private to the individual forming it. No one else can know it, however thorough the inquiry, though it may be inferred. It has no necessary or logical relation to the actions it brings about, as words have with their meaning. As a psychiatrist, one tries to decide whether one believes that the accused knew at the material time, without equivocation, what he intended, and if so, whether this intent can be inferred beyond reasonable doubt.

In the case of G., there are different levels and combinations of intentions. For example:

1. Multiple intention. In such a complex and emotionally laden situation as in this case, it is difficult for the accused to state afterward precisely what he was intending. He might have have had a few desperate intentions.
2. Intention compounded of several levels of consciousness. A particular source of confusion is when conflicting meanings or purposes deriving from different times in the subject's life make an appearance simultaneously in consciousness, and in some people this seems to occur under stress.
3. Changing intention. During the commission of a crime, the intention formed at the outset of the act may change, so that it is not clearly known to the accused exactly what was being attempted at any particular time, e.g., to threaten or to murder.

G. without doubt suffers from schizophrenic illness. It seems from the evidence that his act was planned with criminal intent and was not the result of impulsive or irresistible urges. Which version is more acceptable? Is a statement made to the police by one who is mentally ill when under emotional pressure reliable? Did the patient try to use his illness to cloud his criminal intent, as in the Ganser syndrome or in malingering?

Can we consider the possibility of both criminal intent leading to premeditated murder and of mental illness facilitating the criminal act by lack of adequate emotional control? It is doubtful that in a case like this we can get to the truth. The psychiatrist must be satisfied with a description of the disease and its psychogenesis and clinical symptomatology until such tools are developed as will allow more comprehensive understanding of the connection between the disease and the act.

Case 2. A. was 25 years old, unmarried, the third of nine children; both his parents were alcoholics, and two brothers were drug addicts and criminals. A. had suffered emotional deprivation as a child. He completed 8 years of schooling and was below average at school. A. served 2 years in the army and was discharged early as unable to adapt to army life. He spent 2 years in jail as the result of crimes committed with his brother. During this period there was no evidence of psychiatric disturbance. One week after his release from jail, he became psychotic, was hospitalized, and was diagnosed as suffering from schizophrenic illness. After release from the hospital A. did not continue treatment. He was arrested 6 months after discharge from hospital as the result of attempted armed robbery with an accomplice. He was brought to the hospital for observation under court order.

On psychiatric examination, he reported that his brother was to be brought to trial for robbery and was unable to pay for his defense, and that he had attempted the robbery to provide the money. A. reported that from time to time he had strange feelings that he was someone special and said that he heard a voice that told him he was destined to save his brother.

This case exemplifies a combination of different motivations for a criminal act. There is no doubt as to criminal intent - we know, too, that he had committed such acts in the past, when there was no evidence of psychopathology. But there is also a psychotic determinant in that there was an auditory hallucination which encouraged him to help his brother. Is this enough to free him from responsibility? What are the interconnections between the two motives? Is the psychosis merely language which expresses the criminal intent in a psychotic-sounding way? Or - can we see the act as a response to disease? Or - can we assume that the disease contributed partially to the act by facilitating it?

Case 3. M. was 29 years old, unmarried, the second of nine children of a lower-socioeconomic-group family. His parents did not get along and created a tense family atmosphere. He spent 9 years in primary school and 3 years in vocational school, but never worked in his profession of carpentry. Instead, he helped his parents in their store. He was never inducted in to the army and was hospitalized at the age of 19 in a severe psychotic state. M. left the hospital only partially improved. He was rehospitalized 1 year later by court order after having threatened to kill the Minister of Defense because he had not been inducted into the army and yelled and created a commotion in the street. He remained an inpatient for 7 years, but upon release he continued his vagrancy and committed several robberies. He was recommitted to our institution on a court order as a result of a burglary.

On psychiatric examination he was found to have a neglected appearance and flat and inadequate affect, but no disturbance in thought process and content or in perception. There was no evidence of an active psychotic state. When relating his acts he remembered planning the burglary, and that he had known that it was criminal and tried not to be caught. He explained his act by stating that his National Insurance benefit was inadequate and he needed spending money. It was clear that he did not act as a result of an irresistible urge.

When we attempted to assess his ability to stand trial, we had no doubt that he was able to understand the charges, as well as his rights as an accused person. Regarding the question of legal responsibility, we see two components. The first is criminal intent, which is predominant and stands alone. The second is the partial mental defect, which somewhat diminishes his ability to control, restrain, or even sublimate his drives or impulses. In this case, it is possible that the idea of diminished responsibility could be used to reflect the complexity of intent, even though it is possible that the mental defect played a minor part in the criminl act itself.

When we discuss his capacity to endure imprisonment, a new dilemma arises. Should we tailor the punishment to the crime or to the individual with all his problems? According to our law, as we evaluate his responsibility, we have no power to excuse him from due process of the law. However, to evaluate his ability to stand punishment and to be sent to jail, we have to take into consideration all his mental problems and to recommend hospitalization and treatment. Thus two kinds of considerations are taken into account in establishing the psychiatric evaluation.

To conclude, our objective was to show that even in cases of defined mental illness there are difficulties in forging connections between the illness and the criminal act:

1. We lack tools to reconstruct the mental constellation of the patient at the time of the criminal act.
2. It is difficult to give weight to the different motivations, intents, controls, and cognitive and emotional perceptions of the accused as regards the criminal act.
3. To what extent must we use the different psychiatric considerations, made appropriate to specific legal questions, which are being asked of the psychiatrist by the court?

We see a need for a double process. On the one hand we must sharpen our understanding of the complex components of criminal behavior. On the other, we must find a suitable language to bridge the gap between the psychiatrist's world view when examining the mental state of the patient and the legal profession when examining the criminal aspects of the act. Such a process must be a continuous one related to the change in and development of psychiatric knowledge.

Violence After Severe Provocation

E. Johanson

The formal treatment of well-functioning people who commit severe acts of violence after having been provoked and humiliated seems to be a problem throughout the world. In Sweden, a person who commits a crime under the influence of mental disease, feeblemindedness, or mental abnormality of such a profound nature that it must be considered equivalent to mental disease may not be sentenced to imprisonment but must be surrendered for care in a mental hospital or given a sanction not involving deprivation of liberty. If he acts under the influence of a less profound mental abnormality he may, under certain circumstances, receive a penalty under the minimum appointed for the crime.

There exists a forensic psychiatric organization in Sweden. The work is esentially teamwork by a psychiatrist, a psychologist, and a social worker. The psychiatrist is the one finally responsible for the report. Forensic psychiatric examination is always ordered by the court. It is never obligatory, but most persons who commit serious crimes of violence are examined. The court is not bound to follow the recommendations of a report, but instead of changing them of its own accord, if there is hesitation about the content of the report or its conclusions the court may submit it for the opinion of the National Board of Health and Welfare. If there is hesitation there too, the report may be sent for further scrutiny to one of the members of the Board's Scientific Council. That member then usually performs a personal examination of the individual concerned before answering the Board. In that capacity, in spring 1982, I had to examine the two cases that I am now going to summarize. (Both have given me permission.) The work also gave rise to a study of how similar cases are treated in Sweden and elsewhere.

The subjects had in common that they were socially extremely well functioning, they had never been seriously ill, they had neither abused alcohol nor anything else (although one of them had drunk rather heavily during an earlier period), and they were not intoxicated when they committed their crimes. The first examining psychiatrist in both cases concluded that there was neither mental illness nor abnormality equivalent to mental illness and no need for care in a mental hospital.

The first case was that of a 42-year-old woman who tried to kill her husband with an axe just before Christmas 1981. She was born in a neighboring country but had been living in Sweden for more than 20 years. Her husband shared her nationality; they met shortly after her arrival. One of his legs was amputated. He was always uncommunicative, reticent, without warm relations to anybody. The woman told me she would probably not have married him had she not become pregnant. They had two children, born in 1962 and 1965. From 1969 on, she had night work as a ward orderly in a large hospital, essentially in wards where strenuous work was needed. She was considered very reliable and she liked her work. In the mid 1960s the husband was granted a disability pension. He drank alcohol in increasing quantities; he beat her sometimes; he never respected her needs; he was jealous; he demanded sexual intercourse, sometimes several times a day, and he wanted her to study pornographic pictures with him. In 1975 she wanted a divorce. He agreed but never moved away. In the months before the event he drank excessively – the situation got even worse after she called the police when he had an extremely aggressive outburst some time before the event. The week before the deed she worked a great deal and slept very little. She was expecting her menstrual period that very day (although it did not start until 2 weeks later). She came home from work at about 8 a.m., went to bed, and fell asleep, but was soon waken up by the husband wanting sexual intercourse. She sent him off; he went back to his beer and his pornographic pictures. She was unable to sleep again, and got up to do some household work. He wanted her to look at his pictures, she declined, he insisted; they probably quarrelled – she took the axe and beat him heavily in the back of his head. She called the ambulance (and police?) and was found "very nervous and maybe shocked." He survived but was probably disabled for the future. She was never able to recall completely the details of what happened, although she tried to reconstruct, and for a long time afterward she was tired and could not concentrate. When I met her more than 3 months after the incident she had only been able to collect her thoughts enough to read a book for about a week.

The second case was that of a 35-year-old man who, in the autumn of 1981, killed his 80-year-old mother-in-law (in reality his wife's adoptive mother) by violently and repeatedly beating her against a staircase. He called the ambulance, saying that his mother-in-law had had an accident. She died some hours later in the hospital. At the autopsy it became evident that the cause of death could not have been an accident, so the man was questioned. He denied involvement and was not arrested until 7 weeks later; he confessed after another 5 days but behaved in such a way that police and prosecutor got the impression that he was trying to render their work difficult. He had grown up in socially good conditions, but the father was severe and the children had to obey. The man dared neither oppose nor show aggressivity. His wife had grown up with the mother-in-law and her husband but was not adopted until she was an adult, when the mother-in-law became a widow. There was rivalry between the wife and the mother-in-law's relatives. The mother-in-law was dominating and critical; the wife was extremely sensitive and had to be comforted by her husband. Some months before the incident the mother-in-law came to live with her adoptive daughter and her husband after a period of illness, while awaiting a place in an old people's home. Things worsened; she was quarrelsome and went on criticizing her daughter. The husband tried to mediate; had been working very hard and he was tired. On the day of the deed he had a day off to do some gardening. He wanted to explain the problems to the old lady, but instead they seem to have quarrelled vehemently: he lost his temper and began to beat her. There were no witnesses and he was never able (or could never bring himself) to relate what happened; from her injuries one might judge that he had been completely infuriated.

In Sweden with its more than 8 million inhabitants the number of persons sentenced for murder and manslaughter is about 85 every year. What happens to them? Not everybody undergoes forensic psychiatric examination, but during the 5-year period 1977–1981 altogether 230 persons were examined because of murder or manslaughter. I was able to study 221 of the reports. The nine not accessible seemed to concern men who had been taken care of in a hospital for mentally abnormal patients, and were thus not similar to my cases.

The variables to be considered were operationally defined before the study of the reports. Of the 221, 24 were women. There was no difference in age distribution between the sexes. There were other differences, however. The forensic psychiatric assessments are shown in Table 1; the women were much more often judged to suffer from mental illness (but not from mental abnormality equivalent to mental illness). When they were sentenced to imprisonment they received sanctions considerably under the statutory minimum for manslaughter (which is 6 years in Sweden).

Table 1. Forensic psychiatric assessment of 221 individuals convicted of murder or manslaughter in Sweden, 1977–1981

Assessment	Men		Women			
	n	%	*n*	%	x^2	*p*
Mental illness	45	22.8	13	54.2	9.29	<0.01
Mental abnormality equivalent to mental illness	62	31.5	8	33.3		
Mental abnormality not equivalent to mental illness	90	45.7	3	12.5		
Total	197	100.0	24	100.0		

Table 2. Investigated variables in 221 cases of murder or manslaughter in Sweden. 1977–1981

	Men		Women			
	n	%	*n*	%	x^2	*p*
Victim in near family	79	40.1	18	75.0	9.21	<0.01
Earlier criminality	95	48.2	2	8.3	11.84	<0.001
Abuse of alcohol	130	66.0	7	29.2	10.80	<0.01
Intoxication with alcohol at the time of the deed						
Certain	125	63.5	6	25.0	7.78	<0.01
Possible	11	5.6	3	12.5		
Drug abuse	35	17.8	2	4.2	1.99	NS
Intoxication with drugs at the time of deed						
Certain	14	7.1	2	8.3		NS
Possible	5	2.5	–	–		
Long-term provocation						
Certain	32	16.2	8	33.3	1.76	NS
Possible	13	6.6	1	4.2		
Acute provocation						
Certain	63	33.0	12	50.0	2.68	NS
Possible	31	15.7	1	4.2		

From Table 2 it is seen that they much more often killed members of the immediate family, that they less often had previous convictions, less often abused alcohol, and were less often intoxicated at the time of the deed. The remaining differences were not statistically significant.

In nine cases, one involving a woman, the conditions were similar to those in my cases. If anything, these subjects were older than the rest. In all cases but one, the victim was a member of the immediate family. Of the nine, five were considered to suffer from an abnormality, equivalent to mental illness and one (who had killed three people) from actual mental illness at the time of the act. Those six were surrendered for care in mental hospitals (open care was proposed by the examining psychiatrist in one case but this was changed by the National Board of Health and Welfare). Three were sentenced to imprisonment; none was given a sanction under the statutory minimum for manslaughter.

From a review of the literature it is evident that in the Nordic countries, in continental Europe, and in the Anglo-Saxon world some special provision may be made for these rare cases. They are seldom considered psychotic, but diminished responsibility is sometimes assumed. It is recognized that psychotic episodes may be very short-lasting and there is some literature on clouded consciousness due to strong affect; this is even reflected in the legislation of some countries. The personalities of the perpetrators are sometimes considered healthy, sometimes described as neurotic or borderline, but often stressed as being inhibited, afraid of aggressivity in themselves and in other people. When they explode, the explosion is very violent.

In my two cases I came to different conclusions. The woman's first examining psychiatrist explicitly conceded being uneasy imagining she might get a long prison sentence. I judged the data to be sufficiently convincing to make it possible to assume clouded consciousness at the time of the deed and to consider her mentally ill. She was suffering from exhaustion and a well-masked depression, too. We agreed there was not need for care in a mental hospital. The National Board of Health and Welfare shared my opinions. She was convicted of attempted manslaughter and sentenced to probation, somewhat unexpectedly.

The man, being habitually overcontrolled, and thus in a way abnormal, was maybe more vulnerable. The provocation in his case was less severe, at least as judged from the outside, and he was certainly less profoundly humiliated. I am inclined to interpret his amnesia for the deed as well as his denial and peculiar behavior during questioning as an expression of his need to deny to himself that he had been able to commit such a deed. I could not regard this as a mental illness, however, nor his abnormality as being equivalent to mental illness. I advocated a sentence under the statutory minimum because of the abnormality and the circumstances. In this case the National Board of Health and Welfare disagreed with my conclusion and judged his abnormality to be so profound as to be equivalent to mental illness; a need of care in a mental hospital was assumed. No reason for the change was given. I had to go into court as an expert witness. The man was sentenced to 3 years of imprisonment for manslaughter. It is well possible that he may be conditionally released after half that time.

The defendant or the prosecutor may appeal against a sentence in the court of appeal. In neither of the cases was this right made use of.

It is not and certainly should not be self-evident how cases like these should be judged. Although the two subjects have in common that they were well-adapted, were considered healthy up to the deed, and reacted violently only after severe provocation, they show important differences on several levels. To me it is not psychiatrically correct in these cases to assume an abnormality equivalent to mental illness, as sometimes occurs in Sweden. If anything, there may be a question of a very short-lasting episode of psychotic intensity. It is in agreement with clinical experience and most international literature that this should be an exception. In most cases there seem to be reasons to advocate a sentence under the statutory minimum. If so, this should be made explicit. Sometimes the psychiatrist must have the courage to propose a sentence not involving deprivation of liberty and the court to follow that proposal.

If the forensic psychiatric reports are to furnish data of real benefit to society and the individual in these intricate cases, they must be performed with extreme care. Results will never be unequivocal, however. These cases are difficult to assess and have to remain so. Shared experience might improve assessment.

Staff Injuries Caused by Psychiatric Patients

B. C. Dimond

Introduction

Pressure from human rights groups has recently led to a major change in mental health legislation in England and Wales. An Amendment Act is designed to provide additional guarantees for patients who are compulsorily detained and provides for automatic referral of certain cases to a Mental Health Review Tribunal. It provides for the establishment of a Mental Health Commission to act as a watchdog over all compulsorily detained patients and tightens the rules relating to consent by compulsorily detained patients to certain types of treatment.

I had been conducting in Wales a series of seminars with consultant psychiatrists, senior nursing officers, and administrative officers while the bill was on its progress through Parliament, with the aim of acquainting the professionals with the new proposals and passing on their comments to the law makers. One question asked frequently in every seminar was "What provision is being made for staff safety?" The answer was "None" – it was not included in the Amendment Act, although a holding power was given to trained nurses to restrain a patient for 6 hours before a doctor could attend.

This concern to ensure legislative changes to protect staff safety interested me – was it a hysterical phenomenon not based on any real threat to their safety, or did the concern emanate from a high level of incidents which required further investigation and action? I decided that the best approach was to investigate the "reported accidents," to consider the remedies available to staff who were injured, and to determine whether legislative or managerial changes were required. I limited my investigation to some of the main psychiatric hospitals in South, Mid-, and West Wales. This paper sets out some of my findings and reveals the confused picture as far as the remedies are concerned.

The Size of the Problem

There is a duty (now a statutory duty under the Notification of Accident Regulations) to report accidents to staff. Hospitals have long-established procedures for completing accident forms or an accident report book, partly to provide the information for the Department of Health and Social Security under the industrial injuries scheme, but also for managerial/staff safety reasons.

These accident reports I used as my basic data. There was no uniformity about them – some were filled in in great detail, in others only the bare facts were recorded. I was aware, too, that reporting levels might differ between hospitals – in some hospitals the tiniest incident being recorded in great detail, perhaps even exaggerated, in others such incidents possibly being ignored. However, I hoped that this would become apparent when the overall statistics were looked at.

The size of the hospitals and their activity as showen by occupancy and length of stay are shown in Table 1. The initial accident figures are shown in Table 2.

Table 1. Psychiatric hospitals in Wales investigated to consider patient-related staff accidents (bed use statistics for 1981)

Hospital	No. of beds	% occupancy	Average length of stay (days)
A	422	70	343.5
B	598	75	382.5
C	448	89.2	190.3
D	707	92	360.7
E	441	89	135.4

Table 2. Incidence of patient-related staff accidents

Date	Hospital	1 Total staff accidents	2 Patient-related staff accidents	2 as % of 1
11/1981-11/1982	A	50	18	36
1/1981-11/1982	B	181	54	42.5
1981 and 1982	C	271	76	28
1981 and 1982	D	285	130	45.6
1981 and 1982	E	565	267	47.3

The Term "Patient-Related"

I was initially concerned to track the level of violence/aggression, but discovered that accidents were being caused to staff not only by the deliberately violent patient but also by the unthinking carelessness of a patient: a patient who suddenly relaxed when being walked along by a nursing assistant could cause a severe back injury as the nursing assistant tried to prevent a fall and took the full weight of the patient, and this injury could cause more long-term damage than a bite on the arm by a violent patient. However, the way in which the injury is caused has considerable effect on whether or not the staff member will obtain reasonable compensation. The term "patient-related" is therefore used to cover all those accidents to staff which are caused by the behavior of the patient - whether deliberate, negligent, or unthinking.

Degree of Severity

Only a small proportion of the reported accidents were serious enough to incur time off sick (see Table 3).

Table 3. Psychiatric hospitals in Wales: patient-related staff accidents in 1982. Seriousness of injury measured by failure to return to work

	% not returning to work
Hospital A	11
Hospital B	11
Hospital C	7
Hospital D	1.5
Hospital E	6.6

In Hospital E, for example, nine of the 135 staff who were injured in patient-related accidents in 1982 did not return to work. Their injuries ranged from a near strangling, unconsciousness, and head injuries to a strained back, cuts and bruises, and severe shock. Clearly, whether staff return to work immediately after treatment or are absent for a few days depends on the subjective qualities of the staff concerned – fortitude, courage, or hypochondria – and also on staff morale and on identification with the group. All these factors influence individual rates of sickness and absenteeism.

In Addition, the degree of injury occasionally depends on the assistance which is given to the staff involved in the incident by other staff or patients. For this reason the total number of incidents is perhaps as important as the number of very serious incidents.

In Hospital E, a staff nurse who was injured by a patient and was kicked in the stomach had to answer the question on the accident form. "Was the accident trivial?" and wrote the note "It may be trivial on paper, but it's not trivial to the person receiving it." She, incidentally, was one of those who returned to work – her injuries being reported as a strained abdomen.

Analysis of Patient-Related Staff Accidents by Sex of Patient and Sex of Staff

Table 4 shows the sexes of the patients whose behavior caused the injuries and the sexes of the staff injured. Male staff report significantly few accidents caused by female patients. There are several possible reasons for this.

Table 4. Psychiatric hospitals in Wales. Sex of patient and sex of staff injured (1982)

	Male staff			Female staff		
	Male patient	Female patient	Sex of patient unknown	Male patient	Female patient	Sex of patient unknown
Hospital A	11%	6%	11%	6%	33%	33%
Hospital B	11%	2%		30%	55%	2%
Hospital C	30%	3%	5%	18%	38%	6%
Hospital D	16%	5%	1%	13%	59%	6%
Hospital E	19%	1%	1%	27%	33%	19%

1. Male staff may cope with female aggression and receive no injuries.
2. Male staff may not bother to report minor injuries received from female patients - there are many cultural reasons for this.
3. Male staff may have little contact with female patients.

More concern is, however, generated in certain hospitals by the male patient/female staff problem. Certainly, in Hospital E where female staff had been injured as a result of the behavior of male patients there was often a comment to this effect. A state-enrolled nurse who went to the help of a patient who was being attacked by another patient stated as the cause of her injuries the fact that there were insufficient male staff on the ward - there were only female staff who had to cope with difficult, unpredictable male patients. This occurred at 5.30 in the evening. In another male patient/female staff incident in the same hospital, a female nursing assistant was hit on the head by a male patient. It was suggested that constant supervision, more medication, and more nurses on the ward were necessary to prevent injuries of this kind. Certainly, policies on the use of mixed wards may have implications for the safety and serenity of female staff.

Time of Day of Patient-Related Staff Accidents

The time at which incidents tend to occur appears to differ sharply between the hospitals: in some hospitals the early shift - waking the patients up and getting them dressed and ready for breakfast - appears to be a time of great concern. In other hospitals the night staff are most vulnerable. Levels of night medication could have some relevance here (Table 5).

Table 5. Psychiatric hospitals in Wales. Patient-related staff accidents analyzed by time of day (% of total)

Time of day	Hospital				
	A	B	C	D	E
7.00- 9.00	28	24	12	25	11
9.01-12.00	39	15	18	21	18
12.01-13.30	5	9	6	8	9
13.31-18.00		22	26	14	22
18.01-21.00	11	13	14	14	12
21.01- 7.00	17	17	20	18	27
Unknown			4		1

Compensation

What action is taken as a result of these incidents and what compensation is available to staff? Unless the member of staff is able to show some substantial injury, there is no compensation. Bites, bruises, cuts, and kicks which do not lead to more than a few days' absence or leave permanent scarring do not merit any compensation. The bulk of incidents are therefore not financially compensated. The various forms of compensation which are available are complex, overlap, and have built-in defects (see Table 6).

Table 6. Employee safety and compensation

Criminal law	Civil law	State industrial injuries scheme
Health and Safety at Work Act (health authority exempt from prosecution)	Employer's direct and vicarious duty of care at common law	Injury at work Payment by state
Prosecution of employee or patient	Employee's and patient's personal duty of care	
Criminal Compensation Order by court or compensation by Criminal Injuries Compensation Board		Compensation for disability: percentage for disability and special hardship allowance
Criminal liability	Negligence must be Proved	No negligence or criminal liability, need be proved

The Criminal Injuries Compensation Board

The Criminal Injuries Compensation Board (CICB) is not a statutory scheme but a government scheme designed as follows:

1. There is a minimum payment of £400.
2. Compensation is available only following a criminal act.
3. The scheme is used by trade unions in preference ot authorities because of the difficulty of establishing negligence in civil claims.
4. One trade union referred over 473 claims from England and Wales to the CICB between January 1979 and April 1982; of these 19 related to Wales.
5. The health authority is not wholly concerned with these claims, which are left to the trade union representatives and officers.
6. Aggressive patient behavior would have to be shown and an injury following from the careless and negligent behavior of a patient would not automatically be covered by the CICB. For example, a recent case where an employee was injured by a patient during an epileptic attack was turned down by the CICB.

Civil Litigation

A member of staff who is injured can sue the health authority in several distinct causes of action.

Duty of Care Under the Law of Negligence

There is a duty in law for anyone to take reasonable care to avoid acts or omissions which he can reasonably foresee would be likely to injure his neighbor. This duty of care applies to any employer who has to take reasonable precautions in the light of foreseeable risks to protect the employee. This duty is on the employer personally. He is also vicariously liable for the negligent acts of his employees acting in the course of employment. An empolyee injured by a violent patient where inadequate precautions were taken to protect the employee can sue the employer for breach of his direct duty of care to look after his safety or, if another employee's negligence led to the injuries (for example, where an employee failed to count razor blades accurately and a violent patient obtained one), he can sue the employer for his vicarious liability for that other employee's negligence.

Implied Term in the Contract of Employment

Every employer also has an implied term as part of the contract of employment to look after the safety of his employees. This duty is on the employer personally and he cannot delegate it. If he is in fundamental breach of his contract by failing to perform these duties, then the employee who is put at risk by this failure can regard the employer's conduct as showing that he no longer regards himself as bound by the contract, and the employee has therefore the option of regarding the contract as at an end. In these circumstances the employee who resigns would be considered by an industrial tribunal to have been constructively dismissed. The employee could therefore claim reinstatement or reengagement or compensation for the loss of his job.

As far as the civil law of negligence is concerned one possible defense by the employer is that the employee voluntarily assumed the risk of being injured. There is certainly an ecceptance by many staff I spoke to concerning the risks at work: if you work in a psychiatric hospital you can expect some cuts and bruises. Certainly this was the view taken by the judge in one of the very few cases of patient violence on staff to come to court.

In the one reported case involving violence by a patient against a nurse in a mental hospital, the nurse failed in his action (*Michie v. Shenley and Napsbury General H. M. C.,* 18 March 1952, CLY 1952: 2411). Here a male nurse brought an action for damages against the Hospital Management Committee for injuries he had received when, on sole night duty in a ward of a mental hospital, he was attacked and injured by a patient suffering from epilepsy. The judge (Berry J.) found for the Hospital Management Committee on the following grounds: a mental nurse chose his occupation knowing that it was subject to certain hazards, one of which was the unpredictable conduct of mental patients, epileptics, or others; any person making the care of mental patients his life work must have some expectation of assault and violence. On the night in question the plaintiff had had the clearest possible warning from the patient's behavior that there was a likelihood of his becoming violent. It had not been disputed in evidence that the plaintiff could have obtained assistance, and if he had shown greater care for his own safety he would have obtained help before approaching the patient.

It is extremely unlikely that any court would nowadays take the view that a nurse in a mental hospital voluntarily assumes the risk of being injured by a patient. Certainly, in the light of recent cases (e.g., *Burnett v. British Waterways Board* 1973 2 A11 ER 631) such a defense would not succeed where the health authority had been negligent. A defense of contributory negligence might succeed, however, where (as would appear in *Michie*) the employee failed to follow correct procedures, or take adequate precautions which were reasonably practicable, and as a result of this failure suffered injuries at the hand of the patient. In the school context a suggestion that a schoolteacher ran the risk of being assaulted by parents was not acceptable in a second hearing of the case before magistrates.

Industrial Injuries Benefit

The Industrial Injuries Benefit scheme is administered by the Department of Health and Social Security. It is not concerned with the negligence of the employer but only with whether the accident occurred in the course of authorized work. Rates of compensation are low. Changes are being implemented from April 1983, after which time compensation will not be available for industrial injuries until there has been an absence from work of 8 weeks.

Criminal Laws

The Health and Safety at Work Act 1974 places a duty on every employer - including Crown bodies and therefore health authorities - "to ensure, so far as is reasonably practicable, the health, safety and welfare at work of all his employees" [s. 2 (1)].

Section 2 (2) sets out particular aspects of this duty of safety, including the provision and maintenance of plant and systems at work; the use, handling, storage, and transport of articles and substances; and the provision of such instruction, training, and supervision. The employer also has the duty of preparing and as often as may be appropriate revising a written statement of his general policy and bringing it to the notice of his employees [s. 2 (3)]. Should the employer fail in carrying out these duties, enforcements and prohibition notices can be issued and he can be prosecuted. Such means of enforcement are not available against the Crown and health authorities. Individual officers in the National Health Service could, however, be prosecuted.

The failure to carry out the general duties laid down under the Act cannot be used by an injured employee to bring an action in the civil courts (s. 47). An injured employee would have to rely on the duty of care in the law of tort discussed above.

It is theoretically possible for the injured staff member to prosecute the patient who has caused his injuries, but the prosecution of a mentally ill person is unlikely to succeed and in addition he is unlikely to be able to meet any compensation order made by the court. The employee is far more likely to recover compensation from the CICB.

A recent criminal prosecution of a mentally ill patient for assaulting and wounding two male nurses in separate attacks at Park Lane Hospital, Maghull, Merseyside ended in the conditional discharge of the patient. The solicitor for the patient accused the hospital of bringing a political trial, and held that it was a misuse of the power of the courts (*Guardian*, January 1982). Certainly, since the injured employee can obtain compensation from the CICB without the criminal conviction, to prosecute a patient already under restricted court order is likely to be of very little value.

Department of Health and Social Security Guidance

Department of Health and Social Security Circular HC (76) 11 sets out guidelines on how to prevent, deal with, and review incidents of violence from patients. An appendix prepared by the Royal College of Psychiatrists and the Royal College of Nursing sets out principles of good medical and nursing practice in the management of acts of violence in hispitals.

Advice is given under the following headings:

- Prevention First Objective
- Attitude of Staff to Patients
- Dealing with a Violent Episode
- Reporting Violent Episodes.

Conclusions

1. My initial conclusion is that in the Psychiatric hospitals whose records I investigated there is a high level of tolerance by Management and employees toward minor incidents. The proportion varied greatly between hospitals.

2. There was evidence that as the percentage of patient-related staff accidents increases as a proportion of the total reported staff accidents, staff are more likely to show concern – as expressed in comments on the accident forms.

3. The proportion of very serious injuries is small.

4. Provided either a criminal act by the patient or negligence by the health authority can be shown, the employee suffering from serious injury will be adequately compensated.

5. Where serious injury is caused unintentionally and without negligence, e.g., where a patient has an epileptic attack, no compensation is available to the employee other than the relatively low-level payment of state industrial injury benefit.

6. The bulk of injuries would be classified as trivial, but in terms of staff morale and attitudes and managerial acceptance or lack of action, they require attention and investigation.

7. Psychiatric nursing staff seem prepared to accept a certain risk of minor injury as an occupational hazard, but where patient-related injuries increase as a proportion of the total reported staff accidents, disquiet and unrest develop.

8. Now that the level of payment from the CICB has been increased to £400 (net of Department of Health and Social Security benefits), more staff suffering minor injuries will go without compensation. One possibility, is for health authorities to create a fund for the payment of ex gratia sums where criminal injuries compensation would not be paid - i.e., below £400 or where no criminal act can be established. In addition, extending the role of the Health Service Commission to deal with staff grievances might be considered.

9. As far as prevention of accidents is concerned, the Department of Health and Social Security advice in general, if followed, would assist in preventing injuries caused by patients who are known to be violent; however, it does not eradicate or cope with the incidence of unexpected violence and there is no advice or guidance for staff injured through unintentional aggression.

10. There is need for concern to prevent the multitude of trivial incidents which distress staff. In particular, further detailed investigations could be carried out on the incidents involving male patients and female staff and it could be ensured that sufficient male staff are allocated to wards of mixed patients.

The significance of the times of day at which injuries tend to occur in different hospitals could also be investigated: e.g., is a low incidence level at night accompanied by a high incidence level in the early morning a sign of heavy night medication which leads to aggression when patients are woken up and dressed for breakfast?

Another factor which could be investigated is the age of the employee and his experience in preventing an incident occurring or in restraining a patient with minimum risk to himself. This area requires a study of the training given to all staff with patient contact, including unqualified nursing staff, occupational therapists, and cleaners.

Other detailed studies be undertaken to assess (a) whether there is an increase in tension and therefore higher risk to staff resulting from particular forms of treatment, such as behavior modification, or low medication regimes; and (b) whether there is any substance in the suggestion put to me that economic and social factors can also increase tension and therefore violence, e.g., the increasing cost of cigarettes.

11. My final point is that no health authority whose psychiatric hospitals I studied was able to provide data on the percentage of staff accidents resulting in industrial injury claims, or the percentage resulting in criminal injury claims. Civil claims were better documented because there the health autharity was the potential defendent.

As far as the international significance of this investigation is concerned, I would like to pose the following questions:

- Can one assume that all staff employed in psychiatric hospitals are prepared voluntarily to assume the risk of receiving certain injuries? If so, are staff warned when they take up the employment and are they all given specific training to cope with potential incidents?
- Are staff who are injured in patient-related incidents adequately and speedily compensated?
- Are the data on such injuries closely monitored by assessing the causes of the incidents, and used to prevent further injuries?

D. The Expert Witness

The Trap of the Medical Certificate

A. F. Halmosh

Paperwork such as the provision of medical certificates, attestations and expert opinions has become part of the doctors daily work. Almost every day the mail brings demands for information about patients. Since the physician is bound by his vow of professional secrecy, each demand is accompanied by a legal document, signed by the patient, certifying his waiver of his privilege of privacy.

There are many reasons for seeking information about the health of a person. As long as the information is required by another physician or medical institution in order to continue the treatment for the benefit of that person, there is practically no problem: there is rather an obligation to furnish data as full as possible. However, when the information is sought by non medical agencies, certain problems arise.

Who are, in general, the non medical recipients of medical information? Insurance companies, lawyers, and courts are the most frequent customers, followed by man power departments of large enterprises and institutions. The reasons for it seem, at first sight, obvious. Insurance companies want to protect themselves against unsubstantiatad claims; lawyers want to further their clients' cases; and courts call on the physician as an expert witness. These demands are more or less justified, and so are those made for security reasons for the good of the patient and the public alike, such as requests for authorizations to operate dangerous machinery, for the validation of driving licenses, and for the provision of certificates of health recessary for certain occupations. The doctor in occupational medicine should be able to decide on these questions and give the necessary recommendation to the employer without exposing the medical record of the person to a large number of unqualified people. But why should manpower departments need to know the medical past and present of their white-collar employees, whose own security and work performance is not usually affected by a disease such as diabetes or, for instance, a compensated heart condition?

I am not aware how this works exactly in other countries, but in Israel, which has a very highly developed social legislation, an employee receives a permanent contract of employment after a trial period of 6–12 months. This means that after this time the employer cannot dismiss his employee unless he has committed some grave breach of discipline or criminal offense. After a worker has obtained this status he is entitled to paid sick leave, which in most occupations is a month per year worked and can be accumulated over the years.

This legislation is certainly very progressive and favorable to any worker, who becomes ill while in his permanent job. However, since the employer is interested in days worked and smooth production, he feels justified in not getting involved with workers who have greater chances of needing sick leave than a 100% healthy individual. Thus it becomes quite obvious that anyone seeking employment, who has the bad luck to have some permanent health problem finds himself in an awkward situation: if he refuses to sign the waiver it means that he has something to hide, and therefore his application is not even considered; if he signs and produces the medical certificate, his changes of being chosen are severely reduced.

In discussions I have had with colleagues about the problem of writing medical certificates, several attitudes were voiced. Surgeons usually state the bare facts without any commentary. Internists tend to add some information about the range of function and prognosis. The task of the psychiatrist is more difficult. If he is seeing the patient and examining him for the first time, both know the exact nature of their relationship. It makes no difference whether the psychiatrist is appointed by the court or given the task by one of the litigating sides. If the psychiatrist is asked to write a certificate for a patient who is or has been under his treatment, the situation is much more delicate. He has knowledge that has been given to him in good faith, which in another situation the patient might have withheld. Sometimes it may be necessary so warn the lawyer not to present a psychiatric certificate, because it would be detrimental to the patients' case.

In most cases, however, the patient, naively asks his doctor to write a medical certificate that should help him to achieve his goal. Here the psychiatrist is sometimes in a very difficult position. He has to consider several points which may be antagonistic or counterproductive to either the purpose of the certificate or the therapeutic relationship and its goals and/or his medical integrity. The certificate may sometimes require the inclusion of information that is not known to the patient's family, or interpretations that have not yet been worked through with the patient. Despite the waiver in his hands the psychiatrist may, and perhaps should, hesitate to specify certain diagnoses, such as schizophrenia or severe personality disorder, because of their important social repercussions. Once these facts are printed on paper outside the medical establishment, that information filters out and becomes common knowledge, especially in a small community.

Over the years I have some to the conclusion that if a certificate is required for a patient who is or has been under treatment, the need for that certificate should be used as a therapeitic tool. The different aspects and the aims of the certificate should be frankly discussed with the patient. Usually, we find that the patient has some kind of magic hopes and expectations of what his doctor (or whatever he represents for him symbolically) could or should achieve for him. It sometimes requires quite an effort to bring the patient to an insight which should be seen as an equivalent to what is called "informed consent." The patient should know that a medical certificate to any official body has only an advisory function, but no decision-making power. More often than not, an unfavorable outcome of the patient's plans bring in its wake, at least temporary, a mini-crisis in the patient-doctor relationship.

The following case report illustrates these problems. A 17-year-old girl went with her older sister on a 3-day camping trip with the Society for the Protection of Nature. She made the acquaintance of a young man of 25 and fell in love with him. She gave in to his insistent and exciting words, but was careful not to tell her sister all that happened between the two of them. The man was from another town and she was looking forward to his visit and telephone calls, which, however, did not materialize. This was her first sexual experience and she was quite naive. She became alarmed when her period did not appear and was scared when the tests proved her to be pregnant. She confided in her sister, who arranged for an abortion. Her parents were unaware of what had happened and would have reacted violently had they known. She became slowly more and more depressed, until some 3 months after the abortion she was brought to the psychiatric clinic, but not before she had made her sister swear that she would not tell anyone about the abortion. There was a convenient reason, well understood by the parents and the neighbors: the approaching compulsory military service could be traumatic to a young girl from a traditional family. Since this reason was maintained in therapy there was naturally no improvement, either as a result of anti depressive medication or as a result of psychotherapy. After some 6 weeks she was referred to our day program, and it was decided together with her to recommend release from the recruiting order. As she saw how other patients were able to express their problems in group therapy, she was finally able to confide her secret to her therapist. As they worked through her guilt and shame, disappointment, and fears, she improved. She got a part-time job and decided to complete her matriculation at evening classes. Contact was lost for some 5 years, until she was again brought by her sister to the clinic in a deep acute depressive state.

After her first depression she had apparently entered a phase of slight hyperactivity. She easily completed her matriculation and entered university and obtained a BA degree in economics. She was a good student, and her shyness was gone. She was well liked by all, but she kept the boys at a distance. Then, one day, two problems came up at approximately the same time. First she applied for a job in a large bank and had to fill out an application form, which included the question (which appears on all such forms in Israel): Have you served in the army? The second problem was her engagement to another student at the university. This was a religious boy who accepted her puritanical behavior without question; in the same way he assumed that she was exempt from military service for religious reasons.

The girl came to the clinic in almost the same degree of depression as she has been at the time of the first referral. She was confused because she did not know how to handle the situation. She had practically been accepted for the job. Generally with women the fact of not having served in the army is not taken as seriously as with men. But as she was released on medical grounds, the manpower department asked for a medical certificate. The girl assumed that the psychiatric paragraph would be detrimental to her chances. She would have abandoned her application had it not been for the fact that her future husband had shared with her all the effort of looking for a job.

Up to that time she had completely repressed from her consciousness the crisis that had befallen her when she was 17. Now the feelings of shame and guilt vehemently reupted. The weight of her secret and the feeling of utter helplessness turned this girl almost overnight into a deeply depressed person. She informed her perplexed boyfriend that she was breaking up the engagement and that she was not going to go through with the application for work. In this state she was urgently brought to the clinic. She was again hospitalized under the day program and was assigned the same therapist who had treated her 5 years previously. A good psychotherapeutic relationship was rapidly reestablished and since her anamnesis was known, an aggressive psychotherapy was begun, together with intensive psychopharmacologic therapy. She recovered quickly enough to discuss rationally the immediate and later steps she had to undertake. It was agreed that I would write a certificate for the bank, saying that at that time she had shown an acute stress reaction to a personal crisis and the approaching military service. It was deemed medically advisable that she should not be exposed to further stress, so an exemption from military service was recommended. However, I would also point out that in the meantime she had matured emotionally and had successfully completed her university studies, which indicated that she was able to cope with stressful situations that were within her control.

In my opinion this certificate is compatible with medical ethics and professional integrity. It states the fact that this young woman was reacting to a serious stress situation when she was an immature girl of 17. If the date of her recruitment had not been as close as it was and she had had, let us say,, time to finish her matriculation, she would no doubt, have been drafted. If this had been the case of a young man, he would have obtained a years delay and would have been mobilized, probably with a reduction in profile. It was not necessary to mention the present crisis, which at the time the certificate was wirtten was already tapering off and which was doubtless a reaction to her feeling of helplessness. It was the direct consequence of her first crisis, which she had repressed at that time, instead of working it through in therapy.

The therapist helped her to find a solution for the relationship with her boyfriend. She realized that there was no way in which one could conceal her past relationship from her boy friend, but she could not bring herself to face the possibility of telling him about her abortion, in the same way as she could not work out her guilt feelings about it. Since the patient was absolutely determined about these decisions, there was no mention of this fact in a talk with the couple arranged at their request. When the acute problem was over, the patient again broke up the therapeutic relationship. Two years later I met her at the bank where she was working and she was married. If she should have the bad luck to have problems getting pregnant. I foresee that she will be in for a third crisis.

In conclusion, we have seen that without resorting to lies, through careful wording and in full agreement with the patient, the psychiatrist was able to write a certificate that was helpful to both sides. The bank added a clause to the employment contract, limiting its responsibility in case of psychiatric illness and in turn received an efficient worker. An attempt was made to use the crisis situation for emotional growth by working on the patients neurotic problems. However, because of the constitutional weakness of her personality she preferred not to deal with them.

The Psychiatric Case Register and Confidentiality

S. Schneider and R. Moses

Introduction

Sigmund Freud, in his 1905 paper reporting on the case study of a young hysteric named Dora [6], stated that "now I shall be accused of giving information about my patients which ought not be given." Ernest Jones [9], Freud's biographer, reported that the editor of the *Journal für Psychologie und Neurologie* returned this paper on the grounds that it possibly constituted a breach of medical discretion. Freud, noting the sensitivity of the issue, elaborated in his prefatory remarks on the precautions he had taken to protect his clients' identity. Fifty years later, Stanton and Schwartz [20], in their study of the mental hospital, stated: "... psychoanalytic practice was to use great care in protecting confidence ... on the general principle that only the patient was to decide ..."

Since 1950 the statistical and epidemiological studies carried out by the Israeli Ministry of Health have included the collection of data on psychiatric inpatients [12, 13]. The requirement to provide data on hospitalized patients was enacted by law in 1955 (Treatment of the Mentally Ill Act 1955) – and this with the full knowledge that "this may infringe on the patients' rights to privacy and confidentiality" [13].

In this paper we propose to explore some problems inherent in the conflict between the need to report data on psychiatric patients and the possible abuses of confidentiality.

Confidentiality and Psychiatry

With the recent proliferation of computerized data banks and the standardization of data collection, the issue of confidentiality and psychiatry has been vigorously addressed [7, 10, 18, 19]. The use of a unique identification number, while necessary [13] has met with resistance because of the confidentiality issue [19]. Once the identity number is entered into a collection system and "that button is pushed," *all* the information that has been entered emerges. Selectivity of data is no longer a luxury. The literature is replete with rationalizations and promises of "control of access ... through a sequence of passwords, identification codes, specific user name and codes ..." [7]. However, in reality it is possible for a nonauthorized person to gain access from a computer, even if by haphazard trial and error – "... any security system can be breached and any cryptographic code broken ..." [7].

The need to report diagnoses involves risks other than the loss of confidentiality. There are some clinicians who "fear that categorization is too constraining, or that the patient is depersonalized, or that the thinking of the clinician becomes too fixed" [18]. There are others who are even intimidated by computerization [14]. Nonetheless, this does not inhibit the collection of data – it just allows us to make a token expression of our feelings of guilt.

The moral/ethical issue of confidentiality has been addressed in order to show an "inherent conflict . . . in the psychotherapeutic process with respect to the issue of confidentiality" [16]. Engelhardt and McCullough [5] have gone so far as to state that "unauthorized disclosure of information about patients would . . . be a form of violence against patient autonomy." Stone [21] is amazed that, while confidentiality, is a crucial component of psychiatry, there are "few practitioners (who) seem to recognize the legal and ethical constraints imposed on confidentiality."

Are those involved in mental health blind to the issues? Or is this "inherent contradiction" left as an undefined problem? Two recent articles in the Israeli press [2, 8] have pointed out how legal authorities are concerned about protection of the individual's privacy, while mental health professionals seem to be either less concerned or lax. It is clear that since Freud's time there have been major changes in orientation regarding confidentiality.

Benefit vs Potential Harm

The collection of data on psychiatric patients has to be examined in the light of the type of data being collected and how necessary they are. "The answer must depend upon one's definition of the purposes for which data is being collected" [18]. What must be borne in mind is that, once collected data, run the risk of no longer remaining confidential. People in a bureaucracy tend to talk; with computers, there are greater dangers. We believe that the collection of data must be protected by law so that we do not need to rely upon the judgment of the person in charge with respect to how this information will be used or to whom it will be passed on.

Unless protection is forthcoming, people will continue to fear and may become more afraid of undergoing treatment, in case they be stigmatized. "In order not to jeopardize their immediate employment of future careers, civil service employees, military personnel, corporate executives, politicians, and teachers soon learned not to use their insurance coverage for psychiatric treatment" [4]. Unless the patient feels protected, either he will avoid treatment or there will be "less than frank disclosure by the patient and thus he will seriously compromise the therapeutic process" [5].

The argument that there must be disclosure in order to protect society has to be weighed against the violation of the rights of the individual [16].

If we can allow people to undergo treatment without fear of being unduly stigmatized, or of their rights being compromised, therapists will find it easier to give information if someone is dangerous to himself or others. What we are now faced with is the danger of the therapist overprotecting because society is underprotecting.

Governmental bodies that fund mental health facilities force the divulgence of information by threatening to cut off funding. In New York State the United States District Court, Southern District, recently ruled that complete uniform case records do not have to be turned over city or state agencies if "there is . . . some question as to whether adequate facilities presently exist to insure that access to this information will be limited" [11]. Thus the ethics of confidentiality here takes precedence over the requirement to divulge information - if adequate safeguards are not built in.

The Child, Adolescent, and Stigma

Adolescence is an age of turbulence the transition phase between childhood and adulthood. The adolescent cannot leave the quietude of childhood and enter adulthood without making a "big bang." The method that the adolescent chooses to deal with his internal turmoil is determined by, and will in turn determine, his psychological make up. He may free himself from inner tensions and pressures by acting them out in an impulsive manner, or he may withdraw and avoid dealing with the outside world. Neither extreme is healthy. What is clear is that the "storm and stress" theory of adolescence implies turmoil that is transient. The adolescent looks disturbed at the present time. But since adolescence is a fluid state, changes occur rapidly. If we diagnose him and place his name on the computer, we expose him to possible damage by society - even when his condition changes once he overcomes the transient disturbance. The same problem exists with children. Their personality is so changeable because it has not yet jelled.

Society should treat people on the basis of their level of function. As Freud stated, the essence of health is the ability "to love and to work." If a diagnosis is already in the computer, the individual's future state of functioning is irrelevant. He is stamped with a label without the possibility of change on updating.

In the classic Rosenhan study [15] it was shown that once a diagnosis is made, one is stigmatized for life. To Rosenhan, this labeling rather than focusing on specific problems and behaviors "seems undoubtedly counter-therapeutic."

Quite apart from the fact that the confidentiality of all those undergoing treatment should be safeguarded, adolescents and children should be handled particularly carefully.

The DSM-III (Diagnostic and Statistic Manual of the American Psychiatric Association [1] has attempted to separate the diagnoses of the disorders of children and adolescents from those of the rest of the psychiatric population on the grounds that one should make the least restrictive and least pejorative diagnosis possible in the case of a child or adolescent [17]. A more extreme and stigmatizing diagnosis can be made at a later date, if necessary. In the interim, the child or adolescent will benefit from the least restrictive diagnosis.

It seems ironic to us that the Israeli Ministry of Health should have abandoned in 1978 the DSM classification for the International Classification of Diseases (ICD) [13] - even with its clinical modification to bring it into line with the DSM-III (the ICD-9-CM) - since in 1980 the DSM-III came out with this important distinction between adults and children and adolescents. The DSM-III is quite specific and clear regarding the transient quality of child and adolescent disturbance. The philosophy behind this is an important factor to be reckoned with.

The child and adolescent have a whole life ahead of them - why close it off with a potentially harmful diagnosis? There must be another way to handle children and adolescents. Maybe information on them should not be passed on? Maybe an ongoing review of their condition should be carried out? Maybe their files should be sealed at a certain age, as in juvenile probation cases? These are philosophical issues that must be worked out.

The Legal Argument

What should mental health professionals in Israel do in the present setup in order to protect their patients and act both responsibly and legally? This will be examined under two aspects.

Within Existing Law

Doctors have a number of duties to disclose and report. One general duty to report hospitalization and dismissals of mentally ill people is laid down by section 9 of the Treatment of the Mentally Ill Act 1955. This information is to be held in confidence according to section 28 of the same Act, yet there are at least three statutory exceptions to this guarantee. Under Israeli law, this information may be transferred, and is indeed transferred, to the military authorities, and to the authorities responsible for controlling both firearms licenses and driving licenses. In other words, doctors who comply with the duty to disclose must know that the information may be transferred and used in these ways. In addition, doctors are under a specific duty to disclose if a person they are treating is, in their judgment, too dangerous to carry a gun, or if a person they are treating should not drive a heavy public vehicle [section 12B (a) of the Transportation Ordinance (New Version), as amended in 1979; and section 11A (a) of the Firearms Act 1949, as amended in 1978]. The licensing authorities in both cases ask the Ministry of Health for information, and such reports must be given to these authorities. The mechanism is slightly different in the two cases. The guns authority submits the names of applicants and the Ministry of Health is under an obligation to disclose medical information. The guns licensing authority then, presumably, uses its discretion to make a decision. In fact, however, a license is regularly denied. The driving safety authority, on the other hand, has its own access to the data in the Ministry of Health (and the security system). On the basis of the data they have, they make a recommendation to the licensing authority. In addition, both bodies have legal powers to require a medical examination of all applicants.

The general duty to report is more problematic, since it deals with hospitalization and has a variety of purposes. There is no reason to think that all hospitalization records are relevant to either driving or carrying a gun. In principle, the law may be responsive to these dangers. In the case of guns, the official responsible for the data has discretion as to whether or not to pass it to the licensing authority (see section 11B (b) of the Firearms Act 1949). This discretion (as opposed to the duty to deliver specific reports from doctors about the individual) may suggest that the medical personnel in the ministry may make a judgment about the relevance of the specific hospitalization record to the risks involved in this person's carrying a gun.

As an aside, it is both strange and revealing that there was no discussion in the *Knesset* (Israeli Parliament) about this difference. The law was voted in with no discussion and no reservation; [DK volume 82, 4 April 1979, pp. 2451-2452.] In the case of driving licenses, the medical authority has discretion to see what the implications of the record should be. However, in fact it seems that these guarantees do not work. It seems that discretion is not used in either case, that the disqualification is sweeping, and that the transfer of information is not made selectively.

Section 33 (a) of the Defense Service Act (Consolidated Version) 1959 specifies that the Minister of Defense may, in regulations, require that certain information will be given to a clerk. The 1967 regulations under this section indeed detail a long list of duties of disclosure. The ones which concern us are the duty imposed on the individual himself to report illnesses for which he needed hospitalization or prolonged treatment (regulation 1 (A) 18); the duty of the Ministry of Health to report dates and places of hospitalization [regulation 4 (cl)]; and the obligation on doctors, psychologists, and employees of hospitals to give the army details about dates of hospitalization, medical findings, results of tests, diagnosis, and operations, and the course of illness and treatment given. The defense authorities say that they use these data as "alerters" only, that they conduct their own examinations, and that they are sensitive to the difficult issues involved. We know of no research that can substantiate these claims.

Existing law, and the way it is enforced, is therefore a reason for uneasiness. The doctor must, of course, do what he is obliged to under the law. Yet he should know the possible uses of this information, and act accordingly. The doctor may, and probably must, make disclosure of information conditional upon proof that the information is used discriminately and with discretion, and that those areas of discretion provided for by the existing law should be effectively utilized to protect the privacy and the liberty of mental patients.

The law says nothing about the way information which must be reported is to be kept. It is thus possible to argue, even within the existing law, that the data should be stored manually, and not be fed into the computer. Such an arrangement would reduce the risks of leakage and abuse, and it seems appropriate for the type of sensitive data we are discussing here. However, it is probably hopeless to make such a demand, since the benefits of technology are so great that it is hard to believe they will be given up. We should thus be as ready as we can to protect the data when they are computerized, rather than spending our energies in fighting computerization.

Should Changes Be Made in the Law?

Firstly, administrative changes should be demanded and made at once so that the existing legal framework can be used fully, in line with what has been suggested above. Secondly, the duty to disclose, the liberty to pass on data, and the purposes for which information may be passed on are drafted too broadly. On all questions of disqualification, due process requires that all previous data will serve, at the maximum, as alerters, and that the individual should be given the chance to present his own medical data, or to challenge the accuracy, completeness, and up-to-dateness of the information and its relevance to the matter at hand. Individuals should be told what the reason for disqualification is and, upon demand, they should be entitled to demand an independent examination and subsequently a decision on the merits of their cases. This is especially true for driving licenses and for the military record, which are of central importance to the chances of employment and with regard to stigmatization generally.

The predictive value of psychiatric examinations is especially low in cases of road safety and firearms usage. It is somewhat limited even in areas such as nervous breakdowns in the army. The tendency is to use the existing record system to defend society from those who may infringe upon it, by checking the mental health records of individuals. In this process, data are treated globally rather than differentially. This trend is likely to be strengthened in times of economic inflation, when resources that would allow differential examination of people are not easily available. While a few people may be appropriately disqualified, many will thus be inappropriately disqualified and discriminated against.

There thus seems to be a good basis for proposing that no data on hospitalizations should be computerized or added to any collection. The individual should be required by law to disclose the required information when the applies for a gun license or is drafted, and it then is his responsibility to do so. The relevant authorities can then verify these disclosures by independent examinations. In cases of actual dangerous situations, the professional giving treatment must weigh and share the responsibility. However, as long as society cannot yet accept this, information should only be supplied if we can be sure that such material will be treated not globally and bureaucratically but clinically and differentially. We do not want to bring about a situation where the therapist scales down the diagnosis and people will avoid beginning (or continuing) treatment, or where they will avoid treatment in order to avoid the stigma.

If all these modifications require too much manpower and investment, the whole question of disqualification should be reopened and discussed. With the low predictive value of mental health examinations, a strong case can be made for taking some risk of potential harm in order to protect the privacy and liberty of the many. As mentioned before, if such measures are enacted, medical professionals may be more willing to report the cases in which they believe there is potential danger. Such selective reports might yield a better balance between the need to safeguard others and the rights of the individual seeking emotional help.

Acknowledgement. We gratefully acknowledge the help of Dr. Ruth Gavison (Hebrew University, Faculty of Law and The association for Civil Rights in Israel) in the writing of this paper.

References

1. American Psychiatric Association (1980) Diagnostic and statistical manual (DSM-III). American Psychiatric Association, Washington DC
2. Alon G (1982) Governmental offices forbidden to report data in computers on private citizens. HaAretz, 22 April (Hebrew)
3. American Orthopsychiatric Association Newsletter (1982) Summary reports of 1982 meeting. American Orthopsychiatric Association, New York

4. Beigler JS (1981) Privacy and confidentiality. In: Hofling CK (ed) Law and ethics in the practice of psychiatry. Brunner/Mazel, New York, pp 69-90
5. Engelhardt HT Jr, McCullough LB (1981) Ethics in psychiatry. In: Arieti S (ed) American handbook of psyhiatry, vol VII. Basic Books, New York, pp 795-818
6. Freud S (1905) Fragment of an analysis of a case of hysteria (Dora). In: Richards A (ed) Pelican Freud Library, vol VIII. (1977) Penguin, Harmondsworth, pp 31-164
7. Greist JH, Klein MH (1981) Computers in psychiatry. In: Arieti S (ed), American handbook of psychiatry, vol VII. Basic Books, New York, pp 750-777
8. Harel Z (1982) Personal papers found disgarded. HaAretz, 25 February (Hebrew)
9. Jones E (1955) Sigmund Freud: life and work, vol II. Basic Books, New York
10. Laska EM, Bank R (1975) Safeguarding psychiatric privacy: computer systems and their uses. Wiley, New York
11. New York Coalition for Juvenile Justice and Youth Services Newsletter, March 1982
12. Popper M (1981) The psychiatric information system in Israel. In: Aviram U, Levav I (eds) Community mental health in Israel (Hebrew). Chorikover, Tel Aviv, pp 93-113
13. Rahav M, Popper M, Nahon D (1981) The psychiatric case register of Israel: initial results. Israel Journal of Psychiatry 18 (4): 251-267
14. Reznikoff M, Holland CH, Stroebel CF (1968) Attitudes towards computers among employees of a psychiatric hospital. Hospital and Community Psychiatry 19: 419-425
15. Rosenhan DL (1973) On being sane in insane places. Science 179: 250-258
16. Schneider S (1981) Confidentiality: the moral/legal/treatment conflict. Society and Welfare 4 (2): 119-127 (Hebrew)
17. Schneider S (1982) The DSM-III: a revolution in psychiatric diagnosis. Society and Welfare 4 (3-4): 315-320 (Hebrew)
18. Snyderman B, Magnussen MG, Henderson PB (1979) Standardized data collection. In: Noshpitz JD (ed) Basic handbook of child psychiatry, vol I. Basic Books, New York, pp 657-675
19. Spitzer RL, Endicott J (1975) Computer applications in psychiatry. In: Arieti S (ed) American handbook of psychiatry, vol VI. Basic Books, New York, pp 811-839
20. Stanton AH, Schwartz MS (1954) The mental hospital. Basic Books, New York
21. Stone AA (1978) Psychiatry and the law. In: Nicholi AM Jr (ed) The Harvard guide to modern psychiatry. Belknap/Harvard University Press, Cambridge, Massachusetts
22. US Department of Health and Human Services (1980) International classification of diseases - 9th revision - clinical modification (ICD 9-CM). 3 vols, 2nd edn. US Department of Health and Human Services, Washington DC

Amnesia, Law, and Modern Psychiatry

M. S. Tropper, A. Avnat, and J. Wagner

In day by day dealings with people involved with legal proceedings (lawyers, police, court officials), there is much evidence of a significant lack of basic knowledge of memory problems among these professionals. Among the significant issues involved in the relationship between amnnesia, law, and psychiatry the following should be mentioned:

1. Memory involved in the reconstruction by witnesses of events,
2. Flashbulb memory,
3. Involuntary memory,
4. Semantic, episodic and repisodic memory,
5. Hysterical amnesias,
6. Confabulations
7. Facial recognition
8. Consolidation weakness of memory traces.

At the beginning of the twentieth century, William Stern [5], an outstanding psychologist, convincingly showed that memory problems have serious implications on legal procedure. He was the first to draw attention to the problem of the unreliability of testimony. The practice of the United States Supreme Court, the proceedings of the United States Watergate Investigating Committee, the proceedings of the Kahan Commission of inquiry in Israel, and the files of many other legal procedures studied by us show that memory and related issues of memory pathology represent an underestimated area of great importance for law, medicine, and psychiatry. A problem often encountered is the reconstruction of events by witnesses. In our contemporary world, full of stress and strain, road accidents frequently lead to legal proceedings, which are almost always connected with the testimony of witnesses. In order to illustrate and emphasize the topic we would like to ask: Do we really remember all the details of such complex events as road accidents?

Let us imagine that this or that accident happened in our presence. How will we answer the next three questions, when asked by the police or during the court proceedings: How fast were the cars travelling? What length of time passed between the sounding of the car's horn and the moment of collision? How long did the accident take?

It is well known that people are rather inaccurate in recalling such details as time, distance, speed, and duration of events. When the interrogator asks a person, "How fast were the bus and the car going when they hit each other?" he will receive one answer. However, if he changes only one word in the question and asks "How fast were the bus and the car going when they crashed into each other" This leads to a higher speed estimation [3]. We used this example in order to emphasize that the way a question is phrased can enormously influence the answer that is given. This contradicts the opinion that in interrogation the anticipated answer is based only upon the memory of a concrete event and independent of the circumstances of the interrogation.

This is the place to mention that in analogous situations two kinds of information which enter one's memory play a role. The first is the information gleaned during the direct perception of the original event, the second is the external information supplied after the fact. Over time, information from these two sources may be mixed in such a way that one is unable to tell from which source some concrete detail is recalled. It has been shown that reproductive and recognitory memory are both seriously affected by verbal labels, and consequently that verbal labels may cause significant shifts in human memory. As a result of these and other conclusions, the notion of the leading question in interrogation has been elaborated (Supreme Court Reporter, 1977, 3, Rules of evidence for USA courts and magistrates).

The USA Supreme Court decision concerning the case *Simons* v. *US*. 390, US, 377, 1968 reflects the court's opinion and its awareness of the falibility of eyewitness identification. In this decision it was emphasized that when an identification was incorrectly conducted the witness was apt to retain in his memory the image of the presented photograph rather than of the person actually seen during the event concerned.

Our experience shows that every detail concerning the differentiation between memory for faces and memory for the circumstances of an event should be throughly evaluated. There are cases when witnesses base their indictments on facial recognition alone. The complexity of the memory of witnesses continues to be underestimated, and therefore the assumption that conceptions and interpretations may be based and built completely on the memory of witnesses is far from being correct. Two aspects of the issue should be mentioned here. One is the intactness of the witness's memory and accuracy in ecphoria, especially in elderly persons [6, 7]; the other is the bias induced by mugshots.

One of the concrete cases connected with memory, amnesia, and legal practice is John Dean's testimony before the United States Senate Watergate Investigating Committee. It's scientific significance is unique because the testimony protocol was compared with the White House presidential transcripts, a factual secret record of all conversations held in Richard Nixon's oval office. When John Dean, the former president's councelor, described many meetings he had attended over a period of several years, a series of questions were raised by the Senate Committee members. The doubts were expressed in the principal questions: How much did he really remember? Was he telling the truth? How much did a human being who did not belong to the very rare group of mnemonists (people with outstanding memories, persons possessing astonishing abilities to use mnemonic techniques in recapitulation) really remember? And the question put by Senator Inowye of Hawaii, often cited in the literature, "Have you always had a facility for recalling the details of conversations which took place many months ago" was typical of the doubts among the Watergate Committee members.

The judges of the Israeli Supreme Criminal Court of Appeal also dealt with the subject of witnesses' memories. In the case *Cohen* v. the *State of Israel* (file 950/80, page 568 of volume 36, part 3 we read: the judges saw the witnesses and did not believe them. The judges conclusion was based on the behavior of the witnesses during testimony and their "exaggerated memory" for details. They reasoned that an ordinary person would not have been able to recall these details after such a considerable time had elapsed since the occurence of the event. The judges therefore concluded that the witnesses were perjurers.

The importance of aspects of memory in testimony is clearly seen in the openly published reports of the Kahan commission of inquiry (Israel 1982), where it appears that even highly responsible witnesses responded to questioning with "I can't remember", but not with "I don't know".

In connection with the topic under discussion we would like to emphasize four conceptual issues: first, that memory in stress situations is remarkably influenced by "schemata" [1] for familiar events; second, that a person's semantic memory should be thoroughly differentiated from his episodic memory [11]; third, that memory distortions are often caused by the needs and the character of the individual [2]; fourth, that in the interpretation of medicolegal cases specialists have to make a clear-cut distinction between verbatim recall and memory for gist (of what was said, of the underlying sequence of intentions). Specialists in our branch have already developed methods of assessment and apply these in the qualitative and quantitative evaluation of memory and memories [10].

Both inquiry committees (Watergate and Kahan) raised among the specialists concerned the problem of the nature of memory for conversations as one of great importance. In this connection some pioneers in this field may be mentioned. William [5] Stern warned that even the memories of witnesses under oath should not be trusted. Bartlett [1] drew attention more than 50 years ago to constructive and reconstructive memory and recommended that they be given serious consideration. Tulving [11] emphasized more than 10 years ago the notion of episodic memory, involving the retrieval of individual episodes of one's life, in contrast to semantic memory (the store of facts, meanings and general knowledge). Neisser [4] mentioned the "repisodic memories", resembling screen memories, a set of repeated episodes, experiences, and rehearsed presentations. What sometimes appears to be an episode actually represents a repetition and this is a phenomenon of underestimated importance in the interpretation of the recollections of witnesses. Experience often proves that specificity in the recollections of witnesses actually depends on the repetitive factor per se.

Another legal issue connected with memory is the difficulty of eyewitness identification. Not rarely, eyewitnesses are asked to play the role of a tape recorder on whose tape all the pecularities of an event have left a clear-cut print. Sometimes the prosecution thoroughly searched for stored facts on this "tape", trying to prove that the "tape recorder" was and is made without taking into account age, physical and mental state, signs of overt or latent so-called "organicity signs" typical for dementing processes, affective disorders (various depressive states), manifold stress factors [9], which together or separately influence the witness's ability to recall the detailed events. On the other hand, the defense points out that, there are "failures" in the human tape recorder and "empty intervals in the tape" and as a result of such a complex interaction it becomes clear that the presumption that "every thing is perfectly recorded in a human being's brain and can be arbitrarily played back later" is far from being correct and applicable in legal procedures.

Recent achievements in research show that cognition and memory represent complex information-processing mechanisms, and that consequently a person who sees an accident or withnesses a crime, when asked later in a legal framework to describe what he saw, cannot call up an "instant reply." A witness depends on his memory with all its limitations. In our daily activities limitations of memory may not be of such crucial importance. However, when one is a witness the inaccuracy increases enormously in importance. Apart from the above-mentioned factors, a witness's memory is affected by:

1. Background,
2. Personal abilities,
3. Attitudes,
4. Motives,
5. Beliefs,
6. Environment,
7. Age-related factors,

such as time reaction, vigilance, attention, etc. Experience accumulated by specialists shows that there are factors which significantly limit a witness's ability to give a thorough account of events he once saw or to identify people who were involved.

Among these the following may be mentioned:

1. Insignificance at the time of the events that were observed,
2. Short observation time,
3. Poor observation conditions (darkness, distance, fast movement, presence of a crowd).

The existence of such conditions were interfering at the time when the investigation of Emil Grinzweig's murder (1983) was conducted. Here we would like to mention briefly two notions: stress and mental state. A person under extreme or even moderate stress is a much less than a normally reliable witness, especially when things happened so that the person's own life was threatened and a strong physiological reaction took place, e.g. sudden changes in blood pressure, breathing rate and occurence of various cardio-vascular manifestations. In publications on research with Air Force flight crew members it is reported that even highly trained persons become poor observers under stress. Of no less importance are physical conditions, difficulties in seing, hearing, etc. Among these factors, weakness of consolidation of memory traces, confabulations, topographic memory disorders, amnestic aphasia, transient global amnesia, and last but not least, the phenomenon for which we have coined the name amnemophobia [8], it means the fear of loosing one's memory, should be mentioned.

Let us turn to another issue of importance – the legal and psychiatric view on identification of persons. Often arrays of photographs presented to witnesses are not throughtfully assembled. In cases when one item in the array of photographs is markedly different in height, weight, dress, sex, or quality the likelihood that one will be picked out is significantly greater. We should not forget that in many cases arrays of photographs are like psychological multichoice tests. When the rules for designing the test are ignored, its results become unreliable because the test design contradicted current scientific knowledge. For instance, if there are six photographs the chance should be one in six that one picture will be chosen on the basis of guess work. However, when the test was reduced, as in the often mentioned case of Angela Davis, to four photographs, including three of the suspect, the probability that the witness will pick out the suspect's picture is not 1 to 6, but 3 to 4 (75%), regardless of whether he had seen the suspect on the occasion concerned or not.

Let us examine an excerpt from the Israeli Supreme Criminal Court file 420/81, volume 36, part 2, page 29 (*Cohen* et al. v. *State of Israel*), a case of burglary, attacks on a policeman and use of a stolen vehicle. In this case the defense appeal was based upon a wrong identification: the identification was made by only one police officer. Judge Dov Levin (page 36) stated that "presentation of separate photographs to the witness led the witness to identify the person concerned not because he was registered in his memory during the event's perception but merely because this and other photographs were not presented in the right order." The judge stated that after this photograph had become fixed in the witness's memory every other identification, even the most correct, would be useless in trying to change this. Judge Levin's conclusion was that "we must take care that the quality of the witness should be observed in an objective way as much as possible in order to exclude any external influences ... there is a great danger in identification by eyewitness because at the end such a testimony becomes an evidence of inrooting an external opinion in one's memory." Therefore we can see that no test with photographs or a lineup can be completely free from suggestion. Basic data on eyewitness identification recommend that suggestions, hints, or pressure should not be transmitted to the witness, but experience with criminal investigations in different countries often reveals abuses by zealous police officers.

The research on memory in legal procedures so far carried out justifies us in writing the word "CAUTION" on every file where aspects of amnesia are involved. On the basis of a professional approach we must seek to understand the factors underlying the success as well as the failure of eyewitness testimony.

Another important issue is the "flashbulb memory". Almost everyone in Israel who is not too young remembers how and under what circumstances he first heard that the Yom Kippur war (1973) had broken out. Almost everyone in the United States will remember where and in what circumstances he first heard that President John Kennedy had been assassinated. It should be emphasized that the matter is not the memory of an event but the circumstances on first hearing the news about it. The main features characterizing flashbulb memory are surprise, insufficient illumination, and brevity. Our experience shows that flashbulb memory has definite importance for legal procedures, and therefore some of the notions, belonging to this kind of memory should be mentioned. Important here are: 1. the place in which one first learned about an event, 2. the ongoing activity which was interrupted by learning about the event, 3. the personality of the informant, 4. the affect aroused in others, 5. the own feelings of the subject, 6. the aftermath and 7. the consequences.

Another interesting issue is the interaction between amnesia and disturbances of consciousness. Loss of consciousness may be the cause of involuntary acts which even leads to crimes. Such involuntary acts are often labeled "automatisms." Professionals concerned with the matter should bear in mind that amnesia could be the result of disturbances in any of the stages of remembering:

1. Failure to register,
2. Failure to retain,
3. Failure to recall.

There are two types of involuntary actions which are now recognized by law as absolving from responsibility. The first type concerns "conscious" involuntary movements, reflexes, and instinctive actions; the second type represents "unconscious automatic actions" with no memory for the event. For medicolegal procedures cases belonging to the second type bear more importance, namely head injury, post-epileptic states, sleepwalking, organic brain syndromes, anoxia, drug intoxications, etc. All these states should be taken into consideration, remembering that the current law requires that to be convicted of a crime a person must commit a voluntary act and must also have a guilty mind – *mens rea*. In other words, the defense of automatism warrants the presence of M'Naghten insanity rules.

The issue of amnesia is of interest not only for proceedings in the criminal courts. Experience shows that civil courts encounter these problems quite often. Amnesia is encountered in divorce cases, testamentary cases, contract cases, suits for damages, management cases, etc.

In conclusion, we are aware that we have only touched here on the topic under discussion. We wanted to draw attention to the legal issues of memory, amnesia, and related topics and to point to the necessity of improving the basic knowledge of memory problems among professionals. We feel that a contribution could be made to the judicial system by implementing the latest achievements of memory research, memory assessment, and memory understanding in the forensic decision making process.

References

1. Bartlett FC (1932) Remembering. Cambridge University Press, Cambridge
2. Freud S (1956) Screen memories. In Collected papers of Sigmund Freud vol 5. Hogarth, London
3. Loftus EF, Palmer JC (1974) Reconstruction of automobile destruction: an example of the interaction between language and memory. J Verbal Learning Verbal Behavior 13: 585–589
4. Neisser V (1981) John Dean's memory: a case study. Cognition 9: 1–22
5. Stern W (1904) Wirklichkeitsversuche. Beitr Psych Aussage 2/1: 1–31
6. Tropper M (1977) Memory control as the central issue in psychogeriatrics. J Gerontol (Israel) 10: 42–49 (Hebrew)
7. Tropper M (1978) Memory control in psychogeriatric rehabilitation. In: II International Congress of Gerontology, Tokyo, Abstr, vol. 1, 151
8. Tropper M, Wagner J (1981) Geropsychiatry and the family physician. In: The Family Physician (Israel) 10/2: 208–219 (Hebrew)
9. Tropper M (1983) Dementias as multi-stage processes (conceptual semiological approaches). In: VII World Congress of Psychiatry, Vienna, Abstr, vol I, 192
10. Tropper M (1984) Neuropsychology and psychogeriatrics: new dimensions in assessment, intervention and functional rehabilitation of elderly patients. In: Innovations in Psychogeriatrics, First International Psychogeriatric Association Workshop, Cologne, Germany
11. Tulving E (1972) Episodic and semantic memory. In: Tulving E, Donaldson W (eds) Organization of memory. Academic, New York

E. Children and the Aged

Children's Accidents: Psychological and Legal Dimensions

N. P. Sheehy

The consequences of accidents account for a staggering amount of human suffering. During 1979 more than 17 000 people died in the United Kingdom from injuries accidentally inflicted. During the same year more than 300 000 road users were involved in traffic accidents. The problem is an international one: over 1 600 000 road users were involved in fatal or serious traffic accidents in the European Economic Community during 1979. More than 5000 died from accidents in the home in 1978. The accident rate among children is particularly severe, and accidents constitute the single largest cause of death to children between the ages of 5 and 14 years. By comparison, few accidents occur in the workplace: there were 711 fatal work accidents reported in the United Kingdom in 1979. The disproportionately high interest which workplace accidents has attracted among psychologists is probably a consequence of the fact that industrial accidents have a conspicuous political element. This encourages financial resources for research and prevention. Psychological textbooks dealing with child development typically do not include a comprehensive analysis of child accidents.

There are a number of theories of accident causation which relate to industrial injuries, but few indications as to whether these theories can be generalized to apply to children's accidents. The fact that most of these theories do not include an explicit treatment of developmental factors suggests that they are of limited value in understanding the etiology of children's accidents.

Popular models of accident causation have tended to reflect deep superstitions about the hidden meaning of catastrophic events in our lives. In this regard, popular theories of accident causation have a similar history to folk theories of disease etiology. Both were originally viewed as manifestations of evil. They have been subject to rational analysis only in more recent times. Popular explanations for the vulnerability of children typically assume that children's accidents arise from heedlessness and carelessness on the part of the child. Foot et al. [6] questioned parents, teachers, police officers, and road safety officers regarding their attributions of responsibility for children's road accidents. They found that factors such as the child's lack of attention, impetuousness, unawareness of danger, and lack of road sense figured prominently in attributions of responsibility. On average only 8% mentioned insufficient care and attention on the part of drivers. A study of attitudes toward child and adult pedestrians by Sheehy [14] also supports the hypothesis that children are viewed as relatively incompetent and heedless road users.

Evidence from field investigations of children's perceptions of hazard and behavior in traffic does not support these attitudes. Sheehy [14] examined adults' and children's perceptions of traffic hazard using video sequences of routine street activity as the stimulus material. Children were more conservative in their perceptions of hazard than adults. Children were also more conservative than the adults expected them to be. In a study of pedestrian-driver interaction, Howarth and Lightburn [9] found that in a majority of cases accidents were avoided by action on the part of the child alone. This evidence supports the argument that adults ought to accept a greater burden of responsibility when negotiating children in traffic. For the present it is unlikely that they will do this because of the pervasiveness and strength of attitudes which presume carelessness on the part of the child. Thus legislative changes may have an important but potentially limited role in ensuring a more equitable distribution of responsibility along the lines envisaged in this argument.

Accidents and Blame

Few writers have explored why accidents have such a conspicuous moral character. We offer the following explanation. Accidents are experienced as a consequence of actions executed at a socially immersed level of awareness: by definition, accidents are unexpected and unintended events [3]. When actions which are consciously planned and deliberately executed yield unintended and unexpected results, these are not normally regarded as accidents. For instance, failure to make the desired impression would not be regarded as an accident. Thus accidents are defined by more than expectancy and intentionality. Explanations of accidents typically address context-based motives. Beginning with an intuitive and undefined concept of "situation" [1], then every action occurs in a spatiotemporal situation. Often actions have deictic features which refer to the situation in which the action takes place. The context of actions also includes sociological and psychological variables pertinent to an understanding of the action.

Actions whose meanings are completely determined by their contexts have the quality of having no meaning. This is because meaning implies choice. If observers know in advance what an actor will do, then the actor's actions offer no information when executed. For instance, the fact that a pedestrian is seen to wait at the curb before attempting to cross the road seems quite reasonable, and all that needs to be said about the behavior is that it is used in such interactions. It is not particularly informative to insist on an explanation of its meaning above its use. However, "waiting at the curb" contrasts with "not waiting," and it is in the choice of waiting and not waiting that the action has meaning. Consequently, one can go on and ask about the meaning of each of the potential actions by contrasting it with its alternatives.

It follows from the notion of "choice" that meaning is, in principle, quantifiable with respect to the probability of occurrence in context. This conforms with the idea that the meaningfulness of actions varies inversely with the degree of expectancy in context, and this is also the idea on which theories of information processing are founded (cf. [II]). Precise quantification of meaning depends on the capacity to identify contextual features and their conditional probabilities, and it is very unlikely that meaning can be quantifiable in this sense with precision. Nevertheless, researchers have made extensive use of the concepts of objective and subjective probability distributions, and their interrelationships have been considered important in determining the probability of accidents [2]. Thus one can say that the tendency toward moral blameworthiness is linked with the apparent meaninglessness of accidents. Accident victims appear to break an obligation to maintain the social order and show that their actions are meaningful. In the case of children developmental immaturity shields the child from severe moral sanction, although the child can nevertheless be held responsible for the accident. In the case of traffic accidents a complicating variable is added: road users are encouraged to promote an atmosphere of safety by acting as if other interactants were careless and hazardous. Where accidents to occur this means that to establish their innocence individuals have merely to prove that tehy were strangers to the accident. We would suggest that adults more than children find it possible to distance themselves from accidents. Children live in a world created and managed by adults. When accidents occur involving children and adults, the adults will tend to find themselves in a stronger and privileged position. Usually, it will be more difficult for the child to demonstrate the adult's guilt than vice versa (cf. [15]). The findings of Howarth and Lightburn [9] and Sheehy [14] suggest that children are not as incompetent as adults often believe them to be. Potentially, this evidence will expose the child to greater moral blame and disadvantage the child still further. The legal system can play an important part in ensuring that this will not happen.

Law as an Agent of Change

Foot et al. [6] have shown that neither police nor road safety officers place any emphasis on strengthening legal powers as a practical solution for reducing child pedestrian accidents. In contrast, legal measures are more often mentioned by parents and teachers. This disparity suggests that those professionally involved in road safety doubt the usefulness of legislative changes, while parents and teachers are more hopeful of their contribution. It is not clear whether the attitudes of road safety and police officers are based on experience of the consequences of legislative change, but parents and teachers clearly feel that not enough is being done in this regard.

Psychologists and lawyers who have considered the contribution of legislation in a more comprehensive manner are inclined to share the optimism of the layman. Howarth and Gunn [8] have proposed that some time ought to be devoted to a systematic appraisal of experimental legislation through the courts. Howarth and Lightburn [9] have proposed that the safety of protected pedestrian crossings ought to be generalized to larger sections of roadway in residential areas. However, analysis of pedestrian accidents reveals that, relative to their proportion of roadway, the area on either side of pedestrian crossings is the most hazardous section of roadway (i.e., relatively more accidents happen here). These data raise doubts about the generalizability of legislative countermeasures which are geographically specific. They may lead to a concentration of accidents in other sections of roadway (cf. [7]).

Presently, in cases involving careless driving, different outcomes will result depending on whether the case is criminal or civil in nature. In criminal cases the prosecutor is obliged to prove the case beyond reasonable doubt, but in civil cases the plaintiff need only establish a case on the balance of prohabilities. Thus it is easier for a plaintiff than a prosecutor to establish a case, and reciprocally a defense which works in civil law is even more likely to work in criminal law. Thus children who seek compensation for accidentally inflicted injuries will be more inclined to pursue a case in civil than criminal law. Nevertheless, when faced with the necessity of choosing between the testimony of an adult and that of a child, courts may be more inclined to accept the statements of an adult. In order to redress this bias Howarth and Gunn [8] have proposed a more technical innovation during court proceedings and argue for the introduction of the maxim of *res ipsa loquitur* (the thing speaks for itself).

The evidential burden of proof refers to the obligation on a party to educe relevant evidence pertinent to some fact at issue. Shifting she burden indicates the moving, during the trial, of the burden of proof from one party to another. The operation of the rule contained in the *res ipsa loquitur* maxim illustrates the shifting of the burden. This is a rule of evidence which takes account of the fact that injury is often inflicted during a course of events which suggest lack of care on the part of someone. However, the circumstances often make if difficult for the plaintiff to prove the exact form which the carelessness took. If the circumstances are such that the plaintiff is unable to specify the exact cause of injury but can cite facts which allow a reasonable inference of negligence on the part of the defendant, then there exists a *prima facie* case which it is for the defendant to rebut [10].

Shifting the burden involves much more than is overtly described in the maxim. The obligation to prove a set of facts does not shift. The plaintiff may have an obligation to prove one set of facts and the defendant to refute these facts. In shifting the burden the plaintiff lays down his load and the defendant takes up a new load to prove a different set of facts. Thus the moral and legal character of the dispute alters appreciably. It is for this reason that Cross [4] and others disapprove of the introduction of *res ipsa loquitur* in criminal law, although it is probably more acceptable in civil litigation.

Using the legal system as an agency of social change raises issues beyond technical considerations. The courts may be required to take decisions which would be better taken by other sections of the community. One cannot force adults to meet their responsibilities toward children merely by providing legal guarantees. The issues here are more fundamental and relate to attitudes and behavior toward children and the status of children in society and law. The problem of children's accidents demands a strategic response in which education and information services and medical, engineering, and legal systems can all play a part. An important obstacle to the coordination of psychological and legal approaches rests in the nonequivalence of certain psychological and legal concepts. This nonequivalence is demonstrated in the legal concept of *res gestae*. Literally, *res gestae* refers to things done relevant to the affair being considered by the court. Facts in issue before the court are those facts necessary to establish or refute a case. Admissible statements must explain the fact in issue. However, Curzon [5] and others have argued that the concept of *res gestae* is used as a blanket of respectability for a variety of legal courses to which precise formulae cannot be applied. For instance, in the case of *R.* v. *Bedingfield* [12] X staggered from a room in which she had been with Y, with her throat cut, exclaiming, "See what Y has done to me." This statement was not admitted as part of the *res gestae,* since it consisted of little more than a narration of what had happened. However, in the case of *Ratten* v. *R.* [13] a telephone call to an operator by P, requesting police assistance, shortly before P was stabbed by Q, was held to be admissible as part of *res gestae.* These decisions suggest that much evidence accepted by psychologists as part of the *res gestae* might not be admitted by the courts. The differences between legal and psychological criteria cannot be surmounted by further empirical investigation. The two perspectives reflect different value assumptions which cannot be proved or disproved. There is an unavoidable dialectic between psychological and legal perspectives which must be addressed in the courtroom at a professional level. It should not be treated as a basis for inaction.

In summary, we have argued that one of the most significant aspects of accidents is their moral feature. This feature has not received a level of interest appropriate to its importance. In the case of children's accidents the child may find that he is saved from moral blame but also isolated from justice. Psychologists have an important role to play in assisting the courts to make fair and informed decisions. There is an unavoidable conflict between the perspectives of law and psychology, and neither can be proved or disproved through empirical inquiry. Both perspectives reflect value assumptions. These assumptions can be identified and irregularities and inconsistencies remedied through joint contact.

References

1. Argyle M, Furnham A, Graham JA (1981) Social situations. Cambridge University Press, London
2. Brown ID (1980) The traffic offence as a rational decision: exposure of a problem and suggested countermeasures. In: Lloyd-Bostocksm (ed) Psychology in legal contexts: applications and limitations. Macmillan, London
3. Chapman AJ, Foot HC, Sheehy NP, Wade FM (1982) The social psychology of child pedestrian accidents. In: Eiser JR (ed) Social psychology and behavioral medicine. Wiley, Chichester
4. Cross R (1979) Cross on evidence. Butterworth, London
5. Curzon LB (1978) Law of evidence. Macdonald and Evans, London
6. Foot HC, Chapman AJ, Wade FM (1982) Pedestrian accidents: general issues and approaches. In: Chapman AJ, Wade FM, Foot HC (eds) Pedestrian accidents. Wiley, Chichester
7. Garwood F, Moore RL (1962) Pedestrian accidents. Traffic Engineering and Control 4: 274–276, 279
8. Howarth CI, Gunn MB (1982) Pedestrian safety and the law. In: Chapman AJ, Wade FM, Foot HC (eds) Pedestrian accidents. Wiley, Chichester
9. Howarth CI, Lightburn A (1981) A strategic approach to child pedestrian safety. In: Foot HC, Chapman AJ, Wade FM (eds) Road safety: research and research. Praeger, Eastbourne
10. James PS, Brown DJL (1978) General principles of the law of torts. Butterworths, London
11. Miller G (1967) The psychology of communication. Penguin, Harmondsworth
12. *R.* v. *Beddingfield* (1879). 14 Cox cc 341
13. *Ratten* v. *R.* (1972). AC 378
14. Sheehy NP (1982) The perception of hazard by adults and children in familiar environments. Unpublished PhD thesis, University of Wales
15. Sheehy NP (1982) Children's accidents and tort compensation. Paper presented to the international conference on psychology and law, British Psychological Society, Swansea

The Agony of Phillip Becker: Parental Autonomy Versus the Best Interests of the Child

S. S. Herr

For seven years, American courts have struggled to decide the fate of a boy who was born with Down's syndrome. The internationally publicized case of Phillip Becker seemingly raised a stark issue: the power of absentee parents to deny their child not only life-prolonging medical treatment, but also any chance to live an emotionally satisfying life. At its bleakest juncture, Phillip's case appeared headed for tragedy: a child in the grips of a strangling cyanotic illness, natural parents resistant to medical advice, a court judgment affirmed by the California Supreme Court endorsing the natural parents' right to withhold treatment, and a prognosis that Phillip's congenital heart defect might no longer be operable even if authorization for surgery could be obtained. By shifting the case's focus from parental neglect to a child's beneficial custody, Phillip's advocates dramatically changed the legal, medical, and social outcomes for this youngster and his substitute family. This chapter describes the remarkable results of this case, and the discrimination it exposes. It is also a reminder that the concept of parental autonomy can lead to radical decisions of nonintervention that damage a child's health, emotional development, and lifespan.

This litigation involving Phillip Becker has forced society to consider the value of a retarded child's life and the possibilities for such a child's future. It documented Phillip's abilities as a mildly retarded 15-year-old to learn, to grow, and to give and receive affection. It also revealed problems of low parental expectations and conflicts of interests that can arise from the birth of an infant with Down's syndrome. Ironically, Phillip's natural parents would invest great emotional energy and legal expense in waging a bitter custody fight over a child they never invited to their home until litigation had begun [1].

Phillip's plight is somewhat similar to the so-called right to life-prolonging treatment cases. These cases typically involve the withholding of life-saving surgery or nutrition from handicapped infants as a result of informal decisions made by doctors and parents. In the United States, for example, litigation to save the life of Baby Doe in Bloomington, Indiana, sparked a national furor. There the parents of a Down's syndrome infant refused to consent to the surgical correction of the infant's esophaegal defect. Although local prosecutors contested the parents' decision, a trial court refused to intervene. The state supreme court affirmed the trial court's decision by a 3 to 2 vote, and the baby died before an emergency petition to the U. S. Supreme Court could be filed [2]. The meanest mass-murderer in the United States would receive more due process than that.

The *Doe* and *Becker* cases are not all that exceptional, only better publicized than other life-prolonging treatment cases. Studies at some of the most respected medical centers document the numerous decisions to forego medication, nourishment and other basic life-supports for handicapped children [3]. In addition, Wolf Wolfensberger, a well-known psychologist and university professor, has examined the denial of medical treatment to handicapped adults, and described the resulting loss of life as genocide [4]. Although that characterization may be overstated, it is clear that the label of Down's syndrome or mongolism - as the condition is commonly known - is one that raises the risk of stereotypical thinking and decision-making grossly prejudicial, if not lethal, to the well-being of the individual so classified.

The life of Phillip Becker all too sadly illustrates this point. Within days of his birth, his parents transferred him from the hospital to a board-and-care facility. For the first six years of his life, he received little more than basic care. Even after his transfer to another institution, he had no programs for education or therapy. Although his parents were notified when Phillip was three years old of his ventricular septal defect, they repeatedly refused to consent to corrective urgery. When Phillip was six, they rejected surgery without considering the risks or consulting other physicians. When the boy was eleven, they again ignored medical advice warning of the consequences for Phillip if surgery was not performed and the disease was allowed to progress into its terminal stages. According to their testimony, the natural parents would have authorized such an operation if either of their nonhandicapped sons had had the same problem as Phillip. Indeed, their decision to deny heart surgery for Phillip was motivated primarily by his mental retardation, and their fears that Phillip might outlive them. As Mr. Becker explained: "The motivation for it had to do with the fact he was retarded. In other words, if he wasn't retarded, I don't think there would have been any question about the fact that he would have had the operation" [5]. If courts have any role in intervening to disturb parental autonomy, surely Becker's case cried out for intervention. In outspoken terms, his parents seemed to view his life as having little appreciable value. When Mr. Becker was asked whether he believed it would be better that Phillip were dead rather than alive, he answered affirmatively.

In 1978, district attorneys, acting for the State of California, brought a neglect petition seeking court approval for the surgery. The juvenile court, in a multi-factored analysis of the risks and the parental prerogatives at stake, found that the state had failed to meet its burden of proof and dismissed the petition. The court of appeal affirmed as a matter of law, and the U.S. Supreme Court declined to grant further review [6]. Although commentators sharply criticized this elevation of parental autonomy over the child's best interests, state authorities were unwilling to pursue Phillip's case further [7]. Had this case not received national media attention and provoked the intervention of new actors, Phillip might not have had another day in court. George Will, a *Newsweek* columnist and a parent of a Down's syndrome child, criticized the injustices to handicapped children revealed by cases of this kind [8]. Herbert and Patsy Heath, regular visitors to Phillip who would become his de facto parents, came forward to befriend him and advance his medical, developmental, and emotional interests.

The Heaths also sought the assistance of attorneys and habilitation experts who could present an alternate legal theory to the courts. Under California law, a court can make an award of custody to a nonparent if this is required to serve the child's best interests, and the parents' continued custody would be detrimental to the child. Thus, unlike neglect actions the emphasis shifts from findings of parental unfitness to findings of serious threats of detriment to the child.

Guardianship of Becker succeeded because it emphasized that the harms inflicted on Phillip went far beyond an untreated, damaged heart. In their evidence to the superior court, clinicians clearly documented the injuries to his spirit, emotional well-being, and capacities for living a full and independent life. The court's opinion recognized the profound emotional harm to Phillip when is natural parents decided to terminate his home visits to the Heaths, the only experience of terminate his home visits to the Heaths, the only experience of family life he had ever known. Judge Fernandez cited evidence of further emotional trauma if the Beckers were to carry out their threat of permanently separating Phillip from his psychological parents by sending him to a remote institution. Finding that relationship a source of protection, affection, and satisfaction of the child's emotional needs, the court noted that even its temporary interruption had produced signs of emotional disturbance (e.g., depression, fire-setting, running away, and sullenness) in Phillip. The court also found educational detriments to Phillip's development as a result of parental neglect or deliberate choice in denying him the opportunity for habilitation. Finally, Judge Fernandez found that Phillip had not only suffered medical detriment, but would suffer future medical detriment if left under the Beckers' control [9].

These findings and legal conclusions have been upheld by appellate judges. On 23 January 1983, the California Court of Appeal rendered a landmark decision on the custody of handicapped children. The panel's unanimous opinion affirmed the child's paramount interests, the guardians' legal interests as psychological parents, and the state's interest in enforcing statutory rights to habilitation that must prevail over a natural parent's idiosyncratic but strongly held beliefs. As the court concluded, "When a trial court is called upon to determine the custody of a developmentally disabled or handicapped child ... it must be guided by such overriding policies rather than by the personal beliefs or attitudes of the contesting parties" [10]. Furthermore, the court strongly endorsed the concept of psychological or de facto parental relationship, even when such parents do not provide day-to-day residential care.

The *Becker* case restores the doctrine of the best interests of the child to its proper place. It shows that the presumption that parents act in their child's best interests can be overcome by a sufficiently strong objective and subjective demonstration of harm to the child. Moreover, such findings of detriment need not stigmatize those parents as neglectful or abusive. Nor is institutionalization alone a grounds for a change in custody. As the appellate court stressed, it was not Phillip's institutional confinement but his parents' calculated decision to abandon him emotionally that justified this shift in custody. The court also referred to the Beckers' "passive neglect" of Phillip's medical condition as evidence of possible future reoccurrence of a dangerously passive approach to his future medical needs.

Phillip Becker has finally found a home. He now attends a public school, using public transport, and is making progress in living a life which is as normal as possible. After long years of struggle and anxiety, his psychological parents could obtain diagnostic medical procedures for him. Cardiologists had feared that delayed medical treatment would mean denied medical treatment. Miraculously, when a cardiac catheterization was finally performed, surgeons discovered that his condition was still operable. On 28 September 1983, doctors at the University of California Medical Center repaired a hole between the pumping chambers of Phillip's heart. Phillip's recovery has been complete and he is now firmly a part of a family that sought to adopt him [11]. In January 1985, the adoption of Phillip Becker Heath finally took place.

The responsibility for this agonizing case cannot simply be laid at the feet of natural parents. There is something fundamentally wrong when a 2-day-old infant can be deposited in a board-and-care home, when such prolonged institutionalization can be based on narrow clinical advice, when affluent parents can have such a child maintained at state expense, when state social workers make no effort to free him for adoption, and when effective interventions come not through the state's attorney but through the lucky combination of determined and caring surrogate parents, public-spirited lawyers, and professional associations that wanted a child to live his life to its fullest promise. In averting tragedy and ending harm to a single child, the *Becker* case poses a challenge to professionals to aid many less fortunate children.

It is urgent that the medical and legal professions join together, internationally and in our respective countries, to take effective action to prevent such tragedies - the diminution or destruction of innocent lives. This action may take many forms: education clinicians and parents as to positive expectations for disabled persons, setting humane standards, enacting model legislation, providing informed advocacy for disabled children, and increasing the capacity of child welfare agencies to find new homes for unwanted children [12]. Parental autonomy must not be a license to bury a child's vital best interests.

Notes: * Associate Professor, University of Maryland School of Law. B.A. 1967, Yale College; J.D. 1970, Yale Law School; D.Phil. 1979, Oxford University. The author was of counsel to the *amici curiae* American Association on Mental Deficiency, Association for Retarded Citizens of the United States, Association for Retarded Citizens - California, and Protection and Advocacy, Inc. in *Guardianship of Becker,* 188 Cal. Reptr. 781 (1983).

References

1. Guardian Ad Litem's Answer to Petition for Hearing by Supreme Court, Civ No A 014309 at 15 (Cal Sup Ct, 21 March 1983)
2a. *Baby Dies Before Court Could Be Asked to Save It,* Boston Globe 16 April 1982, at 7, col. 1
2b. *Court Refuses to Order Treatment for a Baby* NY Times, 15 April 1982, at D. 21, col. 3.
3a. Duff R, Campbell A (1983) Moral and ethical dilemmas in the special-care nursery. *New Eng J Med* 289: 890
3b. Affleck B (1980) Physicians' attitudes toward discretionary medical treatment of Down's syndrome infants. *Ment Retard* 18: 79
3c. Robertson J (1975) Involuntary euthanasia of defective newborns: a legal analysis, Stanford Law Review 27: 213
4a. *Psychologist Accuses Society of Genocide of Weak, Helpless,* Toronto Star 25 Aug 1982, at 3
4b. Wolfenberger W (1981) The extermination of handicapped people in World War II Germany. Ment Retard 19: 1
5. Reporter's Transcript 1286, 1812-13, *Guardianship of Becker,* 188 Cal. Rptr. 781 (App. 1983)
6. *In Re Phillip B.*, 92 Cal. App. 3d 796 (1979), *cert. denied sub nom. Bothman v. Becker,* 445 U.S. 949 (1980)

7a. Note (1980) *In Re Philipp B.:* what happened to the best interests of the child. *University of Toledo Law Rev* 12: 151
7b. American Association of Mental Deficiency, Resolution on Value of Life Business Meeting, San Francisco, 14 May 1980
8a. Will G (1980) The case of Phillip Becker. *Newsweek* 14 April, p 112
8b. Will G (1980) A trip toward death. *Newsweek* 31 August, p 72
9. *Guardianship of Becker,* No. 101981 (Cal Super Ct, Santa Clara Co 7 August 1981)
10. *Guardianship of Becker,* 188 Cal. Rptr 781, 792 (Ct App 1983)
11. Herr S (1984) The Phillip Becker case resolved: a chance for habilitation. Ment Retard 22 (Feb): 30
12a. Shapiro R (1983) Medical treatment of defective newborns: an answer to the "Baby Doe" dilemma. Harvard J Leg 20: 137
12b. Sales B, Powell D, Van Duizend R, et al (1982) Disabled persons and the law: state legislative issues Plenum, New York, pp 88–98
12c. Roos P (1979) Custodial care for the subtrainable – revisiting an old myth. Law Psychol Rev 5: 1, 16
12d. Neely D (1982) Handicapped advocacy: inherent barriers and partial solutions in the representation of disabled children. Hastings Law J 33: 1359
12e. Herr S (1983) Rights and advocacy for retarded people. Lexington Books, Lexington

The Child in Court

S. Tyano

In the Bible, as well as in history, many quarrels between brothers or relatives culminate in murder or in violent death. In the past, as in the present, jealousy between brethren or nations have often ended in bloodshed. Yet there is but one sacrifice of Isaac, as the Bible relates it in Genesis 22. Much has been written on the significance of this attempted sacrifice and on the symbolism it carries. However, from the traditional Jewish interpretations we may distill the message: "No more sacrifices of children laid on the altar of various gods for religious, mystical, ritualistic, or other purposes serving parents or other adults." The timing of the ram's appearance emphasizes the necessity of obeying God's order not to spill the child's blood. For even God does not demand such an enormous sacrifice; even he cannot order the sacrifice of a child, because man has preeminence above beast and child above adult. Why? Because among all mammals, only man's child undergoes such a relatively lengthy development, during the various stages of which he is unable to defend himself and his personality. It is precisely on the occasion of the attempted sacrifice of Isaac that the notion of the "child's well-being" was born.

It follows that we must institutionalize our social rules in keeping with the laws of nature and evolution. In the administration of our social institutions in general and of law in particular there must be different standards for children than for adults. This difference resides first in what we may expect of children's contributions to the legal process and, secondly, in the significance for and impact on a child's future when he is called to appear in court as a witness.

In regard to the first point, since Piaget's works on the child's cognitive development, we know that the cognitive development is no less important and decisive than the biological, the emotional, and the social development which were known about before then. During the various stages of his development, the child randomly grasps objects in the same manner by which he relates to the natural laws of balance and facts about life and death. Since his capacity of abstraction develops gradually, his grasp of events taking place around him is developmental. The same questions posed at ages 6,9, or 12 years will elicit different answers according to the stage of development.

As to the second point, we know today that emotionally charged events at an early age may result in traumatic fixations with repercussions on the future development of the child. However, with prompt and correct action the effects of these events can be reversed much more easily in children, than in adults.

In my opinion, with respect to children, both axes of development must guide the legislative approach or, at least, they must be taken into account when a child's testimony is required in court or when a legal verdict involves a child's fate on such issues as we shall discuss in this chapter.

About 2 years ago, I was present in court when a boy about 8 years old was called as a witness to give contributory evidence to that of a state witness – his own father – in a drugs trial. The police needed the boy's evidence in order to convict another drug smuggler. The child was asked questions about the weight of drugs, the kind of scales used, etc. During this trial, I tried to explain the huge disproportion between the child's cognitive capacity to evaluate objectively such data as he was questioned about and the weight attributed to his evidence. The boy was not even aware of the rules of operations and seriation which are among the most basic concepts of intellectual functioning. When I concluded my statement, the judge asked me whether I was implying that the child was lying as a witness. This made me realize at once that all my explanations had been in vain. Everyone knows that when a child hits the table that fell upon him or declares that sky and earth meet at the horizon line, he is just dealing with the facts as he sees them, although his "truth" and our "truth" are not identical.

The judge's task is to evaluate in court to what extent a child is telling the truth or whether he understands the meaning of punishment – and according to this evaluation, he will decide upon the child's credibility and capacity as a witness. In so doing, he is putting himself in a position where even psychiatrists would hardly dare place themselves and then only after carrying out specific cognitive tests.

What are a judge's qualifications in this matter? Is there a Faculty of Law whose curriculum includes Piaget's laws of cognitive development? Does a judge's legal training endow him with the capacity to evaluate such cases? Above all, when and where could he have studied the moral development of children and their internalization of social values according to their stage of development?

The evidence of this 8-year-old boy brought a verdict which sent a number of adults to prison. Did anyone investigate the impact of this experience on the child or consider the moral values internalized by this boy and the significance they would have for him when he reaches the point of understanding – when he will realize the weight his evidence carried?

Adults and adolescents are equipped to consider the significance of their answers when giving evidence and to appraise each answer properly before voicing it, particularly because they can weigh the moral issues and assess the importance of their answers. Are we entitled to place this burden on the shoulders of a 8-year-old child?

Until the age of adolescence, children should be excused from such judicial settings, both because we lack sufficient knowledge regarding the extent of their development, and because we are still inadequately informed about the significance of the residuum which this experience might leave with them: guilt feelings, a sense of omnipotence, etc.

A further problem arises when a child is examined by an expert for the purpose of establishing the degree of invalidity due to injuries sustained in an accident. I was recently asked to examine a little girl and give a psychiatric opinion about her case. I was the ninth doctor to examine her and not the last one, and this was 2 years after the accident.

Whom are we serving? Is this what is called "the best interests of the child" – inhibiting the repression of the trauma, a manifest antitherapeutic act; removing the parents' motivation to repress the trauma until the completion of the judicial process? I have even seen cases prolonged for 4 or 5 years after the trauma. It is evident that the ambivalent situation I have just described makes is totally impossible for the therapist to help the child. Why is it not possible for the law to give priority to juvenile cases?

Children have a better capacity for adapting to injury than adults. When this kind of trauma is fixated at an early age, the change produced is more fundamental and will cause more future damage. A sapling starting its growth in a crooked direction will continue to grow in distorted ways. But a sapling which has grown into an upright tree, if injured, will develop a single crooked branch while its trunk remains erect. Adults have stronger compensation mechanisms at their disposal.

My third field of concern is divorce. Much has been written about the "child's good," with all efforts being directed toward a better development, in the best of conditions, for the child. But what happens in reality? Each of the parents presents his own arguments, witnesses, and experts. The child is tossed about from one expert to on other, each one in turn striving to favor the party by whom he was retained, and thus to extract from the child incriminating data against the other parent. And in trials where expert opinions are presented regarding the same act of the same scenario, the two opinions are often polarized. Then, and only then, does the court decide to appoint an expert on its behalf who will arbitrate on the matter ... and the whole process is back to square one.

Every meeting between the psychiatrist and the child has an impact. The psychiatrist and the analyst determine attitudes during every examination in whith they try to elicit evidence against papa or momma. Can this remain without impact? The same psychiatrist who reports and exhorts on the impact and the therapeutic effect of one session with a child can obliterate this consideration when he is retained professionally.

Why is it that only in matters of sex and morality has a body of youth investigators been established to stand between the child and the court? Are sex and morality the only aspects which have succeeded in bringing the judicial system to begin to understand properly what is authorized and what is forbidden when dealing with the well-being of a child? Could it not be that only in an adult's imagination to matters of sex take priority over relegating a child to live with only one parent - father or mother? Are we not projecting our imaginary world on the child's imagination and enshrining this projection in judicial procedures?

In order to meet the law courts' needs for learned opinions, whether regarding injuries sustained or divorce disputes, permanent professional multidisciplinary teams should be appointed whose members would devote part of their time to this sole function. They would be the only ones authorized to provide expert opinions and submit them in court. Such a multidisciplinary team would be appointed by the court with professionals from the specific scientific field as consultants. The picture thus obtained would be objectively for the child's own good.

To get the best professionals to devote their expertise to this matter, it would certainly be possible to oblige both parties in conflict to provide learned opinions of this kind. Decent fees, befitting the professional level we strive for, will help the court obtain speedy, objective, and high-level answers.

In conclusion, I think that for his own good the child must be totally exempted from the necessity of appearing in court. Children's interests require priority to be given to cases involving a child in damage law. Let us restrict the honour of appearing in court to adults and allow our children to go on exercising their imagination for "trials" at school or in youth clubs, as we all staged in our childhood or adolescence on various subjects for goals which were literary or ideological. Let us not tamper with the enriching and gratifying emotional experiences of the young. Let us not destroy their imagination and so many fantasies and legends in order to punish an adult offender. Even when a court appearance is justifiable, the child's vulnerability may produce sequelae whose significance has not yet been properly investigated.

Thus children should not be seen or heard in court. In cases of invalidity, the child should undergo medical and, if necessary, psychological examination only once and then be left to children's occupations, games, and books, interacting with friends, or just to daydreams and fantasies. A child's experience with the law should be purely theoretical while he internalizes the rules of society according to his own individual maturation process.

The Female Adolescent "Borderline": Psychiatric Disorder, Intellectual Anomaly, or Both?

S. Schneider

1 Introduction

The use of the descriptive term "borderline" has in recent years been applied to a multitude of clinical entities. Confusion centers around its exact definition and whether we are dealing with a psychiatric or intellectual label. It is the thesis of this chapter that there exists, in addition to a psychiatric disorder and an intellectual anomaly, a condition that has elements of both. We will focus on the adolescent girl in this paper, as with girls the condition masks itself in a cloud of emotional complications, whereas with adolescent boys the major focus may move into the "criminal," antisocial realm. Thus the condition of the adolescent female begs for treatment and the behavior of the adolescent boy is met with controls. This may reflect society's double standard: in this case the female gets the better deal.

2 What is a "Borderline?"

2.1 Psychiatric Disorder

In 1959, Melitta Schmideberg wrote the first article on the "borderline" to appear in a psychiatric textbook [14]. Schmideberg, the daughter of Melanie Klein, was a psychoanalyst and was involved in treating criminal offenders. Her definition of the borderline was of "a clinical entity . . . bordering

1. On normality
2. On the neuroses
3. On the psychogenic psychoses
4. On psychopathy.

It contains elements of any, and sometimes all, of these entities" (p. 398). This definition left enough vagueness to encompass almost any type of personality disturbance that could not be more clearly defined or subsumed in another disorder.

Over the years this psychiatric syndrome has received considerable attention in the psychiatric/psychoanalytic writings of Otto Kernberg [10, 11], Michael Stone [18], and James Masterson [13]. The syndrome had gone through a variety of labels including: latent schizophrenia, transient schizophrenia, borderline schizophrenia, and narcissistic character disorder. The latest edition of the Diagnostic and Statistical Manual of the American Psychiatric Association (DSM-III, [1] lists a separate personality disorder, the borderline personality. Previous psychiatric classifications did not list a separate entity called the "borderline."

Regardless of the treatment method that is advocated, there seems to be unanimity on the descriptive features of this psychiatric syndrome.

The DSM-III [1] states (p. 321):

> [The syndrome involves] instability in a variety of areas, including interpersonal behavior, mood and self-image ... Interpersonal relations are often intense and unstable, with marked shifts of attitude over time. Frequently there is impulsive and unpredictable behavior that is potentially physically self-damaging. Mood is often unstable ... A profound identity disturbance may be manifested ... There may be problems tolerating being alone, and chronic feelings of emptiness or boredom.

This definition is usually reserved for individuals over 18 years of age. In those younger than 18 the childhood/adolescent disorder called "identity disorder" may be diagnosed. The DSM-III [1] gives the following definition of identity disorder: "... severe subjective distress regarding inability to reconcile aspects of the self into a relatively coherent and acceptable sense of self. There is uncertainty about a variety of issues relating to identity ..." We tend to use the term borderline personality disorder even for those under 18 years of age because the disorder we see is usually too severe to fall in the category of identity disorder.

2.2 Intellectual Anomaly

In 1916, Terman of Stanford University revised the Binet-Simon Scale for measuring intelligence. This instrument, the Stanfort-Binet, became the standard test for intelligence testing. Terman stated: "All who test below 70 I.Q. ... should be considered feeble-minded" ([19] p. 79). This cut-off point of an IQ of 70 has stood the test of time and has been incorporated into numerous state education laws. The DSM-III [1] states: "Significantly sub-average intellectual functioning is defined as an IQ of 70 or below ... an IQ of 70 is considered to represent a band or zone of 65–75" (p. 36). Thus we see that an IQ of below 70 signifies mental retardation.

When we speak of borderline intelligence, are we talking of scores slightly above 70 or scores slightly below 70? The DSM-III [1] has a special category called "borderline intellectual functioning." This is for "an IQ in the 71–84 range" (p. 332). However, "the differential diagnosis between borderline intellectual functioning and mental retardation ... is especially difficult and important when certain mental disorders co-exist" (p. 332). It is very hard to tease out exactly what the person's intellectual capabilities really are when a psychiatric/psychological condition is also present.

An additional issue to contend with in this realm of "intellectual anomaly" is the social/cultural factor. Here we include "inadequate emotional and intellectual stimulation in economically and educationally deprived families ..." [9]. Frankenstein [7] contrasts three different types of "retardation": actual retardation, retardation due to social factors, and retardation due to cultural factors (pp. 80–85). His thesis is that secondary retardation can mask or distort primary retardation; one may be diagnosed as "retarded" when in reality a correction of social and/or cultural factors can significantly improve intelligence.

When we add to all this the maternal deprivation studies of Spitz [17] and Bowlby [3-5], we see how intelligence is affected by the familial climate. This only compounds the underlying emotional component, which is festering as a result of early maternal deprivation/rejection.

3 Problems in Treatment

It is our thesis that in treating adolescent females who have been characterized as borderline females, we are dealing with borderline intellectual functioning and a borderline psychiatric syndrome. Therefore, we have to take into account the psychological personality factors that have gone into "creating" this problem.

The separation-individuation process that occurs in the young child has been described by Mahler [12], following the study of Bowlby [3]. We see what problems may occur later in life if the initial bonding or attachment between mother and child was defective. This defect may leave a fixation point that may be triggered off at the onset of adolescence [2]. Blos [2] describes the adolescent who acts out having eruptions due to regressive pulls back to childhood dependency and safety. This he calls the second separation-individuation process in adolescence. Masterson [13], on the other hand, feels that the acting-out in adolescence is a result of the fear of abandonment which is precipitated in the borderline who has not yet worked through his first individuation process.

Since we are dealing with a personality component, we are faced with deeply ingrained, maladaptive traits. The person "masks" (cf. Latin, *persona*, actor's mask) his real emotions and feelings, and instead of adaptive personality patterns developing, we see "engraved" (cf. Greek, *charactēr*, distinctive quality, from *charassein*, to scratch), rigid pathological systems.

Borderlines have difficulty with appropriate socialization skills. They need a supportive, therapeutic, "holding" [20] environment. This milieu must provide limits and controls while taking into account their special needs [15]. The borderline has been missing a stable, warm, consistent set of persons in her life. Therefore, "the one thing that has a bad effect on a borderline patient is weakness and detachment" ([14] p.407). There must be clear lines of authority, so that the adolescent realizes who is in control. While the control dynamic is the most difficult aspect of treating adolescents, in this particular disorder it is of crucial importance. However, this control cannot just be wielded indiscriminately. The adolescent must feel that she has a hand in the therapeutic process. Treatment in a therapeutic milieu involves a combination of rules that must be followed (rigid controls) and rules that are negotiable (elastic controls).

While control systems in a therapeutic milieu are necessary, we must remember that a borderline cannot fit into a rigid system. We need to help her with her difficulties in object relations, defiance of rules and routine, and mood instability. All of these are results of the difficulties in the mother-father-child triad.

We cannot expect to fill in all that is missing or distorted. This takes time, patience, and a willingness and ability to be flexible and tolerant. Flexibility is just as difficult for the therapist. Supervision and introspection are very important in order to help the therapeutic personnel free themselves from their countertransference feelings. This is especially true in the sexual sphere. The acting-out and seductive potential of borderline females create many problems for the therapeutic milieu staff [16]. It is important that the restitution of the narcissistic imbalance should not be at the expense of the "giving" therapist. The therapeutic relationship should not be reminiscent either of one with a possessive, dominating parent or of one with the rejecting parent. A therapeutic balance is necessary in order to reach and treat the borderline.

The borderline we have described, combining a borderline intellectual syndrome with a borderline psychiatric syndrome, manifests difficulties that are similar to those of the learning-disabled adolescent with minimal brain dysfunction adolescent.

These may include some or all of the following:

1. Inability to process and adapt to varying levels of sensory stimuli; this may lead to "overload" and behavioral disorganization
2. Destructive behavior - to ward self and/or others and/or objects
3. Restlessness; short attention span; low frustration tolerance
4. Difficulty in tolerating even mild amounts of anxiety
5. Difficulty in accepting change - especially change in identification figures
6. Difficulty in judgment; dichotomy between own abilities and society's expectations.

All of these difficulties must be taken into account in order for us to treat this borderline syndrome. "To influence the patient, we must approach him both intellectually and emotionally" ([14] p. 411). This means reasoning with the adolescent - not an easy task when the level of insight may be low. The adolescent must be motivated for our treatment. The milieu that we offer her must be, in her eyes, better than the milieu she has come from. The relationship and "attachment" will be what will hold her in the therapeutic milieu.

Our aim in treating these borderlines is to strengthen their ego in order to withstand the onslaught from the id [8] and to avoid weakening the defense mechanisms. We must be careful in our interpretations. The adolescent will recognize that a warm, supportive, consistent milieu is her opportunity for growth and change. It is our job to make her use that milieu.

References

1. American Psychiatric Association (1980) Diagnostic and statistical manual, 3rd edn (DSM-III). American Psychiatric Association, Washington DC
2. Blos P (1967) The second individuation process of adolescence. The Psychoanalytic Study of the Child 22: 162-186
3. Bowlby J (1957) Separation from the mother at an early age and its effects on the development of the child. Megamot 8: 3-40, 119-152 (Hebrew)
4. Bowlby J (1969) Attachment and loss. I: Attachment. Basic Books, New York
5. Bowlby J (1973) Attachment and loss. II: Separation. Basic Books, New York
6. Cytryn L, Lourie RS (1975) Mental retardation. In: Freedman AM, Kaplan HI, Sadock BJ (eds) Comprehensive textbook of psychiatry/II, vol. I. Williams and Wilkins, Baltimore
7. Frankenstein C (1975) Impaired intelligence. Hebrew University and the Ministry of Education and Culture, Jerusalem (Hebrew)

8. Freud S (1923) The ego and the id, Standard edn, vol 19. Hogarth, London 1961
9. Group for the Advancement of Psychiatry (GAP) (1972) Psychopathological disorders in childhood. Group for the Advancement of Psychiatry, New York
10. Kernberg O (1967) Borderline personality organization. Journal of the American Psychoanalytic Association 15: 641-685
11. Kernberg O (1975) Borderline conditions and pathological narcissism. Jason Aronson, New York
12. Mahler MS (1968) On human symbiosis and the vicissitudes of individuation. International Universities Press, New York
13. Masterson JF (1972) Treatment of the borderline adolescent. Wiley, New York
14. Schmideberg N (1959) The borderline patient. In: Arieti S (ed) American handbook of psychiatry, vol I. Basic Books, New York, 398-416
15. Schneider S (1979) A proposal for a multi-faceted program for a special population of adolescents and young adults. Society and Welfare 2: 4, 406-413 (Hebrew)
16. Schneider S, Deutsch C (to be published) Adolescent sexuality in a therapeutic community: staff countertransference issues. Adolescence
17. Spitz R (1946) Anaclitic depression. The Psychoanalytic Study of the Child 2: 313-342
18. Stone M (1980) The borderline syndromes. McGraw-Hill, New York
19. Terman L (1916) The measurement of intelligence. Houghton-Mifflin, New York
20. Winnicott DW (1955) Metapsychological and clinical aspects of regression within the psychoanalytical set-up. International Journal of Psychoanalysis 36: 16-26

Legal Problems in Current Geriatric Psychiatry

M. S. Tropper, A. Avnat, and J. Wagner

In recent years, due to demographic trends, the rapidly growing branch of clinical psychiatry named geriatric psychiatry has become a very important field. Among the various issues with which geriatric psychiatry deals are the legal problems of elderly patients with mental disorders. These problems are at present on the agendas of different national and international forums - of psychiatry as well as of gerontology and geriatrics.

This chapter is based on the analysis of the legislation of various countries with respect to admission (institutionalization, hospitalization), relocation, discharge, and other related issues. At the same time our presentation is based on clinical observations and interviews with different interested professionals (physicians, lawyers, psychologists, administrators, nurses, social workers), patients' relatives, and the patients themselves.

Compulsory Institutionalization and Hospitalization

Most aged patients agree to come into a hospital, geriatric center, or old people's home when this becomes necessary. Some of them, however, do refuse, causing a legal problem. The question is raised whether this objection is a result of a psychiatric disorder and represents a serious danger to the patient's health and life or to the safety of others.

There is a widespread tendency of settle old people in geriatric centers and old people's homes, and within these geriatric institutions in permanently closed, locked departments, units, and wards against their will in some cases, when these patients manifest cognitive or behavioral disorders. The current Mental Health Acts do not permit compulsory admission even of old people with personality disorders, but experience shows that neurotic and situationally disturbed old people (diagnostic labels rarely used in geriatric psychiatry) are sometimes compulsorily settled in "closed" frameworks without sufficient legal medical reasons, and without the agreement and knowledge of a psychiatrist. This not only represents a violation of law, but often has a serious impact upon the patient's cognitive level, and leads rapidly to a deeper and more rapid cognitive deterioration. Professionals working in the field of geriatric psychiatry are often confronted with the fact that the role of the psychiatrist remains underestimated in the decision-making related to the issue of primary importance.

We are sorry to say that in many cases we have seen old people with short-term behavioral or cognitive disorders who were unnecessarily detained and deprived of the right to free communication. When the reasons for the resettling of a person are psychiatric (cognition, behavior), the decision-making should not be given into the hands of general practitioners, specialists in internal medicine, or ev Although he must take into consideration the results of the geriatric. tion concerning the patient's physical state, the psychiatrist (or gerop the only authorized specialist for the proper psychiatric assessment of psychopathological state and the professional interpretation of behav. nestic data. This includes the evaluation of the true psychopathological and the prediction of outcome of sometimes even short-term, transient psychotic, hypopsychotic, or subacute confusional states.

Even in emergency cases, when it is not always possible to obtain the opinion of two physicians, one of which must be a psychiatrist, the admission of an old person in a closed geropsychiatric setting ("locked unit") should be limited to 3 days, during which the patient should be seen by a psychiatrist. This is in order to avoid harming the patient's health and violating of the patient's rights.

Confidentiality

We often encounter cases where the failure to observe the patient's and his family's rights causes many troublesome psychogenic traumata. We often forget that sometimes among our geropsychiatric patients there are people who are well known in society, and that by violating confidentiality and leaking information about a patient's present mental state we may cause serious damage to his adult children, other relatives, and colleagues. Therefore, we are deeply convinced that confidentiality in geriatric psychiatry should be preserved in all areas except those where information needs to be given to others, that is, in cases where with holding knowledge would constitute definite harm to the patient or those near to him.

Legal, Moral, and Ethical Aspects of Sex in Old Age

The legal, moral, and ethical aspects of sex in old age constitute an issue of serious importance, which is underestimated and often neglected. Among the staff of geriatric institutions, including geropsychiatric ones, stereotyped attitudes toward sexual behavior in old age continue to dominate. Segregation by sex in nursing homes has a negative impact upon the patient's state and daily activities. The issue of sexual activity even in old age demands proper attention and understanding. The right of an old person to marry or remarry should be preserved. If he is still in possession of his facultes and able to understand the meaning of what he wishes to do, he should be allowed to do it. However, the approach of the staff should be correct and individually based. Staff members should be brought by continuous education, in service and out of it, to better understanding and to a proper tolerance toward sexual arousal in elderly people. Ethics demands that the current, sometimes anecdotal approach of the staff members of become geriatric centers and institutions become more realistic and modern.

ℯ Right of Residents of Geriatric Centers and Old People's Homes to Free Movement

The right to leave the institution for a definite time (hours, sometimes one or more days) can not be restricted or limited by reason of age. If an old person is in possession of all his faculties and his physical state is satisfactory, and if he has loyal relatives, the administration of the home should make it possible for him to come and go freely. In the case of patients under geropsychiatric observation and treatment, the psychiatrist remains the specialist responsible, and must reach a decision on the matter on the basis of past and present psychopathological evaluation. This decision should serve as the basis for the policy adopted by the administration of the institution.

The Authenticity and Credibility of the Information Supplied by Relatives Concerning Old People's Behavior

Our long experience shows that although parents carry a great burden of responsibility for their children's safety, adult children unfortunately do not always show the same feelings of responsibility toward their aged parents, not to mention other relatives. In this connection the issue of "power of attorney" in geriatric psychiatry is worth mentioning. Geropsychiatrists encounter cases where relatives misuse old people, who are persuaded one way or on other to sign documents giving them the right to dispose of their property on a legal basis. One should bear in mind that the information supplied by relatives may be (a) objective and truthful; (b) subjective and false; or (c) intentionally dishonest. When doubts arise, the information supplied should be verified in the interests of the person under treatment before any medicolegal decision is made.

The Right of the Elderly Patient to Refuse Treatment

The right to refuse treatment upheld should be except in those cases where, as a result of impaired judgment, the patient cannot practically be the decision maker in the matter. This issue also concerns terminal cases where the patients' relatives demand that supportive treatment be discontinued. In the field of geriatric psychiatry this especially concerns cases of severe atrophic brain processes (primary degenerative dementia according to DSM-III), when persons become deeply impaired in their mentally vital functions, namely in the so-called highest brain functions (perception, memory, insight, judgment, orientation, decision-making, and others). Unfortunately, specialists working in our field encounter such individuals, whom one of us (M.T.) has defined as "physically alive but cognitively dead" (International Symposium on the Dying Human, Tel-Aviv, 1978, Abstracts volume, page 59). In our opinion all these rights, and their legal-ethical implications should be discussed individually in every case. The decisions should be made by a commission comprising three physicians, including a psychiatrist; a psychologist; and a social worker.

The Role of the District Psychiatrist with Respect to the Field of Geriatric Psychiatry

In day by day practice the District Psychiatrist's office at present has responsibility for geriatric psychiatry. Current statistical, epidemiological data show that more than 65% of residents of geriatric centers and old people's homes are suffering from some kind of mental disorder. There are strong medicolegal grounds for the extension of the authority of the District Psychiatrist to cover all geriatric institutions in his district.

Restructuring of Geriatric Institutions

In order to overcome the serious legal problems mentioned above, there appears to be a strong necessity to change the existing structure of departments and units in geriatric centers. Our experience indicates that in every geriatric center where there are more than 200 residents, an intermediate between the open and closed geropsychiatric departments should be planned and implemented promptly.

Conclusion

We have touched here only on some of the issues of legal and ethical importance in the field of geriatric psychiatry. We are fully aware of the existing difficulties in geriatric psychiatry and their legal implications. One of the unresolved problems is the issue of diminished responsibility of old people with mental disorders in current legislation. Another unresolved problem can be defined as "ambiguities in the notions of normality and abnormality in old age," which are of paramount importance in geriatric psychiatry. This lack of clarity is due to the pecularities in the differential diagnosis of cognitive changes and behavioral patterns in "normal brain ageing" and in the course of "pathological brain ageing" processes. However, the main problem the geropsychiatrist encounters is and remains the one of involuntary institutionalization and relocation. The crucial question is whether within geriatric institutions, where there are thousands of geropsychiatric patients, an old person may be taken by force from his habitual setting and placed in a permanently and strictly locked ("closed") department surrounded by a 2-meter-high fence, in a building nobody apart from the staff can enter or leave. Sometimes a person spends months there or even longer. Such a transition, if undertaken without a psychiatrist's agreement or without the District Psychiatrist's decision, represents an involuntary relocation and, legally speaking, a violation of civil liberties.

This practice, which exists in some countries, is far from being in conformity with current Mental Health Acts, and there are two reasons for this.

1. The geropsychiatric aspects of the day by day activities of geriatric institutions are away from the supervision and away from the sphere of interest of the Mental Health Departments of the Ministries of Health and Mental Health Administrations in different countries.

2. There is a significant lack of clarity in the law and in the interpretation of the current Mental Health Acts with respect to old people with mental disorders.

It is our strong belief that the problems discussed here are urgent, and there is nothing more frustrating for us than that there should be a lot of talk, of the restriction of the freedom of the middle-aged mentally ill while it is forgotten that the matter is much more severe when it concerns the elderly mentally ill, for whom even a short restriction of freedom causes a much more severe social isolation, which in turn leads to a very rapid, often irreversible cognitive deterioration.

Geriatric psychiatry, its needs, demands, and specific issues, is closely related to current legal problems, and therefore all these aspects should be regulated on a proper judicial basis. Patients with mental disorders, regardless of age, should be equal in their rights before the law.

IV. Treatment and Rehabilitation

Iatrogenic Syndromes and Disharmony in the Doctor-Doctor Relationship

M. Torem

Introduction

A recent survey by the Center of Health Services Research and Development of the American Medical Association reveals that the number of group practices among American physicians more than doubled between 1966 and 1980 (from 4287 up to 10762). The greatest period of proliferation in group practice occurred between 1975 and 1980 [1]. Moreover, the survey reveals that, contrary to the case in the early years of group practice, which were characterized by multispecialty groups, this latest growth in group practice among physicians occurred among single-specialty groups.

Impressed by the report of these changes, one may wonder, however, what relevance it has to patient care? This chapter will focus on one aspect of these changes, namely, the changes in the doctor-doctor relationship as a result of group practice and its effect on the care of the patient.

Let us take a look at some differences between the traditional solo practice and the "new" group practice as they are seen in the private general hospital. Under the solo practice system a patient admitted to the hospital has one physician, usually his general practitioner or internist, who has cared for and treated him for years prior to the hospitalization. The workup in the hospital is initiated and conducted by this primary care physician. If consultations with a specialist are indicated, they are requested by this primary care physician, who coordinates all people and efforts involved in the care of "his" patient, and the patient knows well who "his" physician is and who all the others are.

In the group practice mode, even in the outpatient setting the patient may not receive continuity of care, since he may see different physicians at his outpatient visits. When admission to hospital is indicated, the patient is admitted under the name of the group of physicians, which may include eight or more doctors. He may be admitted by one doctor and every day another, different, physician may make the hospital rounds and make important decisions pertinent to the patient's care in the hospital. Some of these physicians will be seeing the patient for the first time, and their attitude and approach to patient care and the practice of medicine may be different from those of the physician who made the rounds the day before. The patient who is faced by a series of physical and psychological investigations thus also has to face a daily change of doctors.

Clinical Syndromes

The following case reports will illustrate the various clinical syndromes that may result from the lack of harmony in the team of doctors involved in the patient's treatment. These syndromes are clearly iatrogenic and naturally put extra responsibility on the physician to prevent or correct them.

Case 1: "Helplessness and a Sense of Abandonment"

J. M. was a 25-year-old married man who was admitted to the hospital for evaluation and treatment of a severe swelling of lymph nodes in the neck. The diagnosis was metastatic squamous cell carcinoma originating from the left maxillary sinus. The patient was shocked by the diagnosis and was determined to do anything to fight for his life. He decided to stop smoking and wanted to learn self-hypnosis to achieve this goal. A psychiatric consultation was requested by the attending internist. The patient was found to be hypnotizable and was highly hopeful that he would achieve full control over the smoking habit. He even believed this would improve his chances of responding to the treatment for his cancer. He was taught self-hypnosis and found it to be a very good method to reduce tension and achieve a state of relaxation.

On a follow-up visit 2 days later he was found to be distressed, anxious, somewhat depressed, and confused about his immediate future. He reported that he had been seen by a consultant radiotherapist, who recommended radiotherapy as the treatment of choice. Later in the day he had been seen by an oncologist, who recommended adding chemotherapy to the treatment. Both consultants wanted to start the treatment the very same day, and one of them, according to the patient, told him he should not stop smoking now because he would be under a lot of stress and probably needed to smoke. The following day the patient was seen by a surgeon, who recommended surgical removal of the swellings in the neck, to be followed by radiation. When asked how he was going to make his decision the patient communicated a sense of loss and confusion and stated that he had many doctors but did not know who his physician was. He wanted to discharge himself from hospital.

A quick intervention by the liaison psychiatrist included a meeting of the attending internist and three of the consultants with the patient. The treatment options were discussed, the patient had a chance to ask clarifying questions, and it was decided that the primary attending internist would coordinate the patient's care. No treatment decisions would be made or communicated directly from the consultant to the patient without a discussion with the coordinating attending internist. The patient's mood improved dramatically and he agreed to stay in the hospital for treatment.

This case demonstrates how disharmony and lack of direction and communication in the medical team may lead the patient to confusion, anger, and a sense of feeling lost and abandoned. Moreover, it demonstrates how quickly intervention can be effective in ameliorating the patient's problem.

Case 2: A Depressive Paranoid Syndrome

A 45-year-old married woman and mother of three was admitted to the hospital for an elective hysterectomy for a fibroid tumor associated with abdominal pain. The operation was performed the day after admission by the physician who had examined her in his consulting rooms. After the operation, it was implied by the physician's assistant (who assisted during surgery) that there had been additional findings. When the patient indicated her desire to know what they were, the physician's assistant responded by saying that it was the responsibility of her physician to discuss them with her. The patient became anxious and began to imagine that the "additional finding" must be cancer. Her sleep that night was disturbed. The following morning she experienced abdominal pain more severe than ever before, and interpreted this to mean that this could be cancer after all. She could hardly wait for the visit of her doctor that day. She was then surprised to see a new doctor entering her room, introducing himself as a partner of the doctor who had performed the operation. He told her that he was covering rounds that day. The patient welcomed him politely and asked about the additional findings made in the course of surgery. She was disappointed to learn that he knew nothing of the details, since he had not been present at the operation and the patient's chart still lacked the surgery report. He attempted to allay her fears by the usual "Don't worry" and "If it were something serious the doctor would have made a point of telling you by now." After the morning rounds the patient became more depressed and suspicious that the doctors were hiding the truth from her. She refused to cooperate with the medical student and resident who came later to take a full history. She said that she would not be a "guinea pig for doctors" and asked them to leave. Only on the third day after surgery did the patient learn that the additional findings mentioned earlier by the physician's assistant were multiple fibroid tumors and endometriosis.

Although she experienced some relief, she continued to be suspicious, and suffered from insomia and poor appetite, which interfered with her recovery. A psychiatric consultation allowed her to tell her story and encouraged her to ventilate her emotions. She gradually recovered emotionally and physically. This case demonstrates how, when group practice is carried out without a clear leader-coordinator, there may be poor communication among the doctors in the group and discontinuous patient care, which may affect the patient's recovery. In this case, in response to ambiguity and confusion the patient developed a clearly iatrogenic paranoid syndrome, a condition previously described by Wanck [2] and Cavenar [3].

Case 3: Paranoia and Confusion

R. L., a 58-year-old insurance agent who was admitted to the hospital for the treatment of an acute myocardial infarction, developed a "sundown" syndrome involving marked diurnal variation in sensorial state. At night he had the usual delusions accompanied by paranoid thinking, seeing himself in a garage and being threatened by strangers. The cardiologist requested a psychiatric consultation. It was found that this was his second myocardial infarction, and had occurred only 3 months after a double bypass of the coronary arteries.

As part of the therapeutic approach, it was agreed with the consulting physician that the patient would be told that the reason for his confusional state was due to enzymes and other intracellular substances released from the infarction area that were reaching the brain. The patient was satisfied with the answer, since for someone with his personality structure control by intellectual knowledge was significant in maintaining mental balance.

The following day the patient was seen by a partner of the first cardiologist and by a resident. The patient told them with a smile that he felt much better because he had finally received a satisfactory answer enabling him to understand why he was getting so confused at night. However, they looked at one another and immediately corrected him, saying that this explanation had not yet been satisfactorily confirmed and that no scientific studies had been undertaken to support it. The answer they gave was simply: "We do not know why," and "Let's not make a big deal out of it . . . what is important is to get your heart in good shape." That night the patient developed a confusional state accompanied by delusions that he was being kept in the hospital to be experimented on as part of a scientific study. He then proclaimed that he had never really had a heart attack, and pressed to discharge himself from the hospital.

This case shows the effects of disharmony in the team of physicians on the treatment of the patient, illustrating that the patient's confusion and helplessness may sometimes be a mere reflection of the condition among the team of doctors treating him.

Case 4: "The Patient Without a Doctor"

E. T., a 48-year-old white married woman and mother of three grown children, was admitted to the hospital for an evaluation and treatment of intractable angina (chest pain). She had a full evaluation and workup, which included repeated ECG and a 24-hour halter monitor for arrhythmias. She was seen on rounds every day by different doctors who were part of a five-member group practice team.

She was referred by one of the team members for consultation to evaluate the psychosocial aspects of chest pain and to suggest treatment. Before the patient was seen by the psychiatric consultant it was reported by the nurses that she became very hostile toward the physician and nurse and insisted on leaving the hospital. It was learned that the patient was getting different messages from the various doctors she saw. Each of them gave her different and inconsistent explanations for her chest pain.

When asked who her doctor was she pointed out that her real doctor was back where she lived, and that though she had many doctors coming in and out, she did not really know which one was in charge and truly was her doctor.

This case shows how a medical group without a leader or coordinator may resemble an orchestra without a conductor. Although each player may be of the first quality, disharmony may very well result. In addition, this patient developed a sense of abandonment, like a lost child without a parent.

Case 5: "Too Many Cooks Spoil the Broth"

A 57-year-old man, a respected member of the community with high socioeconomic status, was admitted to the hospital for reevaluation and possible treatment of a single liver metastasis. The primary lesion was a cancer of the colon, for which the patient had had a hemicolectomy 5 years earlier.

Since the patient also suffered from diabetes and with a cardiologist and a diabetologist was requested hypertension, consultation. One of these consultants was concerned about the patient's symptom of paresthesia and numbness in the legs and decided to call for consultation with a neurologist. The oncologist who originally sent for the cardiologist and diabetologist was not aware of this new consultation. The cardiology group consisted of five partners, the diabetologist's group of three partners, the oncologist's group of two, and the neurologist's group of two partners.

The patient was reported by the nurses to be withdrawn and quiet, hardly talking, which for him was very unusual behavior. A decision had to be made as to what type of approach to take in his treatment, whether to give him chemotherapy, adopt a surgical approach, or use radiation. The patient was by nature an active, aggressive, hard-driving, decisive man. He had personally built up a chain of businesses. In the hospital situation at this time, he could not make the necessary critical decision as to which line of treatment should be carried out. He exhibited hopelessness and helplessness. When asked who his physician was he mentioned his family physician, whom he had known for many, many years, who had transferred him to the specialist but since then had not been involved and had hardly visited.

This case demonstrates a number of points, first that a patient may be "bombarded" by the attentions of many physicians, consultants, and their partners, all eager to help and use their sophisticated knowledge and techniques, but that without coordination all their talent may not only be wasted but may even affect the patient negatively and produce iatrogenic effects. The case also demonstrates the invaluable role of the family physician, who in his absence was greatly missed by the patient. His absence was a loss to the entire medical team.

Discussion

A number of issues are illustrated in common by these cases. First is the fact that these patients suffered unecessary anguish resulting from acts of commission or omission by one or another of the number of physicians practicing in the system providing the patient's care. This is what makes it iatrogenic in nature. The word is made up of two words, *iatros,* meaning "physician" in Greek, and *genesis,* meaning "origin" in Latin. The literature on iatrogenic syndromes is rich in reports and studies of side effects of drugs, diagnostic tests, surgery, and radiation therapy. However, very little has been written on iatrogenic syndromes stemming from a faulty doctor-patient relationship or from disharmony in the medical team or the institution.

The cases presented show how these iatrogenic syndromes originated from fragmented and discontinuous care. Coherence and continuity of care were clearly lacking. What it continuity of care and what are its effects on patient care? A dictionary definition of continuity refers to an uninterrupted unceasing succession of things [7]. In the medical context continuity of care can be defined as the extent to which a single physician manages and coordinates the health care and needs of a patient. This definition has been supported by Sussman [8], Breslan [9], Bice [10], Roos [11], and others. Continuity of care is referred to by the Royal College of General Practitioners in Britain in the role specification for the general practitioner, with the stiputation that patient care is to be "primary, continuing and personal" [12]. It is generally accepted today by such writers as Becker [13], Heagerty [14], and Alpert [15] that continuity of care is a necessary attribute of personalized and high-quality health care. Continuity of care contributes to a better doctor-patient relationship, reduction in relapses in cases of chronic illness, and a reduction in the number of unnecessary diagnostic procedures and hospitalizations. The lack of continuity in the patient's care contributed to the sense of abandonment that some of the patients felt, and specifically to the feeling of not having one pyhsician who could be called "my doctor." All this contributed a great deal to the ambiguity in doctor-patient communication and the lack of clarity and the presence of much uncertainty in the patient. Facing this situation in addition to the regular stresses of the hospital environment may precipitate a paranoid reactive syndrome. Heilburn [16, 17] described a population of people who, when given affectively charged ambiguous information, defended against the anxiety of uncertainty by adopting delusions with which to organize the information. This may very well be the mechanism for the development of a reactive paranoid syndrome of a iatrogenic nature in cases 2, 3, and 5. Any syndrome which is iatrogenic in nature puts a heavy load of responsibility on the physician and the health care system. The old Hippocratic dictum: *Primum non nocere* (First do no harm) is strongly applicable. The physician owes it to his patients and himself to prevent and correct iatrogenic disorders in all circumstances, at all times.

Suggestions for Treatment and Prevention

The cases presented in this chapter are not rare or unusual. I believe that they represent a situation which has to be corrected. What can be done about it? The following are some suggestions.

It is necessary to improve the channels of communication, both among group practice members and between the group and other physicians or other members of the health care team who are not physicians. This can be improved by having each group of physicians elect a medical director whose function will be to coordinate, communicate, and make sure that continuity of care is practiced in the group. This will increase the opportunity for personal doctoring, and not only will the patients be more satisfied but the primary care physicians may very well feel more fulfilled in their work. This idea was also expressed in Britain by Grey [12] from the Royal College of General Practitioners. More awareness of such iatrogenic syndromes and how the physician's behavior may affect the patient's illness, recognition of the vital role of clear communication among doctors and between patient and doctors, the establishment of continuity of care, and the appointment of a medical director to ensure communication and good continuity of care issue will improve the current situation and prevent many other such iatrogenic syndromes in the future.

References

1. Buchert WI (1982) Looking back on group practice. Group Practice Journal 31: 24-29
2. Wanck B (1982) Reactive paranoid psychosis following an ambiguous cancer diagnosis. Psychosomatics 23: 439-440
3. Cavenar JO, Cavenar MG (1980) Iatrogenic illness in a community mental health center. North Carolina Med Journal 41: 93-94
4. Waterhouse BE (1981) The medical director. Group Practice Journal 30: 25-26
5. McEwan J (1978) Practicing together, notes on communication within the practice. The Practitioner 221: 305-311
6. Wall EM (1981) Continuity of care and family medicine; definitions, determinants and relationship to outcome. Journal of Family Practice 13: 655-664
7. Ehrlich E et al. (eds) (1980) Oxford American Dictionary. Oxford University Press, New York, p 138
8. Sussman MB, Caplan EK, Hang MR, et al. (1967) The walking patient: a study in outpatient care. Case Western Reserve University Press, Cleveland, Ohio
9. Breslan N, Reeb KG (1975) Continuity of care in a university-based practice. J Med Educ 50: 965
10. Bice TW, Boxerman SB (1977) A quantitative measure of continuity of care. Med Care 15: 347
11. Roos LL, Roos NP, Gilbert P, et al. (1980) Continuity of care: does it contribute to quality of care? Med Care 18: 194
12. Gray DP (1979) The key to personal care. J Roy Coll Gen Practit 29: 666-678
13. Becker MH, Drachman RH, Kirscht JP (1974) A field experiment to evaluate various outcomes of continuity of care. Am J Public Health 64: 1062
14. Heagerty MC, Robertson LS, Kosa J, et al. (1970) Some comparative costs in comprehensive versus fragmented pediatric care. Pediatrics 46: 596
15. Alpert J, Robertson LS, Kosa J, et al. (1976) Delivery of health care for children: report of an experiment. Pediatrics 57: 917
16. Heilburn AB, Jr (1975) Tolerance for ambiguity in late adolescent males: Implications for a developmental model of paranoid behavior. Develop Psychol 3: 288-294
17. Heilburn AB Jr (1975) A proposed basis for delusion formation within an information-processing model of paranoid development. Br J Soc Clin Psychol 14: 63-71

Ego-Structural Milieu Therapy in the Conception of Ammon's Theory of Dynamic Psychiatry

D. Griepenstroh

Ammon [5] writes,

> Dynamic psychiatry can be seen as a chain of endeavors to understand more and more exactly, with the help of theoretical concepts, what is actually happening in therapy, to develop hypotheses which make it possible for the therapist to act purposefully and systematically and to learn from what he does.

"Milieu treatment," wrote Ammon as early as 1959 [1], "is as old as the human race and is based on the idea that people can be changed through people and environmental factors."

These two central thoughts of Ammon are, as it were, the cornerstones of this chapter, the purpose of which is the description of milieu treatment in Ammonism. Because of the limit which is set by the length of such a chapter, this is a rather difficult task, especially because two different, interdependent levels have to be considered.

Roughtly speaking, I have these two levels in mind:

1. The sphere of practical treatment, i.e., the answer to the question "What is happening in dynamic psychiatry under the heading of milieu treatment?"; and, linked with it (b)
2. The answers to the further questions "Why does just this happen and not something else?" and "How is what is happening to be understood?". This is the level of theory.

To give you a list of all that is happening in our school under the heading of milieu treatment would, to my mind, be beside the point, as would an elaborate, theoretical presentation of the topic, which would involve not only the concepts of illness and of health, but also the models of development and personality in our school, our theory on therapy, and our treatment methodology.

The main point of dynamic psychiatric milieu treatment is the holistic approach: what the patient actually does and what the therapist actually puts into practice from what he has learned is of less importance. What really counts is the attitude of the therapist, the seriousness of his interest in the patient, his readiness to try hard to make contact and keep contact with the patient, and his ability to give the patient what Ammon calls "social energy."

Thus milieu treatment is anything but the performance of a special work program, but rather, as Ammon says, the structuring of the whole day together with the patient in terms of an individual treatment plan which is adapted to the diagnosis, ego-structurally differentiated, and open to change in the course of treatment. The structuring of the day also involves the structuring of the milieu. As Ammon writes [6], the task is to establish a social energy field within the therapeutic, group dynamic context.

To illustrate my point, I want to give an example (cf. [8]). K., a schizophrenically reacting patient who had passed through a number of traditional mental hospitals, had been at our hospital for some time. He mostly kept away from group activities, considering himself to be the saint of all saints, so that it was not necessary for him to speak to normal people. The only person whom he accepted at this time and whom he, at the behest of his God with whom he had a secret union, had declared sacred was Dr. Ammon, the chief counsellor of the hospital. K. would wait for Ammon's arrival, meet him in the hall, deeply bow in front of him, and greet him in a reverential manner. Ammon would stop to meet him and would bow even lower and just a bit more reverentially, so that K., by turns, would try to surpass Ammon's gesture of reverence. When the point was reached that K., who was rather well rounded and had never really been keen on physical exercise, was unable to bow anly lower than Ammon, he threw himself flat on the ground – and so did Ammon. Now K. could no longer maintain the seriousness of his reverence: it had become a game and both of them had to laugh about it. The game served as a bridge to establish contact. They helped each other to stand up again: their relationship had become a real one. Both of them had enjoyed the game. It might be added that K. had been in psychiatric hospitals since adolescence (at the time of the incident described here he was 40 years old), and that until this time he had refused any kind of contact either with the staff or with other patients.

As a vital aspect of the milieu therapeutic field, Ammon [2, 3] stresses that it must be a real one:

> First, the aim is to offer the patient the opportunity of making new experiences, within the setting of the therapeutical milieu and through the direct interaction with the therapist; very often he will experience a successful interaction for the first time, which will give him a positive attitude towards his own existence.

However, a therapeutic situation can be real only if all the people working with the patient behave as real people rather than being reduced to just the doctor or just the nurse and performing their specific functions in an intellectually shut-off way.

Ammon [3] writes,

> The therapist becomes the direct partner of the patient in his present life situation. He becomes one of the most important factors of the patient's life at the given moment. So, with regard to the interaction between therapist and patient, milieu treatment is an active, direct therapy. The interpretation of the conflicts and of the behavior of the patient is only a secondary task of the therapist who works with the patient in the therapeutic milieu. He reacts to, and interprets, the actions and the conflicts of the patient first and above all through his direct response. So, with regard to verbal, analytical interpretation, milieu treatment is an indirect therapy.

In order to be able to perform this task, all the members of the staff need the support of a team, i.e., of a group in which they can freely give vent to their feelings, where everybody can safely question the work of his colleague as well as being questioned about his own work, a group in which each member feels he is taken care of. The more the team is able to support its members emotionally, the more effective will their therapeutic work be. From this it follows that the structuring of the team and the group dynamic work with the team is the most important aspect of milieu therapeutic work as a whole (cf. [1, 2, 3]).

Of course, the patients are an essential topic at the team meetings. In particular, seriously ill patients - Ammon speaks of a spectrum of archaic ego illnesses (cf. [2]) - often behave very differently in different situations and toward different people. Therefore, it is the task of the team meetings to find out the healthy ego components which every patient has, however ill he may be. It is necessary to find them, to encourage them, and to work with them in order then to be able to deal with the destructive components of the patient's personality. This approach to working with the patient has been called and described by Ammon as "ego-structural work" (cf. [4]).

Milieu treatment, in particular, allows man to develop and to unfold as a whole being, in all his essence, with all his abilities and aptitudes, but also within his limits in terms of talents and intelligence. He can try out constructive behavior, give vent to destructive feelings, and let deficits become apparent. He can do all this simultaneously at various places within the group dynamic context. The task of the team meeting is to collect together all impressions to form one picture - a kind of jigsaw puzzle consisting of parts which seem to have no relation to each other, but out of which a perspective can be developed with and for the patient, a perspective which it will be the concern of all to realize.

Milieu treatment, to my mind, is the central element of the methodology of treatment in dynamic psychiatry as a whole. Here what Ammon calls the "social energetic field" becomes obvious, and it is also characterized by the holistic principle, which means that man is seen, treated, and understood as a whole being.

This is not my only concern in this chapter, however. In accordance with Ammon, I understand the criminal offense as a symptom marking out the offender as mentally ill. I regard the criminal offense as nothing else but a specific form of manifestation of psychic disturbance, as an expression of specific suffering, as the result of the lack of opportunity for development in the life history of the delinquent.

Mentally ill people are often put into mental hospitals; criminal offenders are put into penal institutions. In the Federal Republic of Germany the penal institutions are often preferred to the mental hospitals by the people concerned. This, however, is not so much an indication of the high standards of the penal institutions as of the absolutely degrading conditions in some of the mental hospitals.

The purpose and the aim of both kinds of institutions really ought to be one and the same: to help people find their constructive potential, and perhaps to activate some hidden potential in them, while at the same time dealing with their destructive and deficient personality components. In both cases milieu treatment could provide the framework for those people who have been excluded from society and go on excluding themselves to find their way back into society, not as adjusted people who keep silent, but rather as independent-minded personalities.

Some people might consider me an idealist who knows nothing about reality. However, I am of the firm conviction that much more is possible than is actually done. This, to my mind, is a question of morals, of the morals of those who let the prison system continue and new prisons be built: it is a system organized on the basis of resignation and fear. And I think, we must also question the professional ethics of those scientists who analyze and fragmentize man and forget that he is a complex and synthetic being in interaction with his fellowmen.

Werner Müller [9] writes: For the acid of the analyst eats away the flesh from the bones.

> The naked, stark terms of theory face us with something uncanny, something not just incomprehensible, but ghastly, something which is as akin to the dissecting-room of the physician as to the destruction wrought in the laboratory of the physicist ... since the intellectual reduction of real life, a harmless play of the few in the beginning, has paved the way for the juggernaut of the machine age of modern times.

The question of how much this attitude to life endangers our very existence as human beings on this planet is now no longer raised only by scientific outsiders, especially, since our existence is not only threatened from a biological point of view. The question of how to reintegrate into society the so-called fringe groups, to which both the mentally ill and criminal offenders belong, cannot be separated from the question "Into what kind of society are we goint to reintegrate them?"

Berthold Brecht [7] defines disorder as the situation where nothing is in its proper place, as opposed to order, where in the proper place there is nothing. By this I want to say that the "order" which we so-called integrated people try to establish - the legislators through laws, the physicians through diagnoses, and the judges through sentences - must not replace chaos by inner emptiness and meaninglessness. A society in which the average citizen leads a life duller than the delinquent, in which someone who reacts schizophrenically is more creative than the civil servant, desperately needs to question its values.

References

1. Ammon G (1959) Theoretical aspects of milieu therapy. The Menninger School of Psychiatry. Pinel, Berlin, 1977
2. Ammon G (1973) Dynamische Psychiatrie. Luchterhand, Darmstadt
3. Ammon G (1979a) Psychoanalytische Milieutherapie. In: Ammon G (ed) Handbuch der dynamischen Psychiatrie, vol 1. Rheinhardt, Munich, pp 604-621
4. Ammon G (1979b) Das Borderline-Syndrom und das ich - strukturelle Arbeiten. In: Ammon G (ed) Handbuch der dynamischen Psychiatrie, vol 1. Rheinhardt, Munich, pp 295-363
5. Ammon G (1982a) Methodenintegration aus der Sicht der Dynamischen Psychiatrie. In: Ammon G (ed) Handbuch der dynamischen Psychiatrie, vol 2. Rheinhardt, Munich, pp 25-48
6. Ammon G (1982b) Das sozialenergetische Prinzip in der Dynamischen Psychiatrie. In: Ammon G (ed) Handbuch der dynamischen Psychiatrie. vol 2. Rheinhardt, Munich, pp 4-25
7. Brecht B (1961) Flüchtlingsgespräche. Suhrkamp, Frankfurt/Main
8. Griepenstroh D (1982) Zur therapeutischen Bedeutung von Tätigsein - ein Vergleich von der Arbeitstherapie nach Istvan Benedek mit der Milieutherapie nach Günter Ammon. In: Ammon G (ed) Handbuch der dynamischen Psychiatrie, vol 2. Rheinhardt, Munich, pp 407-435
9. Müller W (1981) Indianische Welterfahrung. Klett Cotta, Stuttgart

Contraception and Abortion in Mentally Handicapped Female Adolescents Under German Law

A. Eser

At first sight, the title of this paper seems rather academic, but when we look more closely, it reveals problems of a highly explosive social and political nature. This is particularly so if we think of permanent contraceptive procedures such as sterilization. Since there was awful abuse of this measure during the German national socialist period, this is still a very touchy problem [1]. Nonetheless, we must concede that contraceptive measures with regard to a mentally handicapped yet still sexually fully active adolescent might become very urgent. In such a case, what should parents be allowed to do and to ask for? What measures should homes or other protective institutions for the mentally handicapped be allowed to take? What limitations are imposed in this respect by contemporary German law? The purpose of this survey is to pursue some of these questions. First, however, it will be necessary to identify certain problems arising within the framework of this topic.

Some Necessary Distinctions

Medical Procedures Requiring Differentiation

Medical prodecures exhibiting certain common features by virtue of their sexual reference and on account of specific problems concerning the mentally handicapped are covered under the topic "contraception and abortion," although from a legal point of view questions of a widely differing nature arise, according to the type and aim of the procedure concerned.

Consequently, it becomes necessary at the very outset to distinguish between the following procedures:

1. Temporary contraceptive measures, such as the prescription of ovulation inhibitors, the insertion of spirals, and the injection of contraceptives
2. Much more radical, permanent, contraceptive procedures, such as sterilization.
3. Termination of an already existing pregnancy, a procedure which is fundamentally different from such contraceptive measures as those mentioned above.

"Adolescence" not Equatable with "Minority"

Our topic is restricted to that group of mentally handicapped persons who are "female adolescents." As far as age is concerned, we are here dealing with persons who for biological reasons must already be considered amenable to contraceptive measures, i.e., young persons from about the age of 12. On the attainment of majority in terms of section 2 of the German Civil Code, adolescence in the medical sense does not cease; nevertheless, the legal issues involved assume a new guise. I shall return to this point later.

In the presentation of the topic only female adolescents are mentioned. This corresponds to the state of the debate so far. There has been hardly any discussion of measures for the prevention of fertility in men, although it is incontestable that the male sex ought particularly to be included in reflections on sterilization. This also applies to the mentally handicapped.

"Mentally Handicapped" not Equatable with Absolute Incapacity to Consent

In considering procedures affecting the fertility of the mentally handicapped, we cannot avoid taking a closer look at what is to be understood by "mentally handicapped." From a medical point of view we are here concerned with persons suffering from mental defects indicating a considerable degree of health impairment, where such defects may be inherited or transmissible (but not necessarily so). A mental defect becomes a legal problem mainly because the affected persons themselves are generally unable not only on account of their age but also because of their mental inability to make necessary decisions on birth planning or control. Thus the question arieses whether and to what extent birth prevention measures that appear necessary should be allowed to be taken by others as representatives or even on a mandatory basis. Here an immediate warning must be given against a shortcut equation of "mental infirmity" with "incapacity to consent," for the latter crucially depends on capacity to understand the nature and significance of a concrete measure. Whether capacity to consent is later established or not, mental infirmity as such is already sufficient cause for raising the question whether and to what extent contraceptive precautions or, if necessary, an abortion ought to be considered.

In the examination of this question a number of factors could be taken into account – but without my wishing fully to adopt any one of them:

1. The wish to prevent danger to life or health of the person concerned
2. The wish to avoid the birth of offspring with an hereditary disease
3. The fact that persons suffering from a severe mental infirmity would not themselves be able to look after, educate, and maintain their children, so that the latter, even if healthy themselves, would almost certainly be committed to a life spent in homes
4. The experience that persons of the category being considered here not infrequently exhibit an above-average degree of sexual activity [2]
5. The observation that new conceptions for treatment and integration of the handicapped are connected with greater encouragement to enter into sexual relationships and that, for this very reasons, the danger of sexual abuse is increased [3].

For all these reasons it is to be welcomed when questions of birth control as they affect the mentally handicapped are gradually freed from the taboo resulting from the experience of national socialism, and are instead opened to a new sociopolitical discussion. Clearly, with such factual complexity as is indicated here, legal comprehension cannot be an easy matter. This is all the more the case since even the legal position of adults and persons of sound mind is not yet fully settled. This especially applies to sterilization, which will be dealth with first, since the multiplicity of problems involved comes to light with particular intensity here.

Sterilization

Present Legal Practice: Permissibility of Voluntary Sterilization

Sterilization must be viewed as the most serious contraception procedure that we are goint to consider because it leads to enduring infertility and – at least in the case of women – must be regarded as regularly (still) irreversible. It is all the more regrettable that – at least as far as German law is concerned – the legal position in this field is rather obscure and controversial in certain areas. So as not to burden our consideration fo this topic more than is necessary by dealing with disputed legal points, I shall only refer here to the opinion of the Federal Surpreme Court *(Bundesgerichtshof)*, which constitutes the most decisive guide to legal practice. Following the sensational decision in the case against Dr. Axel Dohrn, this court has taken the view that today voluntary sterilization is no longer an offense under criminal law [4]. The consequences of this are mainly twofold:

1. Informed consent is to be regarded as both a necessary and a sufficient condition for the permissibility of sterilization.
2. Sterilization is not to be subjected to a "morality test," as would be required according to section 226a of the German Penal Code if sterilization were still covered by the penal provision on "physical injury" (S. 223) [5].

In other respects, much remains unsettled. As the Federal Supreme Court has on the whole only hat to concern itself with voluntary sterilization, there has been no clarification at the highest judicial level of the prerequisites for sterilization of minors and/or the mentally handicapped. Consequently, recourse must be had to general principles of consent, and we must work on the basis that the admissibility of a sterilization will depend solely and crucially on there being effective consent. Thus – in addition to the other requirement that a physician should be consulted (which will not be further discussed here) – the capacity to consent of the person to be sterilized will become the central problem of admissibility.

In view of this, the following questions arise regarding the sterilization of mentally handicapped female adolescents:

1. How far are young persons capable of consent at all?
2. To what extent are there special restrictions applicable to the mentally handicapped?
3. How far can a lack of capacity to consent on the part of the mentally handicapped be replaced by the consent of others (in particular by the consent of the parents or some other statutory representative)?

General Capacity of Minors to Consent

It is useless to search statutes for a clear answer even to the question of the general capacity of minors to consent. Given that there is no express statutory regulation of the general prerequisites for consent, it is not surprising that the German Penal Code is also silent on the question of capacity to consent.

Nonetheless, it is possible in the light of settled judicial opinion to work from the following principle:

Capacity of the individual affected to consent, as required for medical procedures, is not to be equated either with "majority" or with "capacity to make legal transactions" under civil law.

What is alone decisive is rather the natural "capacity to understand and discern." This may be related to age and maturity, but does not depend on a fixed age limit. Capacity to consent may (already or still) be assumed if the patient is capable of fully appreciating the nature and significance of the medical procedure to be carried out in her case [6].

This separation of capacity to consent from legal majority obviously has the disadvantage that a physician must establish in each individual case whether or not he is dealing with a patient capable of consenting. So as to give doctors at least some help in making their decision, attempts have been made to find generalizable criteria to which their evaluation can be adjusted. This has also occurred with regard to sterilization, although there are a number of different views as to the conditions – particularly age – under which capacity to give effective personal consent to an operation of such wide significance can be assumed.

According to a very strict view, a decision of this kind entails a degree of life experience which even persons that have just attained their majority do not as a rule possess. Consequently, as long as voluntary sterilization continues to remain unregulated by statute, it will be necessary to proceed according to the example of the Castration Act on the basis of a minimum age of 25 years for capacity to consent [7].

Other authorities, however, adhere to the view that such a "partial minority of persons of full age" [8] is impossible under existing law. Although the 25-year limit is desirable from a legal policy point of view [9], its adoption would require express statutory stipulation. Thus, as far as the present position regarding legal status is concerned, we are compelled to work on the assumption that every person of full age and sound mind is fully capable of consenting and enjoys unlimitted power to make his own arrangements [10].

Yet, if one seriously considers that there is always something arbitrary about age limits, given the individual nature of the maturing process and the diversity of medical issues, then until the legislature undertakes a classification of types through fixed age limits, one will not on principle be able to exclude the possibility that minors might also be able to give effective consent to sterilization in appropriate cases [11].

Absence of Exclusive Capacity To Decide on the Part of the Mentally Handicapped

Thus, if minors are also considered basically capable of consenting, the question arises as to the conditions under which such consent may be given. This is a particularly crucial question as far as a mentally handicapped adolescent's consent to sterilization is concerned. As in the case of other medical measures, capacity to consent does not simply mean the ability to say "yes," but presupposes the capacity adequately to assess pros and cons regarding the significance and extent of the operation to be performed, and of being able to make a decision accordingly [12]. Capacity to consent does not only have an intellectual aspect; life experience and matters of conscience also play a role. As we are not dealing here with quantifiable factors, psychological testing procedures such as intelligence tests do not help much. They are not useful for our purposes, as their results cannot be used to answer concrete questions relating to intellectual abilities and maturity of character, as would be needed for an assessment of the significance of sterilization. At the most, one might take the negative view that below a certain intelligence quotient - to be set at a very low level - we may rule out the possibility that the person concerned will possess the requisite capacities for a personal decision regarding the operation. Care must be taken here as regards positive deductions. Thus it might be possible to draw conclusions relevant to capacity to decide from an examination of the nature and severity of the mental deficiency, and at the some time conclusions relevant to the patient's condition as a whole. Clearly, statements of a more precise nature would necessitate interdisciplinary contacts of ever greater depth so as to reduce lawyers' ignorance and misinformation regarding psychiatric illness and, on the other hand, to eliminate psychiatrists' misunderstandings regarding the legal implications.

It is, however, possible to make the following observations. It cannot in principle be ruled out that the mentally infirm (including those who do not have the capacity to make legal transactions) may themselves be in a position to give effective consent to the execution of a medical procedure having permanent consequences - and may thus be able to give their consent to a sterilization operation; nevertheless, the younger the patient is, the more ignorance, inexperience, and instability related to age must be added to the inadequacies of mental performance resulting from the illness. If the patient is still a minor the risk of an irreversible and mistaken decision being taken is so great that the right to an exclusive personal decision would be indefensible. It is undeniable that in terms of developmental psychology the maturing process is a matter of gradual advance, and that for this reason any temporal caesura has something arbitrary about it. Consequently, there may be rare cases where inappropriate restrictions are placed on a young person's power to decide; however, this price will have to be paid for the sake of averting mistaken decisions of a very serious nature in by far the greater number of cases. This is all the more so since a responsible young person will on principle not take decisions of such importance without first discussing the matter thoroughly with members of the family [13].

Substituted Consent of a Statutory Representative

If a patient is to be deprived of his power to decide himself and it is not intended to dispense with the operation, rules will be needed to provide for substituted consent.

Two possibilities of varying substance are imaginable:

1. The consent of a statutory representative will have to be substituted for personal incapacity to consent.
2. Mandatory sterilization will have to be permitted by statute on specified grounds.

Since the latter method is correctly regarded as taboo after the malpractices of the national socialist period [14], there remains only the possibility of the substituted consent of the parents or some other statutory representative. But as the latter should on no account be permitted to make dispositions regarding the legal interests of others in the manner of a despotic regent, there are two tasks facing the legal regulation of consent by representation: on the one hand, there is the issue of determining the person entitled to act as representative; and, on the other hand, there is the issue of delimiting the powers to be granted to a representative.

Parents are, as we know, authorized to represent their minor children. By virtue of section 1626 of the German Civil Code both father and mother have the right, and are under a duty, to "care for the person" of their child. This includes responsibility for ensuring necessary medical attention [15]. In the case of mentally handicapped children living in homes, the duties of the parents are not infrequently taken over by a guardian [16], as also happens with mentally incapable adults who are unable to run their own affairs [17]. Where there is only a limited need for assistance in such cases, the appointment of a special guardian for the handicapped *(Gebrechlichkeitspfleger)* may suffice [18]. If a doctor has to deal with such a person, there will not as a rule be any need to check the authority of the person claiming the right of care.

The extent of the powers of representation enjoyed by the person with the right of care deserves much closer attention, for only insofar as this person keeps within the limits of his representative powers may a doctor work on the assumption that there has been effective consent to the sterilization. Thus the purpose and limits of the power of representation are crucially important. The key norm in this respect is section 1627, subsection 1 of the German Civil Code, according to which parents – and the same is true of guardians in relation to their wards – exercise "parental care on their own responsibility and in mutual agreement for the welfare of the child," and in doing so are subject to the guardianship court as watchdog [19]. This regulation is also important in the field of medical activity because there are no other special statutory provisions. Obviously, however, it is too generally phrased for one to be able to draw direct conclusions regarding concrete medical treatment. For this reason the interpretation of "welfare of the child" is decisive: only if the assumption can be made that sterilization is in the interests of the welfare of the mentally infirm patient can the statutory representative's consent thereto also have the effect of excluding the possibility of punishment. In order to facilitate an assessment of this question in individual cases, it is advisable to adopt a classification of types based on specific grounds or "indications," which as a rule justify the assumption that sterilization is in the interests of the welfare of the child. The following reasons for sterilization – in some ways parallel to the catalog of indications for abortion contained in section 218 a of the German Penal Code – must be considered.

Medically Indicated Sterilization

Sterilization is at its least problematic if it must be carried out to avert danger to the life or health of a mentally handicapped adolescent, where such danger is greater than the impairment of physical integrity that would result from the sterilization operation itself. This applies in any event to those (not very frequent) cases where a medicotherapeutic indication is present, so that sterilization is necessary for treatment of an existing ailment.

It is much more difficult to give concrete shape to the medico-prophylactic indication. How great must the impending health risks be? What degree of certainty must the prognosis of such dangers display? How far must recourse be had to alternative methods for treatment that are less radical by dint of not being irreversible? The 1972 draft of the Fifth Penal Law Reform Act, which went beyond abortion reform to include sterilization provisions, embodied a very strict requirement [20]. The person concerned would have to be incapable of consenting indefinitely, and treatment would have to be necessary for the elimination of an otherwise unavoidable risk of death or complete collapse of health [21]. The adoption of such a strict requirement was intended to deprive comparisons with the compulsory sterilizations of national socialism of their foundation. However understandable this anxiety may be, it does seem as though too little attention has been paid to the interests of the handicapped themselves. It is certainly correct only to permit sterilization as a measure of last resort, and accordingly to require that the objective pursued should not be attainable by less radical means. However, restriction of sterilization to cases where it is necessary it the complete collapse of the patient's health is to be avoided appears to be a narrow and over-anxious approach [22]. Nor is such a limitation called for by existing law.

As a result it would probably be more appropriate to take one's orientation from section 218 a, subsection 1, no. 2 of the Penal Code. That is to say, medico-prophylactic sterilization would be allowed in a case where a pregnancy termination would be indicated for the avoidance of serious impairment to physical or mental health and where there was no prospect of improvement in the patient's health [23]. Sterilization would be permitted in such cases because it would amount to the lesser evil in comparison with the concrete risk that a pregnancy would have to be terminated [24].

Genetically Indicated Sterilization

While discussion of the medical indication in relation to the mentally handicapped has now become less subject to prejudice in the Federal Republic of Germany, there are still signs that the past has not been overcome as far as the genetic indication is concerned. Thus the draft of the Fifth Penal Law Reform Act was still quite decidedly against allowing sterilization on eugenic grounds in the cases of persons incapable of giving their consent; the 1970 Alternative Draft for a Penal Code also kept this problem out of the realm of the criminal law [25]. On the other hand, those who advocate that some provision be made for substituted consent in this case have recently begun to grow in number [26]. They are agreed that eugenic and population aspects should not play any role here - and not only for purely ethical reasons [27].

Genetically indicated sterilization will have to be seen as running parallel, as it were, to abortion under the law already in force (section 218a, subsection 2, no. 1 of the Criminal Code). As we have already seen in the case of the medico-prophylactic indication, it cannot be ruled out that early sterilization would constitute a lesser evil than a later series of abortions [28]. That the representative whose consent will be required may run into even greater conflict than in the case of the medical indication cannot be overlooked [29].

Sterilization Indicated on Familial and Social Grounds

As in the case of an abortion to avert some other precarious situation (the so-called *allgemeine Notlagenindikation* according to section 218a, subsection 2, no. 3 of the Penal Code), it might also be apposite to permit sterilization in all cases where pregnancy would put the adolescent in a socially unacceptable precarious situation [30]. However, in opposition to this conclusion there is the fact that, particularly in severe cases of mental infirmity, the pregnant female would not herself be burdened with the consequences of seeing her pregnancy through because the child would in any case have to be removed from her care on account of her inability to look after it. Thus sterilization would serve to relieve pressure on the family or society, but would not serve the personal welfare of the adolescent concerned, as required for the operation to be permissible. Insofar as relief of the family cannot necessarily be regarded as indirectly serving the welfare of the mentally handicapped mother, it is not apparent how familial and social grounds for sterilization of the mentally infirm could be established without a prior change in the law. For this reason it is absolutely essential that the legislature should concern itself with the problems involved in sterilization on this indication.

At any rate, in a way parallel to the indication for abortion arising from some other "precarious situations," as mentioned above, sterilization may now be considered for a mentally handicapped adolescent in two cases. These may at first sight appear to be in direct conflict with each other, but actually have a common aspect in the ultimately individual conflict of interests of those concerned.

On the one hand, there is the case where the requirements of section 1747, subsection 4 or section 1748, subsection 3 of the German Civil Code would probably be permanently fulfilled in the event of the pregnancy being brought to completion: the child would be removed from the care of its mother against her will or would, in its own iterests, even have to be taken away. If it were desired in this case to exclude the possibility of legal sterilization, a genuine opportunity would arise for using that nasty expression "birth machine." Not protecting a woman from getting pregnant and then compelling her to give birth to a child in the certain knowledge that she will never be able or allowed to look after the child definitely seems degrading, quite apart from the question of the future prospects of the child itself [31].

On the other hand, sterilization can be considered if it is necessary to avoid denying a handicapped person opportunities of elementary human development. Of course, in such cases, where it is ultimately a question of the integration of the mentally handicapped, the same result can often be achieved with less radical contraceptive measures. In any event, it will always be necessary to examine the question how far a decision on an irreversible sterilization can be deferred until adulthood, in the hope that the person concerned will then display sufficient insight to be able to reach her own decision on such an operation. Above all, however, where representation is unavoidable, there will have to be very careful balancing so as to protect the genuine welfare of the person concerned in the clash between free personality development on the one hand and protection against unwanted offspring on the other [32]. Obviously, it would be too one-sided to view the continual more or less vague expectation of social integration at the expense of reproductive capacity as a fundamentally higher value. Thus sterilization will have to be seen as the lesser evil if the only alternative amounts to permanent medical treatment suppressing the sexual instinct but at the same time changing the personality. Even in the latter case, respect for personal dignity would demand that action should at least not be taken against the express wishes of those involved in such cases, even though they may not be fully aware of all the implications of their refusal. All these difficulties indicate once againt that statutory clarification is urgently desirable.

Institutional Safeguards in Sterilization Procedure

Just as requirements for consent and powers of representation have hardly been determined for sterilization, so too we find hardly any of the institutional safeguards that would be desirable for the decision-making process. Apart from the control of "parental malpractice" by the guardianship court under section 1666 of the German Civil Code – which is more a matter of chance than anything else – the statutory representative is virtually left to make his decision alone [33]. It would therefore be worth considering whether the interests of those concerned should in future be protected through special precautions, such as those provided – even if in an imperfect form – by the draft of the Fifth Penal Law Reform Act of 1972 [34].

Without further elaboration at this point, provision ought to be made for the following measures:

1. The person to be sterilized should participate to the full extent of her mental capacities in the process of reaching a decision.
2. Provision should be made, as in the case of social counseling for abortion under section 218b of the Penal Code, for an effective system of consultation.
3. A method would have to be created for testing the statutory representative's decision in regard to its compatibility with the genuine welfare of the person concerned.

Temporary Contraceptive Measures

As opposed to the usually irreversible infertility procured by sterilization, we are here concerned with measures that are reversible and applicable on flexible time scales. This observation thus leads us to identify their field of application, which arises where the person concerned desires, or where it is in the interests of the welfare of that person, to suspend her reproductive capacity at least temporarily but if possible not permanently. Such measures are of particular relevance in cases where contraception is advisable but the question of sterilization is not ready for decision.

The admissibility of such contraceptive procedures may be amenable to a rather more generous assessment than has been the case with sterilization, given that their consequences are less radical. Clearly, careful consideration of individual cases and precise investigation of the necessity for applying a measure - for example, in relation to measures restricting liberty - will be required. This may be particularly difficult not only where it is a matter of warding off dangers to the person concerned but also where it is desired to attain an improvement in her status. Although there will also be a number of problems of balance here, it will scarcely be possible to solve them by statutory regulation of a necessarily general nature. A doctor may, in this field, run into conflict with the criminal law when there has been an obvious abuse of the right of care on the part of the statutory representative.

Abortion

In relation to the measures discussed up to now, two major differences concerning abortion must be emphasized. First, in view of the nature of the operation it is no longer merely a matter of preventing pregnancy but now concerns the destruction of unborn life and thus is detrimental to another legally protected interest. Second, the statutory regulation of abortion has already been reformed (sections 218-219d of the Penal Code), although there are considerable lacunae, especially with regard to the minors and persons incapable of consent with whom we have been dealing here.

This affects, above all, three questions of practical importance:

- Problems relating to indications where a pregnant female is mentally handicapped
- Minors' capacity to consent,
- Substituted consent of the statutory representatives.

Problems of Indication Relating to Mentally Handicapped Pregnant Adolescents

By contrast with Danish and Austrian law, under which an abortion is allowed, even beyond the 3-month limit, where the pregnant female is immature or under age [35], the German Penal Code has no provision for abortion related specifically to the handicapped. This applies even to cases where it is feared that harm to the child will occur - here a provision is made by section 218a, subsection 2, no. 1 of the German Penal Code, which should on no account be misunderstood as eugenic in intent. Neither the infirmity of the pregnant female nor the apprehended harm to the child constitutes in itself a reason for abortion: this only arises when the pregnant adolescent cannot reasonably be expected to see her pregnancy through on account of apprehended irreparable harm to the child [36]. If the unreasonableness of such an expectation is understood in a strictly individual sense, this might even suggest that the more limited a handicapped pregnant adolescent's horizon of experience is, the less an abortion may be considered to be indicated for such a person [37]. It is clear that indications are to be determined in relation to the individual situation of the persons concerned [38]; nevertheless, it is also a matter here of statutory anticipation of conflict situations in accordance with objective criteria [39]. Accordingly, not only the strict medical indication of section 218, subsection 1, no. 2 of the German Penal Code but also the general indication for a precarious situation of section 218 a, subsection 2, no. 3 of the Penal Code are conceivable in relation to the handicapped, the considerations that arise with regard to the demands that can be made of a handicapped pregnant adolescent being similar to those that arise in the case of contraception through sterilization. At any rate the possibility of adoption cannot without more ado be regarded as a reasonable alternative to an abortion [40].

Finally, the so-called criminological indication (section 218 a, subsection 2, no. 2 of the German Penal Code) may become significant where impregnation of a mentally handicapped person takes place. Insofar as inability to resist arising from the illness of the handicapped adolescent is misused for the purpose of sexual intercourse and the resulting pregnancy is thus based on an unlawful act under section 179 of the German Penal Code, there is automatically ground for the performance of an abortion without there being need for a special finding that the pregnancy cannot reasonably be expected to be brought to completion [41]. The same applies, to an obviously even greater extent, in the more serious case of rape (section 177 of the German Penal Code) or sexual duress (section 178 of the German Penal Code).

Requirement of the Pregnant Adolescent's Consent

Even if one of the indications just mentioned is present, an abortion is not justified for this reason alone. The consent of the pregnant female is also required before an abortion can be performed (section 218 a, subsection 1, no. 1 of the German Penal Code). Thus the same issues regarding the capacity of the mentally handicapped to decide arise here as in the matter of sterilization.

In spite of this, the answers to the question of capacity to decide need not necessarily be the same, since the requirements are different in each case. Whereas in the case of sterilization the most important requirement for consent is that the person concerned must be in a position to recognize the permanent effect of the irreversible loss of her reproductive capacity, in the case of abortion it is crucial that the mentally handicapped adolescent be capable of realizing the particular significance of destroying unborn life and consequently should not only conceive of an abortion as interference with her physical integrity alone [42]. It might be easier to make this comprehensible, with the result that a mentally handicapped female adolescent's personal capacity to decide may be assumed with greater likelihood in the case of abortion than in the case of sterilization.

Codecision of the Statutory Representative

As a rule it will be necessary to proceed on the basis of a need for representation [43]. The required (substituted or additional) consent of the parents or some other statutory representative will scarcely be easier to attain than in the case of sterilization; here, too, a high degree of empathy will be required to establish what is genuinely best for the pregnant person. She has a natural right to the child on the one hand, but there are also the interests embodied in the indications enumerated in section 218a of the German Penal Code [44] to be protected.

Where the pregnant female expressly opposes the consent of the statutory representative and thus the performance of an abortion, it will be necessary to proceed as for sterilization. If her veto can at least be based on a certain conception of the difficulties she is bound to face, this will lead - except where there is a strict medical indication - to the assertion that consent by the statutory representative can no longer regarded as being as in the interests of her welfare. This, in turn, will mean that effective consent is lacking [45].

Concluding Remarks

The problems relating to contraception and abortion in mentally handicapped female adolescents have clearly not been exhaustively dealth with in this rather cursory examination. Nonetheless, some of the essential points affecting doctors have been touched upon. If guidance in making decisions has not turned out to be as concrete as doctors may have hoped for particular cases, there is not only a disadvantage but also an advantage in this, namely, that freedom of evaluation, decision, and action on an individual's own responsibility is thereby conceded. In spite of an understandable desire for legal certainty, doctors ought to be able to appreciate this discretion, for, particularly as far as this subject is concerned, we in Germany have indeed had other and by no means better experiences.

Acknowledgement. For valuable assistance I am indepted to Assessor H.-G. Koch

References

1. In this respect, other countries are much better off, since they are able to discuss these problems untouched by the dark shadows of their history: an impressive example is the Working Paper 2.4, Sterilization: implications for mentally retarded and mentally ill persons, by the Law Reform Commission of Canada, 1979.
2. But not necessarily of such a nature that one could speak of an "abnormal sexual instinct" in the sense of the German Castration Act of 15 August 1969 (*Gesetz über die freiwillige Kastration und andere Behandlungsmethoden:* BGBl. I 1143). Treatment measures in terms of this Act are not dealt with here. A corresponding application of rules of procedure under this Act to the fields of inquiry to be considered here is impossible [LG Düsseldorf FamRZ 1981, 95; AG Kaiserslautern MDR 1981, 229; see also Henke, Neue Juristische Wochenschrift (1976) Ergänzende Maßnahmen zur Neuregelung des Schwangerschaftsabbruchs - advocating an extensive adoption of the provisions of the *Kastrationsgesetz (KastrG),* from a legal policy point of view]. Cf also Hanack (1959) Die strafrechtliche Zulässigkeit künstlicher Unfruchtbarmachung, pp 320ff and note 33

3. See Wimmer (1976) Ärztliche Sterilisation von Einwilligungsfähigen und Nichteinwilligungsfähigen. Renovatio, p 127
4. BGHSt (*Entscheidungen des Bundesgerichtshofs in Strafsachen:* Decisions of the Federal Court in Penal Matters) 20 (1966) 81
5. For this reason there is at present no real foundation for the repeatedly expressed fear that a so-called "acommodating sterilization" *(Gefälligkeitssterilisation)* must be seen as *contra bonos mores* (immoral) in view of section 6 of the professional rules for doctors *(Berufsordnung für Ärzte)* and could accordingly be punishable under section 226a of the German Criminal Code. On this subject and for further details see Eser in Eser, Hirsch (eds) (1980) Sterilisation und Schwangerschaftsabbruch, pp 55ff
6. For individual references to this now generally recognized view in German theory and practice see Lenckner in Schönke, Schröder (eds) (1982) Kommentar zum StGB, 21st edn, prenotes 39ff to section 32, and also Eser in Schönke and Schröder, section 223, notes 37ff
7. Cf section 2, subsection 1, no 3 *KastrG* (note 2 above). See further, for example, Hirsch's view in Leipziger Kommentar zum StGB, 10th edn, 1981, section 226a, note 41
8. Lenckner's term, in Eser and Hirsch (note 5 above), p 188
9. Cf section 226b of the 1972 draft of a Fifth Criminal Law Reform Act and section 112, subsection 2 *Alternativ-Entwurf* (Alternative Draft) (cf note 25 below). See further Hanack (1979) Die strafrechtliche Zulässigkeit künstlicher Unfruchtbarmachung, p 339, and Wimmer (note 3 above), pp 129ff
10. This, in particular, is Lenckner's view (note 8 above)
11. See Eser in Schönke and Schröder (note 6 above), section 223, note 62 (but also note 38 below). Capacity to consent cannot "automatically" be attributed to persons of full age. To the extent that an attempt may be made to avoid a minor's possible capacity to consent by reference to the *contra bonos mores* provision of section 226a of the German Penal Code - so that a minor's power to make his own arrangements is disputed either generally or only with regard to sterilization carried out as a favor [cf Lenckner in Eser and Hirsch (note 5 above) p 189] - it must be countered that according to the German Civil Code there is no room for considerations relating to *contra bonos mores,* either on principle or with reference to age
12. This definition of capacity to consent is commonly used in the courts and in theory; certain nuances, however, may be passed over here. Cf instead BGHSt 12 (1959) 379/382 and Eser in Schönke and Schröder (note 6 above), section 223, note 38 with further references
13. Even if by virtue of section 1626, subsection 2 of the German Civil Code parents must take into account the "growing ability and desire of children to act independently and on their own responsibility," such a need for personal decision-making (without parents, participation) will probably have to be disavowed at least in the cases of irreversible operations that we are dealing with here
14. Cf *Bundestags-Drucksache* (Government Publication) VI/3434, p 41, and Lenckner in Eser and Hirsch (note 5 above), p 174, who correctly takes the view that article 1 of the West German Constitution *(Grundgesetz)* has excluded the possibility of provisions being enacted on the model of the Hereditary Health Act *(Erbgesundheitsgesetz)* of 1933/41
15. Cf Hinz in Münchner Kommentar zum BGB, 1978, section 1626, note 44
16. Cf sections 1773 and 1793 of the German Civil Code
17. Cf sections 6 and 1896ff of the German Civil Code
18. Cf section 1910, subsection 2 of the German Civil Code. In practice special guardianship of the handicapped is preferred, as indicated by the endeavor as far as possible to allow those affected themselves to collaborate in the taking of fateful decisions. On this see Goerke in Münchner Kommentar, section 1910, note 16ff
19. Cf section 1666, subsection 1, sentence 1 of the German Civil Code. *De lege ferenda,* an opportunity for preventive control - which is nonexistent under the present law - ought to be created. Cf also note 33 below
20. *Bundestags-Drucksache* VI/3434, section 226b
21. This suggestion was silent on the question of the requisite degree of risk
22. See Lenckner in Eser and Hirsch (note 5 above), p 190; Henke (1976) Ergänzende Maßnahmen zur Neuregelung des Schwangerschaftsabbruchs. Neue Juristische Wochenschrift, p 1776; Becker (1972) Das Sterilisationsproblem im neuen Strafgesetzentwurf. Zeitschrift für Evangelische Ethik, p 334

23. Also Lenckner's view (see note 22 above). Cf also LG Berlin, Zeitschrift für das Gesamte Familienrecht 1971, p 668 (where, however, the decision was incorrectly based on section 4, subsection 2, *KastrG*)
24. At any rate this argument cannot be controverted on the basis that sterilization is not an *ultima ratio* because an abortion may, if necessary, also be considered. In contradistinction to the comparison between sterilization and other less radical and therefore preferable contraceptive measures, a legal interest (unborn life) not relating to the patient herself in also affected through performance of an abortion
25. According to the *Alternativ-Entwurf, Strafsachen gegen die Person*, vol 1 1970, p 53, the whole complex of sterilization and castration of the mentally ill who are incapable of giving their consent ought to be dealth with in a special administrative law
26. Cf Wimmer (note 3 above), p 130
27. Cf Jürgens in Eser and Hirsch (note 5 above), p 16
28. For a similar view see Lenckner in Eser and Hirsch (note 5 above), pp 190ff
29. See Kohlhaas (1968) Zur Sterilisation bei Minderjährigen aus eugenischen Gründen. Deutsche Medizinische Wochenschrift 229. Kohlhaas also concludes in favor of allowing prophylactic sterilization on eugenic grounds of minors incapable of consenting; he calls for the intervention of the guardianship court and of the juvenile court service *(Jugendgerichtshilfe)* under existing law, without, however, indicating the legal basis for this. *De lege lata*, there is at the most the possibility of a voluntary application to the guardianship court in accordance with section 1631, subsection 3 of the German Civil Code
30. In this sense Lenckner, in Eser and Hirsch (note 5 above), p 191ff
31. It is common knowledge that adoption can scarcely be procured for children of mentally handicapped parents
32. Wimmer (note 3 above), p 131, correctly takes a cautious view
33. This also applies to foster children and minors under the age of 16 who are living in homes. Although by virtue of sections 31 and 79 of the Juvenile Welfare Act *(Jugendwohlfahrtsgesetz: JWG)* such persons are subject to the supervision of the juvenile welfare office, effective preventive control is nevertheless not guaranteed, since the duty of foster parents to notify the authorities pursuant to section 32 *JWG* only relates to the taking in, handing over, change of address, and death of the child. In state legislation these duties have been partly extended (see for instance section 14, subsection 2, sentence 2 of the Baden-Württemberg *Landes-JWG:* duty to notify any change crucial to the granting of permission to act as foster parent that affects the situation of the foster child or parent). The extension of these duties does not, however, cover measures relating to the care of the child. As regards the decision to sterilize a mentally infirm adult, some guardianship courts consider it necessary in an analogous application of section 4, subsection 2, and section 6 *KastrG* that the consent of the authorized special guardian should be approved. Whether this approach is correct need not be decided here; in any event it is not applicable to minors under parental control
34. Cf *Bundestags-Drucksache* VI/3434, sections 226b and 226c
35. Cf section 3 of the Danish abortion statute of 1973, under which an abortion is, inter alia, permissible when the woman as a result of physical or mental affliction or of weakness of aptitude (no 4) or in consequence of her youthful age or immaturity (no 5) is not in a position to care for her child in a satisfactory manner. See also section 97 of the Austrian Penal Code of 1975, according to which the minority of the pregnant woman at the time of her pregnancy constitutes a ground for abortion
36. See Eser in Schönke and Schröder (note 6 above), section 218a, note 6; Lenckner in Eser and Hirsch (note 5 above), p 178
37. For this view see *Bundestags-Drucksache* VI/3434, pp 29ff on the 1972 draft of a Fifth Penal Law Reform Act
38. See Eser in Schönke and Schröder (note 6 above), section 218a, note 6; Lenckner in Eser and Hirsch (note 5 above), p 178
39. Eser, Lenckner (note 36 above)
40. For further details regarding the general indication for a precarious situation, including problems of adoption, see Eser in Eser and Hirsch (note 5 above), pp 160ff
41. Cf Eser in Schönke and Schröder (note 6 above), section 218a, note 38
42. See Lenckner in Eser and Hirsch (note 5 above), p 177

43. Competence to act as representative in case of incapacity to consent is not restricted to particular indications but is general: see Eser in Schönke and Schröder (note 6 above), section 218a, note 58
44. Apart from the control of abuse under section 1666 of the German Civil Code, there is no provision under existing law for participation by the guardianship court in making the decision; cf also note 33 above, and regarding legal policy Henke (note 22 above)
45. Cf Lenckner in Eser and Hirsch (note 5 above), p 179

Victim Workers as Therapists for Incarcerated Sex Offenders

L. V. Annis, L. Mathers, G. Dixon, and C. A. Baker

Convicted sex offenders are often sentenced to prison terms, the length of which seems to be determined more by the vagaries of judge and jurisdiction than by characteristics of the offense or offender. Most of these persons then enter the general convict pool of state penitentiaries, at the end of which they may be more sociopathic and better able to evade capture than before incarceration, but just as likely to commit a sex offense.

A minority of convicted sex offenders – fewer than 5% – enter treatment programs for mentally disordered sex offenders (MDSOs). These usually are administered either within the penitentiary system or on the premises of state hospitals. There they participate in rather diverse programs designed to reduce the likelihood of their reoffending. Although they tend to serve about the same time behind bars as untreated offenders, their risk of recidivism is appreciably less than that of incarcerated but untreated sexual aggressives [1, 2]. This is particularly important for MDSOs, many of whom are multiple offenders who would thus be expected to display high rates of reoffending upon release.

The term "sexual aggression" denotes divergent behaviors, ranging from preadolescent voyeurism to brutal and sadistic rape. The individual history, personality, demography, and psychopathology of sexual offenders also vary considerably [1, 3, 4]. Quite different intrapsychic and interpersonal events may result in very similar inappropriate behaviors. As a consequence, especially considering the degree to which individual treatment needs change over time, treating sexually aggressive persons becomes a complex task.

Common threads do, nevertheless, pervade treatment of most offenders [5–7]. Among the foci of treatment of the MDSO at Florida State Hospital is the promotion of the offender's concern for past and potential future victims, an area in which most offenders are notably weak. This concern is largely prompted through group psychotherapy. The offender is encouraged to personalize men and women in general and victims in particular. Efforts are directed at the offender's accepting personal responsibility for his behavior, both the consequences to himself and others. When successful, the arousal valence of deviant sexual and other aggressive behaviors should decline, with a corresponding reduction in further offending. Perceptions of victims as people are further explored in individual therapy sessions, where acceptance of women, men, and children as fellow humans as, it is hoped, enhanced by discussing the qualities they share with the offender. Identification with the plight of victims may be prompted through media presentations, including videotapes, films, and assigned readings. Some of these are dramas or decomentaries displaying the effects of sexual offenses on the victims. Others are productions, such as police rape prevention pamphlets and films like "Rape, A Preventive Inquiry," that were originally designed to reduce the risk of sexual assault to potential victims. The manner of their presentation diminishes their titillation potential, as it is unlikely that new assault techniques will be taught to persons who have shared years of incarceration with other sexual and criminal offenders. Guided discussion following such presentations often emphasizes the offender's own potential – and sometimes actual – response to being sexually assaulted.

Unfortunately, talking with therapists and peers and viewing media products often seem to fail to reach offenders emotional levels. This may particularly be the case for offenders characterized as showing signs of the syndrome typically labeled "antisocial personality disorder" [8], to many of whom victims remain abstract entities.

An alternative treatment for this affliction emerged in the course of a university conference on rape. During their participation on panels, community victim workers met members of the treatment team for MDSO at a nearby state hospital. Each group realized its ignorance of the other's programs and clients. Following considerable discussion, and after securing the approval of agency administrators, face-to-face encounters were initiated between offenders and persons who work with the victims of sexual assault.

Program

Offenders

Florida State Hospital contains a large Forensic Unit, in which a premium is placed on security. Tall, barbed-wire-topped, chain-link fences, numerous locked steel doors, and access points controlled by guards, video cameras, and remotely operated entrances enhance the air of a correctional facility. The Forensic Unit contains its own kitchen and dining areas, activity centers and workshops, library, school, medical and dental clinic, and recreational facilities.

About 400 patients reside within the Forensic Unit. Most of their time is spent on 36- to 42-bed wards that resemble those typically found in mental hospitals of the 1950s and 1960s. These expansive, somewhat bleak wards are divided by 4-ft-high partitions into smaller bays on either side of a single board passage. Six patients reside in each bay, each assigned a 40-ft^2 living area. Furniture is limited to a bed, chair, table, and small bookcase for each patient, with two patients sharing every chest of drawers. Besides the nursing station, a ward also contains a porch and two small, barren therapy rooms which double as recreation spaces, seclusion areas, and laundry rooms.

Most forensic patients are committed as "incompetent to stand trial" or "not-guilty by reason of insanity," but one ward contains only men committed as MDSOs. While some offenders are selected for treatment from within the correctional system, others are committed at the discretion of the court following evaluation by expert examiners. Psychotics and mentally retarded, legally insane, and otherwise incompetent patients are excluded from the MDSO program. All MDSOs have been found guilty of felonious sexual offenses and recommended to the program as likely to benefit from treatment. Participation in the treatment program is voluntary. Offenders must recognize they have a sexual problem and express a desire for rehabilitation prior to their being accepted as potential candidates for transfer to the program. About half are eventually returned to court or prison as unlikely to gain from therapy. The other half are discharged back to court or prison as no longer likely to commit sexual or other offenses (the much sought-after "good" report), usually receiving probation, reduction of sentence, or assignment to a less restrictive correctional institution. Persons receiving unfavorable reports and returned to the correctional system generally remain for their ordinary terms, although some sentences have been increased when the hospital determined that the offender was not amenable to treatment.

The victim workers were involved in the treatment of 25 offenders. These patients ranged in age from 20 to 46 years. They had been sentenced to periods as long as three terms of natural life plus 60 additional years. Many were multiple offenders, and included persons convicted of committing or attempting rape, child molestation, incest, indecent assault, and exhibitionism.

Therapists

The group and individual psychotherapy sessions were conducted by treatment team members usually referred to as "therapists." The two male and three female therapists involved in this project included two psychologists and three clinical social workers. Educational backgrounds ranged from bachelors' degrees to a doctorate. Three staff were white, two black. Some therapists reported that they were survivors of sexual assault, although this was generally unknown among the offenders.

Victim Workers

Three women involved in services to victims of assault participated in the encounters. All indentified themselves to the offenders, giving their names and titles as well as describing what they actually did with victims. One person was a former worker and agency director for rape crisis programs, who was at that time providing consultative and direct service to victims through a private counseling agency. The other two women were police officers who both investigated sexual assault cases and managed rape prevention programs for their respective police departments. One officer wore a uniform during the meetings with offenders.

Guest Participation

The victim workers served as "guest participants" in ongoing group and individual therapy sessions with offenders. Workers and treatment team members met for 15–30 minutes prior to and following each day's therapy sessions to discuss developments in specific cases as well as group progress. The group therapy sessions lasted from 1 to 1½ hours per day, and usually each worker met with two groups daily. Structurally, the groups remained the same: the usual therapist and patient population were present during these meetings. They were held in their typical ward locations.

Each group consisted of one or two therapists and five to eight offenders. The therapy program might be loosely described as "cognitive behavioral," but the basic orientations of the various therapy groups ranged from supportive and therapist guided to highly peer-confrontative.

Guest met with each group one to five times. Sometimes a single guest was present in a group, while at other times two guests attended. Guests also joined with therapists in individual therapy sessions with offenders, and participated in a general ward meeting with all of the offenders.

The first meeting with each worker began with all present introducing themselves. The workers indicated why they were attending, and the offenders described why they were incarcerated. From that point, general question, answer, confrontation, and discussion ensued.

Confidentiality was protected by requiring offenders and guests to cosign agreements limiting release of information.

Results and Discussion

Initially, group meetings generally emphasized information exchanges: offenders described their sexual assault and other victimization experiences, while guests detailed the immediate and long-term effects on victims. These discussions later evolved into highly personal, often very intense, interactions with considerable disclosure by both offenders and guests. Individual meetings usually focused on particular, often highly emotional, concerns raised by the offenders. These frequently seemed to be based on issues introduced earlier in group sessions, although they also included topics that the offenders felt uncomfortable with in group sessions.

The outcome of the program was assessed by self-reports before, during, and after the visits, and by follow-up questionnaires. Results are reported here separately for offenders, therapists, and guests.

Offenders

Prior to the guests' arrival, many offenders held rather strong expectancies, most of them somewhat divergent from those of the therapists. These expectations may be classified as focusing on staff, guests, victims, or themselves. For themselves, offenders anticipated opportunities to talk with someone new. More specifically, they viewed the program as a chance to talk to women who were neither staff nor other patients. Reported staff-centered foci were largely anticipating of impressing therapists with their skills and healthiness, and trepidation about looking bad in front of people who wielded considerable influence over their daily lives and future prospects.

Guest-centered expectations seemed related to anticipating that the guests would take a rather passive role in the therapy groups. Some offenders expected that presenting their side of sexual assault would lead to the guests understanding the motivations of offenders in general, and themselves in particular, better. Impressing guests with their efforts to improve themselves seemed especially important to several offenders. Others stated their intention to assist guests in preventing sexual assault and in dealing with victims. A minority expressed fear that the staff were using them as human guinea pigs to show off to the guests. Victim-centered expectancies emphasized cognitive changes. Many offenders said they expected enhanced insight into the effects of sexual assault on victims. Some stated they were looking for knowledge about the feelings toward assailants held by victims, police, and society in general.

Most offenders viewed the guests as underinformed about sex offender treatment programs before their visit. While most offenders believed the guests to have some preconceptions, they also indicated they felt them to be somewhat open-minded. Guests were expected by many of the offenders to be skeptical about the effects of treatment and, by some offenders, to view the patients as criminals who were avoiding "hard time." Some offenders expected the guests to view them, at least initially, in a very bad light. Adjectives used to describe the guests' previous views of offenders included "cruel," "vicious," "sexually obsessed," "sick," "inhuman," "animal," and "unrepentant." A small minority of offenders stated their expectations of guests' intense dislike for them as freaks, perverts, and jerks, who "deserved to be taken out and shot."

After the program, the offenders believed the guests' views had changed. Hearing the assailant's side and seeing the benefits of treatment were seen as increasing the accuracy of the guests' perceptions. Offenders advised that they were now more likely to be viewed as human beings who, while individuals, were basically the same as everyone else. They appeared particularly anxious to be seen as working hard, aware of people, and concerned for their own and others' victims.

Offenders indicated a number of ways in which they felt helped by the program, most of them unanticipated by the therapists. Some offenders reported improved communication skills. The program allowed the opportunity to apply new social skills outside of the usual cadre of peers and staff. The experience aided in desensitizing them to sharing thoughts and feelings with other persons, especially women. The guests were seen as models of openness, caring, and appropriate emotional expression. Indeed, some patients complained that they experienced more sharing and candor with the guests than among the therapists.

A second area of self-perceived improvement might be labeled feminization. Offenders reported that interacting with the guests led to their perception of women as fellow humans and less as objects. Women were viewed as more honest, expressive, assertive, and courageous. This increased personalization by offenders promoted the view of women as socially and emotionally equal to men.

Offenders seemed increasingly to personalize victims as well. They indicated increased knowledge of the experiences and feelings of citims, often appearing startled at the long-term effects of sexual assault. Several offenders stated they felt enhanced emotional involvement with victims, with significantly more remorse for their offenses. Offenders seemed more sympathetic toward victims' plights and to perceive more accurately the multigenerational effects of sexual assault.

A fourth improvement area was socialization. Offenders indicated increased accuracy of their notions about the views held by society of sexual assailants. The idea that rape was a "sick" act seemed reinforced. Police appeared to be viewed less negatively and more as humans, although "armed neutrals" might be a better description than "friend." In addition, information, particularly about dating and sexual behaviors, was improved.

The final benefit reported by offenders was enhanced therapy responses. Offenders reported that viewing interactions of other group members with guests gave them a new perspective on their peers. They often indicated renewed interest in therapy, reduced boredom, and excitement from the novelty and new topics introduced. Many of the issues initiated during these sessions served as stimulation for new avenues of self-exploration. Concerns long felt to have been resolved were reexamined.

No offender reported feeling that his treatment was impaired by the project. Most of the offenders indicated their desire that these guests return, with different offenders stating their preference for different guests. Many also expressed interest in other police and rape workers, as well as guests from other facets of the community: legislators, students, and citizens in general. Sexual offenders stated that the visits indicated to them that someone outside the immediate circle of friends, family, and therapists cared. Enhanced community involvement and concern, it was felt, could promote effective treatment as well as increase the likelihood of their successful return to the community following incarceration.

Therapists

Compared with the offenders, the therapists had few expectations for the project. Their primary announced goal was to increase the offenders' personalization of victims. A secondary concern was to promote the interest of the community in treating sex offenders rather than merely incarcerating them. The offenders' indications of ways in which the program benefited their rehabilitation was largely supported by the therapists' observations. In general, however, the therapists were somewhat skeptical about the degree of improvement reported by offenders and suggested that modification in thoughts, feelings, and behaviors were somewhat more subtle than the dramatic alterations offenders reported.

The therapists themselves may have gained from the program. The general community sometimes seems to identify helpers with their clients. This misidentification, combined with perceptions of public hostility toward sex offenders, remoteness of the hospital from population centers, and dearth of public support for treatment programs enhanced a feeling of professional isolation among the therapists. The guest program promoted interaction between the therapists and persons in the community, reducing isolation and initiating personal and professional relationships which continue. The therapists may also have benefited from information about victims, and may have become more interested in treatment due to the novelty in group participation and membership and in seeing their client's behavior under unusual circumstances.

Victim Workers

Guest participants had several objectives in entering the program. They were primarily looking for information that would be useful in treating victims and preventing future sexual victimization. A secondary goal was to deter reoffending by the offenders in treatment by presenting victims as thinking, feeling fellow humans. More personal objectives were enhancing their therapeutic skills and promoting their professional credentials with peers, superiors, and clients. Interest was also expressed in increasing cooperation among agencies and agents dealing with sex crimes.

These goals appear to have been largely satisfied. In addition, guests seemed surprised by the frequency and intensity of personal interaction between themselves and many - though not all - of the offenders. Such personalization seemed most evident in the individual therapy meetings, many of which were scheduled at the offenders' requests.

Visitors generally indicated that while their notions about offenders were accurate in some areas, other preconceptions proved to be erroneous. Identifying offenders as past victims seemed to support the visitors in promoting prevention, early intervention, and victim counseling, especially in cases of incest and child molesting. The strength and pervasiveness of the cycle of victim becoming victimizer was unexpected. The popular myth ascribing extensive sexual experiences and considerable libido to sexual offenders was thoroughly debunked by the group members. Instead, visitors reported viewing offenders increasingly as relatively inexperienced persons whose history held few rewarding social or sexual contacts with either men or women. Visitors subsequently encouraged the treatment team to develop a more comprehensive program for training offenders in human anatomy and sexuality.

Finally, the guests who had themselves veen victims of sexual assault reported their own therapeutic gains from the project. Personalizing offenders, disclosing their own victim status in a public forum, and interacting in a largely positive manner with rapists and child molesters seemed to help these guests to reestablish a sense of personal power and control which they had felt to be diminished following their assault experiences.

Recommendations

A number of modifications might have improved the guest participant program. Some prior discussion with the target groups seems to be indicated, but lengthy preparation appears unwarranted. Offenders who were advised of the project the day of the first visit suggested that previous discussions might have reduced anxiety. Nevertheless, considerable anxiety was displayed among the two groups that had been notified of and had discussed the visit for 6 weeks prior to the guests arriving. This would suggest that a middle course might be helpful in promoting effective, early group interaction. In addition, of course, some degree of anxiety tends to be helpful in promoting group participation.

The group sessions always seemed rushed, regardless of the schedule used. This may indicate the interest of offenders, therapists, and visitors in the discussions, but also suggest that 50-minute sessions were too brief. Group sessions lasting 90 minutes seemed about right to all concerned. In addition, spacing visits over time might be helpful. In referring to one group series, an offender remarked that "so much happened in a 1-week period it was hard to grasp everything that was experienced." Initial sessions were often devoted to developing mutual trust and sharing, severely diminshing time available for group exchanges. This suggests that the number of sessions should be increased.

Some offenders seemed to gain more from individual sessions than from group participation. In these cases, more than one individual session with a visitor and therapist might be useful. Thirty-minute contact often seemed too brief, while sessions lasting 50 minutes seemed more satisfactory.

Finally, some form of follow-up seems advisable. Many group members requested one or more future visits by the same guests. Some offenders expressed interest in telling the guests about recent interpersonal or intrapsychic events, others about ways in which the offender felt changed by the experience, and several stated that they wanted to indicate their feelings of indebtedness to the guests. In addition, the superiority of distributed learning to massed learning has been clearly demonstrated [9], and follow-up meetings could serve as boosters to promote incorporation of new, tentatively held beliefs and skills.

Overall, evaluation indicates that the project was beneficial to offenders, therapists, and guests. One would thus expect to find similar programs as standard treatment tools in sex offenders rehabilitation programs. In truth, however, only a few MDSO programs presently employ similar projects. A survey of 44 rehabilitation programs for incarcerated rapists indicated just four which presently employ rape victims or those who work with survivors in treatment roles.[1] A few indicated that such projects had been discontinued or had been considered but rejected. In some cases, concern was expressed for the mental health of victims and that of victim workers, who conceivably closely identify with their clients. Therapy meetings were seen as too emotion-provoking for most victimized women. Some treatment personnel indicated fears that such encounters could allow victims to be mentally abused by rapists, with ill effects for both victims and offenders. Others advised that interactive programs were extraneous. Victims were said to be sufficiently personalized through discussion focused on victims' plights, including women on treatment teams, and encouraging offenders to identify with women on the basis of their own victimization and resulting pain, guilt, shame, and feelings of dehumanization.

Nevertheless, victim workers seem to present a pool of potential offender therapists who are alert, skilled, and mentally healthy enough to function effectively in MDSO treatment programs. In addition, the approach described in this paper to treating sex offenders seems particularly cost effective. As a result, a summary recommendation of this paper must be that those who treat offenders and those who assist victims should attempt enhanced communication in order to achieve their congruent goal: reducing sexual attack on innocent persons.

---

[1] Connecticut Correctional Institution, Somers; Fulton State Hospital, Fulton, Missouri; North Dakota State Penitentiary, Bismark; and Minnesota Correctional Institution, Lino Lakes

Acknowlegment. The authors wish to express their appreciation to colleagues without whom this project would not have been possible: Robert Alcorn, Donna Campbell, Mary Dykes, Faye Edwards, Linda Presnell, Charles Schaefer, Connie Smith, and Lois Stevens.

References

1. Groth AN (1979) Men who rape: the psychology of the offender. Plenum, New York
2. Groth AN (1982) Treatment of the sexual offender in a correctional institution. Unpublished manuscript, Connecticut Correctional Institution, Somers, Connecticut
3. Groth AN, Burgess AW, Holstrom LL (1977) Rape: power, anger and sexuality. Am J Psychiatry 134: 1239–1243
4. Seghorn TK (1981) The decision tree: factors in the clinical subtyping of dangerous persons. Paper presented at the annual convention of the American Psychological Association, Los Angeles, August 1981
5. Abel GG, Blanchard EB, Becker JV (1976) An integrated treatment program for rapists. In: Rada R (ed) Clinical aspects of the rapist. Grune and Stratton, New York
6. Dowling AK, Annis LV (1982) A residential treatment program for male sex offenders. Paper presented at the international conference on psychology and law, Swansea, July 1982
7. Witt P (1981) Treating the repetitive offender. Treatment for Sexual Aggressives News 4 (3): 1–2
8. American Psychiatric Association (1980) Diagnostic and statistical manual of mental disorders, 3rd edn. APA, Washington
9. Kimble GA (1961) Hilgard and Marquis conditioning and learning. Appleton-Century-Crofts, New York

V. Psychiatry and Ethics

Ethics and Psychiatry

N. Laor

Common Sense Psychiatry and Common Sense Ethics in Conflict

Prevailing ethical principles forbid enforced medical treatment in the recognition of the individual's choice as to whether to get cured or to remain ill. Prevailing medical practice, especially in psychiatry, includes at times the imposition of medical treatment. Can prevailing medical practice be reconciled with prevailing ethical principles? These are burning ethical questions and they are on the agenda today. They have been vociferously pressed, and rightly so, especially since recently the view of mental illness as, among other things, a deliberately chosen way of life, is gaining legitimization these days. Indeed, the argument seems at times convincing. Although the principles upon which an individual sets up his life-style may seem to us bizarre, this does not permit us to deem him defective in autonomy. He should still be considered fully and unconditionally autonomous. Moreover, it has been claimed, perhaps with some justice, that we should not even deem him mentally ill. His bizarre life-style is no license for us to impose on him any sort of physical or mental treatment. Hence, by the same token, when he transgresses the law, he should not be stripped of his autonomy – he should then bear the full responsibility for his actions. All this, of course, is part-and-parcel of individualistic ethics which, as is well known, constitutes the view of the individual as autonomous and hence as the agent exclusively responsible for his actions, for better or for worse. And this view of the bizarre life-style is endorsed by all individualists. This view, to repeat, is still largely controversial; it was introduced into the filed of psychiatry about twenty years ago by Thomas S. Szasz [1] and is a particular challenge to the individualist.

Let me here pause and explain why the challenge is so difficult, yet so unavoidable. The claim that the mentally ill are fully autonomous seems to have consequences which clash with our common sense on plain psychology. The opposite view, the claim that the autonomy of the mentally ill is defective if at all existent, has consequences which clash with our common sense on plainly moral matters.

This conflict between commonly accepted practice and commonly accepted ethics is unbearable. Indeed, quite possibly the changes of ethical standards in the U.S., which have been introduced over the past twenty years in standards for involuntary psychiatric treatment of mental patients, owe much to Dr. Szasz's views on the autonomy of the mentally ill. Yet at Szaszian arguments call for much more: they call for a total revolution in our world view as well as in our practice.

The inability to accept the Szaszian arguments concerning the autonomy of the mentally ill coupled with the inability to ignore their moral and clinical implications (and their being so wide in their scope) suggest a deep-seated fault in the current conceptual framework. This suggests that philosophical research is in order into the commonsense assumption that enforced medical treatment – physical as well as mental - may be permitted at times. We shall question, then, the reconcilability of enforced treatment with the individualistic principle, of common sense psychiatry and common sense ethics, with the accent on the possible invalidity of the latter.

Classical Individualism and the Two Conflicting Views

The chief question before us is the following: Is every individual necessarily fully autonomous, or may he be defective in autonomy at times? An examination of the moral philosphies of the important moral philosophers of the Enlightenment, which still serve the foundations of western culture to the present day, reveals that all of them hold similar views on the matter. Their views reflect the paradoxical ethical common sense concerning the autonomy of the individual: on the one hand, they hold a view - which will be termed here the extreme view - that the individual is always autonomous, even when he is constrained by his circumstances. For, indeed, he always is, by actual chains, or by constraints such as budgetary limitations, physical or mental illness, etc., so that it is only the individual's field of action that is constricted thereby. On the other hand, according to the view of the same moral philosophers (which will here be termed the moderate view) the individual is always defective in autonomy, even when he behaves most rationally. This is because his rationality is always partial at best, due to intellectually and/or emotionally limited capacity, let alone confusions, obsessions, or worse than that, mental illnesses of all sorts. To deny that both views are common sense is difficult; to accept both is impossible. The *extreme* view takes autonomy as the same for every individual, whereas the *moderate* view takes the individual as always defective in autonomy, since he is always defective in rationality.

The moral philosophers of the Enlightenment take human autonomy to be the supreme, if not the only, human value. However, we see here that, in dealing with questions concerning human autonomy, to the extent that both their extreme and moderate views are commonsense, their ethics rarely rise above the level of prevailing common sense. Yet, to the extent that both their extreme and their moderate views are anticommonsense, they fail to account for their rejection of common sense. The paradoxical nature of their views, their adherence at one and the same time to both conflicting views, the extreme and the moderate, makes it impossible to pursue the avenue they open.

We are left then to our own paradoxical common sense. Has Szasz solved the paradox? No. Szasz's views seem conflict-free and coherent; this he achieves by merely adhering to one pole of the paradox and discarding the other. How, then, does Szasz know which pole to choose? Both may be justified by the same ethics. What is needed here, then, and as a preliminary step, is a commonsense account for both the prevailing paradoxical moral intuitions and for any rejection of either of the two.

It seems, then, that we have here reached an impasse. The impasse may be broken through only when new possible solutions are found; in our case, new solutions for the paradox. Such a possible solution exists.

It was offered as a critique, improvement, and modification of individualistic ethics two centuries ago by Solomon Maimon, the individualistic philosopher, who was both highly praised and highly maligned by Kant, who viewed Maimon both as the best student of his writings and as a mere parasite [2].

Unity of Clinical and Ethical Common Sense

The philosophy of Immanuel Kant serves as the starting line for Maimon's philosophical investigations. It sets Man as a free agent, rational and thus responsible, a citizen of the Kingdom of Freedom, above the kingdom of the physical and of the animal [3]. Now, if Man's humanity is his rationality which comes together with his freedom and with his duty, then depriving him of his duty may also be depriving him of his very humanity! This exemption, says Szasz, happens in practice all too often even today, when the person declared mentally ill is freed of this responsibility yet also is deprived of his human rights [4]. Kant regards the madman as still human and also expels him from the common pale of humanity. Thus, Kantian ethics, too, was entrenched in prevailing common sense. The madman was viewed as close to both his mentally healthy fellow human beings and to the merely animal or physical.

When the *a priori* notion of the absolute freedom of the human spirit is rejected, while the Kantian framework is still maintained, then obviously human beings and animals end up being on a par: predetermined machines. Traditionally, commonsensical psychiatry advocates this view and clashes with common sense on plain ethics. Antipsychiatry, or commonsensically coherent ethics, still holds to the opposite, namely, that all human beings are machines yet are self-determined, and thus autonomous. Hence, antipsychiatry clashes with common sense on plain psychology. Both views are impossible, of course. As we have seen, they are both entrenched in a paradoxical view of Man as well as in a paradoxical ethical framework, and both are met by Maimon's commonsensical critique and modification and improvement.

Maimon rejects Kant's transcendental metaphysics and approaches the difficult problem of free will quite empirically; evading the metaphysical difficulties, he observes the obvious fact that no one is completely free. Yet we all have some degree of control. Hence, he says, "the concept of *absolute freedom cannot be presented in the empirical world* . . . We must then regard absolute freedom only as an idea to which we can approach closer and closer by the more perfect use of theoretical reason but never to reach" [5]. Here we find an idea of degrees of freedom, not found elsewhere in the literature of the Enlightenment. What is, then, the meaning of autonomy in a framework where freedom does not show up except in this or that degree? Naturally, we take autonomy to be the capacity to perceive one's control and to act appropriately in the world, i. e., to exercise the controls one has, and to do so with some measure of awareness. This is common sense. And, indeed, this is Maimon's view of autonomy as well as of mental health. The novelty of it is its introduction of degrees of autonomy from the very start.

Maimon recommends that a certain minimal level of autonomy be required of a person we recognize as sane. This may be required of every individual in society, though we may demand different levels at different occasions. The required level should be determined, according to him, by socially accepted standards of autonomy. That is to say, one would be regarded as empirically sufficiently autonomous if every other rational being in one's society would, if in one's place, desire decisions or actions similar to one's own. This is Maimon's proposed improvement on Kant's ethical theory. Maimon replaces the categorical imperative "do not do unto others what you would not like done unto you" (Babylonian Talmud Shabbat 31a) by "judge not your fellow until you come into his position" (Ethics of the Fathers, 2:4). Both dicta are, as is well known, ascribed to Hillel in the oldest Talmudic text extant.

That is to say, whereas the imperative quoted first is categorical, i.e., independent of any circumstances, Maimon proposed an imperative which prescribes the employment of rational empathy in the domain of ethical inter-personal relations. Duty, he says, prescribes that we first take into consideration the constraints on the individual and only then proffer a judgement. Hence, still according to Maimon, but only by implication, both psychiatry and the legal system should serve a regulative function in society; both should be based on ethical considerations of specific conditions and in the light of changing standards. This may make us wonder as to the very possibility of Maimon's view to relieve the problem at hand. For even the demarcation between the violator of the law on moral grounds and on other grounds, between the criminal and the madman, in a given society, is not clear-cut within Maimon's view. For this demarcation is grounded in variable interpersonally determined standards of responsibility and of the diagnosis of various levels of autonomy. This criticism, however, may be adequately met. As different standards may apply to different societies and they also may and should change (for the better, let us hope), it would be undesirable to propose fixed standards.

To conclude, Maimon views mental health an ideal, the idea of absolute human freedom. It is a mere regulative idea toward which and by the guidance of which, the individual is striving for. Apparently the ideal is the increase of one's degree of autonomy. Hence, all human beings are to some degree defective in autonomy, that is, they are mentally ill to certain differing degrees. According to Maimon there are all sorts of mental illnesses and he carefully depicts and differentiates between them. However, I will not elaborate on this as it takes us beyond the scope of the present essay. Here suffice it to say that Maimon views all mental illness as deliberately chosen and self-imposed hindrances of freedom. Hence the individual can always improve on his given degree of autonomy, and psychotherapy, then, can be effected only on a voluntary basis, never by coercion. Coercion in psychotherapy is both morally and clinically wrong practice, thus justifiable only in times when the mentally ill are in immediate danger to themselves or to others, or else neglect is imposed.

Avoiding Commonly Permitted Enforced Treatment and Universal Total Szasz-Style Neglect

Szasz and Maimon have much in common. Yet Maimon would never accept the finality of Szasz's argument on the autonomy and responsibility of the mentally ill; especially when for their own good, so Szasz says, they are required to pay the price – even when the price is their own death – for Szasz's own arguments. Such a requirement is incompatible with Maimon's moral imperative which commends rational empathy in interpersonal relations. Such a requirement, I think, commends sheer neglect. It is also explicitly paternalistic, and paternalism it what individualism opposes most. Is there a place, then, between paternalism and neglect? Is there a place, then, between commonsense psychiatry and commonsense ethics?

What is needed here are institutional strategies for research in the domain of human autonomy and responsibility. Maimon offers the ethico-clinical framework for such research which may lay the ground for the social implementation of new standards of responsibility; and we may try different modes reflecting different standards of responsibility. In fact, even Szasz's actual recommendation concerning the status of autonomy and responsibility of the mentally ill can serve as one of the strategies to be empirically tested against other alternatives in various domains. This, as any other social research, calls for checked studies so as to avoid both the commonly permitted enforced treatment as well as the universal total Szasz-style neglect.

References

1. Szasz TS (1974) The myth of mental illness, rev. ed. Harper and Row, New York
2. Kant I (1967) Philosophical correspondence. University of Chicago Press, Chicago, pp 155, 212
3. Kant I (1964) Groundwork of the metaphysics of morals. Harper and Row, New York
4. Szasz TS (1963) Law, liberty and psychiatry. Macmillan, New York
5. Maimon S (1797) Kritische Untersuchungen über den menschlichen Geist. Gerhard Fleischer dem Jüngern, Leipzig, p 289. English translation in: Bergman S (1967) The philosophy of Solomon Maimon. The Magnus Press, The Hebrew University, Jerusalem, p 207

Ethics and Depth Psychology

G. Dreifuss

Ethical behavior is commonly thought to be simply obeying the law and avoiding conflict with the penal code. The child is educated by parents, teachers, and youth leaders to a behavior that is regarded as ethical by the society he lives in. To educate means, in this connection, to develop and strengthen the ego, the center of consciousness, and the willpower of the individual to such an extent that it will not deviate from the common law, the "cultural canon" [2]. This means that behavior accepted by a certain culture at a certain time in history will change in the course of time (for instance, polygamy was permitted in biblical times but is forbidden today).

Ethics belongs to theology, philosophy, sociology, and psychology. Usually it is considered to belong to the psychology of consciousness, i. e., to a rational will that adheres to cultural morals. Depth psychology has brought a new dimension to ethics by stressing the influence of the unconscious on consciousness. Deviations from the ethical values of the society one lives in are looked upon not only as a conflict with the penal code, but also as a conflict between the conscious and the unconscious. The question then arises whether these deviations are pathological.

The adaptation to the ethics of the collective is usually a goal for psychotherapy, but at times there can be such an obstinate conflict between conscious and unconscious tendencies that long-term analysis is indicated, which may lead to a new ethical attitude first of the individual and later of the collective.

A conflict is often unconscious, expressing itself in different symptoms, such as phobias, depressions, and psychosomatic disturbances. When the conflict becomes conscious the symptoms can recede, but are replaced by intense suffering. "Since real moral problems all begin where the penal code leaves off, their solution can seldom or never depend on precedent, much less on precepts or commandments. The real moral problems spring from conflicts of duty" [1]. In all these conflicts there is no certainty about what is good or bad, what is right or wrong, positive or negative. This brings us to the relativity of good and evil.

Let me illustrate this with an example. A mother spoils her child but is convinced that she is a good mother sacrificing herself for the benefit of the child. She is unaware of her overprotectiveness and its damaging effect on the child. In psychotherapy she could be made aware that the unconscious motivation for her overprotecting the child is a deep-seated fear of losing the love of the child and thus remaining alone. The exaggerated love is in fact a power drive, a negative side, a shadow, a need to chain the child to herself. In therapy she has to work on her fears, facing the fact that she has to find a meaning in life in herself, not only through the child. In a process of inner development, she has to deal with the opposites in her psyche (love and power in this case), and thus enlarge her consciousness.

Of course, there are cases such as premeditated murder in which the penal code and depth psychology are in accordance. We, as healthy individuals, "know," by an inner voice, what is right and wrong. Also with regard to the Holocaust, there is no doubt about its evil. But with regard to wars, for instance, the good and the "right" of one side are set against the good and the "right" of the other side, and each side accuses the other of doing evil, of being wrong.

Psychologically, evil is easily projected and not seen as belonging to one's own psyche. To make the evil, the shadow, in oneself conscious and to find a way to live with it without being overpowered by it is an important task of the individual and the collective. However, in ordinary life situations, good and bad are experienced as an ethical problem of the individual.

Let me give you a clinical example. A young man, a scientist, the only son of a widowed mother who is a victim of the Holocaust, who lost all her family except this son, gets an invitation to a distinguished university in the United States. He cannot take his sickly mother with him. He is not capable of deciding what to do, gets into a state of anxiety, and seeks help. His ethical problem is clear: leaving his mother is against his innermost feeling of love, compassion, and duty, yet staying with his mother means renouncing his development and advancement as a scientist. Here two values stand one against the other: love and consideration for the mother as a human being, which is faithfulness to the Erosprinciple, or faithfulness to the scientific career, to the professional development, to the Logosprinciple. This is a real conflict of duties which my analysand could not resolve by a clear-cut decision.

Deciding or choosing between two possibilities means leaving out one possibility, giving one up for the other, sacrificing. A therapist or friend, looking at the conflict, may easily be seduced to take a stand for one or the other possible solutions of the conflict. A feeling type will tend to prefer the love and the compassion for the mother, whereas a thinking type may prefer the solution of the professional career. However, a therapist who takes the unconscious seriously must try to understand the psychological significance and the meaning of the conflict. Behind the moral conflict stands a bigger, encompassing entity, an archetype, which Jung called the self. This self wants to embody, to realize itself, to become conscious in our patient. The self forces him to come to a new attitude and to accept a psychoid entity representing the opposites in his own psyche.

The conflict cannot be solved by the ego because it transcends the ego. Therefore, the patient has to understand the inner meaning of his conflict by working on and understanding his dreams, which are the language of the unconscious.

In these conflicts of duty it often happens that they find an unexpected solution "by fate," so to speak, if only the individual has enough patience to to see the conflict through. This happened in the case of the scientist mentioned above. After a year his conflict of duties resolved itself by the unexpected sudden death of his mother. This resolution of the conflict was experienced as numinous, since it was not the result of a conscious decision. Although saddened by his mother's death, he nevertheless felt relieved that he had endured the conflict and remained close to his mother. With the moral conflict resolved, he was now free to follow his professional career.

In summary, from a psychological point of view ethical behavior means accepting the fact that the ego is not the sole master in our psyche. Other components of our personality, usually unconscious, have to be taken into account and experienced. Depth psychology has taken moral problems from philosophical heights into everyday life. The opposites, good and evil, ego and shadow, have to be acknowledged as existing in one's own psyche; projections have to be taken back and integrated. Thus a new attitude, a deeper ethical responsibility of the individual to himself and to others, may become the leading force in his life.

References

1. Jung CG (1959) Aion. In: Collected works, vol 9. Pantheon, New York
2. Neumann E (1969) Depth psychology and a new ethic. Hodder and Stoughton, London

The Right to Suicide - Ethical, Legal, and Psychiatric Approaches

F. Weil

Suicide is a subject which causes grave concern to each and every one of us. It can be regarded from two opposite points of view. On the one hand, suicide is a tragedy which arises from extreme feelings of distress and comprises an act of irrevocable destruction. On the other hand, this voluntary act is frequently envisaged as a liberation from an unbearable situation - and the knowledge of the possibility of committing suicide may in itself reduce anguish and feelings of helplessness in a given situation. Suicide is sometimes the result of an acutely pathological mental state - but under certain cricumstances the contemplation of one's own suicide is regarded as a part of the normal thought process in the distressed individual.

In the fields of ethics, law, and medicine the subject of suicide has long been pondered, with heated discussions regarding both the fear of suicide resulting from pathological mental states of individuals and reservations as regards its prevention by mandatory hospitalization.

The ethical viewpoint may differ from one culture to another or within a given culture. Suicide may be regarded as totally unacceptable. This attitude is based on the belief that life is the supreme gift of God, which can only be withdrawn by him. Therefore, any person who takes his own life commits a crime not only against himself but against humanity as a whole. If, however, the quality of life rather than its duration is valued, then suicide is accepted as the individual's final rejection of a life whose worth is totally diminished - as in the case of an incurable disease, an intolerable permanent disability, or prolonged unbearable suffering. In certain Eastern cultures, suicide enhances the acquisition of rights in the world to come, or protects traditional group honor. In our society, certain cases of suicide are recognized as cases of self-punishment - especially among leaders who have failed in their tasks. At the other end of the spectrum, suicide can be regarded as an act of bravery or heroism, where self-sacrifice is for the sake of an ideology, as in the books of Maccabees and at Masada, or as a protest against an oppressive regime, or to ensure silence in the face of torture.

As a matter of principle, the ethical approach requires respect for individual human liberty on the one hand and the right of the endangered person to be assisted on the other. The problem is particularly subtle when it is suspected that insanity is at the root of the intention to commit suicide. In such a case the safest means of assistance necessarily involves the deprivation of freedom, at least temporarily.

The judical approach regards suicide as a criminal act. The law relating to the mentally ill does not distinguish between danger to oneself and danger to someone else. In the case of attempted suicide, two conflicting elements - the roles of perpetrator and of victim - exist simultaneously in the same individual. Hence the legislator has to consider the legal responsibility of the "murderer " and, at the same time, the protection of the "victim."

In practice, the Halakic code excommunicates a person who has committed suicide. The criminal code, on the other hand, no longer prosecutes those who have attempted suicide, except in a few countries such as Britain and Japan and in New York State. However, the individual who aids someone else in committing suicide or who practices euthanasia is prosecuted. It may appear paradoxical that an individual can decide his own death only to the extent of his ability to execute it by himself, while if handicapped, and thus unable to carry out the decision by himself, he is not legally allowed to obtain assistance from a third party. The rationale usually put forward to justify this is the need to prevent all possible errors or abuses.

The Mental Health Act, which aims at preventing suicide, can only intervene through "commitment," which infringes upon the individual's civil right to settle his own fate. Faced with a grave decision, the legislator has had to formulate the conditions under which medical intervention is mandatory. The final criterion retained is the diagnosis of mental illness. The law also determines joint control of medical and legal components affecting decisions on commitment.

The medical approach regards suicide as a symptom in every case. For a long period every case of suicide was regarded as pathological. Esquirol (1838) thought that "man acts against his own existence only in a state of delirium – the person who commits suicide is alien." Achille Delmas, as late as 1932, maintained the same approach. Durkheim (1897) and Halbwachs (1930) regarded the pathology as the result of conflicts between the individual and his environment. It is society which grants or withdraws the desire to live. In their opinion the individual achieves an objective cognition of his place in society. Schneider saw a link between these two concepts: Psychopathology renders the individual more susceptible to social pressures or frustrations, and reciprocally sociological problems may weaken the individual's objective assessment of a given situation. The psychoanalytic school evokes the "universal" existence of the death instinct and primary sadomasochism, from which may evolve the desire for one's own death or the death of someone else. This is in accordance with the judicial concern about the danger to oneself or to others. This physiological basis of the death wish also leads us to accept the concept that suicide may be a lucid act in an individual with no mental pathology.

In practice, in the face of an attempted suicide the psychiatrist must try to determine whether or not the act arises from a pathological state. He bases his assessment on symptoms, such as the relation of the patient to death, his capacity to reason and judge, his reality testing, and his degree of self-control. The doctor must also determine a double prognosis, both as to the danger of immediate death and as to the danger of further attempts. Psychiatrists have tried to differentiate between serious intentions of suicide and manipulative behavior. In fact, it appears that even in the latter case the individual expresses distress, and the "cry for help" must be taken to seriously.

The therapeutic goals which must guide the psychiatrist's attitude are manifold:

- Treatment of the pathological component, if it exists
- Close surveillance to prevent the suicide attempt and to prevent its recurrence in the immediate future
- Prevention of repetition of the attempt in the long run. Here, the psychiatrist tries to reinforce the will to live through reinvestment of constructive goals with the

development of positive relations between the patient and the therapist. The psychiatrist must decide whether he is to intervene – and if so, how.

With a cooperative patient willing to accept assistance, the decision is relatively simple. But when the patient refuses treatment and continues to strive for his own death, the psychiatrist differentiates between a lucid and a pathological subject. The psychiatrist has no right to intervene in the decision of a lucid person. The delicate problem of euthanasia is raised when a lucid terminal patient asks for the doctor's help to precipitate his death. Some doctors oppose this vehemently, considering that the doctor's task is to cure or to prolong life; other doctors consider that life and death constitute an indivisible entity and that the doctor who strives to improve the conditions of life must not shy away from striving to improve the conditions of death. Others still accept the principle but are opposed to its application because of the fear of abuse.

In the case of a mentally ill person the doctor is obliged to intervene, but the choice of approach is sometimes difficult. Commitment maximally reduces the immediate risk, but causes additional stress to the individual and turns the doctor-patient relationship to one of conflict. On the other hand, taking a calculated risk preserves the future relationship but lays grave responsibilities upon the doctor in the immediate present with respect to the patient, his family, and his own medicolegal status.

At first sight, there seems to be a consensus of the ethical, judicial, and medical approaches to the practical attitude in the handling of suicide attempts, and this is exemplified in the consideration of the two clear options open to one. When the case is one of a mentally ill patient, there is a moral obligation to help somebody in danger, there is a need to treat the patient, and the law imposes treatment even against the patient's will. The lucid individual, if seen as a separate entity, retains the right to dispose of his life; he cannot legally be committed and the doctor must honor his refusal of treatment. There is an exception to this when the individual is seen as belonging to his community or to God, in which case the right to commit suicide does not exist.

These ethical, judicial, and medical approaches do not overlap entirely, however. A first example is the criterion of mental pathology. Jurists retain the use of the term "mental illness", while leaving with the doctors the decision about the existence of mental pathology. In fact, this concept is difficult to define, since the opposing concept of mental health has such diffused borders. Jurists use the term "mental illness," which implies a diagnosis, while psychiatrists regards suicide as pathological mainly on the basis of concomitant symptoms found at the time of the examination. These include disturbed powers of reasoning and judgment or loss of self-control. For instance, after bereavement or disappointment in love the patient might convince himself that his life is empty or wasted, and hopeless, and would want then to commit suicide. His reality analysis is disturbed as a transient reaction to his loss: in our opinion he needs help but he is not mentally ill.

From the practical point of view, the psychiatrist must make his decision after an examination whose precision is limited by an atmosphere of urgency, a lack of cooperation on the part of the individual being examined, and sometimes an impairment of his consciousness due to the means used to attempt suicide. Consequently, there are cases in which the psychiatrist cannot immediately reach a conclusion. The law dictates on the one hand the obligation to hospitalize, even against his will, every dangerous mental patient, and on the other hand demands that the refusal of the non-mentally-ill individual be honored, and hence leaves no room for hesitation.

Another bone of contention is the effect of commitment as a therapeutic tool. All agree that commitment is the safest immediate preventive measure available. Jurists and psychiatrists also agree as to the gravity of the deprivation of the right to dispose of oneself, the distressing condition of closed wards, the deep damage to one's self-image, and the exposure to further rejection by society. However, the jurists stress the responsibility of the psychiatrist to the risk of error or abuse, but in the final analysis demand that, in the absence of doubt as to the diagnosis, commitment be mandatory.

The psychiatrist, who also appreciates the negative consequences, sees that commitment damages the doctor-patient relationship at a time when the patient is particularly suffering from emotional isolation. Because of this, the psychiatrist would at times like to preserve the right to accept the calculated risk of allowing the patient to stay free, without involuntary hospitalization, with in the framework of a positive relationship and more intensive therapy. This is demonstrated in two cases in which it would be preferable to avoid, as far as possible, imposed hospitalization. The first is that of the borderline personality who, through self-mutilation, invites commitment. The actualization of commitment would only reinforce his feeling that, as always, the outside world oppresses him, at a time when he is in need of help. The second example is that of the psychotic in a state of remission who, on the basis of previous admissions, has difficulty in being rehabilitated in society and consequently attempts suicide. Here also, commitment will increase the risk of recurrence. Many doctors believe that one cannot prevent suicide merely by attempting to prevent its execution, but rather by enhancing the will to live and aiding in the rehabilitation of the patient.

In conclusion, the decision in regard to the individual who is in danger of commiting suicide bears grave responsibilities and also demands delicate judgment. It is highly desirable that this decision be made jointly by doctors and lawyers on the basis of their respective professional ethics. Coordination and cooperation between these two branches is the best guarantee of serving the patient's interests. However, if differences between the two are debated in court or presented as scandals in the news media, the danger exists that the psychiatrist may relate in a narrow obsessional way to the rigid formulations of the law, to the detriment of the proper consideration of the nuances of each patient's state. This in turn will prejudice the fine balance when a decision is made on the patient's right to dispose of himself, including the right to commit suicide, or on the obligation to receive treatment even against one's will.

References

1. The Mental Health Act in Israel
2. Cahiers de santé publique, no. 58: Le suicide et les tentatives de suicide. World Health Organization, Geneva, 1975
3. Deshaies G (1947) Psychologie du suicide. Presses Universitaires de France, Paris
4. Durkheim (1897) Le suicide. Études de sociologie. Alan, Paris
5. Eggens JB (1959) Les doctrines scientifiques sur le suicide problèmes. pp 17-21
6. Stengel E (1964) Suicide and attempted suicide. Penguin, Harmondsworth

Ethical Issues in Forensic Psychiatry

J. R. Rappeport

I first became involved in looking at the ethical issues in forensic psychiatry for the American Academy of Psychiatry and the Law when the Academy decided to see about developing ethical standards or guidelines. This chapter represents my experience in working to develop such guidelines, which then developed into a chapter in the book on psychiatric ethics by Block and Chodoff [1]. Since then, I have had time to reflect further on ethical problems of forensic psychiatry.

The basic issue which I believe is at the core of the problem faced by the psychiatrist in the forensic arena is one related to the question: Whom are we serving? We may wish to serve the patient, but we must also serve the court and society. During this Congress, we have heard about double-agentry or serving two masters, and we have also heard *primum non nocere,* first do no harm. The original use of that phrase did not apply to the subtle issues we speak of here but dealt more with the problem of surgical interventions such as trephining, which were dangerous to the patient and frequently fatal. The choices were ones that were likely to do real harm. When we use this phrase to speak of the possible harm caused by forensic psychiatry, the dangers are generally not nearly as severe, although damage can be done. Nevertheless, if we are to be honest, and in that sense ethical we cannot be the patient's agent or function in a patient-centered role unless we make this clear to the court. Our professional integrity requires that we reveal our biases to the court.

Judge David Bazelon has accused us of not always revealing these biases [2]. When we do not make it clear that we are biased, we are then being unethical. It is our duty to tell the court that we are patient-oriented and that our opinion is so biased, rather than let the court believe that what we are presenting is a "scientific" and thus unbiased opinion.

Now let us look at some areas of forensic psychiatry that may exemplify some of the double-agentry and other ethical problems in a more pragmatic sense. We might think of civil and criminal issues and the issue of testifying. Taking thestifying first, we must decide our position on the witness stand. Are we to be an advocate or adversary when testifying? In my opinion and that of Halleck, absolutely not [3]. We are under oath to tell the absolute truth, which also means that we must reveal our bias as well. I believe we should be an advocate when assisting the attorney in his preparation. We should help him prepare his direct examination of us, pointing out the strong points and weak points of our testimony, and the strong and weak points in the report of the opposing expert. However, when we are on the witness stand, it is the attorney's job to bring out what he wants and to deal with what he may not like in his own way. That is his job; ours is to present our findings as clearly and honestly as the legal system will allow.

Another part of this testifying issue is related to the rendering of opinions without examination. As you know, this arises frequently in will contests when the issue of testamentary capacity arises. We cannot examine the dead man. We can obtain records, interview people, and do a psychological autopsy. We might then render an opinion about the deceased's testamentary capacity. However, I believe that it is our responsibility to be certain that the court understands that our opinion is not based on an actual examination of the deceased. If asked whether an examination might have made a difference, I do not see how we can answer otherwise. The clinical examination is the basis of medicine. Even the pathologist has his tissue to examine.

A similar situation arises with the use of the hypothetical question as used in many jurisdictions. Here the attorney will present, hypothetically, a series of facts about the individual in question and ask for an opinion. Often such questions do not actually contain the full information necessary to enable a professional opinion to be reached. This is a serious defect with hypothetical questions and arises unless the expert helps to prepare or actually prepares the question. Is it ethical to answer an incomplete or inaccurate hypothetical question? A recent case, *Barefoot* v. *Estelle,* is shortly to be heard by the Supreme Court [4]. The lower court found no problem with this type of question, even when used in the death penalty phase of sentencing. In Texas, after a guilty finding in certain cases, the jury hears about mitigating or aggravating circumstances as related to treatability, danger to society in the future, etc. Psychiatrists testify to these issues. The American Psychiatric Association (APA) will file an amicus brief in this case, stating that the death penalty is so serious that psychiatric testimony should only be based on a thorough clinical examination and not on a hypothetical question. If the defendant cannot be examined, then there should be no psychiatric testimony in such a serious situation. In any situation where the individual could possibly be examined, he should be, Not to examine, where this is possible, and then to render an opinion is, I believe, unethical.

Another issue is that which arises around examination prior to arraignment and prior to an attorney's appointment. While the APA Code of Ethics says that no such examination should be carried out, their own Ethics Committee apparently found nothing wrong when a psychiatrist interviewed a defendant at 1.30 a.m. after he had been interrogated for 6 hours by the police. The interview was recorded, furnishing the prosecutor with additional data. Even though the patient had received his so-called Miranda warnings, I believe that such behavior on the psychiatrist's part may be unethical. The defendant had not consulted with his attorney. This, however, is a delicate point. If you wait too long, a psychotic individual could recover and be amnesic for his psychotic behavior and thus lose the advantage of an insanity plea. On the other hand, his attorney could coach him about insanity and possibly fool the examiner. I am less concerned about the latter, since I believe few people successfully malinger. In fact, if there is error, I believe it is in the direction of our belief that someone is malingering when he is not. Regardless of which way we look at the prearraignment (no attorney contact) examination, it is fraught with problems. The greatest unethical issue in such situations is still that of our being "used" by the prosecutor while the defendant does not truly understand our role.

Although I have only briefly covered a few examples of ethical problems, it should be clear that the major issue confronting the forensic psychiatrist is whom does he serve – the patient, the lawyer, or the court – and how can he most effectively function and still maintain his intergrity while not taking advantage of his role?

References

1. Rappeport JR (1981) Ethics and forensic psychiatry in psychiatric ethics. Block S, Chodoff P (eds) Oxford University Press, London, pp 225–276
2. Bazelon D (1978) The role of the psychiatrist in the criminal justice system. American Academy of Psychiatry and the Law Bulletin 6: 139–146
3. Halleck S (1980) Law in the practice of psychiatry: a handbook for clinicians. Plenum, New York
4. *Barefoot* v. *Estelle* 103 S. Ct. 3383 (1983)

Research in Human Structurology

I. Burbiel

Any research work or scientific investigation is inseparably linked with the persons who undertake it, with their conception of their science, with their particular interest in discovery and their particular notion of the nature of man. Any concept of human nature involves or presupposes elements of judgment or evaluation such that the findings reflect this view of the nature of man, whether explicitly or implicitly.

Hence scientific research on man and the question of its ethical implications form complementary parts, and have consequences on theory, on the conception of science, and on day-to-day research and its results. The reflection on and disputation of the ethical views we hold in human structurology are an integral part of our research work. This paper will therefore discuss some of these views and their consequences for science and research.

Günter Ammon's scientific concept of dynamic psychiatry or, in a wider sense, of human structurology, provides an explicitly formulated concept of the nature of man. It is based on a holistic concept of man [4, 7, 11, 19]. Man is conceived in all the dimensions of his being and behavior. They comprise his unconscious and conscious: his sound and creative and his pathological life-forbidding sides:. his biological, neurophysiological, mental, and social dimensions as a group member and societal being. They include all his abilities, his skills, and the entire scope of his activities. Man is conceived as being primarily constructive [2]. He is a free and thus responsible person, who lives with an innate interest in "struggling for his personal identity, experiencing himself in the face of, and through, others, expressing himself in groups, developing himself in contact and confrontation with other members in the group" [6], in terms of energy, through social energetic exchange within the group [6]. Man is conceived as a being who changes and matures in groups throughout his life. The schism between individual and group has thus been abolished; the inseparability of man and relationship has been postulated.

The concept of identity forms the heart and nub of the holistic concept of man in dynamic psychiatry [4, 5, 7, 8]. Man wants, and must have, identity - this is the evaluating dimension of the identity concept. The interconnection of identity and ethics is accounted for in Ammon's concept of human structurology in that it links the philosophical-ethical with the psychological aspect.

A holistic school of thought, focusing on man in all his dimensions of life, has changeability and his development potentials cannot but constitute a living organism undergoing continuous development, or its efforts will be misguided. Any person or any group we encounter, no matter whether in a diagnostic examination or in a therapeutic setting, can provide us with new insights requiring integration into our theoretical concept.

In the light of a conception so open toward the variety of human existence, dynamic psychiatric theory will never be a closed, rigid system, but will continue to develop in a process linking theory and practice [10]. In this process a new step in the development of theory is often initiated by so-called border situations, as is the case when the treatment of a patient gets blocked or when particular interpersonal events cannot yet be explained by the theoretical state of the art.

This, however, means that the researcher must be able and willing to leave rutted roads, move on to untrodden ground, and have the courage to admit new lines of thought. This goes to show that rigid closed circuit theories inhibit, if not obstruct, advanced scientific discovery either, as Feyerabend [18] explains, by simply eliminating facts that contradict the theory or by adapting these facts in terms of extra hypotheses that are in compliance with the theory. Such a procedure, of course, adjusts human reality to theory and serves to maintain traditional lines of thought and research.

An example of this is the doctrine of endogenous heritage held by traditional psychiatry, whose representatives have retreated to an ivory tower of closed circuit theory and thus reject contact patients with suffering pathologically. They simply desert them [14]. This applies to any school of scientific thought that resists new findings and is principally unwilling to question its concept of man when a problem continues to recur. This calls for us to focus our attention on all those who have it upon themselves to promote the development of theoretical research. Our school of dynamic psychiatry conceives of the researcher as an immediate participant, in conscious and unconscious terms, in the group dynamic field of the investigation setting. If man is conceived as being born into a group, and living and realizing himself in groups, then all the manifestations of his life are part of the framework of interpersonal relationships and also scientific results can only be explained by interpersonal relationship [16].

Any empirical insight is thus interpersonal insight, conveying, in fact, an interpersonal relationship between the researcher and the person being investigated. It implies that the aim, the method and result of the research effort, cannot be dissociated from the researcher's identity, and that he as a person must be open to full scientific discourse and face the personal responsibility for his activities. The practice of splitting the person off from the scientist, which has become so common this century, is thus eliminated.

This goes to show that the researcher's scientific achievement is inevitably linked with his achievements in developing his identity. The more profound his identity, the more humane is his research effort and the more humane he is himself. To quote Günter Ammon in another context: "Identity and humanity are inseparable" [8]: this applies to the researcher as well.

The development of human identity, including its group dynamic and social energetic history, present state, and future, is the focus of our dynamic psychiatric research.

> The ego and identity development precipitates in group-dependent ego structures, the most important of which are the central ego functions in the unconscious, linked by interdependent relations to the secondary ego functions representing the abilities and skills and to the ego functions of the primary ego, i.e., the biological and neurophysiological functions of man with the brain as the material representation of conscious and unconscious experiences of human life [8].

Our research work in human structurology focuses on the exploration of the unconscious with its holistic texture of central ego functions, since they are the ones that determine the sound or pathological development of the person. The unconscious determines the potentialities of human life, to what extent man can creatively satisfy his needs or build up rewarding activities, and how much Lebensraum he is able to claim for himself. In the therapeutic process, work focuses on the unconscious and the development of the creative potentials. The ego structure development in the central ego determines the degree of the patient's recovery from life-obstructing restraints and his progress toward his own identity [3, 5].

In the dynamic psychiatric hospital Menterschwaige in Munich, where we do our work, the entire therapeutic field is available for investigation into the diverse manifestations of the unconscious; this involves team and case conferences. The data are recorded and evaluated by means of videotape and tape, observation questionnaires, sociograms, protocols, etc. In addition, psychological, medical, and psychiatric methods of investigation are used. Ammon's ego structure test and the autokinetic light test have proved to be of particular importance in our work and for some time there have been our brain stream experiments.

Ammon's ego structure test has been developed on the basis of his ego structural model to serve the quantitative assessment of central ego functions [9, 13, 15]. The tests assessing the ego functions of aggression, anxiety, ego demarcation, and new also the function of narcissism [17] have been validated and statistically evaluated. In combination with other diagnostic methods, the tests render surprisingly good results on the development of the patient's identity and reflect the changes in the ego structure during the therapeutic process. The results are not compiled in additive terms, but evaluated to result in integrated personality profiles in accordance with the ego structure and group concept. The results are returned to the therapeutic team to direct and help them check their work and improve effectiveness. Of course, they also help the patient to face the current state of his development. They also serve the therapeutic process, act as an means of efficiency evaluation, and contribute to the further development our of concepts. They have been published in the second volume of the *Handbook of Dynamic Psychiatry*, edited by Günter Ammon [9].

The ego structure test has confirmed the interdependency of the ego functions of anxiety, aggression, ego demarcation, and narcissism as laid down in theory, and also the various manifestations of these ego functions in the various diagnostic groups. Analysis of the therapeutic process showed that the central ego functions of aggressions, anxiety, and ego demarcation significantly develop from deficient and destructive elements toward their constructive manifestations.

Nevertheless, the unconscious cannot, as yet, be measured by a direct approach; we can only secure approximate data. Here the autokinetic light test and our brain stream measurements have their particular importance, as they permit a more direct access to the manifestations of ego structural elements of the unconscious.

The autokinetic light test derives its existence from the autokinetic phenomenon of perception. If a person fixes his eyes on an objectively fixed minute source of light in a completely dark room, this light point will, in the eye of the observer, start moving about. The type and range of its motion will vary considerably from observer to observer. The importance of this phenomenon lies in the fact that it is the observer himself who causes the motion of the light point. It was Ammon [1] who first pointed out the connection between autokinetics and the unconscious and introduced this test into human structurological research. We assume that the motion of the point is a direct reflection of the observer's unconscious dynamics. Hitherto, results have basically confirmed this assumption [9, 12].

We found that two groups, the one causing extremely little and the one causing an extremely high amount of autokinetic motion, can be discerned by their ego structure. Patients with little autokinetic effect revealed the deficient ego-structural elements to be predominant, whereas patients with an extremely high degree of autokinetics showed more destructive ego-structural elements in terms of aggression, anxiety, ego demarcation, and narcissism. Besides, we found out that the way the observer observed the light point reflected important information on the way this person observed himself. The retest reliability is significant, which led us to make use of the test also in ego-structural diagnostics and efficiency investigations. The autokinetic light test reveals its particular prognostic value where prepsychotic states of ego structures and tendency to suicide are suspected. The autokinetic light test is being examined for further valid applications and studies are under way to combine it with the brain stream measurements.

Exploring the unconscious will continue to be our research. There is a demand for the investigation of completely new approaches that lie beyond our rationalistic cognition, rule out the laws of Aristotelian logic, and include "the resources of awareness and cognition in the unconscious" [7]. A permeable school of thought will always admit new ideas, and we are convinced that, in a few decades, hitherto unthought of research potentials will have been developed. Scientists should get together in an attitude that does not create pointless borders to scientific thought, but questions them and tears them down for the benefit of man. Such a union could create immense potentials for the development of human identity and of our communal life.

References

1. Ammon G (1959) Theoretical aspects of milieutherapy. The Menninger School of Psychiatry, Topeka/Kansas. Pinel, Berlin, 1977
2. Ammon G (1970) Gruppendynamik der Aggression – Beiträge zur psychoanalytischen Theorie. Pinel, Berlin. Kindler, Munich, 1973, 1981
3. Ammon G (1978) Das Verständnis eines Entwicklungsdefizits von Ich-Strukturen in Persönlichkeit und umgebender Gruppe als Grundlage der Wissenschaft und Praxis einer Dynamischen Psychiatrie. Dynamische Psychiatrie 11: 120–137
4. Ammon G (1979) Was ist dynamische Psychiatrie. In: Ammon G (ed) Handbuch der dynamischen Psychiatrie, vol 1. Reinhardt, Munich
5. Ammon G (1979) Entwurf eines Dynamisch-Psychiatrischen Ich-Struktur-Konzepts – zur Integration von funktional-struktureller Ich-Psychologie, analytischer Gruppendynamik und Narzißmustheorie. In: Ammon G (ed) Handbuch der dynamischen Psychiatrie, vol 1. Reinhardt, Munich
6. Ammon G (1982) Das sozialenergetische Prinzip in der Dynamischen Psychiatrie. In: Ammon G (ed) Handbuch der dynamischen Psychiatrie, vol 2. Reinhardt, Munich
7. Ammon G, Griepenstroh D, Harlander U (1982) Methodenintegration aus der Sicht der dynamischen Psychiatrie. In: Ammon G (ed) Handbuch der dynamischen Psychiatrie, vol 2. Reinhardt, Munich
8. Ammon G (1982) Identität – ein Geschehen an der Grenze von Raum und Zeit. Dynamische Psychiatrie 15: 114–128

9. Ammon G, Burbiel I, Finke G, Wagner H (1982) Ergebnisse Dynamisch Psychiatrischer Forschung. In: Ammon G (ed) Handbuch der dynamischen Psychiatrie, vol 2. Reinhardt, Munich
10. Ammon G, Griepenstroh D (1982) Methodenintegration, Möglichkeit und Verfahren aus der Sicht der Psychoanalyse. In: Petzold H (ed) Methodenintegration in der Psychotherapie. Junfermann, Paderborn
11. Ammon G (1983) Das Prinzip der Sozialenergie im holistischen Denken der dynamischen Psychiatrie. Dynamische Psychiatrie 16: 169-191
12. Ammon G, Burbiel I, Stuck U (1983) Der Autokinetische Lichttest in der Humanstrukturologischen Forschung. In: Dynamische Psychiatrie 16: 63-109
13. Bott C, Beck A, Rock W, Wiehl-Volbehr A (1978) Methodische Ansätze zu einer objektivierenden ich-strukturellen Diagnostik im Rahmen des Ammon'schen Ich-Struktur-Modells am Beispiel der zentralen Ich-Funktion der Aggression. Dynamische Psychiatrie 11: 152-164
14. Bott C, Burbiel I (1981) Wissenschafts- und erkenntnistheoretische Diskussion zur Persönlichkeitstheorie Günter Ammon. Paper read at the 13th international symposium of the Deutsche Akademie für Psychoanalyse, Munich
15. Burbiel I, Vogelbusch W (1981) Die Persönlichkeitstheorie nach Günter Ammon als Grundlage psychometrischer Untersuchungen. Dynamische Psychiatrie 14: 16-37
16. Burbiel I, Bott C, Finke G (1982) Wissenschaftstheoretische Grundlagen und Forschungsmethodik der Dynamischen Psychiatrie. In: Ammon G (ed) Handbuch der dynamischen Psychiatrie, vol 2. Reinhardt, Munich
17. Finke G, Wagner H (1983) Der Ich-Struktur-Test des Narzißmus nach Ammon. Dynamische Psychiatrie 16: 221-253
18. Feyerabend P (1976) Wider den Methodenzwang. Suhrkamp, Frankfurt
19. Mönnich H (1983) Ammon und Jantsch - Pioniere eines neuen wissenschaftlichen Paradigmas. Paper read at the 2nd world congress of the World Association for Dynamic Psychiatry, December 1983, Munich

Subject Index

Medicolegal Library

Editor: **A. Carmi**

Volume 1

Child Abuse

Editors: A. Carmi, H. Zimrin

1984. 39 figures. X, 216 pages
ISBN 3-540-12471-3

Child Abuse is the first volume in Springer-Verlag's important new series **Medicolegal Library.** An interdisciplinary approach to one of modern society's most appalling phenomena, it shows that child abuse is not the result of uniform behavior patterns, but rather has many causes requiring many different types of treatment. The contributions focus on legal, pathologic, sexual, psychiatric, and familial aspects of the problem and show how they are dealt with in various Western countries.

Volume 2

Euthanasia

Editor: A. Carmi

1984. X, 185 pages. ISBN 3-540-13251-1

The second volume in the Medicolegal Library, **Euthanasia** provides a cross-cultural view of the dignity of life and the right to die. The authors trace the phenomena of euthanasia from its earliest recorded instances to the present and consider it from the points of view of law, medicine, psychology, sociology, philosophy, and religion.

Volume 3

Disability

Editors: A. Carmi, E. Chigier, S. Schneider

1984. 5 figures, 20 tables. XIV, 253 pages
ISBN 3-540-13421-2

The authors of this third volume in the series **Medicolegal Library** bring together legal, medical and psychosocial aspects of disability to allow those involved in the care and integration of the disabled to benefit from the experiences of others. Their contributions include such topics as problems with the implementation of antidiscrimination laws, compensation for chronic pain, the rehabilitation of heroin addicts, and medicolegal problems of sterilization for the mentally ill.

Volume 4

Nursing Law and Ethics

Editors: A. Carmi, S. Schneider

1985. XI, 246 pages. ISBN 3-540-15253-9

In this monograph experts from all over the world – nurses, physicians, and jurists – contribute their critical essays on the legal, ethical, cultural and religious aspects of nursing. The rights, responsibility and accountability of nurses, the moral dilemmas they face, standards of treatment in difficult medical cases, ethical aspects of nursing education and research, and the decision making process itself are all topics included in this interdisciplinary look at the nursing profession today.

Springer-Verlag Berlin Heidelberg New York Tokyo